Information-Theoretic Methods in Deep Learning: Theory and Applications

Information-Theoretic Methods in Deep Learning: Theory and Applications

Guest Editors

Shuangming Yang
Shujian Yu
Luis Gonzalo Sánchez Giraldo
Badong Chen

Basel • Beijing • Wuhan • Barcelona • Belgrade • Novi Sad • Cluj • Manchester

Guest Editors

Shuangming Yang
School of Electrical and
Information Engineering
Tianjin University
Tianjin
China

Shujian Yu
Department of Computer
Science
Vrije Universiteit
Amsterdam
Netherland

Luis Gonzalo Sánchez Giraldo
Department of Electrical and
Computer Engineering
University of Kentucky
Lexington
United States

Badong Chen
Institute of Artificial
Intelligence and Robotics
Xi'an Jiaotong University
Xi'an
China

Editorial Office
MDPI AG
Grosspeteranlage 5
4052 Basel, Switzerland

This is a reprint of the Special Issue, published open access by the journal *Entropy* (ISSN 1099-4300), freely accessible at: www.mdpi.com/journal/entropy/special_issues/IQDPF89J1Z.

For citation purposes, cite each article independently as indicated on the article page online and using the guide below:

Lastname, A.A.; Lastname, B.B. Article Title. *Journal Name* **Year**, *Volume Number*, Page Range.

ISBN 978-3-7258-2982-8 (Hbk)
ISBN 978-3-7258-2981-1 (PDF)
https://doi.org/10.3390/books978-3-7258-2981-1

© 2025 by the authors. Articles in this book are Open Access and distributed under the Creative Commons Attribution (CC BY) license. The book as a whole is distributed by MDPI under the terms and conditions of the Creative Commons Attribution-NonCommercial-NoDerivs (CC BY-NC-ND) license (https://creativecommons.org/licenses/by-nc-nd/4.0/).

Contents

Ravid Shwartz Ziv and Yann LeCun
To Compress or Not to Compress—Self-Supervised Learning and Information Theory: A Review
Reprinted from: *Entropy* 2024, 26, 252, https://doi.org/10.3390/e26030252 1

Justin Veiner, Fady Alajaji and Bahman Gharesifard
A Unifying Generator Loss Function for Generative Adversarial Networks
Reprinted from: *Entropy* 2024, 26, 290, https://doi.org/10.3390/e26040290 29

Denis Ullmann, Olga Taran and Slava Voloshynovskiy
Multivariate Time Series Information Bottleneck
Reprinted from: *Entropy* 2023, 25, 831, https://doi.org/10.3390/e25050831 54

Shachar Shayovitz, Koby Bibas and Meir Feder
Deep Individual Active Learning: Safeguarding against Out-of-Distribution Challenges in Neural Networks
Reprinted from: *Entropy* 2024, 26, 129, https://doi.org/10.3390/e26020129 103

Kristoffer K. Wickstrøm, Sigurd Løkse, Michael C. Kampffmeyer, Shujian Yu, José C. Príncipe and Robert Jenssen
Analysis of Deep Convolutional Neural Networks Using Tensor Kernels and Matrix-Based Entropy
Reprinted from: *Entropy* 2023, 25, 899, https://doi.org/10.3390/e25060899 120

Xueling Pan, Guohe Li and Yifeng Zheng
Ensemble Transductive Propagation Network for Semi-Supervised Few-Shot Learning
Reprinted from: *Entropy* 2024, 26, 135, https://doi.org/10.3390/e26020135 141

Sibo Gai, Shangke Lyu, Hongyin Zhang and Donglin Wang
Continual Reinforcement Learning for Quadruped Robot Locomotion
Reprinted from: *Entropy* 2024, 26, 93, https://doi.org/10.3390/e26010093 163

Chenguang Zhang, Tian Liu and Xuejiao Du
A Deep Neural Network Regularization Measure: The Class-Based Decorrelation Method
Reprinted from: *Entropy* 2023, 26, 7, https://doi.org/10.3390/e26010007 179

Jinfeng Zhou, Xiaoqin Zeng, Yang Zou and Haoran Zhu
Position-Wise Gated Res2Net-Based Convolutional Network with Selective Fusing for Sentiment Analysis
Reprinted from: *Entropy* 2023, 25, 740, https://doi.org/10.3390/e25050740 194

Pascal A. Schirmer and Iosif Mporas
PyDTS: A Python Toolkit for Deep Learning Time Series Modelling
Reprinted from: *Entropy* 2024, 26, 311, https://doi.org/10.3390/e26040311 213

Review

To Compress or Not to Compress—Self-Supervised Learning and Information Theory: A Review

Ravid Shwartz Ziv [1,*] and Yann LeCun [1,2]

1 Center of Data Science, New York University, New York, NY 10011, USA
2 FAIR at Meta, Broadway, New York, NY 10003, USA
* Correspondence: ravid.shwartz.ziv@nyu.edu

Abstract: Deep neural networks excel in supervised learning tasks but are constrained by the need for extensive labeled data. Self-supervised learning emerges as a promising alternative, allowing models to learn without explicit labels. Information theory has shaped deep neural networks, particularly the information bottleneck principle. This principle optimizes the trade-off between compression and preserving relevant information, providing a foundation for efficient network design in supervised contexts. However, its precise role and adaptation in self-supervised learning remain unclear. In this work, we scrutinize various self-supervised learning approaches from an information-theoretic perspective, introducing a unified framework that encapsulates the self-supervised information-theoretic learning problem. This framework includes multiple encoders and decoders, suggesting that all existing work on self-supervised learning can be seen as specific instances. We aim to unify these approaches to understand their underlying principles better and address the main challenge: many works present different frameworks with differing theories that may seem contradictory. By weaving existing research into a cohesive narrative, we delve into contemporary self-supervised methodologies, spotlight potential research areas, and highlight inherent challenges. Moreover, we discuss how to estimate information-theoretic quantities and their associated empirical problems. Overall, this paper provides a comprehensive review of the intersection of information theory, self-supervised learning, and deep neural networks, aiming for a better understanding through our proposed unified approach.

Keywords: self-supervised learning; information theory; representation learning; deep neural networks

Citation: Shwartz Ziv, R.; LeCun, Y. To Compress or Not to Compress—Self-Supervised Learning and Information Theory: A Review. *Entropy* **2024**, *26*, 252. https://doi.org/10.3390/e26030252

Academic Editors: Shuangming Yang, Shujian Yu, Luis Gonzalo Sánchez Giraldo, Badong Chen and Sotiris Kotsiantis

Received: 6 December 2023
Revised: 12 February 2024
Accepted: 26 February 2024
Published: 12 March 2024

Copyright: © 2024 by the authors. Licensee MDPI, Basel, Switzerland. This article is an open access article distributed under the terms and conditions of the Creative Commons Attribution (CC BY) license (https://creativecommons.org/licenses/by/4.0/).

1. Introduction

Deep neural networks (DNNs) have revolutionized fields such as computer vision, natural language processing, and speech recognition due to their remarkable performance in supervised learning tasks [1–3]. However, the success of DNNs is often limited by the need for vast amounts of labeled data, which can be both time-consuming and expensive to acquire. By using unlabeled data, supervised learning costs can be reduced, especially in fields that require expensive annotations. As an example, biomedical task labels must be provided by domain experts, who are costly to hire. Besides the hiring cost, labeling tasks are often labor-intensive. For example, video data labels require the review of many frames. Self-supervised learning (SSL) emerges as a promising direction, enabling models to learn from data without explicit labels by leveraging the underlying structure and relationships within the data.

Recent advances in SSL have been driven by joint embedding architectures, such as Siamese Nets [4], DrLIM [5,6], and SimCLR [7]. These approaches define a loss function that encourages representations of different versions of the same image to be similar while pushing representations of distinct images apart. After optimizing the surrogate objective, the pre-trained model can be employed as a feature extractor, with the learned features serving as inputs for downstream supervised tasks, like image classification, object detection, instance segmentation, or pose estimation [7–10]. Although SSL methods have shown promising results in practice, the theoretical underpinnings behind their effectiveness remain an open question [11,12].

Information theory has played a crucial role in understanding and optimizing deep neural networks, from practical applications like the variational information bottleneck [13] to theoretical investigations of generalization bounds induced by mutual information [14,15]. Building upon these foundations, several researchers have attempted to enhance self-supervised and semi-supervised learning algorithms using information-theoretic principles, such as the Mutual Information Neural Estimator (MINE) [16] combined with the information maximization (InfoMax) principle [17]. However, the plethora of objective functions, contradicting assumptions, and various estimation techniques in the literature can make it challenging to grasp the underlying principles and their implications.

In this paper, we aim to achieve two objectives. First, we propose a unified framework that synthesizes existing research on self-supervised and semi-supervised learning from an information-theoretic standpoint. This framework allows us to present and compare current methods, analyze their assumptions and difficulties, and discuss the optimal representation for neural networks in general and self-supervised networks in particular. Second, we explore different methods and estimators for optimizing information-theoretic quantities in deep neural networks and investigate how recent models optimize various theoretical-information terms.

By reviewing the literature on various aspects of information-theoretic learning, we provide a comprehensive understanding of the interplay between information theory, self-supervised learning, and deep neural networks. We discuss the application of the information bottleneck principle [18], connections between information theory and generalization, and recent information-theoretic learning algorithms. Furthermore, we examine how the information-theoretic perspective can offer insights into the design of better self-supervised learning algorithms and the potential benefits of using information theory in SSL across a wide range of applications.

In addition to the main structure of this paper, we dedicate a section to the challenges and opportunities in extending the information-theoretic perspective to other learning paradigms, such as energy-based models. We highlight the potential advantages of incorporating these extensions into self-supervised learning algorithms and discuss the technical and conceptual challenges that must be addressed.

The structure of this paper is as follows. Section 2 introduces the key concepts in supervised, semi-supervised, and self-supervised learning, information theory, and representation learning. Section 3 presents a unified framework for multiview learning based on information theory. We first discuss what an optimal representation is and why compression is beneficial for learning. Next, we explore optimal representation in single-view supervised learning models and how they can be extended to unsupervised, semi-supervised, and multiview contexts. The focus then shifts to self-supervised learning, where the optimal representation remains an open question. Using the unified framework, we compare recent self-supervised algorithms and discuss their differences. We analyze the assumptions behind these models, their effects on the learned representation, and their varying perspectives on important information within the network.

Section 5 addresses several technical challenges, discussing both theoretical and practical issues in estimating theoretical information terms. We present recent methods for estimating these quantities, including variational bounds and estimators. As part of Section 6, we examine a wide range of review papers that cover information theory and self-supervised learning thoroughly. Section 7 concludes this paper by offering insights into potential future research directions at the intersection of information theory, self-supervised learning, and deep neural networks. Our aim is to stimulate further research that leverages information theory to advance our understanding of self-supervised learning and to develop more efficient and effective models for a broad range of applications.

2. Background and Fundamental Concepts

2.1. Multiview Representation Learning

Multiview learning, which utilizes complementary information from multiple features or modalities, has gained increasing attention and achieved great practical success. The multiview learning paradigm divides the input variable into multiple views from which the target variable should be predicted [19]. Using this paradigm, one can eliminate hypotheses that contradict predictions from other views and provide a natural semi-supervised and self-supervised learning setting. A multiview dataset consists of data captured from multiple sources, modalities, and forms but with similar high-level semantics [20]. This mechanism was initially used for natural-world data, combining image, text, audio, and video measurements. For example, photos of objects are taken from various angles, and our supervised task is to identify the objects. Another example is identifying a person by analyzing the video stream as one view and the audio stream as the other.

Although these views often provide different and complementary information about the same data, directly integrating them does not produce satisfactory results due to biases between multiple views [20]. Thus, multiview representation learning involves identifying the underlying data structure and integrating the different views into a common feature space, resulting in a high performance. In recent decades, multiview learning has been used for many machine learning tasks and influenced many algorithms, such as co-training mechanisms [21], subspace learning methods [22], and multiple kernel learning (MKL) [23]. Li et al. [24] proposed two categories for multiview representation learning: (i) multiview representation fusion, which combines different features from multiple views into a single compact representation, and (ii) the alignment of multiview representation, which attempts to capture the relationships among multiple different views through feature alignment. In this case, a learned mapping function embeds the data of each view, and the representations are regularized to form a multiview-aligned space. In this research direction, an early study is the canonical correlation analysis (CCA) [25] and its kernel extensions [23,26,27]. In addition to CCA, multiview representation learning has penetrated a variety of learning methods, such as dimensionality reduction [28], clustering analysis [29], multiview sparse coding [30–32], and multimodal topic learning [33]. However, despite their promising results, these methods use handcrafted features and linear embedding functions, which cannot capture the nonlinear properties of multiview data.

Deep learning provides a powerful way to learn complex, nonlinear, and hierarchical representations of data. By incorporating multiple hierarchical layers, deep learning algorithms can learn complex, subtle, and abstract representations of target data. The success of deep learning in various application domains has led to a growing interest in deep multiview methods, which have shown promising results. Examples of these methods include deep multiview canonical correlation analysis [34] as an extension of CCA, multiview clustering via deep matrix factorization [35], and the deep multiview spectral network [36]. Moreover, deep architectures have been employed to generate effective representations in methods such as multiview convolutional neural networks [37], multimodal deep Boltzmann machines [38], multimodal deep autoencoders [39,40], and multimodal recurrent neural networks [41–43].

2.2. Self-Supervised Learning

Self-supervised learning (SSL) is a powerful technique that leverages unlabeled data to learn useful representations. In contrast to supervised learning, which relies on labeled data, SSL employs self-defined signals to establish a proxy objective between the input and the signal. The model is initially trained using this proxy objective and subsequently fine-tuned on the target task. Self-supervised signals, derived from the inherent co-occurrence relationships in the data, serve as self-supervision. Various such signals have been used to learn representations, including generative and joint embedding architectures [7,44–47].

Two main categories of SSL architectures exist: (1) generative architectures based on reconstruction or prediction and (2) joint embedding architectures [48]. Both architecture classes can be trained using either contrastive or non-contrastive methods.

We begin by discussing these two main types of architectures:

1. **Generative architecture:** Generative architectures employ an objective function that measures the divergence between input data and predicted reconstructions, such as squared error. The architecture reconstructs data from a latent variable or a corrupted version, potentially with a latent variable's assistance. Notable examples of generative architectures include autoencoders, sparse coding, sparse autoencoders, and variational autoencoders [49–51]. As the reconstruction task lacks a single correct answer, most generative architectures utilize a latent variable, which, when varied, generates multiple reconstructions. The latent variable's information content requires regularization to ensure the system reconstructs regions of high data density while avoiding a collapse by reconstructing the entire space. PCA regularizes the latent variable by limiting its dimensions, while sparse coding and sparse autoencoders restrict the number of non-zero components. Variational autoencoders regularize the latent variable by rendering it stochastic and maximizing the entropy of the distribution relative to a prior. Vector quantized variational autoencoders (VQ-VAEs) employ binary stochastic variables to achieve similar results [52].

2. **Joint embedding architectures (JEAs):** These architectures process multiple views of an input signal through encoders, producing representations of the views. The system is trained to ensure that these representations are both informative and mutually predictable. Examples include Siamese networks, where two identical encoders share weights [7,53–55], and methods permitting encoders to differ [56]. A primary challenge with JEA is preventing informational collapse, in which the representations contain minimal information about the inputs, thereby facilitating their mutual prediction. JEA's advantage lies in the encoders' ability to eliminate noisy, unpredictable, or irrelevant information from the input within the representation space.

To train these architectures effectively, it is essential to ensure that the representations of different signals are distinct. This can be achieved through either contrastive or non-contrastive methods:

- **Contrastive methods:** Contrastive methods utilize data points from the training set as *positive samples* and generate points outside the region of high data density as *contrastive samples*. The energy (e.g., reconstruction error for generative architectures or representation predictive error for JEA) should be low for positive samples and higher for contrastive samples. Various loss functions involving the energies of pairs or sets of samples can be minimized to achieve this objective.

- **Non-contrastive methods:** Non-contrastive methods prevent the energy landscape's collapse by limiting the volume of space that can take low energy, either through architectural constraints or through a regularizer in the energy or training objective. In latent-variable generative architectures, preventing collapse is achieved by limiting or minimizing the information content of the latent variable. In JEA, collapse is prevented by maximizing the information content of the representations.

We now present a few concrete examples of popular models that employ various combinations of generative architectures, joint embedding architectures, contrastive training, and non-contrastive training:

The **denoising autoencoder** approach in generative architectures [57–59] uses a triplet loss, which utilizes a positive sample, which is a vector from the training set that should be reconstructed perfectly, and a contrastive sample consisting of data vectors, one from the training set and the other being a corrupted version of it. In SSL, the combination of *JEA* models with *contrastive learning* has proven highly effective. In contrastive learning, the objective is to attract different augmented views of the same image (positive points) while repelling dissimilar augmented views (negative points). Recent self-supervised visual representation learning examples include MoCo [54] and SimCLR [7]. The InfoNCE loss is a commonly used objective function in many contrastive learning methods:

$$\mathbb{E}_{x,x^+,x^-}\left[-\log\left(\frac{e^{f(x)^T f(x^+)}}{\sum k=1^K e^{f(x)^T f(x^k)}}\right)\right] \quad (1)$$

where $x+$ is a sample similar to x, x^k are all the samples in the batch, and f is an encoder. This loss, inspired by NCE [60], uses categorical cross-entropy loss to distinguish the positive sample amongst a set of unrelated noise samples in the batch. In this formulation, the numerator represents the output of a positive pair, while the denominator sums the values of both positive and negative pairs. This straightforward loss function aims to increase the value of positive pairs (driving the logarithmic term towards 1, thereby reducing the loss towards 0) and separate the negative pairs further.

However, contrastive methods heavily depend on all other samples in the batch and require a large batch size. Additionally, Jing et al. [61] have shown that contrastive learning can lead to dimensional collapse, where the embedding vectors span a lower-dimensional subspace instead of the entire embedding space. Although positive and negative pairs should repel each other to prevent dimensional collapse, augmentation along feature dimensions and implicit regularization cause the embedding vectors to fall into a lower-dimensional subspace, resulting in low-rank solutions.

To address these problems, recent works have introduced *JEA* models with *non-contrastive methods*. Unlike contrastive methods, these methods employ regularization to prevent the collapse of the representation and do not explicitly rely on negative samples. For example, several papers use stop gradients and extra predictors to avoid collapse [53,55], while Caron et al. [62] employed an additional clustering step. VICReg [56] is another non-contrastive method that regularizes the covariance matrix of representation. Consider two embedding batches $Z = [f(x_1), \ldots, f(x_N)]$ and $Z' = [f(x'_1), \ldots, f(x'_N)]$, each of size $(N \times K)$. Denote by C the $(K \times K)$ covariance matrix obtained from $[Z, Z']$. The VICReg triplet loss is defined by the following:

$$\mathcal{L} = \frac{1}{K}\sum_{k=1}^{K}\left(\alpha \max\left(0, \gamma - \sqrt{C_{k,k} + \epsilon}\right) + \beta \sum_{k' \neq k}(C_{k,k'})^2\right) + \gamma \|Z - Z'\|_F^2 / N. \quad (2)$$

The variance loss (the diagonal terms) encourages high variance in the learned representations, thereby promoting the learning of a wide range of features. The covariance loss (the off-diagonal terms), however, aims to minimize redundancy in the learned features by reducing the overlap in information captured by different dimensions of the representation.

2.3. Semi-Supervised Learning

Semi-supervised learning employs both labeled and unlabeled data to enhance the model performance [63]. Consistency regularization-based approaches [64–66] ensure that predictions remain stable under perturbations in input data and model parameters. Certain techniques, such as those proposed by Grandvalet and Bengio [67] and Miyato et al. [65], involve training a model by incorporating a regularization term into a supervised cross-entropy loss. In contrast, Xie et al. [68] utilizes suitably weighted unsupervised regularization terms, while Zhai et al. [69] adopts a combination of self-supervised pretext loss terms. Moreover, pseudo-labeling can generate synthetic labels based on network uncertainty to further aid model training [70].

2.4. Representation Learning

Representation learning is an essential aspect of various computer vision, natural language processing, and machine learning tasks, as it uncovers the underlying structures in data [71]. Extracting relevant information for classification and prediction tasks from the data improves the performance and reduces computational complexity [72]. However, defining an effective representation remains a challenging task. In probabilistic models, a useful representation often captures the posterior distribution of explanatory factors beneath the observed input [2]. Bengio and LeCun [73] introduced the idea of learning highly structured yet complex dependencies for AI tasks, which require transforming high-dimensional input structures into low-dimensional output structures or learning low-level representations. Consequently, identifying relevant input features is challenging because most input entropy does not relate to the output. [74]. Ben-Shaul et al. [75] demonstrated that self-supervised learning inherently promotes the clustering of samples based on semantic labels. Intriguingly, this clustering is driven by the objective's regularization term and aligns with semantic classes across multiple hierarchical levels.

2.4.1. Minimal Sufficient Statistic

A possible definition of an effective representation is based on *minimal sufficient statistics*.

Definition 1. *Given $(X, Y) \sim P(X, Y)$, let $T := t(X)$, where t is a deterministic function. We define T as a sufficient statistic of X for Y if $Y - T - X$ forms a Markov chain.*

A sufficient statistic is defined relative to the statistics of the data, or a probabilistic function, and provides all the information in the data about that model or the parameters of that model.

Intuitively, a sufficient statistic captures all the information about Y in X. Cover [76] proved this property:

Theorem 1. *Let T be a probabilistic function of X. Then, T is a sufficient statistic for Y if and only if $I(T(X); Y) = I(X; Y)$.*

However, the sufficiency definition also encompasses trivial identity statistics that only "copy" rather than "extract" essential information. To prevent statistics from inefficiently utilizing observations, the concept of minimal sufficient statistics was introduced:

Definition 2. *(Minimal sufficient statistic (MSS).) A sufficient statistic T is minimal if, for any other sufficient statistic S, there exists a function f such that $T = f(S)$ almost surely (a.s.).*

In essence, MSSs are the simplest sufficient statistics, inducing the coarsest sufficient partition on X. In MSSs, the values of X are grouped into as few partitions as possible without sacrificing information. MSSs are statistics with the maximum information about Y while retaining the least information about X as possible [77].

2.4.2. The Information Bottleneck

The majority of distributions lack exact minimal sufficient statistics, leading Tishby et al. [18] to relax the optimization problem in two ways: (i) allowing the map to be stochastic, defined as an encoder $P(T|X)$, and (ii) permitting the capture of only a small amount of $I(X; Y)$. The information bottleneck (IB) was introduced as a principled method to extract relevant information from observed signals related to a target. This framework finds the optimal trade-off between the accuracy and complexity of a random variable $y \in \mathcal{Y}$ with a joint distribution for a random variable $x \in \mathcal{X}$. The IB has been employed in various fields, such as neuroscience [78,79], slow feature analysis [80], speech recognition [81], molecular relational learning [82], and deep learning [13,74].

Let X be an input random variable, Y a target variable, and $P(X, Y)$ their joint distribution. A representation T is a stochastic function of X defined by a mapping $P(T \mid X)$. This mapping transforms $X \sim P(X)$ into a representation of $T \sim P(T) := \int P_{T|X}(\cdot \mid x) dP_X(x)$. The triple $Y - X - T$ forms a Markov chain in that order with respect to the joint probability measure $P_{X,Y,T} = P_{X,Y} P_{T|X}$ and the mutual information terms $I(X; T)$ and $I(Y; T)$.

Within the IB framework, our goal is to find a representation $P(T \mid X)$ that extracts as much information as possible about Y (high performance) while compressing X maximally (keeping $I(X;T)$ small). This can also be interpreted as extracting only the relevant information that X contains about Y.

The data processing inequality (DPI) implies that $I(Y;T) \leq I(X;Y)$, so the compressed representation T cannot convey more information than the original signal. Consequently, there is a trade-off between compressed representation and the preservation of relevant information about Y. The construction of an efficient representation variable is characterized by its encoder and decoder distributions, $P(T \mid X)$ and $P(Y \mid T)$, respectively. The efficient representation of X involves minimizing the complexity of the representation $I(T;X)$ while maximizing $I(T;Y)$. Formally, the IB optimization involves minimizing the following objective function:

$$\mathcal{L} = \min_{P(t|x); p(y|t)} I(X;T) - \beta I(Y;T), \qquad (3)$$

where β is the trade-off parameter controlling the complexity of T and the amount of relevant information it preserves. Intuitively, we pass the information that X contains about Y through a "bottleneck" via the representation T. It has been shown that

$$I(T;Y) = I(X;Y) - \mathbb{E}_{x \sim P(X), t \sim P(T|x)}[D[P(Y|x)||P(Y|t)]]. \qquad (4)$$

2.5. Representation Learning and the Information Bottleneck

Information theory traditionally assumes that underlying probabilities are known and do not require learning. For instance, the optimality of the initial IB work [18] relied on the assumption that the joint distribution of input and labels is known. However, a significant challenge in machine learning algorithms is inferring an accurate predictor for the unknown target variable from observed realizations. This discrepancy raises questions about the practical optimality of the IB and its relevance in modern learning algorithms. The following section delves into the relationship between the IB framework and learning, inference, and generalization.

Let $X \in \mathcal{X}$ and a target variable $Y \in \mathcal{Y}$ be random variables with an unknown joint distribution $P(X,Y)$. For a given class of predictors $f : \mathcal{X} \to \hat{\mathcal{Y}}$ and a loss function $\ell : \mathcal{Y} \to \hat{\mathcal{Y}}$ measuring discrepancies between true values and model predictions, our objective is to find the predictor f that minimizes the *expected population risk*:

$$\mathcal{L}_{P(X,Y)}(f, \ell) = \mathbb{E}_{P(X,Y)}[\ell(Y, f(X))]. \qquad (5)$$

Several issues arise with the expected population risk. Firstly, it remains unclear which loss function is optimal. A popular choice is the logarithmic loss (or error's entropy), which has been numerically demonstrated to yield better results [83]. This loss has been employed in various algorithms, including the InfoMax principle [17], tree-based algorithms [84], deep neural networks [85], and Bayesian modeling [86]. Painsky and Wornell [87] provided a rigorous justification for using the logarithmic loss and showed that it is an upper bound to any choice of the loss function that is smooth, proper, and convex for binary classification problems.

In most cases, the joint distribution $P(X,Y)$ is unknown, and we have access to only n samples from it, denoted by $\mathcal{D}_n := (x_i, y_i) \mid i = 1, \ldots, n$. Consequently, the population risk cannot be computed directly. Instead, we typically choose the predictor that minimizes the empirical population risk on a training dataset:

$$\hat{\mathcal{L}}_{P(X,Y)}(f, \ell, \mathcal{D}_n) = \frac{1}{n} \sum_{i=1}^{n} [\ell(y_i, f(x_i))]. \qquad (6)$$

The generalization gap, defined as the difference between empirical and population risks, is given by

$$Gen_{P(X,Y)}(f, \ell, \mathcal{D}_n) := \mathcal{L}_{P(X,Y)}(f, \ell) - \hat{\mathcal{L}}_{P(X,Y)}(f, \ell, \mathcal{D}_n). \qquad (7)$$

Interestingly, the relationship between the population risk and the empirical risk can be bounded using the information bottleneck term. Shamir et al. [88] developed several finite sample bounds for the generalization gap. According to their study, the IB framework exhibited good generalizability even with small sample sizes. In particular, they developed non-uniform bounds adaptive to the model's complexity. They demonstrated that for the discrete case, the error in estimating mutual information from finite samples is bounded by $O\left(\frac{|X|\log n}{\sqrt{n}}\right)$, where $|X|$ is the cardinality of X (the number of possible values that the random variable X can take). The results support the intuition that simpler models generalize better, and we would like to compress our model. Therefore, optimizing Equation (3) presents a trade-off between two opposing forces. On the one hand, we want to increase our prediction accuracy in our training data (high β).

On the other hand, we would like to decrease β to narrow the generalization gap. Vera et al. [89] extended their work and showed that the generalization gap is bounded by the square root of mutual information between training input and model representation times $\frac{\log n}{n}$. Furthermore, Russo and Zou [90] and Xu and Raginsky [14] demonstrated that the square root of the mutual information between the training input and the parameters inferred from the training algorithm provides a concise bound on the generalization gap. However, these bounds critically depend on the Markov operator that maps the training set to the network parameters, whose characterization is not trivial.

Achille and Soatto [91] explored how applying the IB objective to the network's parameters may reduce overfitting while maintaining invariant representations. Their work showed that flat minima, which have better generalization properties, bound the information with the weights, and the information in the weights bound the information in the activations. Chelombiev et al. [92] found that the generalization precision is positively correlated with the degree of compression of the last layer in the network. Shwartz-Ziv et al. [93] showed that the generalization error depends exponentially on the mutual information between the model and the input once it is smaller than $\log 2n$—the query sample complexity. Moreover, they demonstrated that M bits of compression of X are equivalent to an exponential factor of 2^M training examples. Piran et al. [94] extended the original IB to the dual form, which offers several advantages in terms of compression. As an example, when the data can be modeled in a parametric form, the dual IB preserves this structure and obtains the representation based on the original parameters, resulting in a more efficient compression.

These studies illustrate that the IB leads to a trade-off between prediction and complexity, even for the empirical distribution. With the IB objective, we can design estimators to find optimal solutions for different regimes with varying performances, complexity, and generalization.

3. Information-Theoretic Objectives

Before delving into the details, this section aims to provide an overview of the information-theoretic objectives in various learning scenarios, including supervised, unsupervised, and self-supervised settings. We will also introduce a general framework to understand better the process of learning optimal representations and explore recent methods working towards this goal.

Developing a novel algorithm entails numerous aspects, such as architecture, initialization parameters, learning algorithms, and pre-processing techniques. A crucial element, however, is the objective function. As demonstrated in Section 2.4.2, the IB approach, originally introduced by Tishby et al. [18], defines the optimal representation in supervised scenarios, enabling us to identify which terms to compress during learning by explicitly defining the relevant information $I(T;Y)$ that we want to optimize. However, determining the optimal representation and deriving information-based objective functions in self-supervised settings are more challenging. In this section, we introduce a general framework to understand the process of learning optimal representations and explore recent methods striving to achieve this goal.

3.1. Setup and Methodology

Using a two-channel input allows us to model complex multiview learning problems. In many real-world situations, data can be observed from multiple perspectives or modalities, making it essential to develop learning algorithms capable of handling such multiview data.

Consider a two-channel input, X_1 and X_2, and a single-channel label Y for a downstream task, all possessing a joint distribution $P(X_1, X_2, Y)$. We assume the availability of n labeled examples $S = (x_1^i, x_2^i, y^i)_{i=1}^n$ and t unlabeled examples $U = (x_1^i, x_2^i)_{i=n+1}^{n+t}$, both independently and identically distributed. Our objective is to predict Y using a loss function.

In our model, we use a learned encoder with a prior $P(Z)$ to generate a conditional representation (which may be deterministic or stochastic) $Z_i | X_i = P_{\theta_i}(Z_i | X_i)$, where $i = 1, 2$ represents the two views. Subsequently, we utilize various decoders to "decode" distinct aspects of the representation.

For the supervised scenario, we have a joint embedding of the label classifiers from both views, $\hat{Y}_{1,2} = Q_\rho(Y | Z_1, Z_2)$, and two decoders predicting the labels of the downstream task based on each individual view, $\hat{Y}_i = Q_{\rho_i}(Y | Z_i)$ for $i = 1, 2$.

For the unsupervised case, we have direct decoders for input reconstruction from the representation, $\bar{X}_i = Q_{\psi_i}(X_i | Z_i)$ for $i = 1, 2$.

For self-supervised learning, we utilize two cross-decoders, $\tilde{Z}_1 | Z_2 = q_{\eta_1}(Z_1 | Z_2)$ and $\tilde{Z}_2 | Z_1 = q_{\eta_2}(Z_2 | Z_1)$, attempting to predict one representation based on the other. Figure 1 illustrates this structure.

The information-theoretic perspective of self-supervised networks has led to confusion regarding the information being optimized in recent work. In supervised and unsupervised learning, only one "information path" exists when optimizing information-theoretic terms: the input is encoded through the network, and then the representation is decoded and compared to the targets. As a result, the representation and corresponding information always stem from a single encoder and decoder.

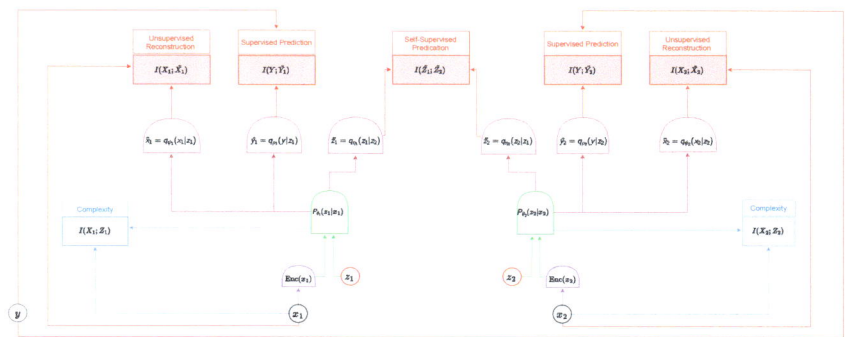

Figure 1. Multiview information bottleneck diagram for self-supervised, unsupervised, and supervised learning.

However, in the self-supervised multiview scenario, we can construct our representation using various encoders and decoders. For instance, we need to specify the associated random variable to define the information involved in $I(X_1; Z_1)$. This variable could either be based on the encoder of $X_1 - P_{\theta_1}(Z_1 | X_1)$ or based on the encoder of $X_2 - P_{\theta_2}(Z_2 | X_2)$, which is subsequently passed to the cross-decoder $Q_{\eta_1}(Z_1 | Z_2)$ and then to the direct decoder $Q_{\psi_1}(X_1 | Z_1)$.

To fully understand the information terms, we aim to optimize and distinguish between various "information path"; we marked each information path differently. For example, $I_{,P(X_1),P(Z_1|X_1),P(Z_2|Z_1)}(X_1, Z_2)$ is based on the path $P(X_1) \to P(Z_1|X_1) \to P(Z_2|Z_1)$.

In the following section, we will "translate" previous work into our present framework and examine the loss function.

3.2. Optimization with Labels

After establishing our framework, we can now incorporate various learning algorithms. We begin by examining classical single-view supervised information bottleneck algorithms for deep networks that utilize labeled data during training and extend them to the multiview scenario. Next, we broaden our perspective to include unsupervised learning, where input reconstruction replaces labels, and semi-supervised learning, where information-based regularization is applied to improve predictions.

3.2.1. Single-View Supervised Learning

In classical single-view supervised learning, the task of representation learning involves finding a distribution $p(z|x)$ that maps data observations $x \in \mathcal{X}$ to a representation $z \in \mathcal{Z}$, capturing only the relevant features of the input [95]. The goal is to predict a label $y \in \mathcal{Y}$ using the learned representation. Achille and Soatto [91] defined the sufficiency of Z for Y as the amount of label information retained after passing data through the encoder:

Definition 3. *Sufficiency: A representation Z of X is sufficient for Y if and only if* $I(X;Y|Z) = 0$.

Federici et al. [96] showed that Z is sufficient for Y if and only if the amount of information regarding the task remains unchanged by the encoding procedure.

$$I(X;Y|Z) = 0 \Leftrightarrow I(X;Y) = I(Y;Z). \tag{8}$$

A sufficient representation can predict Y as accurately as the original data X. In Section 2.4, we saw a trade-off between prediction and generalization when there is a finite amount of data. To reduce the generalization gap, we aim to compress X while retaining as much predicate information on the labels as possible. Thus, we relax the sufficiency definition and minimize the following objective:

$$\mathcal{L} = I(X;Z) - \beta I(Z;Y). \tag{9}$$

The mutual information $I(Y;Z)$ determines how much label information is accessible and reflects the model's ability to predict performance on the target task. $I(X;Z)$ represents the information that Z carries about the input, which we aim to compress. However, $I(X;Z)$ contains both relevant and irrelevant information about Y. Therefore, using the chain rule of information, Federici et al. [96] proposed splitting $I(X,Z)$ into two terms:

$$I(X;Z) = \underbrace{I(X;Z|Y)}_{\text{superfluous information}} + \underbrace{I(Z;Y)}_{\text{predictive information}}. \tag{10}$$

The conditional information $I(X,Z|Y)$ represents information in Z that is not predictive of Y, i.e., superfluous information. The decomposition of input information enables us to compress only irrelevant information while preserving the relevant information for predicting Y. Several methods are available for evaluating and estimating these information-theoretic terms in the supervised case (see Section 5 for details).

3.2.2. The Information Bottleneck Theory of Deep Learning

The IB hypothesis for deep learning proposes two distinct phases of training neural networks [74]: the fitting and compression phases. The fitting phase involves extracting information from the input and converting it into learned representations, characterized by increased mutual information between inputs and hidden representations. Conversely, the compression phase, which is much longer, concentrates on discarding unnecessary information for target prediction, decreasing mutual information between learned representations and inputs. In contrast, the mutual information between representations and targets increases. For more information, see Geiger [97]. Despite the elegance and plausibility of the IB hypothesis, empirically investigating it remains challenging [98].

The study of representation compression in deep neural networks (DNNs) for supervised learning has shown inconsistent results. For instance, Chelombiev et al. [92] discovered a positive correlation between generalization accuracy and the compression level of the network's final layer. Shwartz-Ziv et al. [93] also examined the relationship between generalization and compression, demonstrating that generalization error exponentially depends on mutual information, $I(X; Z)$. Furthermore, Achille et al. [99] established that flat minima, known for their improved generalization properties, constrain the mutual information. However, Saxe et al. [100] showed that compression was not necessary for generalization in deep linear networks. Basirat et al. [101] revealed that the decrease in mutual information is essentially equivalent to geometrical compression. Other studies have found that the mutual information between training inputs and inferred parameters provides a concise bound on the generalization gap [14,102]. Lastly, Achille and Soatto [91] explored using an information bottleneck objective on network parameters to prevent overfitting and promote invariant representations.

3.2.3. Multiview IB Learning

The IB principle offers a rigorous method for learning encoders and decoders in supervised single-view problems. However, it is not directly applicable to multiview learning problems, as it assumes only one information source as the input. A common solution is to concatenate multiple views, though this neglects the unique characteristics of each view. To address this issue, Xu et al. [103] introduced the large-margin multiview IB (LMIB) as an extension of the original IB problem. The LMIB employs a communication system where multiple senders represent various views of examples. The system extracts specific components from different senders by compressing examples through a "bottleneck", and the linear projectors for each view are combined to create a shared representation. The large-margin principle replaces the maximization of mutual information in prediction, emphasizing the separation of samples from different classes. For the complexity, they used the Rademacher complexity, which is defined as follows:

Definition 4. *Rademacher complexity Given a sample $S = \{X_1, \ldots, X_n\} \in \mathcal{X}^n$ and a real-valued function class $\mathcal{F}$ defined on a space $\mathcal{X}$, the empirical Rademacher complexity of $\mathcal{F}$ is defined as*

$$\hat{R}_n(\mathcal{F}) = \mathbb{E}_\sigma \left[\sup_{f \in \mathcal{F}} \left| \frac{2}{n} \sum_{j=1}^n \sigma_j f(X_j) \right| \middle| X_1, \ldots, X_n \right],$$

where $\sigma = (\sigma_1, \ldots, \sigma_n)$ are i.i.d. Rademacher variables (taking values $+1$ or -1 with equal probability).

In the LMIB framework, limiting the Rademacher complexity improves the solution's accuracy and generalization error bounds. Moreover, the algorithm's robustness is enhanced when accurate views counterbalance noisy views.

However, the LMIB method has a significant limitation: it utilizes linear projections for each view, which can restrict the combined representation when the relationship between different views is complex. To overcome this limitation, Wang et al. [104] proposed using deep neural networks to replace linear projectors. Their model first extracts concise latent representations from each view using deep networks and then learns the joint representation of all views using neural networks. They minimize the objective:

$$\mathcal{L} = \alpha I_{P(X_1), P(Z_1|X_1)}(X_1; Z_1) + \beta I_{P(X_2), P(Z_2|X_2)}(X_2; Z_2) - I_{P(Z_2|X_2), P(Z_1|X_1)}(Z_{1,2}; Y). \quad (11)$$

Here, α and β are trade-off parameters, Z_1 and Z_2 are the two neural networks' representations, and $Z_{1,2}$ is the joint embedding of Z_1 and Z_2. The first two terms decrease the mutual information between a view's latent representation and its original data representation, resulting in a simpler and more generalizable model. The final term forces the joint representation to maximize the discrimination ability for the downstream task.

3.2.4. Semi-Supervised IB Learning: Leveraging Unlabeled Data

Obtaining labeled data can be challenging or expensive in many practical scenarios, while many unlabeled samples may be readily available. Semi-supervised learning addresses this issue by leveraging the vast amount of unlabeled data during training in conjunction with a small set of labeled samples. Common strategies to achieve this involve adding regularization terms or adopting mechanisms that promote better generalization. Berthelot et al. [105] grouped regularization methods into three primary categories: entropy minimization, consistency regularization, and generic regularization.

Voloshynovskiy et al. [106] introduced an information-theoretic framework for semi-supervised learning based on the IB principle. In this context, the semi-supervised classification problem involves encoding input X into the latent space Z while preserving only **class-relevant information**. A supervised classifier can achieve this if there are sufficient labeled data. However, when the number of labeled examples is limited, the standard label classifier $p(y|z)$ becomes unreliable and requires regularization.

To tackle this issue, the authors assumed a prior on the class label distribution $p(y)$. They introduced a term to minimize the D_{KL} between the assumed marginal prior and the empirical marginal prior, effectively regularizing the conditional label classifier with the labels' marginal distribution. This approach reduces the classifier's sensitivity to the scarcity of labeled examples. They proposed two variational IB semi-supervised extensions for the priors:

Handcrafted priors: These priors are predefined for regularization and can be based on domain knowledge or statistical properties of the data. Alternatively, they can be learned using other networks. Handcrafted priors in this context are similar to priors used in the variational information bottleneck (VIB) formalism [13,104].

Learnable priors: Voloshynovskiy et al. [106] also suggests using learnable priors as an alternative to handcrafted regularization priors on the latent representation. This method involves regularizing Z through another IB-based regularization with two components: (i) latent space regularization and (ii) observation space regularization. In this case, an additional hidden variable M is introduced after the representation to regulate the information flow between Z and Y. An autoencoder $q(m|z)$ is employed, and the optimization process aims to compress the information flowing from Z to M while retaining only label-relevant information. The IB objective is defined as follows:

$$\mathcal{L} = D_{KL}(q(m|z)||p(m|z)) - \beta D_{KL}(q(x|m)||p(x|m)) - \beta_y D_{KL}(p(y|z)||p(y)) \\ \Leftrightarrow I(M;Z) - \beta I(M;X) - \beta_y I(Y;Z). \tag{12}$$

Here, β and β_y are hyperparameters that balance the trade-off between the relevance of M to the labels and the compression of Z into M.

Furthermore, Voloshynovskiy et al. [106] demonstrated that various popular semi-supervised methods can be considered special cases of the optimization problem described above. Notably, the semi-supervised AAE [107], CatGAN [108], SeGMA [109], and VAE [110] can all be viewed as specific instantiations of this framework.

3.2.5. Unsupervised IB Learning

In the unsupervised setting, data samples are not directly labeled by classes. Voloshynovskiy et al. [106] defined the unsupervised IB as a "compressed" parameterized mapping of X to Z, which preserves some information in Z about X through the reverse decoder $\tilde{X} = Q(X|Z)$. Therefore, the Lagrangian of the unsupervised IB can be defined as follows:

$$I_{P(X),P(Z|X)}(X;Z) - \beta I_{P(Z),Q(X|Z)}(Z;\tilde{X}), \qquad (13)$$

where $I(X;Z)$ is the information determined by the encoder $q(z|x)$ and $I(Z;\tilde{X})$ is the information determined by the decoder $q(x|z)$, i.e., the reconstruction error. In other words, the unsupervised IB is a special case of the supervised IB, where labels are replaced with the reconstruction performance of the training input. Alemi et al. [13] showed that the variational autoencoder (VAE) [111] and β-VAE [112] are special cases of the unsupervised variational IB. Voloshynovskiy et al. [106] extended their results and showed that many models, including adversarial autoencoders [107], InfoVAEs [113], and VAE/GANs [114], could be viewed as special cases of the unsupervised IB. The main difference between them is the bounds on the different mutual information of the IB. Furthermore, the unsupervised IB was used by Uğur et al. [115] to derive lower bounds for their unsupervised generative clustering framework, while Roy et al. [116] used it to study vector-quantized autoencoders.

Voloshynovskiy et al. [106] pointed out that for the classification task in the supervised IB, the latent space Z should have sufficient statistics for Y, whose entropy is much lower than X. This results in a highly compressed representation where sequences close in the input space might be close in the latent space, and the less significant features will be compressed. In contrast, in the unsupervised setup, the IB suggests compressing the input to the encoded representation so that each input sequence can be decoded uniquely. In this case, the latent space's entropy should correspond to the input space's entropy, and compression is much more difficult.

4. Self-Supervised Multiview Information Bottleneck Learning

How can we learn without labels and still achieve good predictive power? Is compression necessary to obtain an optimal representation? This section analyzes and discusses how to achieve an optimal representation for self-supervised learning when labels are not available during training. We review recent methods for self-supervised learning and show how they can be integrated into a single framework. We compare their objective functions, implicit assumptions, and theoretical challenges. Finally, we consider the information-theoretic properties of these representations, their optimality, and different ways of learning them.

One approach to enhance deep learning methods is to apply the *InfoMax principle* in a multiview setting [17,117]. As one of the earliest approaches, Linsker [17] proposed maximizing the information transfer from input data to its latent representation, showing its equivalence to maximizing the determinant of the output covariance under the Gaussian distribution assumption. Becker and Hinton [118] introduced a representation learning approach based on maximizing an approximation of the mutual information between alternative latent vectors obtained from the same image. The most well-known application is the Independent Component Analysis (ICA) InfoMax algorithm [119], designed to separate independent sources from their linear combinations. The ICA-InfoMax algorithm aims to maximize the mutual information between mixtures and source estimates while imposing statistical independence among outputs. The Deep InfoMax approach [120] extends this idea to unsupervised feature learning by maximizing the mutual information between input and output while matching a prior distribution for the representations. Recent work has applied this principle to a self-supervised multiview setting [46,120–122], wherein these works maximize the mutual information between the views Z_1 and Z_2 using the classifier $q(z_1|z_2)$, which attempts to predict one representation from the other.

However, Tschannen et al. [123] demonstrated that the effectiveness of InfoMax models is more attributable to the inductive biases introduced by the architecture and estimators than to the training objectives themselves, as the InfoMax objectives can be trivially maximized using invertible encoders. Moreover, a fundamental issue with the *InfoMax principle* is that it retains irrelevant information about the labels, contradicting the core concept of the IB principle, which advocates compressing the representation to enhance generalizability.

Going beyond the InfoMax principle requires us to tackle the crucial question: How do we discern between relevant and irrelevant information? A foundational concept in addressing this challenge is partial information decomposition (PID), as outlined by Williams and Beer [124] and further explored in Gutknecht et al. [125]. PID provides an elegant framework for categorizing the information provided by a set of source variables about a target variable into distinct types: unique, shared (redundant), and synergistic information.

PID enables us to leverage the complexity of information interactions. For example, shared information refers to common information across multiple sources, valuable for tasks that aggregate information from multiple sources or utilize redundancy in the data. Unique information, conversely, is knowledge exclusive to a specific source, enhancing the diversity of representations, and is particularly useful for tasks requiring specialized knowledge. Synergistic information arises from the combination of sources, unveiling insights unattainable when sources are considered individually.

For example, Sridharan and Kakade [126] proposed the *multiview IB framework*, which uses the shared information as the way to compress. According to this framework, in the multiview without labels setting, the IB principle of preserving relevant data while compressing irrelevant data requires assumptions regarding the relationship between views and labels. They presented the *multiview assumption*, which asserts that either view (approximately) would be sufficient for downstream tasks. By this assumption, they define the relevant information as the shared information between the views. Therefore, augmentations (such as changing the image style) should not affect the labels.

Additionally, the views will provide most of the information in the input regarding downstream tasks. We improve generalization without affecting the performance by compressing the information not shared between the two views. Their formulation is as follows:

Assumption 1. *The **multiview assumption:** There exists a ϵ_{info} (which is assumed to be small) such that*

$$I(Y; X_2 | X_1) \leq \epsilon_{info}$$
$$I(Y; X_1 | X_2) \leq \epsilon_{info}.$$

As a result, when the information sharing parameter, ϵ_{info}, is small, the information shared between views includes task-relevant details. For instance, in self-supervised contrastive learning for visual data [120], views represent various augmentations of the same image. In this scenario, the *multiview* assumption is considered mild if the downstream task remains unaffected by the augmentation [127]. Image augmentations can be perceived as altering an image's style without changing its content. Thus, Tsai et al. [128] contends that the information required for downstream tasks should be preserved in the content rather than the style. This assumption allows us to separate the information into relevant (shared information) and irrelevant (not shared) components and to compress only the unimportant details that do not contain information about downstream tasks. Based on this assumption, we aim to maximize the relevant information $I(X_2; Z_1)$ and minimize $I(X_1; Z_1 \mid X_2)$—the exclusive information that Z_1 contains about X_1, which cannot be predicted by observing X_2. This irrelevant information is unnecessary for the prediction task and can be discarded. In the extreme case, where X_1 and X_2 share only label information, this approach recovers the supervised IB method without labels. Conversely, if X_1 and X_2 are identical, this method collapses into the InfoMax principle, as no information can be accurately discarded.

Federici et al. [96] used the relaxed Lagrangian objective to obtain the minimal sufficient representation Z_1 for X_2 as follows:

$$\mathcal{L}_1 = I_{P(Z_1|X_1)}(Z_1; X_1 \mid X_2) - \beta_1 I_{P(X_2|Z_2)P(Z_2|Z_1)P(Z_1|X_1)}(X_2; Z_1), \tag{14}$$

and the symmetric loss to obtain the minimal sufficient representation Z_2 for X_1:

$$\mathcal{L}_2 = I_{P(Z_2|X_2)}(Z_2; X_2 \mid X_1) - \beta_2 I_{P(X_1|1), Q(Z_1|Z_2), P(Z_2|X_2)} I(X_1; Z_2), \tag{15}$$

where β_1 and β_2 are the Lagrangian multipliers introduced by the constraint optimization. By defining Z_1 and Z_2 on the same domain and re-parameterizing the Lagrangian multipliers, the average of the two loss functions can be upper-bounded as follows:

$$\mathcal{L} = -I_{P(Z_1|X_1), Q(Z_2|Z_1), P(Z_2|X_2), Q(Z_1|Z_2)}(Z_1; Z_2) + \beta D_{\text{SKL}}[p(z_1 \mid x_1) || P(z_2 \mid x_2)], \tag{16}$$

where D_{SKL} represents the symmetrized KL divergence obtained by averaging the expected values of $D_{\text{KL}}(p(z_1 \mid x_1) || p(z_2 \mid x_2))$ and $D_{\text{KL}}(p(z_2 \mid x_2) || p(z_1 \mid x_1))$. Note that when the mapping from X_1 to Z_1 is deterministic, $I(Z_1; X_1 \mid X_2)$ minimization and $H(Z_1 \mid X_2)$ minimization are interchangeable and the algorithms of Federici et al. [96] and Tsai et al. [128] minimize the same objective. Another implementation of the same idea is based on the conditional entropy bottleneck (CEB) algorithm [129] and proposed by Lee et al. [130]. This algorithm adds the residual information as a compression term to the InfoMax objective using the reverse decoders $q(z_1 \mid x_2)$ and $q(z_2 \mid x_1)$.

In conclusion, all the algorithms mentioned above are based on the multiview assumption. Utilizing this assumption, they can distinguish relevant information from irrelevant information. As a result, all these algorithms aim to maximize the information (or the predictive ability) of one representation with respect to the other view while compressing the information between each representation and its corresponding view. The key differences between these algorithms lie in the decomposition and implementation of these information terms.

Dubois et al. [131] offers another theoretical analysis of the IB for self-supervised learning. Their work addresses the question of the minimum bit rate required to store the input but still achieve a high performance on a family of downstream tasks $Y \in \mathcal{Y}$. It is a rate-distortion problem, where the goal is to find a compressed representation that will give us a good prediction for every task. We require that the distortion measure is bounded:

$$D_{\mathcal{T}}(X, Z) = \sup_{Y \in \mathcal{Y}} H(Y \mid Z_1) - H(Y \mid X_1) \leq \delta.$$

Accessing the downstream task is necessary to find the solution during the learning process. As a result, Dubois et al. [131] considered only tasks invariant to some equivalence relation, which divides the input into disjoint equivalence classes. An example would be an image with labels that remain unchanged after augmentation. This is similar to the *multiview assumption* where $\epsilon_{info} \to 0$. By applying Shannon's rate-distortion theory, they concluded that the minimum achievable bit rate is the rate-distortion function with the above invariance distortion. Thus, the optimal rate can be determined by minimizing the following Lagrangian:

$$\mathcal{L} = \min_{P(Z_1|X_1)} I_{P(Z_1|X_1)}(X_1; Z_1) + \beta H(Z_2 \mid X_1). \tag{17}$$

Using this objective, the maximization of information with labels is replaced by maximizing the prediction ability of one view from the original input, regularized by direct information from the input. Similarly to the above results, we would like to find a representation Z_1 that compresses the input X_1 so that Z_1 has the maximum information about X_2.

4.1. Implicit Compression in Self-Supervised Learning Methods

While the optimal IB representation is based on the multiview assumption, most self-supervised learning models only use the InfoMax principle and maximize the mutual information $I(Z_1; Z_2)$ without an explicit regularization term. However, recent studies have shown that contrastive learning creates compressed representations that include only relevant information [132,133]. The question is why is the learned representation compressed? The maximization of $I(Z_1; Z_2)$ could theoretically be sufficient to retain all the information from both X_1 and X_2 by making the representations invertible. In this section, we attempt to explain this phenomenon.

We begin with the InfoMax principle [17], which maximizes the mutual information between the representations of random variables Z^1 and Z^2 of the two views. We can lower-bound it using the following:

$$I(Z_1; Z_2) = H(Z) - H(Z_1 \mid Z_2) \geq H(Z_1) + \mathbb{E}[\log q(z_1 \mid z_2)]. \tag{18}$$

The bound is tight when $q(z_1|z_2) = p(z_1|z_2)$, in which case $\mathbb{E}[\log q(z_1 \mid z_2)]$, or the negative reconstruction error, equals the conditional entropy $H(Z_1|Z_2)$.

In the supervised case, where Z is a learned stochastic representation of the input and Y is the label, we aim to optimize

$$I(Y; Z) \geq H(Y) + \mathbb{E}[\log q(Y \mid Z)]. \tag{19}$$

Since Y is constant, optimizing the information $I(Z; Y)$ requires only minimizing the prediction term $\mathbb{E}[\log q(Y|Z)]$ by making Z more informative about Y. This term is the cross-entropy loss for classification or the square loss for regressions. Thus, we can minimize the log loss without any other regularization on the representation.

In contrast, for the self-supervised case, we have a more straightforward option to minimize $H(Z_1|Z_2)$: making Z_1 easier to predict by Z_2, which can be achieved by reducing its variance along specific dimensions. If we do not regularize $H(Z_1)$, it will decrease to zero, and we will observe a collapse. This is why, in contrastive methods, the variance in the representation (large entropy) is significant only in the directions with a high variance in the data, which is enforced by data augmentation [61]. According to this analysis, the network benefits from making the representations "simple" (easier to predict). Hence, even though our representation does not have explicit information-theoretical constraints, the learning process will compress the representation.

4.2. Beyond the Multiview Assumption

According to the multiview IB analysis presented in Section 4, the optimal way to create a useful representation is to maximize the mutual information between the representations of different views while compressing irrelevant information in each representation. In fact, as discussed in Section 4.1, we can achieve this optimal compressed representation even without explicit regularization. However, this optimality is based on the *multiview assumption*, which states that the relevant information for downstream tasks comes from the information shared between views. Therefore, Tian et al. [133] concluded that when a minimal sufficient representation has been obtained, the optimal views for self-supervised learning are determined by downstream tasks.

However, the *multiview assumption* is highly constrained, as all relevant information must be shared between all views. In cases where this assumption is incorrect, such as with aggressive data augmentation or multiple downstream tasks or modalities, sharing all the necessary information can be challenging. For example, if one view is a video stream while the other is an audio stream, the shared information may be sufficient for object recognition but not for tracking. Furthermore, relevant information for downstream tasks may not be contained within the shared information between views, meaning that removing non-shared information can negatively impact the performance.

Kahana and Hoshen [134] identified a series of tasks that violate the *multiview assumption*. To accomplish these tasks, the learned representation must also be invariant to unwanted attributes, such as bias removal and cross-domain retrieval. In such cases, only some attributes have labels, and the objective is to learn an invariant representation for the domain for which labels are provided while also being informative for all other attributes without labels. For example, for face images, only the identity labels may be provided, and the goal is to learn a representation that captures the unlabeled pose attribute but contains no information about the identity attribute. The task can also be applied to fair decisions, cross-domain matching, model anonymization, and image translation.

Wang et al. [132] formalized another case where the *multiview assumption* does not hold when non-shared task-relevant information cannot be ignored. In such cases, the minimal sufficient representation contains less task-relevant information than other sufficient representations, resulting in an inferior performance. Furthermore, their analysis shows that in such cases, the learned representation in contrastive learning is insufficient for downstream tasks, which may overfit the shared information.

As a result of their analysis, Wang et al. [132] and Kahana and Hoshen [134] proposed explicitly increasing mutual information between the representation and input to preserve task-relevant information and prevent the compression of unshared information between views. In this case, the two regularization terms of the two views are incorporated into the original InfoMax objective, and the following objective is optimized:

$$\mathcal{L} = \min_{P(Z_1|X_1), p(Z_2|X_2)} -I_{P(Z_1|X_1)}(X_1; Z_1) - I_{P(Z_2|X_2)}(X_2; Z_2) - \beta I_{P(Z_1|X_1), P(Z_2|Z_1)}(Z_1; Z_2). \quad (20)$$

Wang et al. [132] demonstrated the effectiveness of their method for SimCLR [7], BYOL [55], and Barlow Twins [135] across classification, detection, and segmentation tasks.

4.3. To Compress or Not to Compress?

As seen in Equation (20), when the *multiview assumption* is violated, the objective for obtaining an optimal representation is to **maximize** the mutual information between each input and its representation. This contrasts with the situation in which the *multiview assumption* holds, or the supervised case, where the objective is to **minimize** the mutual information between the representation and the input. In both supervised and unsupervised cases, we have direct access to the relevant information, which we can use to separate and compress irrelevant information. However, in the self-supervised case, we depend heavily on the *multiview assumption*. If this assumption is violated due to unshared information between views that is relevant for the downstream task, we cannot separate relevant and irrelevant information. Furthermore, the learning algorithm's nature requires that this information be protected by explicitly maximizing it.

As datasets continue to expand in size and models are anticipated to serve as base models for various downstream tasks, the *multiview assumption* becomes less pertinent. Consequently, compressing irrelevant information when the *multiview assumption* does not hold presents one of the most significant challenges in self-supervised learning. Identifying new methods to separate relevant from irrelevant information based on alternative assumptions is a promising avenue for research. It is also essential to recognize that empirical measurement of information-theoretic quantities and their estimators plays a crucial role in developing and evaluating such methods.

5. Optimizing Information in Deep Neural Networks: Challenges and Approaches

Recent years have seen information-theoretic analyses employed to explain and optimize deep learning techniques [74]. Despite their elegance and plausibility, empirically measuring and analyzing information in deep networks presents challenges. Two critical problems are (1) information in deterministic networks and (2) estimating information in high-dimensional spaces.

5.1. Information in Deterministic Networks

Information-theoretic methods have significantly impacted deep learning [13,15,74]. However, a key challenge is addressing the source of randomness in deterministic DNNs.

The mutual information between the input and representation is infinite, leading to ill-posed optimization problems or piecewise constant outcomes [136,137]. To tackle this issue, researchers have proposed various solutions. One common approach is to discretize the input distribution and real-valued hidden representations by binning, which facilitates non-trivial measurements and prevents the mutual information from always taking the maximum value of the log of the dataset size, thus avoiding ill-posed optimization problems [74].

However, binning and discretization are essentially equivalent to geometrical compression and serve as clustering measures [137]. Moreover, this discretization depends on the chosen bin size and does not track the mutual information across varying bin sizes [137,138]. To address these limitations, researchers have proposed alternative approaches, such as interpreting binned information as a weight decay penalty [139], estimating mutual information based on lower bounds assuming a continuous input distribution without making assumptions about the network's output distribution properties [140–142], injecting additive noise, and considering data augmentation as the source of noise [74,130,131,137].

5.2. Measuring Information in High-Dimensional Spaces

Estimating mutual information in high-dimensional spaces presents a significant challenge when applying information-theoretic measures to real-world data. This problem has been extensively studied [143,144], revealing the inefficiency of solutions for large dimensions and the limited scalability of known approximations with respect to the sample size and dimension. Despite these difficulties, various entropy and mutual information estimation approaches have been developed, including classic methods like k-nearest neighbors (KNNs) [145] and kernel density estimation techniques [146], as well as more recent efficient methods.

Chelombiev et al. [92] developed adaptive mutual information estimators based on entropy equal bins and the scaled noise kernel density estimator. Generative decoder networks, such as PixelCNN++ [147], have been employed to estimate a lower bound on mutual information [148–150]. Another strategy includes ensemble dependency graph estimators (EDGEs), adaptive mutual information estimation methods by merging randomized locality-sensitive hashing (LSH), dependency graphs, and ensemble bias reduction techniques [151]. The Mutual Information Neural Estimator (MINE) [152] maximizes KL divergence using the dual representation of Donsker and Varadhan [153] and has been employed for direct mutual information estimation [154]. Shwartz-Ziv and Alemi [155] developed a controlled framework that utilized the neural tangent kernels [156], in order to obtain tractable information measures.

Recent work by Poole et al. [157] introduced a framework for variational bounds of mutual information (MI), addressing bias and variance in existing estimators. This approach unifies recent developments and proposes a continuum of lower bounds that flexibly trades off bias and variance. In contrast, McAllester and Stratos [158] highlighted the statistical limitations inherent in all MI measuring methods. They suggest a difference-of-entropies estimator as a feasible alternative for estimating large MI.

Improving mutual information estimation can be achieved using larger batch sizes, although this may negatively impact the generalization performance and memory requirements. Alternatively, researchers have suggested employing surrogate measures for mutual information, such as log-determinant mutual information (LDMI), based on second-order statistics [159,160], which reflects linear dependence. Goldfeld and Greenewald [161] proposed the Sliced Mutual Information (SMI), defined as an average of MI terms between one-dimensional projections of high-dimensional variables. SMI inherits many properties of its classic counterpart. It can be estimated with optimal parametric error rates in all dimensions by combining an MI estimator between scalar variables with an MC integrator [161]. The k-SMI, introduced by Goldfeld et al. [162], extends the SMI by projecting to a k-dimensional subspace, which relaxes the smoothness assumptions, improves the scalability, and enhances the performance.

In conclusion, estimating and optimizing information in deep neural networks present significant challenges, particularly in deterministic networks and high-dimensional spaces. Researchers have proposed various approaches to address these issues, including discretization, alternative estimators, and surrogate measures. As the field continues to evolve, it is expected that more advanced techniques will emerge to overcome these challenges and facilitate the understanding and optimization of deep learning models.

6. Related Work

This work lies at the intersection of information theory and SSL, aiming to enhance machine learning models through the principles of encoding, compression, and generalization.

6.1. Information Theory Reviews

Information theory has been crucial in machine learning's evolution, starting with Shannon [163], who introduced key concepts like entropy and mutual information. Further reviews by Cover and Thomas [164] and Yeung [165] extended these ideas, incorporating computational advances to address data transmission and decoding challenges. Recent studies, such as those by Wilde [166] and Dimitrov et al. [167], have explored information theory's application in quantum computing and neuroscience.

Significant review works on the IB principle include Slonim [168], which thoroughly reviewed the IB method and its extensions, including the multivariate IB. Recent research by Goldfeld and Polyanskiy [169] and Shwartz-Ziv and Tishby [74] has applied IB theory to deep learning, optimizing feature representations to balance informativeness and compression. This research underscores the theory's importance in advancing machine learning algorithms and deep learning, seeking to bridge theory and practice.

6.2. Self-Supervised Learning Reviews

SSL represents a significant shift, allowing for the use of unlabeled data to learn valuable representations. Jaiswal et al. [170] covers SSL's progress, especially in contrastive learning's application to computer vision, NLP, and beyond. It provides an overview of various methods, showcasing how SSL improves learning representations for diverse tasks, and evaluates the potential and limitations of current methods.

Liu et al. [48] and Gui et al. [171] give detailed analyses of SSL techniques across several domains, including computer vision, NLP, and graph learning. They details how SSL, using input data for supervision, overcomes supervised learning's limitations, enhancing representation learning without manual labeling. This survey classifies methods into generative, contrastive, and generative–contrastive (adversarial) categories, providing theoretical insights.

Patil and Gudivada [172] and Wang et al. [173] delve into SSL-enhanced language models and their application to non-sequential tabular data, respectively. Meanwhile, Xie et al. [174] highlights the parallels between graph neural networks and SSL algorithms, and Hojjati et al. [175] discusses SSL's impact on anomaly detection in fields such as cybersecurity, finance, and healthcare. Moreover, Schiappa et al. [176] and Yu et al. [177] reviewed SSL in videos and recommendation systems.

Our work compiles these insights, offering a comprehensive review that combines the theoretical rigor of information theory with the practical advancements of SSL. Our goal is to pave the way for future research that leverages this interdisciplinary approach to uncover new efficiencies and applications in machine learning.

7. Future Research Directions

Despite the solid foundation established by existing self-supervised learning methods from an information theory perspective, several potential research directions warrant exploration:

- **Self-supervised learning with non-shared information.** As discussed in Section 4, the separation of relevant (preserved) and irrelevant (compressed) information relies on the *multiview assumption*. This assumption, which states that only shared information is essential for downstream tasks, is rather restrictive. For example, situations may arise where each view contains distinct information relevant to a downstream task or multiple tasks necessitate different features. Some methods have been proposed to tackle this problem, but they mainly focus on maximizing the network's information without explicit constraints. Formalizing this scenario and exploring differentiating between relevant and irrelevant data based on non-shared information represents an intriguing research direction.

- **Self-supervised learning for tabular data.** At present, the internal compression of self-supervised learning methods may compress relevant information due to improper augmentation (Section 4.1). Consequently, we must heavily rely on generating the two views, which must accurately represent information related to the downstream process. Custom augmentation must be developed for each domain, taking into account extensive prior knowledge on data augmentation. While some papers have attempted to extend self-supervised learning to tabular data [178,179], further work is necessary from both theoretical and practical standpoints to achieve a high performance with self-supervised learning for tabular data [180]. The augmentation process is crucial for the performance of current vision and text models. In the case of tabular data, employing information-theoretic loss functions that do not require information compression may help harness the benefits of self-supervised learning.

- **Integrating other learning methods into the information-theoretic framework.** Prior works have investigated various supervised, unsupervised, semi-supervised, and self-supervised learning methods, demonstrating that they optimize information-theoretic quantities. However, state-of-the-art methods employ additional changes and engineering practices that may be related to information theory, such as the stop gradient operation utilized by many self-supervised learning methods today [53,55]. The Expectation–Maximization (EM) algorithm [181] can be employed to explain this operation when one path is the E-step and the other is the M-step. Additionally, Elidan and Friedman [182] proposed an IB-inspired version of the EM algorithm, which could help develop information-theoretic-based objectives using the stop gradient operation.

- **Expanding the analysis to usable information.** While information theory offers a rigorous conceptual framework for describing information, it neglects essential aspects of computation. Conditional entropy, for example, is directly related to the predictability of a random variable in a betting game where agents are rewarded for accurate guesses. However, the standard definition assumes that agents have no computational bounds and can employ arbitrarily complex prediction schemes [76]. In the context of deep learning, predictive information $H(Y|Z)$ measures the amount of information that can be extracted from Z about Y given access to all decoders $p(y|z)$ in the world. Recently, Xu et al. [183] introduced *predictive V-information* as an alternative formulation based on realistic computational constraints.

- **Extending self-supervised learning's information-based perspective to energy-based model optimization.** Until now, research combining self-supervised learning with information theory has focused on probabilistic models with tractable likelihoods. These models enable the specific optimization of model parameters concerning the tractable log-likelihood [184–187] or a tractable lower bound of the likelihood [13,111]. Although models with tractable likelihoods offer certain benefits, their scope is limited and necessitates a particular format. Energy-based models (EBMs) present a more flexible, unified framework. Rather than specifying a normalized probability, EBMs define inference as minimizing an unnormalized energy function and learning as minimizing a loss function. The energy function does not require integration and can be parameterized with any nonlinear regression function. Inference typically involves finding a low-energy configuration or sampling from all possible configurations such that the probability of selecting a specific configuration follows a Gibbs distribution [188,189].

Investigating energy-based models for self-supervised learning from both theoretical and practical perspectives can open up numerous promising research directions. For instance, we could directly apply tools developed for energy-based models and statistical machines to optimize the model, such as Maximum Likelihood Training with

MCMC [190], score matching [191], denoising score matching [192,193], and score-based generation models [194].

- **Expanding the multiview framework to accommodate more views and tasks.** The multiview self-supervised IB framework can be extended to cases involving more than two views $(X_1, \cdots, X_n)$ and multiple downstream tasks $(Y_1, \cdots, Y_K)$. A simple extension of the multiview IB framework can be achieved by setting the objective function to maximize the joint mutual information of all views' representations $I(Z_1; \cdots Z_n)$ and compressing the individual information for each view $I(X_i; Z_i)$, $1 \leq i \leq N$. However, to ensure the optimality of this objective, we must expand the *multiview assumption* to include more than two views. In this scenario, we need to assume that relevant information is shared among all different views and tasks, which might be overly restrictive. As a result, defining and analyzing a more refined version of this naive solution is essential. One potential approach involves utilizing the multi-feature information bottleneck (MfIB) [195], which extends the original IB. The MfIB processes multiple feature types simultaneously and analyzes data from various sources. This framework establishes a joint distribution between the multivariate data and the model. Rather than solely preserving the information of one feature variable maximally, the MfIB concurrently maintains multiple feature variables' information while compressing them. The MfIB characterizes the relationships between different sources and outputs by employing the multivariate information bottleneck [196] and setting Bayesian networks.

8. Conclusions

In this study, we delved deeply into the concept of optimal representation in self-supervised learning through the lens of information theory. We synthesized various approaches, highlighting their foundational assumptions and constraints, and integrated them into a unified framework. Additionally, we explored the key information-theoretic terms that influence these optimal representations and the methods for estimating them.

While supervised and unsupervised learning offer more direct access to relevant information, self-supervised learning depends heavily on assumptions about the relationship between data and downstream tasks. This reliance makes distinguishing between relevant and irrelevant information considerably more challenging, necessitating further assumptions.

Despite these challenges, information theory stands out as a robust and versatile framework for analysis and algorithmic development. This adaptable framework caters to a range of learning paradigms and elucidates the inherent assumptions underpinning data and model optimization.

With the rapid growth of datasets and the increasing expectations placed on models to handle multiple downstream tasks, the traditional multiview assumption might become less reliable. One significant challenge in self-supervised learning is the precise compression of irrelevant information, especially when these assumptions are compromised.

Future research avenues might involve expanding the multiview framework to include more views and tasks and deepening our understanding of information theory's impact on facets of deep learning, such as reinforcement learning and generative models.

In summary, information theory is a crucial tool in our quest to better understand and optimize self-supervised learning models. By harnessing its principles, we can more adeptly navigate the intricacies of deep neural network development, paving the way for creating more effective models.

Funding: This research received no external funding.

Data Availability Statement: Data is contained within the article.

Conflicts of Interest: Author Yann LeCun was employed by the company Meta AI-FAIR. The remaining authors declare that the research was conducted in the absence of any commercial or financial relationships that could be construed as a potential conflict of interest.

References

1. Alam, M.; Samad, M.D.; Vidyaratne, L.; Glandon, A.; Iftekharuddin, K.M. Survey on deep neural networks in speech and vision systems. *Neurocomputing* **2020**, *417*, 302–321. [CrossRef]
2. LeCun, Y.; Bengio, Y.; Hinton, G.E. Deep Learning. *Nature* **2015**, *521*, 436–444. [CrossRef]
3. He, K.; Zhang, X.; Ren, S.; Sun, J. Deep Residual Learning for Image Recognition. *arXiv* **2015**, arXiv:1512.03385.
4. Bromley, J.; Guyon, I.; LeCun, Y.; Säckinger, E.; Shah, R. Signature verification using a "siamese" time delay neural network. In *Advances in Neural Information Processing Systems*; Curran Associates, Inc.: Red Hook, NY, USA, 1993; Volume 6.
5. Chopra, S.; Hadsell, R.; LeCun, Y. Learning a similarity metric discriminatively, with application to face verification. In Proceedings of the 2005 IEEE Computer Society Conference on Computer Vision and Pattern Recognition (CVPR'05), San Diego, CA, USA, 20–25 June 2005; Volume 1, pp. 539–546.
6. Hadsell, R.; Chopra, S.; LeCun, Y. Dimensionality reduction by learning an invariant mapping. In Proceedings of the 2006 IEEE Computer Society Conference on Computer Vision and Pattern Recognition (CVPR'06), New York, NY, USA, 17–22 June 2006; Volume 2, pp. 1735–1742.
7. Chen, T.; Kornblith, S.; Norouzi, M.; Hinton, G. A simple framework for contrastive learning of visual representations. In Proceedings of the International Conference on Machine Learning, PMLR, Virtual, 13–18 July 2020; pp. 1597–1607.
8. Caron, M.; Touvron, H.; Misra, I.; Jégou, H.; Mairal, J.; Bojanowski, P.; Joulin, A. Emerging properties in self-supervised vision transformers. In Proceedings of the IEEE/CVF International Conference on Computer Vision, Montreal, BC, Canada, 11–17 October 2021; pp. 9650–9660.
9. Misra, I.; van der Maaten, L. Self-supervised learning of pretext-invariant representations. In Proceedings of the IEEE/CVF Conference on Computer Vision and Pattern Recognition, Seattle, WA, USA, 13–19 June 2020; pp. 6707–6717.
10. Shwartz-Ziv, R.; Goldblum, M.; Souri, H.; Kapoor, S.; Zhu, C.; LeCun, Y.; Wilson, A.G. Pre-train your loss: Easy bayesian transfer learning with informative priors. In *Advances in Neural Information Processing Systems*; Curran Associates, Inc.: Red Hook, NY, USA, 2022; Volume 35, pp. 27706–27715.
11. Arora, S.; Khandeparkar, H.; Khodak, M.; Plevrakis, O.; Saunshi, N. A theoretical analysis of contrastive unsupervised representation learning. *arXiv* **2019**, arXiv:1902.09229.
12. Lee, J.D.; Lei, Q.; Saunshi, N.; Zhuo, J. Predicting what you already know helps: Provable self-supervised learning. In *Advances in Neural Information Processing Systems*; Curran Associates, Inc.: Red Hook, NY, USA, 2021; Volume 3.
13. Alemi, A.A.; Fischer, I.; Dillon, J.V.; Murphy, K. Deep Variational Information Bottleneck. In Proceedings of the International Conference on Learning Representations, Toulon, France, 24–26 April 2017.
14. Xu, A.; Raginsky, M. Information-theoretic analysis of generalization capability of learning algorithms. In *Advances in Neural Information Processing Systems*; Curran Associates, Inc.: Red Hook, NY, USA, 2017; Volume 30.
15. Steinke, T.; Zakynthinou, L. Reasoning about generalization via conditional mutual information. In Proceedings of the Conference on Learning Theory, PMLR, Graz, Austria, 9–12 July 2020; pp. 3437–3452.
16. Belghazi, M.I.; Baratin, A.; Rajeshwar, S.; Ozair, S.; Bengio, Y.; Courville, A.; Hjelm, D. Mutual Information Neural Estimation. In Proceedings of the 35th International Conference on Machine Learning, Stockholm, Sweden, 10–15 July 2018; Dy, J., Krause, A., Eds.; Volume 80, pp. 531–540.
17. Linsker, R. Self-organization in a perceptual network. *Computer* **1988**, *21*, 105–117. [CrossRef]
18. Tishby, N.; Pereira, F.; Biale, W. The Information Bottleneck method. In Proceedings of the 37th Annual Allerton Conference on Communication, Control, and Computing, Monticello, IL, USA, 22–24 September 1999; pp. 368–377.
19. Zhao, J.; Xie, X.; Xu, X.; Sun, S. Multi-view learning overview: Recent progress and new challenges. *Inf. Fusion* **2017**, *38*, 43–54. [CrossRef]
20. Yan, X.; Hu, S.; Mao, Y.; Ye, Y.; Yu, H. Deep multi-view learning methods: A review. *Neurocomputing* **2021**, *448*, 106–129. [CrossRef]
21. Kumar, A.; Daumé, H. A co-training approach for multi-view spectral clustering. In Proceedings of the 28th International Conference on Machine Learning (ICML-11), Citeseer, Bellevue, DC, USA, 28 June–2 July 2011; pp. 393–400.
22. Xue, Z.; Du, J.; Du, D.; Lyu, S. Deep low-rank subspace ensemble for multi-view clustering. *Inf. Sci.* **2019**, *482*, 210–227. [CrossRef]
23. Bach, F.R.; Jordan, M.I. Kernel independent component analysis. *J. Mach. Learn. Res.* **2002**, *3*, 1–48.
24. Li, Y.; Yang, M.; Zhang, Z. A survey of multi-view representation learning. *IEEE Trans. Knowl. Data Eng.* **2018**, *31*, 1863–1883. [CrossRef]
25. Hotelling, H. Relations Between Two Sets of Variates. *Biometrika* **1936**, *28*, 321–377. [CrossRef]
26. Hardoon, D.R.; Szedmak, S.; Shawe-Taylor, J. Canonical Correlation Analysis: An Overview with Application to Learning Methods. *Neural Comput.* **2004**, *16*, 2639–2664. [CrossRef]
27. Sun, S. A survey of multi-view machine learning. *Neural Comput. Appl.* **2013**, *23*, 2031–2038. [CrossRef]
28. Sun, L.; Ceran, B.; Ye, J. A scalable two-stage approach for a class of dimensionality reduction techniques. In Proceedings of the 16th ACM SIGKDD International Conference on Knowledge Discovery and Data Mining, Washington, DC, USA, 25–28 July 2010; pp. 313–322.
29. Yan, X.; Ye, Y.; Lou, Z. Unsupervised video categorization based on multivariate information bottleneck method. *Knowl.-Based Syst.* **2015**, *84*, 34–45. [CrossRef]

30. Jia, Y.; Salzmann, M.; Darrell, T. Factorized Latent Spaces with Structured Sparsity. In *Advances in Neural Information Processing Systems*; Lafferty, J., Williams, C., Shawe-Taylor, J., Zemel, R., Culotta, A., Eds.; Curran Associates, Inc.: Red Hook, NY, USA, 2010; Volume 23.
31. Cao, T.; Jojic, V.; Modla, S.; Powell, D.; Czymmek, K.; Niethammer, M. Robust Multimodal Dictionary Learning. In *Medical Image Computing and Computer-Assisted Intervention—MICCAI 2013: 16th International Conference, Nagoya, Japan, 22–26 September 2013*; Proceedings, Part III; Mori, K., Sakuma, I., Sato, Y., Barillot, C., Navab, N., Eds.; Springer: Berlin/Heidelberg, Germany, 2013; pp. 259–266.
32. Liu, W.; Tao, D.; Cheng, J.; Tang, Y. Multiview Hessian discriminative sparse coding for image annotation. *Comput. Vis. Image Underst.* **2014**, *118*, 50–60. [CrossRef]
33. Pu, S.; He, Y.; Li, Z.; Zheng, M. Multimodal Topic Learning for Video Recommendation. *arXiv* **2020**, arXiv:2010.13373.
34. Andrew, G.; Arora, R.; Bilmes, J.; Livescu, K. Deep canonical correlation analysis. In Proceedings of the International Conference on Machine Learning, PMLR, Atlanta, GA, USA, 17–19 June 2013; pp. 1247–1255.
35. Zhao, H.; Ding, Z.; Fu, Y. Multi-view clustering via deep matrix factorization. In Proceedings of the Thirty-First AAAI Conference on Artificial Intelligence, San Francisco, CA, USA, 4–9 February 2017.
36. Huang, Z.; Zhou, J.T.; Peng, X.; Zhang, C.; Zhu, H.; Lv, J. Multi-view Spectral Clustering Network. In Proceedings of the IJCAI, Macao, China, 10–16 August 2019; pp. 2563–2569.
37. Liu, S.; Xia, Y.; Shi, Z.; Yu, H.; Li, Z.; Lin, J. Deep learning in sheet metal bending with a novel theory-guided deep neural network. *IEEE/CAA J. Autom. Sin.* **2021**, *8*, 565–581. [CrossRef]
38. Srivastava, N.; Salakhutdinov, R. Multimodal Learning with Deep Boltzmann Machines. *J. Mach. Learn. Res.* **2014**, *15*, 2949–2980.
39. Ngiam, J.; Khosla, A.; Kim, M.; Nam, J.; Lee, H.; Ng, A.Y. Multimodal Deep Learning. In Proceedings of the 28th International Conference on International Conference on Machine Learning, ICML'11, Madison, WI, USA, 28 June–2 July 2011; pp. 689–696.
40. Wang, W.; Arora, R.; Livescu, K.; Bilmes, J. On Deep Multi-View Representation Learning. In Proceedings of the 32nd International Conference on International Conference on Machine Learning, ICML'15, Lille, France, 7–9 July 2015; Volume 37, pp. 1083–1092.
41. Karpathy, A.; Fei-Fei, L. Deep visual-semantic alignments for generating image descriptions. In Proceedings of the IEEE Conference on Computer Vision and Pattern Recognition, Boston, MA, USA, 7–12 June 2015; pp. 3128–3137.
42. Mao, J.; Xu, W.; Yang, Y.; Wang, J.; Huang, Z.; Yuille, A. Deep captioning with multimodal recurrent neural networks (m-rnn). *arXiv* **2014**, arXiv:1412.6632.
43. Donahue, J.; Anne Hendricks, L.; Guadarrama, S.; Rohrbach, M.; Venugopalan, S.; Saenko, K.; Darrell, T. Long-term recurrent convolutional networks for visual recognition and description. In Proceedings of the IEEE Conference on Computer Vision and Pattern Recognition, Boston, MA, USA, 7–12 June 2015; pp. 2625–2634.
44. Zhu, J.; Shwartz-Ziv, R.; Chen, Y.; LeCun, Y. Variance-Covariance Regularization Improves Representation Learning. *arXiv* **2023**, arXiv:2306.13292.
45. Chen, X.; Fan, H.; Girshick, R.; He, K. Improved baselines with momentum contrastive learning. *arXiv* **2020**, arXiv:2003.04297.
46. Bachman, P.; Hjelm, R.D.; Buchwalter, W. Learning representations by maximizing mutual information across views. In *Advances in Neural Information Processing Systems*; Curran Associates, Inc.: Red Hook, NY, USA, 2019; Volume 32.
47. Bar, A.; Wang, X.; Kantorov, V.; Reed, C.J.; Herzig, R.; Chechik, G.; Rohrbach, A.; Darrell, T.; Globerson, A. Detreg: Unsupervised pretraining with region priors for object detection. In Proceedings of the IEEE/CVF Conference on Computer Vision and Pattern Recognition, New Orleans, LA, USA, 18–24 June 2022; pp. 14605–14615.
48. Liu, X.; Zhang, F.; Hou, Z.; Mian, L.; Wang, Z.; Zhang, J.; Tang, J. Self-supervised learning: Generative or contrastive. *IEEE Trans. Knowl. Data Eng.* **2021**, *35*, 857–876. [CrossRef]
49. Kingma, D.P.; Welling, M. Auto-encoding variational bayes. *arXiv* **2014**, arXiv:1312.6114.
50. Lee, H.; Battle, A.; Raina, R.; Ng, A. Efficient sparse coding algorithms. In *Advances in Neural Information Processing Systems*; Schölkopf, B., Platt, J., Hoffman, T., Eds.; MIT Press: Cambridge, MA, USA, 2006; Volume 19.
51. Ng, A. Sparse autoencoder. *CS294A Lect. Notes* **2011**, *72*, 1–19.
52. Van Den Oord, A.; Vinyals, O.; Kavukcuoglu, K. Neural discrete representation learning. In *Advances in Neural Information Processing Systems*; Curran Associates, Inc.: Red Hook, NY, USA, 2017; Volume 30.
53. Chen, X.; He, K. Exploring simple siamese representation learning. In Proceedings of the IEEE/CVF Conference on Computer Vision and Pattern Recognition, Nashville, TN, USA, 20–25 June 2021; pp. 15750–15758.
54. He, K.; Fan, H.; Wu, Y.; Xie, S.; Girshick, R. Momentum contrast for unsupervised visual representation learning. In Proceedings of the IEEE/CVF Conference on Computer Vision and Pattern Recognition, Seattle, WA, USA, 13–19 June 2020; pp. 9729–9738.
55. Grill, J.B.; Strub, F.; Altché, F.; Tallec, C.; Richemond, P.; Buchatskaya, E.; Doersch, C.; Avila Pires, B.; Guo, Z.; Gheshlaghi Azar, M.; et al. Bootstrap your own latent-a new approach to self-supervised learning. In *Advances in Neural Information Processing Systems*; Curran Associates, Inc.: Red Hook, NY, USA, 2020; Volume 33, pp. 21271–21284.
56. Bardes, A.; Ponce, J.; LeCun, Y. Vicreg: Variance-invariance-covariance regularization for self-supervised learning. *arXiv* **2021**, arXiv:2105.04906.
57. Vincent, P.; Larochelle, H.; Bengio, Y.; Manzagol, P.A. Extracting and composing robust features with denoising autoencoders. In Proceedings of the 25th International Conference on Machine Learning, Helsinki, Finland, 5–9 July 2008; pp. 1096–1103.

58. Devlin, J.; Chang, M.W.; Lee, K.; Toutanova, K. BERT: Pre-training of Deep Bidirectional Transformers for Language Understanding. In Proceedings of the North American Chapter of the Association for Computational Linguistics, Minneapolis, MN, USA, 2–7 June 2019.
59. He, K.; Chen, X.; Xie, S.; Li, Y.; Dollár, P.; Girshick, R. Masked autoencoders are scalable vision learners. In Proceedings of the IEEE/CVF Conference on Computer Vision and Pattern Recognition, New Orleans, LA, USA, 18–24 June 2022; pp. 16000–16009.
60. Gutmann, M.; Hyvärinen, A. Noise-contrastive estimation: A new estimation principle for unnormalized statistical models. In Proceedings of the Thirteenth International Conference on Artificial Intelligence and Statistics, Sardinia, Italy, 13–15 May 2010; Teh, Y.W., Titterington, M., Eds.; Volume 9, pp. 297–304.
61. Jing, L.; Vincent, P.; LeCun, Y.; Tian, Y. Understanding dimensional collapse in contrastive self-supervised learning. *arXiv* **2021**, arXiv:2110.09348.
62. Caron, M.; Misra, I.; Mairal, J.; Goyal, P.; Bojanowski, P.; Joulin, A. Unsupervised learning of visual features by contrasting cluster assignments. In *Advances in Neural Information Processing Systems*; Curran Associates, Inc.: Red Hook, NY, USA, 2020; Volume 33, pp. 9912–9924.
63. Chapelle, O.; Scholkopf, B.; Zien, A. Semi-supervised learning (chapelle, o. et al., eds.; 2006)[book reviews]. *IEEE Trans. Neural Netw.* **2009**, *20*, 542. [CrossRef]
64. Laine, S.; Aila, T. Temporal ensembling for semi-supervised learning. *arXiv* **2016**, arXiv:1610.02242.
65. Miyato, T.; Maeda, S.i.; Koyama, M.; Ishii, S. Virtual adversarial training: A regularization method for supervised and semi-supervised learning. *IEEE Trans. Pattern Anal. Mach. Intell.* **2018**, *41*, 1979–1993. [CrossRef]
66. Sohn, K.; Berthelot, D.; Carlini, N.; Zhang, Z.; Zhang, H.; Raffel, C.A.; Cubuk, E.D.; Kurakin, A.; Li, C.L. Fixmatch: Simplifying semi-supervised learning with consistency and confidence. In *Advances in Neural Information Processing Systems*; Curran Associates, Inc.: Red Hook, NY, USA, 2020; Volume 33, pp. 596–608.
67. Grandvalet, Y.; Bengio, Y. Entropy Regularization. 2006. Available online: https://www.researchgate.net/profile/Y-Bengio/publication/237619703_9_Entropy_Regularization/links/0f3175320aaecbde17000000/9-Entropy-Regularization.pdf (accessed on 8 May 2023).
68. Xie, Q.; Dai, Z.; Hovy, E.; Luong, T.; Le, Q. Unsupervised data augmentation for consistency training. In *Advances in Neural Information Processing Systems*; Curran Associates, Inc.: Red Hook, NY, USA, 2020; Volume 33, pp. 6256–6268.
69. Zhai, X.; Oliver, A.; Kolesnikov, A.; Beyer, L. S4l: Self-supervised semi-supervised learning. In Proceedings of the IEEE/CVF International Conference on Computer Vision, Seoul, Republic of Korea, 27 October–2 November 2019; pp. 1476–1485.
70. Lee, D.H. Pseudo-label: The simple and efficient semi-supervised learning method for deep neural networks. In Proceedings of the Workshop on Challenges in Representation Learning, ICML, Daegu, Republic of Korea, 3–7 November 2013; Volume 3, p. 896.
71. Bengio, Y.; Courville, A.; Vincent, P. Representation learning: A review and new perspectives. *IEEE Trans. Pattern Anal. Mach. Intell.* **2013**, *35*, 1798–1828. [CrossRef]
72. Goodfellow, I.; Bengio, Y.; Courville, A. *Deep Learning*; MIT Press: Cambridge, MA, USA, 2016.
73. Bengio, Y.; LeCun, Y. Scaling Learning Algorithms towards AI. In *Large Scale Kernel Machines*; Bottou, L., Chapelle, O., DeCoste, D., Weston, J., Eds.; MIT Press: Cambridge, MA, USA, 2007.
74. Shwartz-Ziv, R.; Tishby, N. Opening the black box of deep neural networks via information. *arXiv* **2017**, arXiv:1703.00810.
75. Ben-Shaul, I.; Shwartz-Ziv, R.; Galanti, T.; Dekel, S.; LeCun, Y. Reverse Engineering Self-Supervised Learning. In *Advances in Neural Information Processing Systems*; Curran Associates, Inc.: Red Hook, NY, USA, 2023.
76. Cover, T.M. *Elements of Information Theory*; John Wiley & Sons: Hoboken, NJ, USA, 1999.
77. Koopman, B.O. On distributions admitting a sufficient statistic. *Trans. Am. Math. Soc.* **1936**, *39*, 399–409. [CrossRef]
78. Buesing, L.; Maass, W. A spiking neuron as information bottleneck. *Neural Comput.* **2010**, *22*, 1961–1992. [CrossRef]
79. Palmer, S.E.; Marre, O.; Berry, M.J.; Bialek, W. Predictive information in a sensory population. *Proc. Natl. Acad. Sci. USA* **2015**, *112*, 6908–6913. [CrossRef] [PubMed]
80. Turner, R.; Sahani, M. A maximum-likelihood interpretation for slow feature analysis. *Neural Comput.* **2007**, *19*, 1022–1038. [CrossRef]
81. Hecht, R.M.; Noor, E.; Tishby, N. Speaker recognition by Gaussian information bottleneck. In Proceedings of the Tenth Annual Conference of the International Speech Communication Association, Brighton, UK, 6–10 September 2009.
82. Lee, N.; Hyun, D.; Na, G.S.; Kim, S.; Lee, J.; Park, C. Conditional Graph Information Bottleneck for Molecular Relational Learning. *arXiv* **2023**, arXiv:2305.01520.
83. Erdogmus, D. *Information Theoretic Learning: Renyi's Entropy and Its Applications to Adaptive System Training*; University of Florida: Gainesville, FL, USA, 2002.
84. Quinlan, J.R. *C4. 5: Programs for Machine Learning*; Elsevier: Amsterdam, The Netherlands, 2014.
85. Zhang, Z.; Sabuncu, M. Generalized cross entropy loss for training deep neural networks with noisy labels. In *Advances in Neural Information Processing Systems*; Curran Associates, Inc.: Red Hook, NY, USA, 2018; Volume 31.
86. Wenzel, F.; Roth, K.; Veeling, B.S.; Świkatkowski, J.; Tran, L.; Mandt, S.; Snoek, J.; Salimans, T.; Jenatton, R.; Nowozin, S. How good is the bayes posterior in deep neural networks really? *arXiv* **2020**, arXiv:2002.02405.
87. Painsky, A.; Wornell, G.W. On the Universality of the Logistic Loss Function. *arXiv* **2018**, arXiv:1805.03804.
88. Shamir, O.; Sabato, S.; Tishby, N. Learning and generalization with the information bottleneck. *Theor. Comput. Sci.* **2010**, *411*, 2696–2711. [CrossRef]

89. Vera, M.; Piantanida, P.; Vega, L.R. The role of information complexity and randomization in representation learning. *arXiv* **2018**, arXiv:1802.05355.
90. Russo, D.; Zou, J. How much does your data exploration overfit? controlling bias via information usage. *IEEE Trans. Inf. Theory* **2019**, *66*, 302–323. [CrossRef]
91. Achille, A.; Soatto, S. Emergence of invariance and disentanglement in deep representations. *J. Mach. Learn. Res.* **2018**, *19*, 1947–1980.
92. Chelombiev, I.; Houghton, C.; O'Donnell, C. Adaptive estimators show information compression in deep neural networks. *arXiv* **2019**, arXiv:1902.09037.
93. Shwartz-Ziv, R.; Painsky, A.; Tishby, N. Representation Compression and Generalization in Deep Neural Networks. 2018. Available online: https://arxiv.org/pdf/2202.06749.pdf#page=56 (accessed on 12 December 2023).
94. Piran, Z.; Shwartz-Ziv, R.; Tishby, N. The dual information bottleneck. *arXiv* **2020**, arXiv:2006.04641.
95. Shwartz-Ziv, R. Information flow in deep neural networks. *arXiv* **2022**, arXiv:2202.06749.
96. Federici, M.; Dutta, A.; Forré, P.; Kushman, N.; Akata, Z. Learning robust representations via multi-view information bottleneck. *arXiv* **2020**, arXiv:2002.07017.
97. Geiger, B.C. On Information Plane Analyses of Neural Network Classifiers—A Review. *IEEE Trans. Neural Netw. Learn. Syst.* **2020**, *33*, 7039–7051. [CrossRef]
98. Amjad, R.A.; Geiger, B.C. How (Not) To Train Your Neural Network Using the Information Bottleneck Principle. *arXiv* **2018**, arXiv:1802.09766.
99. Achille, A.; Rovere, M.; Soatto, S. Critical learning periods in deep neural networks. *arXiv* **2019**, arXiv:1711.08856.
100. Saxe, A.M.; Bansal, Y.; Dapello, J.; Advani, M.; Kolchinsky, A.; Tracey, B.D.; Cox, D.D. On the information bottleneck theory of deep learning. *J. Stat. Mech. Theory Exp.* **2019**, *2019*, 124020. [CrossRef]
101. Basirat, M.; Geiger, B.C.; Roth, P.M. A Geometric Perspective on Information Plane Analysis. *Entropy* **2021**, *23*, 711. [CrossRef] [PubMed]
102. Pensia, A.; Jog, V.; Loh, P.L. Generalization error bounds for noisy, iterative algorithms. In Proceedings of the 2018 IEEE International Symposium on Information Theory (ISIT), Vail, CO, USA, 17–22 June 2018; pp. 546–550.
103. Xu, C.; Tao, D.; Xu, C. Large-Margin Multi-ViewInformation Bottleneck. *IEEE Trans. Pattern Anal. Mach. Intell.* **2014**, *36*, 1559–1572. [CrossRef] [PubMed]
104. Wang, Q.; Boudreau, C.; Luo, Q.; Tan, P.N.; Zhou, J. Deep Multi-view Information Bottleneck. In Proceedings of the 2019 SIAM International Conference on Data Mining (SDM), Calgary, AB, Canada, 2–4 May 2019; pp. 37–45. [CrossRef]
105. Berthelot, D.; Carlini, N.; Goodfellow, I.; Papernot, N.; Oliver, A.; Raffel, C.A. Mixmatch: A holistic approach to semi-supervised learning. In *Advances in Neural Information Processing Systems*; Curran Associates, Inc.: Red Hook, NY, USA, 2019; Volume 32.
106. Voloshynovskiy, S.; Taran, O.; Kondah, M.; Holotyak, T.; Rezende, D. Variational Information Bottleneck for Semi-Supervised Classification. *Entropy* **2020**, *22*, 943. [CrossRef] [PubMed]
107. Makhzani, A.; Shlens, J.; Jaitly, N.; Goodfellow, I.; Frey, B. Adversarial autoencoders. *arXiv* **2015**, arXiv:1511.05644.
108. Springenberg, J.T. Unsupervised and Semi-supervised Learning with Categorical Generative Adversarial Networks. *arXiv* **2015**, arXiv:1511.06390.
109. Śmieja, M.; Wołczyk, M.; Tabor, J.; Geiger, B.C. SeGMA: Semi-Supervised Gaussian Mixture Autoencoder. *IEEE Trans. Neural Netw. Learn. Syst.* **2019**, *32*, 3930–3941. [CrossRef]
110. Kingma, D.P.; Mohamed, S.; Jimenez Rezende, D.; Welling, M. Semi-supervised learning with deep generative models. In *Advances in Neural Information Processing Systems*; Curran Associates, Inc.: Red Hook, NY, USA, 2014; Volume 27.
111. Kingma, D.P.; Welling, M. An introduction to variational autoencoders. *Found. Trends® Mach. Learn.* **2019**, *12*, 307–392. [CrossRef]
112. Higgins, I.; Matthey, L.; Pal, A.; Burgess, C.; Glorot, X.; Botvinick, M.; Mohamed, S.; Lerchner, A. beta-vae: Learning basic visual concepts with a constrained variational framework. In Proceedings of the ICLR, Toulon, France, 24–26 April 2017.
113. Zhao, S.; Song, J.; Ermon, S. Infovae: Information maximizing variational autoencoders. *arXiv* **2019**, arXiv:1706.02262.
114. Larsen, A.B.L.; Sønderby, S.K.; Larochelle, H.; Winther, O. Autoencoding beyond pixels using a learned similarity metric. In Proceedings of the International Conference on Machine Learning, PMLR, New York, NY, USA, 20–22 June 2016; pp. 1558–1566.
115. Uğur, Y.; Arvanitakis, G.; Zaidi, A. Variational information bottleneck for unsupervised clustering: Deep gaussian mixture embedding. *Entropy* **2020**, *22*, 213. [CrossRef]
116. Roy, A.; Vaswani, A.; Neelakantan, A.; Parmar, N. Theory and experiments on vector quantized autoencoders. *arXiv* **2018**, arXiv:1805.11063.
117. Wiskott, L.; Sejnowski, T.J. Slow Feature Analysis: Unsupervised Learning of Invariances. *Neural Comput.* **2002**, *14*, 715–770. [CrossRef] [PubMed]
118. Becker, S.; Hinton, G.E. Self-organizing neural network that discovers surfaces in random-dot stereograms. *Nature* **1992**, *355*, 161–163. [CrossRef] [PubMed]
119. Bell, A.J.; Sejnowski, T.J. An information-maximization approach to blind separation and blind deconvolution. *Neural Comput.* **1995**, *7*, 1129–1159. [CrossRef] [PubMed]
120. Hjelm, R.D.; Fedorov, A.; Lavoie-Marchildon, S.; Grewal, K.; Bachman, P.; Trischler, A.; Bengio, Y. Learning deep representations by mutual information estimation and maximization. *arXiv* **2019**, arXiv:1808.06670.

121. Henaff, O. Data-efficient image recognition with contrastive predictive coding. In Proceedings of the International Conference on Machine Learning, PMLR, Virtual, 13–18 July 2020; pp. 4182–4192.
122. Tian, Y.; Krishnan, D.; Isola, P. Contrastive multiview coding. In Proceedings of the European Conference on Computer Vision, Glasgow, UK, 23–28 August 2020; pp. 776–794.
123. Tschannen, M.; Djolonga, J.; Rubenstein, P.K.; Gelly, S.; Lucic, M. On mutual information maximization for representation learning. *arXiv* **2020**, arXiv:1907.13625.
124. Williams, P.L.; Beer, R.D. Nonnegative decomposition of multivariate information. *arXiv* **2010**, arXiv:1004.2515.
125. Gutknecht, A.J.; Wibral, M.; Makkeh, A. Bits and pieces: Understanding information decomposition from part-whole relationships and formal logic. *Proc. R. Soc. A* **2021**, *477*, 20210110. [CrossRef]
126. Sridharan, K.; Kakade, S. An Information Theoretic Framework for Multi-View Learning. In Proceedings of the 21st Annual Conference on Learning Theory—COLT 2008, Helsinki, Finland, 9–12 July 2008.
127. Geiping, J.; Goldblum, M.; Somepalli, G.; Shwartz-Ziv, R.; Goldstein, T.; Wilson, A.G. How Much Data Are Augmentations Worth? An Investigation into Scaling Laws, Invariance, and Implicit Regularization. *arXiv* **2023**, arXiv:2210.06441.
128. Tsai, Y.H.H.; Wu, Y.; Salakhutdinov, R.; Morency, L.P. Self-supervised learning from a multi-view perspective. *ICLR 2021* **2020**.
129. Fischer, I. The conditional entropy bottleneck. *Entropy* **2020**, *22*, 999. [CrossRef]
130. Lee, K.H.; Arnab, A.; Guadarrama, S.; Canny, J.; Fischer, I. Compressive visual representations. In *Advances in Neural Information Processing Systems*; Curran Associates, Inc.: Red Hook, NY, USA, 2021; Volume 34.
131. Dubois, Y.; Bloem-Reddy, B.; Ullrich, K.; Maddison, C.J. Lossy compression for lossless prediction. In *Advances in Neural Information Processing Systems*; Curran Associates, Inc.: Red Hook, NY, USA, 2021; Volume 34.
132. Wang, H.; Guo, X.; Deng, Z.H.; Lu, Y. Rethinking Minimal Sufficient Representation in Contrastive Learning. In Proceedings of the Proceedings of the IEEE/CVF Conference on Computer Vision and Pattern Recognition (CVPR), New Orleans, LA, USA, 18–24 June 2022.
133. Tian, Y.; Sun, C.; Poole, B.; Krishnan, D.; Schmid, C.; Isola, P. What makes for good views for contrastive learning? In *Advances in Neural Information Processing Systems*; Curran Associates, Inc.: Red Hook, NY, USA, 2020; Volume 33, pp. 6827–6839.
134. Kahana, J.; Hoshen, Y. A Contrastive Objective for Learning Disentangled Representations. In *Computer Vision—ECCV 2022*; Springer: Cham, Switzerland, 2022.
135. Zbontar, J.; Jing, L.; Misra, I.; LeCun, Y.; Deny, S. Barlow twins: Self-supervised learning via redundancy reduction. In Proceedings of the International Conference on Machine Learning, PMLR, Virtual, 18–24 July 2021; pp. 12310–12320.
136. Amjad, R.A.; Geiger, B.C. Learning representations for neural network-based classification using the information bottleneck principle. *IEEE Trans. Pattern Anal. Mach. Intell.* **2019**, *42*, 2225–2239. [CrossRef] [PubMed]
137. Goldfeld, Z.; van den Berg, E.; Greenewald, K.; Melnyk, I.; Nguyen, N.; Kingsbury, B.; Polyanskiy, Y. Estimating Information Flow in Neural Networks. *arXiv* **2018**, arXiv:1810.05728.
138. Ross, B.C. Mutual Information between Discrete and Continuous Data Sets. *PLoS ONE* **2014**, *9*, e87357. [CrossRef]
139. Elad, A.; Haviv, D.; Blau, Y.; Michaeli, T. The Effectiveness of Layer-by-Layer Training Using the Information Bottleneck Principle. 2019. Available online: https://openreview.net/forum?id=r1Nb5i05tX (accessed on 12 February 2024).
140. Wang, T.; Isola, P. Understanding contrastive representation learning through alignment and uniformity on the hypersphere. In Proceedings of the International Conference on Machine Learning, PMLR, Virtual, 13–18 July 2020; pp. 9929–9939.
141. Zimmermann, R.S.; Sharma, Y.; Schneider, S.; Bethge, M.; Brendel, W. Contrastive learning inverts the data generating process. In Proceedings of the International Conference on Machine Learning, PMLR, Virtual, 18–24 July 2021; pp. 12979–12990.
142. Shwartz-Ziv, R.; Balestriero, R.; LeCun, Y. What Do We Maximize in Self-Supervised Learning? *arXiv* **2022**, arXiv:2207.10081.
143. Paninski, L. Estimation of Entropy and Mutual Information. *Neural Comput.* **2003**, *15*, 1191–1253. [CrossRef]
144. Gao, S.; Ver Steeg, G.; Galstyan, A. Efficient estimation of mutual information for strongly dependent variables. In Proceedings of the Artificial Intelligence and Statistics, San Diego, CA, USA, 9–12 May 2015; pp. 277–286.
145. Kozachenko, L.F.; Leonenko, N.N. Sample estimate of the entropy of a random vector. *Probl. Peredachi Informatsii* **1987**, *23*, 9–16.
146. Hang, H.; Steinwart, I.; Feng, Y.; Suykens, J.A. Kernel density estimation for dynamical systems. *J. Mach. Learn. Res.* **2018**, *19*, 1260–1308.
147. Van den Oord, A.; Kalchbrenner, N.; Espeholt, L.; Vinyals, O.; Graves, A. Conditional image generation with pixelcnn decoders. In *Advances in Neural Information Processing Systems*; Curran Associates, Inc.: Red Hook, NY, USA, 2016; Volume 29.
148. Darlow, L.N.; Storkey, A. What Information Does a ResNet Compress? *arXiv* **2020**, arXiv:2003.06254.
149. Nash, C.; Kushman, N.; Williams, C.K.I. Inverting Supervised Representations with Autoregressive Neural Density Models. In Proceedings of the International Conference on Artificial Intelligence and Statistics, Playa Blanca, Lanzarote, 9–11 April 2018.
150. Shwartz-Ziv, R.; Balestriero, R.; Kawaguchi, K.; Rudner, T.G.; LeCun, Y. An Information-Theoretic Perspective on Variance-Invariance-Covariance Regularization. In *Advances in Neural Information Processing Systems*; Curran Associates, Inc.: Red Hook, NY, USA, 2023.
151. Noshad, M.; Zeng, Y.; Hero, A.O. Scalable Mutual Information Estimation Using Dependence Graphs. In Proceedings of the ICASSP 2019–2019 IEEE International Conference on Acoustics, Speech and Signal Processing (ICASSP), Brighton, UK, 12–17 May 2019; pp. 2962–2966. [CrossRef]
152. Belghazi, M.I.; Baratin, A.; Rajeshwar, S.; Ozair, S.; Bengio, Y.; Hjelm, R.D.; Courville, A.C. Mutual Information Neural Estimation. In Proceedings of the ICML, Stockholm, Sweden, 10–15 July 2018.

153. Donsker, M.D.; Varadhan, S.S. Asymptotic evaluation of certain Markov process expectations for large time, I. *Commun. Pure Appl. Math.* **1975**, *28*, 1–47. [CrossRef]
154. Elad, A.; Haviv, D.; Blau, Y.; Michaeli, T. Direct validation of the information bottleneck principle for deep nets. In Proceedings of the IEEE International Conference on Computer Vision Workshops, Seoul, Republic of Korea, 27–28 October 2019.
155. Shwartz-Ziv, R.; Alemi, A.A. Information in infinite ensembles of infinitely-wide neural networks. In Proceedings of the Symposium on Advances in Approximate Bayesian Inference, PMLR. 2020; pp. 1–17. Available online: http://proceedings.mlr.press/v118/shwartz-ziv20a.html (accessed on 8 May 2023).
156. Jacot, A.; Gabriel, F.; Hongler, C. Neural tangent kernel: Convergence and generalization in neural networks. In *Advances in Neural Information Processing Systems*; Curran Associates, Inc.: Red Hook, NY, USA, 2018; Volume 31.
157. Poole, B.; Ozair, S.; Van Den Oord, A.; Alemi, A.; Tucker, G. On variational bounds of mutual information. In Proceedings of the International Conference on Machine Learning, PMLR, Long Beach, CA, USA, 9–15 June 2019; pp. 5171–5180.
158. McAllester, D.; Stratos, K. Formal limitations on the measurement of mutual information. In Proceedings of the International Conference on Artificial Intelligence and Statistics, PMLR, Online, 26–28 August 2020, pp. 875–884.
159. Ozsoy, S.; Hamdan, S.; Arik, S.; Yuret, D.; Erdogan, A. Self-supervised learning with an information maximization criterion. In *Advances in Neural Information Processing Systems*; Curran Associates, Inc.: Red Hook, NY, USA, 2022; Volume 35, pp. 35240–35253.
160. Erdogan, A.T. An information maximization based blind source separation approach for dependent and independent sources. In Proceedings of the ICASSP 2022-2022 IEEE International Conference on Acoustics, Speech and Signal Processing (ICASSP), Virtual, 23–27 May 2022; pp. 4378–4382.
161. Goldfeld, Z.; Greenewald, K. Sliced mutual information: A scalable measure of statistical dependence. In *Advances in Neural Information Processing Systems*; Curran Associates, Inc.: Red Hook, NY, USA, 2021; Volume 34, pp. 17567–17578.
162. Goldfeld, Z.; Greenewald, K.; Nuradha, T.; Reeves, G. k-sliced mutual information: A quantitative study of scalability with dimension. In *Advances in Neural Information Processing Systems*; Curran Associates, Inc.: Red Hook, NY, USA, 2022.
163. Shannon, C.E. A mathematical theory of communication. *Bell Syst. Tech. J.* **1948**, *27*, 379–423. [CrossRef]
164. Cover, T.M.; Thomas, J.A. *Elements of Information Theory (Wiley Series in Telecommunications and Signal Processing)*; Wiley-Interscience: Hoboken, NJ, USA, 2006.
165. Yeung, R.W. Information Theory and Network Coding (Yeung, R.W.; 2008) [Book review]. *IEEE Trans. Inf. Theory* **2009**, *55*, 3409. [CrossRef]
166. Wilde, M.M. *Quantum Information Theory*; Cambridge University Press: Cambridge, UK, 2013.
167. Dimitrov, A.G.; Lazar, A.A.; Victor, J.D. Information theory in neuroscience. *J. Comput. Neurosci.* **2011**, *30*, 1–5. [CrossRef]
168. Slonim, N. The Information Bottleneck: Theory and Applications. Ph.D. Thesis, Hebrew University of Jerusalem, Jerusalem, Israel, 2002.
169. Goldfeld, Z.; Polyanskiy, Y. The Information Bottleneck Problem and its Applications in Machine Learning. *IEEE J. Sel. Areas Inf. Theory* **2020**, *1*, 19–38. [CrossRef]
170. Jaiswal, A.; Babu, A.R.; Zadeh, M.Z.; Banerjee, D.; Makedon, F. A survey on contrastive self-supervised learning. *Technologies* **2020**, *9*, 2. [CrossRef]
171. Gui, J.; Chen, T.; Cao, Q.; Sun, Z.; Luo, H.; Tao, D. A survey of self-supervised learning from multiple perspectives: Algorithms, theory, applications and future trends. *arXiv* **2023**, arXiv:2301.05712.
172. Patil, R.; Gudivada, A. A Review of Current Trends, Techniques, and Challenges in Large Language Models (LLMs). *Appli. Sci.* **2024**, *14*, 20. [CrossRef]
173. Wang, W.Y.; Du, W.W.; Xu, D.; Wang, W.; Peng, W.C. A Survey on Self-Supervised Learning for Non-Sequential Tabular Data. *arXiv* **2024**, arXiv:2402.01204.
174. Xie, Y.; Xu, Z.; Zhang, J.; Wang, Z.; Ji, S. Self-supervised learning of graph neural networks: A unified review. *IEEE Trans. Pattern Anal. Mach. Intell.* **2023**, *45*, 2412–2429. [CrossRef] [PubMed]
175. Hojjati, H.; Ho, T.K.K.; Armanfard, N. Self-supervised anomaly detection: A survey and outlook. *arXiv* **2023**, arXiv:2205.05173.
176. Schiappa, M.C.; Rawat, Y.S.; Shah, M. Self-supervised learning for videos: A survey. *ACM Comput. Surv.* **2023**, *55*, 1–37. [CrossRef]
177. Yu, J.; Yin, H.; Xia, X.; Chen, T.; Li, J.; Huang, Z. Self-supervised learning for recommender systems: A survey. *IEEE Trans. Knowl. Data Eng.* **2023**, *36*, 335–355. [CrossRef]
178. Ucar, T.; Hajiramezanali, E.; Edwards, L. Subtab: Subsetting features of tabular data for self-supervised representation learning. In *Advances in Neural Information Processing Systems*; Curran Associates, Inc.: Red Hook, NY, USA, 2021; Volume 34, pp. 18853–18865.
179. Arik, S.Ö.; Pfister, T. Tabnet: Attentive interpretable tabular learning. *AAAI Conf. Artif. Intell.* **2021**, *35*, 6679–6687. [CrossRef]
180. Shwartz-Ziv, R.; Armon, A. Tabular data: Deep learning is not all you need. *Inf. Fusion* **2022**, *81*, 84–90. [CrossRef]
181. Dempster, A.P.; Laird, N.M.; Rubin, D.B. Maximum likelihood from incomplete data via the EM algorithm. *J. R. Stat. Soc. Ser. B (Methodol.)* **1977**, *39*, 1–22. [CrossRef]
182. Elidan, G.; Friedman, N. The information bottleneck EM algorithm. *arXiv* **2012**, arXiv:1212.2460.
183. Xu, Y.; Zhao, S.; Song, J.; Stewart, R.; Ermon, S. A theory of usable information under computational constraints. *arXiv* **2020**, arXiv:2002.10689.
184. Graves, A. Generating sequences with recurrent neural networks. *arXiv* **2013**, arXiv:1308.0850.

185. Germain, M.; Gregor, K.; Murray, I.; Larochelle, H. Made: Masked autoencoder for distribution estimation. In Proceedings of the International Conference on Machine Learning, PMLR, Lille, France, 7–9 July 2015; pp. 881–889.
186. Dinh, L.; Sohl-Dickstein, J.; Bengio, S. Density estimation using real nvp. *arXiv* **2017**, arXiv:1605.08803.
187. Rezende, D.; Mohamed, S. Variational inference with normalizing flows. In Proceedings of the International conference on machine learning, PMLR, Lille, France, 7–9 July 2015; pp. 1530–1538.
188. Huembeli, P.; Arrazola, J.M.; Killoran, N.; Mohseni, M.; Wittek, P. The physics of energy-based models. *Quantum Mach. Intell.* **2022**, *4*, 1–13. [CrossRef]
189. Song, Y.; Kingma, D.P. How to train your energy-based models. *arXiv* **2021**, arXiv:2101.03288.
190. Younes, L. On The Convergence Of Markovian Stochastic Algorithms With Rapidly Decreasing Ergodicity Rates. *Stochastics Stochastics Model.* **1999**, *65*, 177–228. [CrossRef]
191. Hyvärinen, A. Some Extensions of Score Matching. 2006. Available online: https://www.sciencedirect.com/science/article/abs/pii/S0167947306003264 (accessed on 12 February 2024).
192. Song, Y.; Sohl-Dickstein, J.; Kingma, D.P.; Kumar, A.; Ermon, S.; Poole, B. Score-based generative modeling through stochastic differential equations. *arXiv* **2021**, arXiv:2011.13456.
193. Vincent, P. A Connection Between Score Matching and Denoising Autoencoders. *Neural Comput.* **2011**, *23*, 1661–1674. [CrossRef] [PubMed]
194. Song, Y.; Ermon, S. Generative Modeling by Estimating Gradients of the Data Distribution. In *Advances in Neural Information Processing Systems*; Wallach, H., Larochelle, H., Beygelzimer, A., d'Alché-Buc, F., Fox, E., Garnett, R., Eds.; Curran Associates, Inc.: Red Hook, NY, USA, 2019; Volume 32.
195. Lou, Z.; Ye, Y.; Yan, X. The multi-feature information bottleneck with application to unsupervised image categorization. In Proceedings of the Twenty-Third International Joint Conference on Artificial Intelligence, Beijing, China, 3–9 August 2013.
196. Friedman, N.; Mosenzon, O.; Slonim, N.; Tishby, N. Multivariate information bottleneck. *arXiv* **2001**, arXiv:1301.2270.

Disclaimer/Publisher's Note: The statements, opinions and data contained in all publications are solely those of the individual author(s) and contributor(s) and not of MDPI and/or the editor(s). MDPI and/or the editor(s) disclaim responsibility for any injury to people or property resulting from any ideas, methods, instructions or products referred to in the content.

Article

A Unifying Generator Loss Function for Generative Adversarial Networks

Justin Veiner [1], Fady Alajaji [1,*] and Bahman Gharesifard [2]

[1] Department of Mathematics and Statistics, Queen's University, Kingston, ON K7L 3N6, Canada; justin.veiner@queensu.ca

[2] Department of Electrical and Computer Engineering, University of California, Los Angeles, CA 90095, USA; gharesifard@ucla.edu

* Correspondence: fa@queensu.ca

Abstract: A unifying α-parametrized generator loss function is introduced for a dual-objective generative adversarial network (GAN) that uses a canonical (or classical) discriminator loss function such as the one in the original GAN (VanillaGAN) system. The generator loss function is based on a symmetric class probability estimation type function, $\mathcal{L}_\alpha$, and the resulting GAN system is termed $\mathcal{L}_\alpha$-GAN. Under an optimal discriminator, it is shown that the generator's optimization problem consists of minimizing a Jensen-f_α-divergence, a natural generalization of the Jensen-Shannon divergence, where f_α is a convex function expressed in terms of the loss function $\mathcal{L}_\alpha$. It is also demonstrated that this $\mathcal{L}_\alpha$-GAN problem recovers as special cases a number of GAN problems in the literature, including VanillaGAN, least squares GAN (LSGAN), least kth-order GAN (LkGAN), and the recently introduced (α_D, α_G)-GAN with $\alpha_D = 1$. Finally, experimental results are provided for three datasets—MNIST, CIFAR-10, and Stacked MNIST—to illustrate the performance of various examples of the $\mathcal{L}_\alpha$-GAN system.

Keywords: generative adversarial networks; deep learning; parameterized loss functions; f-divergence; Jensen-f-divergence

Citation: Veiner, J.; Alajaji, F.; Gharesifard, B. A Unifying Generator Loss Function for Generative Adversarial Networks. *Entropy* **2024**, *26*, 290. https://doi.org/10.3390/e26040290

Academic Editor: Boris Ryabko

Received: 23 February 2024
Revised: 18 March 2024
Accepted: 22 March 2024
Published: 27 March 2024

Copyright: © 2024 by the authors. Licensee MDPI, Basel, Switzerland. This article is an open access article distributed under the terms and conditions of the Creative Commons Attribution (CC BY) license (https://creativecommons.org/licenses/by/4.0/).

1. Introduction

Generative adversarial networks (GANs), first introduced by Goodfellow et al. in 2014 [1], have a variety of applications in media generation [2], image restoration [3], and data privacy [4]. GANs aim to generate synthetic data that closely resemble the original real data with (unknown) underlying distribution $P_\mathbf{x}$. The GAN is trained such that the distribution of the generated data, $P_\mathbf{g}$, approximates $P_\mathbf{x}$ well. More specifically, low-dimensional random noise is fed to a generator neural network G to produce synthetic data. Real data and the generated data are then given to a discriminator neural network D that scores the data between 0 and 1, with a score close to 1 meaning that the discriminator thinks the data belong to the real dataset. The discriminator and generator play a minimax game, where the aim is to minimize the generator's loss and maximize the discriminator's loss.

Since its initial introduction, several variants of GAN have been proposed. Deep convolutional GAN (DCGAN) [5] utilizes the same loss functions as VanillaGAN (the original GAN) while combining GANs with convolutional neural networks, which are helpful when applying GANs to image data as they extract visual features from the data. DCGANs are more stable than the baseline model but can suffer from mode collapse, which occurs when the generator learns that a select number of images can easily fool the discriminator, resulting in the generator only generating those images. Another notable issue with VanillaGAN is the tendency for the generator network's gradients to vanish. In the early stages of training, the discriminator lacks confidence and assigns generated data values close to zero. Therefore, the objective function tends to zero, resulting in small gradients and a lack of learning. To mitigate this issue, a non-saturating generator loss function was proposed in [1] so that gradients do not vanish early on in training.

In the original (VanillaGAN) problem setup, the objective function, expressed as a negative sum of two Shannon cross-entropies, is to be minimized by the generator and maximized by the discriminator. It is demonstrated that if the discriminator is fixed to be optimal (i.e., as a maximizer of the objective function), the GAN's minimax game can be reduced to minimizing the Jensen-Shannon divergence (JSD) between the real and generated data's probability distributions [1]. An analogous result was proven in [6] for RényiGANs, a dual-objective GAN using distinct discriminator and generator loss functions. More specifically, under a canonical discriminator loss function (as in [1]) and a generator loss function expressed in terms of two Rényi cross-entropies, it is shown that the RényiGAN optimization problem reduces to minimizing the Jensen-Rényi divergence, hence extending VanillaGAN's results.

Nowozin et al. generalized VanillaGAN by formulating a class of loss functions in [7] parametrized by a lower semicontinuous convex function f, devising f-GAN. More specifically, the f-GAN problem consists of minimizing an f-divergence between the true data distribution and the generator distribution via a minimax optimization of a Fenchel conjugate representation of the f-divergence, where the VanillaGAN discriminator's role (as a binary classifier) is replaced by a variational function estimating the ratio of the true data and generator distributions. The f-GAN loss function may be tedious to derive, as it requires computation of the Fenchel conjugate of f. It can be shown that f-GAN can interpolate between VanillaGAN and HellingerGAN, among others [7].

More recently, α-GAN was presented in [8], for which the aim is to derive a class of loss functions parameterized by $\alpha > 0$ and expressed in terms of a class probability estimation (CPE) loss between a real label $y \in \{0,1\}$ and predicted label $\hat{y} \in [0,1]$ [8]. The ability to control α as a hyperparameter is beneficial to be able to apply one system to multiple datasets, as two datasets may be optimal under different α values. This work was further analyzed in [9] and expanded in [10] by introducing the dual-objective (α_D, α_G)-GAN, which allowed for the generator and discriminator loss functions to have distinct α parameters with the aim of improving training stability. When $\alpha_D = \alpha_G$, the α-GAN optimization reduces to minimizing an Arimoto divergence, as originally derived in [8]. Note that α-GAN can recover several f-GANs, such as HellingerGAN, VanillaGAN, WassersteinGAN, and total variation GAN [8]. Furthermore, in their more recent work [11] that unifies [8–10], the authors establish, under some conditions, a one-to-one correspondence between CPE-loss-based GANs (such as α-GANs) and f-GANs that use a symmetric f-divergence (see Theorems 4–5 and Corollary 1 in [11]). They also prove various generalization and estimation error bounds for (α_D, α_G)-GANs and illustrate their ability to mitigate training instability for synthetic Gaussian data as well as the Celeb-A and LSUN Classroom image datasets. The various (α_D, α_G)-GAN equilibrium results do not provide an analogous result to JSD and Jensen-Rényi divergence minimization for the VanillaGAN [1] and RényiGAN [6] problems, respectively, as they do not involve a *Jensen-type divergence*. More specifically given a divergence measure $\mathcal{D}(p\|q)$ between distributions p and q (i.e., a positive-definite bivariate function: $\mathcal{D}(p\|q) \geq 0$ with equality if and only if (iff) $p = q$ almost everywhere (a.e.)), a *Jensen-type divergence of $\mathcal{D}$* is given by

$$\frac{1}{2}\mathcal{D}(p\|\frac{p+q}{2}) + \frac{1}{2}\mathcal{D}(q\|\frac{p+q}{2});$$

i.e., it is the arithmetic average of two $\mathcal{D}$-divergences: one between p and the mixture $(p+q)/2$ and the other between q and $(p+q)/2$.

The main objective of our work is to present a unifying approach that provides an axiomatic framework to encompass several existing GAN generator loss functions so that GAN optimization can be simplified in terms of a Jensen-type divergence. In particular, our framework classifies the set of α-parameterized CPE-based loss functions $\mathcal{L}_\alpha$, generalizing the α-loss function in [8–11]. We then propose $\mathcal{L}_\alpha$-GAN: a dual-objective GAN that uses a function from this class for the generator and uses any canonical discriminator loss function that admits the same optimizer as VanillaGAN [1]. We show that under some regularity (convexity/concavity) conditions on $\mathcal{L}_\alpha$, the minimax game played with these two loss functions is equivalent to the minimization of a Jensen-f_α-divergence: a Jensen-type divergence and another natural extension of the Jensen-Shannon divergence (in addition to the Jensen-Rényi divergence [6]), where the generating function f_α of the divergence is directly computed from the CPE loss function $\mathcal{L}_\alpha$. This result recovers various prior dual-objective GAN equilibrium results, thus unifying them under one parameterized generator loss function. The newly obtained Jensen-f_α-divergence, which is noted to belong to the class of symmetric f-divergences with different generating functions (see Remark 1), is a useful measure of dissimilarity between distributions as it requires a convex function f with a restricted domain given by the interval $[0,2]$ (see Remark 2) in addition to its symmetry and finiteness properties.

The rest of the paper is organized as follows. In Section 2, we review f-divergence measures and introduce the Jensen-f-divergence as an extension of the Jensen-Shannon divergence. In Section 3, we establish our main result regarding the optimization of our unifying generator loss function (Theorem 1) and show that it can be applied to a large class of known GANs (Lemmas 2–4). We conduct experiments in Section 4 by implementing different manifestations of $\mathcal{L}_\alpha$-GAN on three datasets: MNIST, CIFAR-10, and Stacked MNIST. Finally, we conclude the paper in Section 5.

2. Preliminaries

We begin by presenting key information measures used throughout the paper. Let $f : [0, \infty) \to (-\infty, \infty]$ be a convex continuous function that is strictly convex at 1 (i.e., $f(\lambda u_1 + (1-\lambda)u_2) < \lambda f(u_1) + (1-\lambda)f(u_2)$ for all $u_1, u_2 \geq 0$, $u_1 \neq u_2$, and $\lambda \in (0,1)$ such that $\lambda u_1 + (1-\lambda)u_2 = 1$) and satisfying

$$f(1) = 0.$$

Note that the convexity of f already implies its continuity on $(0, \infty)$. Here, the continuity of f at 0 is extended, setting $f(0) = \lim_{u \downarrow 0} f(u)$, which may be infinite. Otherwise, $f(u)$ is assumed to be finite for $u > 0$.

Definition 1 ([12–14]). *The **f-divergence** between two probability densities p and q with common support $\mathcal{R} \subseteq \mathbb{R}^d$ on the Lebesgue measurable space $(\mathcal{R}, \mathcal{B}(\mathcal{R}), \mu)$ is denoted by $D_f(p\|q)$ and given by*

$$D_f(p\|q) = \int_\mathcal{R} q\, f\left(\frac{p}{q}\right) d\mu, \tag{1}$$

where we have used the shorthand $\int_\mathcal{R} g\, d\mu := \int_\mathcal{R} g(x)\, d\mu(x)$, where g is a measurable function; we follow this convention from now on. Here, f is referred to as the generating function of $D_f(p\|q)$.

For simplicity, we consider throughout densities with common supports. A comprehensive definition of f-divergence for arbitrary distributions can be found in Section III of [15]. We require that f is strictly convex around 1 and that it satisfies the normalization condition $f(1) = 0$ to ensure positive-definiteness of the f-divergence, i.e., $D_f(p\|q) \geq 0$ with equality holding iff $p = q$ (a.e.). We present examples of f-divergences under various choices of their generating function f in Table 1. We will be invoking these divergence measures in different parts of the paper.

Table 1. Examples of f-divergences.

f-Divergence	Symbol	Formula	$f(u)$
Kullback–Leiber [16]	KL	$\int_{\mathcal{R}} p \log\left(\frac{p}{q}\right) d\mu$	$u \log u$
Jensen-Shannon [17]	JSD	$\frac{1}{2}\text{KL}\left(p\|\|\frac{p+q}{2}\right) + \frac{1}{2}\text{KL}\left(q\|\|\frac{p+q}{2}\right)$	$\frac{1}{2}\left(u \log u - (u+1) \log \frac{u+1}{2}\right)$
Pearson χ^2 [18]	χ^2	$\int_{\mathcal{R}} \frac{(q-p)^2}{p} d\mu$	$\left(\sqrt{x} - \frac{1}{\sqrt{x}}\right)^2$
Pearson–Vajda ($k > 1$) [18]	$\|\chi\|^k$	$\int_{\mathcal{R}} \frac{\|q-p\|^k}{p^{k-1}} d\mu$	$u^{1-k}\|1-u\|^k$
Arimoto ($\alpha > 0, \alpha \neq 1$) [15,19,20]	$\mathcal{A}_\alpha$	$\frac{\alpha}{\alpha-1}\left(\int_{\mathcal{R}}(p^\alpha + q^\alpha)^{\frac{1}{\alpha}} d\mu - 2^{\frac{1}{\alpha}}\right)$	$\frac{\alpha}{\alpha-1}\left((1+u)^{\frac{1}{\alpha}} - (1+u) - 2^{\frac{1}{\alpha}} + 2\right)$
Hellinger ($\alpha > 0, \alpha \neq 1$) [15,21,22]	$\mathcal{H}_\alpha$	$\frac{1}{\alpha-1}\left(\int_{\mathcal{R}} p^\alpha q^{1-\alpha} d\mu - 1\right)$	$\frac{u^\alpha - 1}{\alpha - 1}$

The Rényi divergence of order α ($\alpha > 0$, $\alpha \neq 1$) between densities p and q with common support $\mathcal{R}$ is used in [6] in the RényiGAN problem; it is given by [23,24]

$$D_\alpha(p\|q) = \frac{1}{\alpha - 1} \log\left(\int_{\mathcal{R}} p^\alpha q^{1-\alpha} d\mu\right). \tag{2}$$

Note that the Rényi divergence is not an f-divergence; however, it can be expressed as a transformation of the Hellinger divergence (which is itself an f-divergence):

$$D_\alpha(p\|q) = \frac{1}{\alpha - 1} \log(1 + (\alpha - 1)\mathcal{H}_\alpha(p\|q)). \tag{3}$$

We now introduce a new measure, the Jensen-f-divergence, which is analogous to the Jensen-Shannon and Jensen-Rényi divergences.

Definition 2. *The **Jensen-f-divergence** between two probability distributions p and q with common support $\mathcal{R} \subseteq \mathbb{R}^d$ on the Lebesgue measurable space $(\mathcal{R}, \mathcal{B}(\mathcal{R}), \mu)$ is denoted by $\text{JD}_f(p\|q)$ and given by*

$$\text{JD}_f(p\|q) = \frac{1}{2} D_f\left(p \left\|\frac{p+q}{2}\right.\right) + \frac{1}{2} D_f\left(q \left\|\frac{p+q}{2}\right.\right), \tag{4}$$

where $D_f(\cdot\|\cdot)$ is the f-divergence.

We next verify that the Jensen-Shannon divergence is a Jensen-f-divergence.

Lemma 1. *Let p and q be two densities with common support $\mathcal{R} \subseteq \mathbb{R}^d$, and consider the function $f : [0, \infty) \to (-\infty, \infty]$ given by $f(u) = u \log u$. Then we have that*

$$\text{JD}_f(p\|q) = \text{JSD}(p\|q). \tag{5}$$

Proof. As f is convex (and continuous) on its domain with $f(1) = 0$, we have that

$$\begin{aligned}
\text{JSD}(p\|q) &= \frac{1}{2}\text{KL}\left(p\left\|\frac{p+q}{2}\right.\right) + \frac{1}{2}\text{KL}\left(q\left\|\frac{p+q}{2}\right.\right) \\
&= \frac{1}{2}\int_{\mathcal{R}} p \log\left(\frac{2p}{p+q}\right) d\mu + \frac{1}{2}\int_{\mathcal{R}} q \log\left(\frac{2q}{p+q}\right) d\mu \\
&= \frac{1}{2}\int_{\mathcal{R}} \frac{p+q}{2} \left(\frac{2p}{p+q} \log\left(\frac{2p}{p+q}\right)\right) d\mu \\
&\quad + \frac{1}{2}\int_{\mathcal{R}} \frac{p+q}{2}\left(\frac{2q}{p+q} \log\left(\frac{2q}{p+q}\right)\right) d\mu \\
&= \text{JD}_f(p\|q).
\end{aligned}$$

□

Remark 1 (*Jensen-f-divergence is a symmetric f-divergence*). Note that $\mathrm{JD}_f(p\|q)$ is itself a symmetric f-divergence (with a modified generating function). Indeed, given the continuous convex function f that is strictly convex around 1 with $f(1) = 0$, consider the functions

$$f_1(u) := \frac{u+1}{2} f\left(\frac{2u}{u+1}\right), \qquad u \geq 0,$$

and

$$f_2(u) := \frac{u+1}{2} f\left(\frac{2}{u+1}\right), \qquad u \geq 0,$$

which are both continuous convex, strictly convex around 1, and satisfy $f_1(1) = f_2(1) = 0$. Now, direct calculations yield that

$$D_f\left(p \middle\| \frac{p+q}{2}\right) = D_{f_1}(p\|q)$$

and

$$D_f\left(q \middle\| \frac{p+q}{2}\right) = D_{f_2}(p\|q).$$

Thus,

$$\mathrm{JD}_f(p\|q) = \frac{1}{2} D_{f_1}(p\|q) + \frac{1}{2} D_{f_2}(p\|q) = D_{\tilde{f}}(p\|q),$$

where $\tilde{f} := \frac{1}{2}(f_1 + f_2)$, i.e.,

$$\tilde{f}(u) = \frac{u+1}{4}\left(f\left(\frac{2u}{u+1}\right) + f\left(\frac{2}{u+1}\right)\right), \qquad u \geq 0, \qquad (6)$$

is also continuous convex, strictly convex around 1, and satisfies $\tilde{f}(1) = 0$. Since by (4),

$$\mathrm{JD}_f(p\|q) = \mathrm{JD}_f(q\|p),$$

we conclude that the Jensen-f-divergence is a symmetric $\tilde{f}$-divergence. An equivalent argument is to note that $\tilde{f} = \tilde{f}^\star$, where $\tilde{f}^\star(u) := u\tilde{f}(\frac{1}{u})$, $u \geq 0$ (with $\tilde{f}^\star(0) := \lim_{t\to\infty} \tilde{f}(t)/t$), which is a necessary and sufficient condition for the $\tilde{f}$-divergence to be symmetric (see p. 4399 in [15]).

Remark 2 (*Domain of f*). Examining (4), we note that the Jensen-f-divergence between p and q involves the f-divergences between either p or q and their mixture $(p+q)/2$. In other words, to determine $\mathrm{JD}_f(p\|q)$, we only need $f\left(\frac{2p}{p+q}\right)$ and $f\left(\frac{2q}{p+q}\right)$ when taking the expectations in (1). Thus, it is sufficient to restrict the domain of the convex function f to the interval $[0, 2]$.

3. Main Results

We now present our main theorem that unifies various generator loss functions under a CPE-based loss function $\mathcal{L}_\alpha$ for a dual-objective GAN, $\mathcal{L}_\alpha$-GAN, with a canonical discriminator loss function that is optimized as in [1]. Under some regularity conditions on the loss function $\mathcal{L}_\alpha$, we show that under the optimal discriminator, our generator loss becomes a Jensen-f-divergence.

Let $(\mathcal{X}, \mathcal{B}(\mathcal{X}), \mu)$ be the measured space of $n \times n \times m$ images (where $m = 1$ for black and white images and $m = 3$ for RGB images), and let $(\mathcal{Z}, \mathcal{B}(\mathcal{Z}), \mu)$ be a measured space such that $\mathcal{Z} \subseteq \mathbb{R}^d$. The discriminator neural network is given by $D : \mathcal{X} \to [0, 1]$, and the generator neural network is given by $G : \mathcal{Z} \to \mathcal{X}$. The generator's noise input is sampled from a multivariate Gaussian distribution $P_\mathbf{z} : \mathcal{Z} \to [0, 1]$. We denote the probability distribution of the real data by $P_\mathbf{x} : \mathcal{X} \to [0, 1]$ and the probability distribution of the generated data by $P_\mathbf{g} : \mathcal{X} \to [0, 1]$. We also set $P_\mathbf{x}$ and $P_\mathbf{g}$ as the densities corresponding to $P_\mathbf{x}$ and $P_\mathbf{g}$, respectively. We begin by introducing the $\mathcal{L}_\alpha$-GAN system.

Definition 3. Fix $\alpha \in \mathcal{A} \subseteq \mathbb{R}$ and let $\mathcal{L}_\alpha : \{0,1\} \times [0,1] \to [0,\infty)$ be a loss function such that $\hat{y}\mathcal{L}_\alpha\left(1, \frac{\hat{y}}{2}\right)$ is a continuous function that is either convex or concave in $\hat{y} \in [0,2]$ with strict convexity (respectively, strict concavity) around $\hat{y} = 1$ and such that $\mathcal{L}_\alpha$ is symmetric in the sense that

$$\mathcal{L}_\alpha(1, \hat{y}) = \mathcal{L}_\alpha(0, 1 - \hat{y}), \qquad \hat{y} \in [0,1]. \tag{7}$$

Then the $\mathcal{L}_\alpha$-**GAN** system is defined by $(V_D, V_{\mathcal{L}_\alpha, G})$, where $V_D : \mathcal{X} \times \mathcal{Z} \to \mathbb{R}$ is the discriminator loss function, and $V_{\mathcal{L}_\alpha, G} : \mathcal{X} \times \mathcal{Z} \to \mathbb{R}$ is the generator loss function, which is given by

$$V_{\mathcal{L}_\alpha, G}(D, G) = \mathbb{E}_{\mathbf{A} \sim P_\mathbf{x}}[-\mathcal{L}_\alpha(1, D(\mathbf{A}))] + \mathbb{E}_{\mathbf{B} \sim P_\mathbf{g}}[-\mathcal{L}_\alpha(0, D(\mathbf{B}))]. \tag{8}$$

Moreover, the $\mathcal{L}_\alpha$-**GAN problem** is defined by

$$\sup_D V_D(D, G) \tag{9}$$

$$\inf_G V_{\mathcal{L}_\alpha, G}(D, G). \tag{10}$$

We now present our main result about the $\mathcal{L}_\alpha$-GAN optimization problem.

Theorem 1. For a fixed $\alpha \in \mathcal{A} \subseteq \mathbb{R}$ and $\mathcal{L}_\alpha : \{0,1\} \times [0,1] \to [0,\infty)$, let $(V_D, V_{\mathcal{L}_\alpha, G})$ be the loss functions of $\mathcal{L}_\alpha$-GAN and consider joint optimization in (9)–(10). If V_D is a canonical loss function in the sense that it is maximized at $D = D^*$, where

$$D^* = \frac{P_\mathbf{x}}{P_\mathbf{x} + P_\mathbf{g}}, \tag{11}$$

then (10) reduces to

$$\inf_G V_{\mathcal{L}_\alpha, G}(D^*, G) = \inf_G 2a \mathrm{JD}_{f_\alpha}(P_\mathbf{x} \| P_\mathbf{g}) - 2ab, \tag{12}$$

where $\mathrm{JD}_{f_\alpha}(\cdot \| \cdot)$ is the Jensen-f_α-divergence, and $f_\alpha : [0,2] \to \mathbb{R}$ is a continuous convex function that is strictly convex around 1 and is given by

$$f_\alpha(u) = -u\left(\frac{1}{a}\mathcal{L}_\alpha\left(1, \frac{u}{2}\right) - b\right), \tag{13}$$

where a and b are real constants chosen so that $f_\alpha(1) = 0$ with $a < 0$ (respectively, $a > 0$) if $u\mathcal{L}_\alpha\left(1, \frac{u}{2}\right)$ is convex (respectively, concave). Finally, (12) is minimized when $P_\mathbf{x} = P_\mathbf{g}$ (a.e.).

Proof. Under the assumption that V_D is maximized at $D^* = \frac{P_\mathbf{x}}{P_\mathbf{x} + P_\mathbf{g}}$, we have that

$$\begin{aligned}
V_{\mathcal{L}_\alpha, G}(D^*, G) &= \mathbb{E}_{\mathbf{A} \sim P_\mathbf{x}}[-\mathcal{L}_\alpha(1, D^*(\mathbf{A}))] + \mathbb{E}_{\mathbf{B} \sim P_\mathbf{g}}[-\mathcal{L}_\alpha(0, D^*(\mathbf{B}))] \\
&= -\int_\mathcal{X} P_\mathbf{x} \mathcal{L}_\alpha(1, D^*) \, d\mu - \int_\mathcal{X} P_\mathbf{g} \mathcal{L}_\alpha(0, D^*) \, d\mu \\
&= -\int_\mathcal{X} P_\mathbf{x} \mathcal{L}_\alpha\left(1, \frac{P_\mathbf{x}}{P_\mathbf{x} + P_\mathbf{g}}\right) d\mu - \int_\mathcal{X} P_\mathbf{g} \mathcal{L}_\alpha\left(0, \frac{P_\mathbf{x}}{P_\mathbf{x} + P_\mathbf{g}}\right) d\mu \\
&= -2 \int_\mathcal{X} \left(\frac{P_\mathbf{x} + P_\mathbf{g}}{2}\right) \frac{P_\mathbf{x}}{P_\mathbf{x} + P_\mathbf{g}} \mathcal{L}_\alpha\left(1, \frac{P_\mathbf{x}}{P_\mathbf{x} + P_\mathbf{g}}\right) d\mu \\
&\quad - 2 \int_\mathcal{X} \left(\frac{P_\mathbf{x} + P_\mathbf{g}}{2}\right) \frac{P_\mathbf{g}}{P_\mathbf{x} + P_\mathbf{g}} \mathcal{L}_\alpha\left(0, \frac{P_\mathbf{x}}{P_\mathbf{x} + P_\mathbf{g}}\right) d\mu \\
&\stackrel{(a)}{=} -2 \int_\mathcal{X} \left(\frac{P_\mathbf{x} + P_\mathbf{g}}{2}\right) \frac{P_\mathbf{x}}{P_\mathbf{x} + P_\mathbf{g}} \mathcal{L}_\alpha\left(1, \frac{P_\mathbf{x}}{P_\mathbf{x} + P_\mathbf{g}}\right) d\mu \\
&\quad - 2 \int_\mathcal{X} \left(\frac{P_\mathbf{x} + P_\mathbf{g}}{2}\right) \frac{P_\mathbf{g}}{P_\mathbf{x} + P_\mathbf{g}} \mathcal{L}_\alpha\left(1, \frac{P_\mathbf{g}}{P_\mathbf{x} + P_\mathbf{g}}\right) d\mu
\end{aligned}$$

$$\stackrel{(b)}{=} -2\int_{\mathcal{X}}\left(\frac{P_{\mathbf{x}}+P_{\mathbf{g}}}{2}\right)\frac{P_{\mathbf{x}}}{P_{\mathbf{x}}+P_{\mathbf{g}}}\left(\frac{-af_{\alpha}\left(\frac{2P_{\mathbf{x}}}{P_{\mathbf{x}}+P_{\mathbf{g}}}\right)}{\frac{2P_{\mathbf{x}}}{P_{\mathbf{x}}+P_{\mathbf{g}}}}+ab\right)d\mu$$

$$-2\int_{\mathcal{X}}\left(\frac{P_{\mathbf{x}}+P_{\mathbf{g}}}{2}\right)\frac{P_{\mathbf{g}}}{P_{\mathbf{x}}+P_{\mathbf{g}}}\left(\frac{-af_{\alpha}\left(\frac{2P_{\mathbf{g}}}{P_{\mathbf{x}}+P_{\mathbf{g}}}\right)}{\frac{2P_{\mathbf{g}}}{P_{\mathbf{x}}+P_{\mathbf{g}}}}+ab\right)d\mu$$

$$=2a\left(\frac{1}{2}\int_{\mathcal{X}}\frac{P_{\mathbf{x}}+P_{\mathbf{g}}}{2}f_{\alpha}\left(\frac{2P_{\mathbf{x}}}{P_{\mathbf{x}}+P_{\mathbf{g}}}\right)d\mu\right.$$

$$\left.+\frac{1}{2}\int_{\mathcal{X}}\frac{P_{\mathbf{x}}+P_{\mathbf{g}}}{2}f_{\alpha}\left(\frac{2P_{\mathbf{g}}}{P_{\mathbf{x}}+P_{\mathbf{g}}}\right)d\mu\right)-2ab$$

$$=2a\,\mathrm{JD}_{f_{\alpha}}(P_{\mathbf{x}}\|P_{\mathbf{g}})-2ab,$$

where:

- (a) holds since $\mathcal{L}_{\alpha}(1,u) = \mathcal{L}_{\alpha}(0,1-u)$ by (7), where $u = \frac{P_{\mathbf{x}}}{P_{\mathbf{x}}+P_{\mathbf{g}}}$.
- (b) holds by solving for $\mathcal{L}_{\alpha}(1,u)$ in terms of $f_{\alpha}(2u)$ in (13), where $u = \frac{P_{\mathbf{x}}}{P_{\mathbf{x}}+P_{\mathbf{g}}}$ in the first term and $u = \frac{P_{\mathbf{g}}}{P_{\mathbf{x}}+P_{\mathbf{g}}}$ in the second term.

The constants a and b are chosen so that $f_{\alpha}(1) = 0$. Finally, the continuity and convexity of f_{α} (as well as its strict convexity around 1) directly follow from the corresponding assumptions imposed on the loss function $\mathcal{L}_{\alpha}$ in Definition 3 and on the condition imposed on the sign of a in the theorem's statement. □

Remark 3. *Note that not only D^* given in (11) is an optimal discriminator of the (original) VanillaGAN discriminator loss function, but it also optimizes the LSGAN/LkGAN discriminators loss functions when their discriminators' labels for fake and real data, γ and β, respectively satisfy $\gamma = 1$ and $\beta = 0$ (see Section 3.3).*

We next show that the $\mathcal{L}_{\alpha}$-GAN of Theorem 1 recovers as special cases a number of well-known GAN generator loss functions and their equilibrium points (under an optimal classical discriminator D^*).

3.1. VanillaGAN

VanillaGAN [1] uses the same loss function V_{VG} for the both generator and discriminator, which is

$$V_{\mathrm{VG}}(D,G) = \mathbb{E}_{\mathbf{A}\sim P_{\mathbf{x}}}[-\log D(\mathbf{A})] + \mathbb{E}_{\mathbf{B}\sim P_{\mathbf{g}}}[-\log(1-D(\mathbf{B}))] \tag{14}$$

and can be cast as a saddle point optimization problem:

$$\inf_{G}\sup_{D}V_{\mathrm{VG}}(D,G). \tag{15}$$

It is shown in [1] that the optimal discriminator for (15) is given by $D^* = \frac{P_{\mathbf{x}}}{P_{\mathbf{x}}+P_{\mathbf{g}}}$, as in (11). When $D = D^*$, the optimization reduces to minimizing the Jensen-Shannon divergence:

$$\inf_{G}V_{\mathrm{VG}}(D^*,G) = \inf_{G}2\mathrm{JSD}(P_{\mathbf{x}}\|P_{\mathbf{g}}) - 2\log 2. \tag{16}$$

We next show that (16) can be obtained from Theorem 1.

Lemma 2. *Consider the optimization of VanillaGAN given in (15). Then we have that*

$$V_{\mathrm{VG}}(D^*,G) = 2\mathrm{JSD}(P_{\mathbf{x}}\|P_{\mathbf{g}}) - 2\log 2 = V_{\mathcal{L}_{\alpha},G}(D^*,G),$$

where $\mathcal{L}_{\alpha}(y,\hat{y}) = -y\log(\hat{y}) - (1-y)\log(1-\hat{y})$ for all $\alpha \in \mathcal{A} = \mathbb{R}$.

Proof. For any fixed $\alpha \in \mathbb{R}$, let the function $\mathcal{L}_\alpha$ in (8) be as defined in the statement:

$$\mathcal{L}_\alpha(y, \hat{y}) = -y \log(\hat{y}) - (1-y) \log(1-\hat{y}).$$

Note that $\mathcal{L}_\alpha$ is symmetric, since for $\hat{y} \in [0,1]$, we have that

$$\mathcal{L}_\alpha(1, \hat{y}) = -\log(\hat{y}) = \mathcal{L}_\alpha(0, 1-\hat{y}).$$

Instead of showing the continuity and convexity/concavity conditions imposed on $\hat{y}\mathcal{L}_\alpha\left(1, \frac{\hat{y}}{2}\right)$ in Definition 3, we implicitly verify them by directly deriving f_α from $\mathcal{L}_\alpha$ using (13) and showing that it is continuous convex and strictly convex around 1. Setting $a = 1$ and $b = \log 2$, we have that

$$f_\alpha(u) = -u\left(\frac{1}{a}\mathcal{L}_\alpha\left(1, \frac{u}{2}\right) - b\right)$$
$$= -u\left(-\log\frac{u}{2} - \log 2\right) = u \log u.$$

Clearly, f is convex (actually strictly convex on $(0, \infty)$ and hence strictly convex around 1) and continuous on its domain (where $f(0) = \lim_{u \to 0} u \log(u) = 0$). It also satisfies $f(1) = 0$. By Lemma 1, we know that under the generating function $f(u) = u \log(u)$, the Jensen-f divergence reduces to the Jensen-Shannon divergence. Therefore, by Theorem 1, we have that

$$V_{\mathcal{L}_\alpha, G}(D^*, G) = 2a\mathrm{JD}_{f_\alpha}(P_\mathbf{x}\|P_\mathbf{g}) - 2ab$$
$$= 2\mathrm{JSD}(P_\mathbf{x}\|P_\mathbf{g}) - 2\log 2$$
$$= V_\mathrm{VG}(D^*, G),$$

which finishes the proof. □

3.2. α-GAN

The notion of α-GANs is introduced in [8] as a way to unify several existing GANs using a parameterized loss function. We describe α-GANs next.

Definition 4 ([8]). *Let $y \in \{0,1\}$ be a binary label, $\hat{y} \in [0,1]$, and fix $\alpha > 0$. The **α-loss** between y and $\hat{y}$ is the map $\ell_\alpha : \{0,1\} \times [0,1] \to [0, \infty)$ given by*

$$\ell_\alpha(y, \hat{y}) = \begin{cases} \frac{\alpha}{\alpha-1}\left(1 - y\hat{y}^{\frac{\alpha-1}{\alpha}} + (1-y)(1-\hat{y})^{\frac{\alpha-1}{\alpha}}\right), & \alpha \in (0,1) \cup (1, \infty) \\ -y \log \hat{y} - (1-y) \log(1-\hat{y}), & \alpha = 1. \end{cases} \quad (17)$$

Definition 5 ([8]). *For $\alpha > 0$, the **α-GAN** loss function is given by*

$$V_\alpha(D, G) = \mathbb{E}_{A \sim P_\mathbf{x}}[-\ell_\alpha(1, D(A))] + \mathbb{E}_{B \sim P_\mathbf{g}}[-\ell_\alpha(0, D(B))]. \quad (18)$$

Joint optimization of the α-GAN problem is given by

$$\inf_G \sup_D V_\alpha(D, G). \quad (19)$$

It is known that α-GAN recovers several well-known GANs by varying the α parameter: notably, VanillaGAN ($\alpha = 1$) [1] and HellingerGAN ($\alpha = \frac{1}{2}$) [7]. Furthermore, as $\alpha \to \infty$, V_α recovers a translated version of the WassersteinGAN loss function [25]. We now present the solution to the joint optimization problem presented in (19).

Proposition 1 ([8]). *Let $\alpha > 0$ and consider joint optimization of the α-GAN presented in (19). The discriminator D^* that maximizes the loss function is given by*

$$D^* = \frac{P_\mathbf{x}^\alpha}{P_\mathbf{x}^\alpha + P_\mathbf{g}^\alpha}. \tag{20}$$

Furthermore, when $D = D^*$ is fixed, the problem in (19) reduces to minimizing an Arimoto divergence (as defined in Table 1) when $\alpha \neq 1$:

$$\inf_G V_\alpha(D^*, G) = \inf_G \mathcal{A}_\alpha(P_\mathbf{x}\|P_\mathbf{g}) + \frac{\alpha}{\alpha-1}\left(2^{\frac{1}{\alpha}} - 2\right) \tag{21}$$

and a Jensen-Shannon divergence when $\alpha = 1$:

$$\inf_G V_1(D^*, G) = \inf_G \mathrm{JSD}(P_\mathbf{x}\|P_\mathbf{g}) - 2\log 2, \tag{22}$$

where (21) and (22) achieve their minima iff $P_\mathbf{x} = P_\mathbf{g}$ (a.e.).

Recently, α-GAN was generalized in [10] to implement a dual-objective GAN, which we describe next.

Definition 6 ([10]). *For $\alpha_D > 0$ and $\alpha_G > 0$, the (α_D, α_G)-GAN's optimization is given by*

$$\sup_D V_{\alpha_D}(D, G) \tag{23}$$

$$\inf_G V_{\alpha_G}(D, G) \tag{24}$$

where V_{α_D} and V_{α_G} are defined in (18), with α replaced by α_D and α_G, respectively.

Proposition 2 ([10]). *Consider the joint optimization in (23) and (24). Let parameters $\alpha_D, \alpha_G > 0$ satisfy*

$$\left(\alpha_D \leq 1, \alpha_G > \frac{\alpha_D}{\alpha_D + 1}\right) \text{ or } \left(\alpha_D > 1, \frac{\alpha_D}{2} < \alpha_G \leq \alpha_D\right). \tag{25}$$

The discriminator D^* that maximizes V_{α_D} is given by

$$D^* = \frac{P_\mathbf{x}^{\alpha_D}}{P_\mathbf{x}^{\alpha_D} + P_\mathbf{g}^{\alpha_D}}. \tag{26}$$

Furthermore, when $D = D^*$ is fixed, the minimization of V_{α_G} in (24) is equivalent to the following f-divergence minimization:

$$\inf_G V_{\alpha_G}(D^*, G) = \inf_G D_{f_{\alpha_D,\alpha_G}}(P_\mathbf{x}\|P_\mathbf{g}) + \frac{\alpha}{\alpha-1}\left(2^{\frac{1}{\alpha}} - 2\right), \tag{27}$$

where $f_{\alpha_D,\alpha_G} : [0, \infty) \to \mathbb{R}$ is given by

$$f_{\alpha_D,\alpha_G}(u) = \frac{\alpha_G}{\alpha_G - 1}\left(\frac{u^{\alpha_D\left(1 - \frac{1}{\alpha_G}\right)+1} + 1}{(u^{\alpha_D} + 1)^{1 - \frac{1}{\alpha_G}}}\right). \tag{28}$$

We now apply the (α_D, α_G)-GAN to our main result in Theorem 1 by showing that (12) can recover (27) when $\alpha_D = 1$ (which corresponds to a VanillaGAN discriminator loss function).

Lemma 3. *Consider the (α_D, α_G)-GAN given in Definition 6. Let $\alpha_D = 1$ and $\alpha_G = \alpha > \frac{1}{2}$. Then, the solution to (24) presented in Proposition 2 is equivalent to minimizing a Jensen-f_α-divergence: specifically, if D^* is the optimal discriminator given by (26), which is equivalent to (11) when $\alpha_D = 1$, then $V_{\alpha,G}(D^*, G)$ in (27) satisfies*

$$V_{\alpha,G}(D^*,G) = 2^{\frac{1}{\alpha}} \mathrm{JD}_{f_\alpha}(P_\mathbf{x}\|P_\mathbf{g}) + \frac{\alpha}{\alpha-1}(2^{\frac{1}{\alpha}}-2) = V_{\mathcal{L}_\alpha,G}(D^*,G), \tag{29}$$

where $\mathcal{L}_\alpha(y,\hat{y}) = \ell_\alpha(y,\hat{y})$, and

$$f_\alpha(u) = \frac{\alpha}{\alpha-1}\left(u^{2-\frac{1}{\alpha}} - u\right), \quad u \geq 0. \tag{30}$$

Proof. We show that Theorem 1 recovers Proposition 2 by setting $\mathcal{L}_\alpha(y,\hat{y}) = \ell_\alpha(y,\hat{y})$. Note that ℓ_α is symmetric since

$$\ell_\alpha(1,\hat{y}) = \frac{\alpha}{\alpha-1}(1-\hat{y}^{1-\frac{1}{\alpha}}) = \ell_\alpha(0,1-\hat{y}).$$

As in the proof of Lemma 2, instead of proving the conditions imposed on $\hat{y}\mathcal{L}_\alpha(1,\frac{\hat{y}}{2})$ in Definition 3, we derive f_α directly from $\mathcal{L}_\alpha$ using (13) and show that it is continuous convex and strictly convex around 1. From Lemma 2, we know that when $\alpha = 1$, $f_\alpha(u) = u\log u$ (which is strictly convex and continuous). For $\alpha \in (0,1) \cup (1,\infty)$, setting $a = 2^{\frac{1}{\alpha}-1}$ and $b = \frac{\alpha}{\alpha-1}\left(2^{1-\frac{1}{\alpha}}-1\right)$ in (13), we have that

$$f_\alpha(u) = -u\left(\frac{1}{a}\mathcal{L}_\alpha\left(1,\frac{u}{2}\right) - b\right)$$
$$= -u\left(2^{1-\frac{1}{\alpha}}\frac{\alpha}{\alpha-1}\left(1-\left(\frac{u}{2}\right)^{1-\frac{1}{\alpha}}\right) - \frac{\alpha}{\alpha-1}(2^{1-\frac{1}{\alpha}}-1)\right)$$
$$= \frac{\alpha}{\alpha-1}(-u)[2^{1-\frac{1}{\alpha}} - u^{1-\frac{1}{\alpha}} - (2^{1-\frac{1}{\alpha}}-1)]$$
$$= \frac{\alpha}{\alpha-1}(u^{2-\frac{1}{\alpha}} - u).$$

Clearly, $f_\alpha(1) = 0$. Furthermore for $\alpha \neq 1$, we have that

$$f_\alpha''(u) = \frac{(2\alpha-1)u^{\frac{-1}{\alpha}}}{\alpha}, \quad u \geq 0,$$

which is positive for $\alpha > \frac{1}{2}$, and f_α is convex for $\alpha > \frac{1}{2}$ (as well as continuous on its domain and strictly convex around 1). Thus, by Theorem 1, we have that

$$V_{\mathcal{L}_\alpha,G}(D^*,G) = 2a\mathrm{JD}_{f_\alpha}(P_\mathbf{x}\|P_\mathbf{g}) - 2ab$$
$$= 2 \cdot 2^{\frac{1}{\alpha}-1}\mathrm{JD}_{f_\alpha}(P_\mathbf{x}\|P_\mathbf{g}) - 2\frac{\alpha}{\alpha-1}2^{\frac{1}{\alpha}-1}(2^{1-\frac{1}{\alpha}}-1)$$
$$= 2^{\frac{1}{\alpha}}\mathrm{JD}_{f_\alpha}(P_\mathbf{x}\|P_\mathbf{g}) + \frac{\alpha}{\alpha-1}(2^{\frac{1}{\alpha}}-2).$$

We now show that the above Jensen-f_α-divergence is equal to the $f_{1,\alpha}$-divergence originally derived for the $(1,\alpha)$-GAN problem of Proposition 2 (note from Proposition 2 that if $\alpha_D = 1$, then $\alpha_G = \alpha > \frac{1}{2}$, so the range of α concurs with the range required above for the convexity of f_α). For any two distributions p and q with common support $\mathcal{X}$, we have that

$$D_{f_{1,\alpha}}(p\|q) = \frac{\alpha}{\alpha-1}\int_\mathcal{X} q\frac{\left(\frac{p}{q}\right)^{2-\frac{1}{\alpha}}+1}{\left(\frac{p}{q}+1\right)^{1-\frac{1}{\alpha}}} d\mu - \frac{\alpha}{\alpha-1}2^{\frac{1}{\alpha}}$$

$$= \frac{\alpha}{\alpha-1}\int_\mathcal{X} q\frac{\left(\frac{p}{q}\right)^{2-\frac{1}{\alpha}}+1}{\left(\frac{p+q}{q}\right)^{1-\frac{1}{\alpha}}} d\mu - \frac{\alpha}{\alpha-1}2^{\frac{1}{\alpha}}$$

$$
\begin{aligned}
&= \frac{\alpha}{\alpha-1} \int_{\mathcal{X}} \left((p+q)\left(\frac{p}{p+q}\right)^{2-\frac{1}{\alpha}} + (p+q)\left(\frac{q}{p+q}\right)^{2-\frac{1}{\alpha}} \right) d\mu \\
&\quad - \frac{\alpha}{\alpha-1} 2^{\frac{1}{\alpha}} \\
&= \frac{\alpha}{\alpha-1} \frac{2}{2^{2-\frac{1}{\alpha}}} \int_{\mathcal{X}} \left(\frac{p+q}{2}\left(\frac{2p}{p+q}\right)^{2-\frac{1}{\alpha}} + \frac{p+q}{2}\left(\frac{2q}{p+q}\right)^{2-\frac{1}{\alpha}} \right) d\mu \\
&\quad - \frac{\alpha}{\alpha-1} 2^{\frac{1}{\alpha}} \\
&= \frac{\alpha}{\alpha-1} 2^{\frac{1}{\alpha}-1} \int_{\mathcal{X}} \left(\frac{p+q}{2}\left(\left(\frac{2p}{p+q}\right)^{2-\frac{1}{\alpha}} - \frac{2p}{p+q} \right) + p \right) d\mu \\
&\quad + \frac{\alpha}{\alpha-1} 2^{\frac{1}{\alpha}-1} \int_{\mathcal{X}} \left(\frac{p+q}{2}\left(\left(\frac{2q}{p+q}\right)^{2-\frac{1}{\alpha}} - \frac{2q}{p+q} \right) + q \right) d\mu \\
&\quad - \frac{\alpha}{\alpha-1} 2^{\frac{1}{\alpha}} \\
&= \frac{\alpha}{\alpha-1} 2^{\frac{1}{\alpha}} \frac{1}{2} \left(\int_{\mathcal{X}} \frac{p+q}{2}\left(\left(\frac{2p}{p+q}\right)^{2-\frac{1}{\alpha}} - \frac{2p}{p+q} \right) d\mu + 1 \right) \\
&\quad + \frac{\alpha}{\alpha-1} 2^{\frac{1}{\alpha}} \frac{1}{2} \left(\int_{\mathcal{X}} \frac{p+q}{2}\left(\left(\frac{2q}{p+q}\right)^{2-\frac{1}{\alpha}} - \frac{2q}{p+q} \right) d\mu + 1 \right) \\
&\quad - \frac{\alpha}{\alpha-1} 2^{\frac{1}{\alpha}} \\
&= 2^{\frac{1}{\alpha}} \text{JD}_{f_\alpha}(p\|q) + \frac{\alpha}{\alpha-1} 2^{\frac{1}{\alpha}-1}(2) - \frac{\alpha}{\alpha-1} 2^{\frac{1}{\alpha}} \\
&= 2^{\frac{1}{\alpha}} \text{JD}_{f_\alpha}(p\|q).
\end{aligned}
$$

Therefore, $V_{\mathcal{L}_\alpha,G}(D^*,G) = V_\alpha(D^*,G)$. □

Note that this lemma generalizes Lemma 2; VanillaGAN is a special case of $(1,\alpha)$-GAN for $\alpha = 1$.

3.3. Shifted LkGANs and LSGANs

Least squares GAN (LSGAN) was proposed in [26] to mitigate the vanishing gradient problem with VanillaGAN and to stabilize training performance. LSGAN's loss function is derived from the squared error distortion measure, whereby we aim to minimize the distortion between the data samples and a target value we want the discriminator to assign the samples to. LSGAN was generalized with LkGAN in [6] by replacing the squared error distortion measure with an absolute error distortion measure of order $k \geq 1$, therefore introducing an additional degree of freedom to the generator's loss function. We first state the general LkGAN problem. We then apply the result of Theorem 1 to the loss functions of LSGAN and LkGAN.

Definition 7 ([6]). *Let $\gamma, \beta, c \in [0,1]$, and let $k \geq 1$. **LkGAN's loss functions**, denoted by $V_{LSGAN,D}$ and $V_{k,G}$, are given by*

$$V_{LSGAN,D}(D,G) = -\frac{1}{2}\mathbb{E}_{A \sim P_x}[(D(A) - \beta)^2] - \frac{1}{2}\mathbb{E}_{B \sim P_g}[(D(B) - \gamma)^2] \tag{31}$$

$$V_{k,G}(D,G) = \mathbb{E}_{A \sim P_x}[|D(A) - c|^k] + \mathbb{E}_{B \sim P_g}[|D(B) - c|^k]. \tag{32}$$

*The **LkGAN problem** is the joint optimization*

$$\sup_D V_{LSGAN,D}(D,G) \tag{33}$$

$$\inf_G V_{k,G}(D,G). \tag{34}$$

We next recall the solution to (33), which is a minimization of the Pearson–Vajda divergence $|\chi|^k(\cdot\|\cdot)$ of order k (as defined in Table 1).

Proposition 3 ([6]). *Consider the joint optimization for LkGAN presented in (33). Then the optimal discriminator D^* that maximizes $V_{LSGAN,D}$ in (31) is given by*

$$D^* = \frac{\gamma P_{\mathbf{x}} + \beta P_{\mathbf{g}}}{P_{\mathbf{x}} + P_{\mathbf{g}}}. \tag{35}$$

Furthermore, if $D = D^*$ and $\gamma - \beta = 2(c - \beta)$, the minimization of $V_{k,G}$ in (32) reduces to

$$\inf_G V_{k,G}(D,G) = \inf_G |c - \beta|^k |\chi|^k (P_{\mathbf{x}} + P_{\mathbf{g}} \| 2 P_{\mathbf{g}}). \tag{36}$$

Note that LSGAN [26] is a special case of LkGAN, as we recover LSGAN when $k = 2$ [6].

By scrutinizing Proposition 3 and Theorem 1, we observe that the former cannot be recovered from the latter. However, we can use Theorem 1 by slightly modifying the LkGAN generator's loss function. First, for the dual-objective GAN proposed in Theorem 1, we need $D^* = \frac{P_{\mathbf{x}}}{P_{\mathbf{x}} + P_{\mathbf{g}}}$. By (35), this is achieved for $\gamma = 1$ and $\beta = 0$. Then, we define the intermediate loss function

$$\tilde{V}_{k,G}(D,G) = \mathbb{E}_{\mathbf{A} \sim P_{\mathbf{x}}}[|D(\mathbf{A}) - c_1|^k] + \mathbb{E}_{\mathbf{B} \sim P_{\mathbf{g}}}[|D(\mathbf{B}) - c_2|^k]. \tag{37}$$

Comparing the above loss function with (8), we note that setting $c_1 = 0$ and $c_2 = 1$ in (37) satisfies the symmetry property of $\mathcal{L}_\alpha$. Finally, to ensure the generating function f_α satisfies $f_\alpha(1) = 0$, we shift each term in (37) by 1. Putting these changes together, we propose a revised generator loss function denoted by $\hat{V}_{k,G}$ and given by

$$\hat{V}_{k,G}(D,G) = \mathbb{E}_{\mathbf{A} \sim P_{\mathbf{x}}}[|D(\mathbf{A})|^k - 1] + \mathbb{E}_{\mathbf{B} \sim P_{\mathbf{g}}}[|1 - D(\mathbf{B})|^k - 1]. \tag{38}$$

We call a system that uses (38) as a generator loss function a **Shifted LkGAN (SLkGAN)**. If $k = 2$, we have a shifted version of the LSGAN generator loss function, which we call **Shifted LSGAN (SLSGAN)**. Note that none of these modifications alter the gradients of $V_{k,G}$ in (32), since the first term is independent of G, the choice of c_1 is irrelevant, and translating a function by a constant does not change its gradients. However, from Proposition 3, for $\gamma = 0$, $\beta = 1$, and $c = 1$, we do not have that $\gamma - \beta = 2(c - \beta)$, and as a result, this modified problem does not reduce to minimizing a Pearson–Vajda divergence. Consequently, we can relax the condition on k in Definition 7 to just $k > 0$. We now show how Theorem 1 can be applied to $\mathcal{L}_\alpha$-GAN using (38).

Lemma 4. *Let $k > 0$. Let V_D be a discriminator loss function, and let $\hat{V}_{k,G}$ be the generator's loss function defined in (38). Consider the joint optimization*

$$\sup_D V_D(D,G) \tag{39}$$

$$\inf_G \hat{V}_{k,G}(D,G) \tag{40}$$

If V_D is optimized at $D^* = \frac{P_{\mathbf{x}}}{P_{\mathbf{x}} + P_{\mathbf{g}}}$ (i.e., V_D is canonical), then we have that

$$\hat{V}_{k,G}(D^*, G) = \frac{1}{2^{k-1}} \mathrm{JD}_{f_k}(P_{\mathbf{x}} \| P_{\mathbf{g}}) + \frac{1}{2^{k-1}} - \frac{1}{2},$$

where f_k is given by

$$f_k(u) = u(u^k - 1), \qquad u \geq 0.$$

Examples of $V_D(D,G)$ that satisfy the requirements of Lemma 4 include the LkGAN discriminator loss function given by (31) with $\gamma = 1$ and $\beta = 0$ and the VanillaGAN discriminator loss function given by (14).

Proof. Let $k > 0$. We can restate SLkGAN's generator loss function in (38) in terms of $V_{\mathcal{L}_\alpha,G}$ in (8): we have that $V_{\mathcal{L}_\alpha,G}(D^*,G) = \hat{V}_{k,G}(D^*,G)$, where $\alpha = k$, and $\mathcal{L}_k : \{0,1\} \times [0,1] \to [0,\infty)$ is given by

$$\mathcal{L}_k(y,\hat{y}) = -(y(\hat{y}^k - 1) + (1-y)((1-\hat{y})^k - 1)). \tag{41}$$

We have that $\mathcal{L}_k$ is symmetric, since

$$\mathcal{L}_k(1,\hat{y}) = -(\hat{y}^k - 1) = \mathcal{L}_k(0, 1-\hat{y}).$$

We derive f_α from $\mathcal{L}_\alpha$ via (13) and directly check that it is continuous convex and strictly convex around 1. Setting $a = \frac{1}{2^k}$ and $b = 2^k - 1$ in (13), we have that

$$\begin{aligned}
f_k(u) &= -u\left(\frac{1}{a}\mathcal{L}_k\left(1, \frac{u}{2}\right) - b\right) \\
&= -u\left(2^k\left(1 - \left(\frac{u}{2}\right)^k\right) - (2^k - 1)\right) \\
&= -u(2^k - u^k - 2^k + 1) \\
&= u(u^k - 1).
\end{aligned}$$

We clearly have that $f_k(1) = 0$ and that f_k is continuous. Furthermore, we have that $f_k''(u) = k(k+1)u$, which is non-negative for $u \geq 0$. Therefore, f_k is convex (as well as strictly convex around 1). As a result, by Theorem 1, we have that

$$\begin{aligned}
\hat{V}_{k,G}(D^*,G) &= \frac{1}{2^{k-1}}\mathrm{JD}_{f_k}(P_\mathbf{x}\|P_\mathbf{g}) - \frac{1}{2^{k-1}}(2^k - 1) \\
&= \frac{1}{2^{k-1}}\mathrm{JD}_{f_k}(P_\mathbf{x}\|P_\mathbf{g}) + \frac{1}{2^{k-1}} - \frac{1}{2}.
\end{aligned}$$

□

We conclude this section by emphasizing that Theorem 1 serves as a unifying result recovering the existing loss functions in the literature and, moreover, provides a way for generalizing new ones. Our aim in the next section is to demonstrate the versatility of this result in experimentation.

4. Experiments

We perform two experiments on three different image datasets that we describe below.

Experiment 1: In the first experiment, we compare (α, α)-GAN with $(1, \alpha)$-GAN while controlling the value of α. Recall that $\alpha_D = 1$ corresponds to the canonical VanillaGAN (or DCGAN) discriminator. We aim to verify whether or not replacing an α-GAN discriminator with a VanillaGAN discriminator stabilizes or improves the system's performance depending on the value of α. Note that the result of Theorem 1 only applies to the (α_D, α_G)-GAN for $\alpha_D = 1$. We herein confine the comparison of $(1, \alpha)$-GAN with (α, α)-GAN only so that both systems have the same tunable free parameter α. The results obtained in [10] for the Stacked MNIST dataset show that (α_D, α_G)-GAN provides consistently robust performance when $\alpha_D = \alpha_G$. Other experiments illustrating the performance of (α_D, α_G)-GAN with $\alpha_D \neq 1$ are carried for the Celeb-A and LSUN Classroom image datasets in [11] and show improved training stability for $\alpha_D < 1$ values.

Experiment 2: We train two variants of SLkGAN with the generator loss function as described in (38) and parameterized by $k > 0$. We then utilize two different canonical discriminator loss functions to align with Theorem 1. The first is the VanillaGAN discriminator loss given by (14); we call the resulting dual-objective GAN **Vanilla-SLkGAN**. The second is the LkGAN discriminator loss given by (31), where we set $\gamma = 1$ and $\beta = 0$ such that the optimal discriminator is given by (11). We call this system **Lk-SLkGAN**. We compare the two variants to analyze how the value of k and choice of discriminator loss impacts the system's performance.

4.1. Experimental Setup

We run both experiments on three image datasets: MNIST [27], CIFAR-10 [28], and Stacked MNIST [29]. The MNIST dataset is a dataset of black and white handwritten digits between 0 and 9 and with a size of $28 \times 28 \times 1$. The CIFAR-10 dataset is an RGB dataset of small images of common animals and modes of transportation with a size of $32 \times 32 \times 3$. The Stacked MNIST dataset is an RGB dataset derived from the MNIST dataset and constructed by taking three MNIST images, assigning each to one of the three color channels, and stacking the images on top of each other. The resulting images are then padded so that each one of them has a size of $32 \times 32 \times 3$.

For Experiment 1, we use α values of 0.5, 5.0, 10.0, and 20.0. For each value of α, we train (α, α)-GAN and $(1, \alpha)$-GAN. We additionally train DCGAN, which corresponds to $(1, 1)$-GAN. For Experiment 2, we use k values of 0.25, 1.0, 2.0, 7.5, and 15.0. Note that when $k = 2$, we recover LSGAN. For the MNIST dataset, we run 10 trials with the random seeds 123, 500, 1600, 199,621, 60,677, 20,435, 15,859, 33,764, 79,878, and 36,123 and train each GAN for 250 epochs. For the RGB datasets (CIFAR-10 and Stacked MNIST), we run five trials with the random seeds 123, 1600, 60,677, 15,859, and 79,878 and train each GAN for 500 epochs. All experiments utilize an Adam optimizer for the stochastic gradient descent algorithm with a learning rate of 2×10^{-4} and parameters $\beta_1 = 0.5$, $\beta_2 = 0.999$, and $\epsilon = 10^{-7}$ [30]. We also experiment with the addition of a gradient penalty (GP); we add a penalty term to the discriminator's loss function to encourage the discriminator's gradient to have a unit norm [31].

The MNIST experiments were run on one 6130 2.1 GHz 1xV100 GPU, 8 CPUs, and 16 GB of memory. The CIFAR-10 and Stacked MNIST experiments were run on one Epyc 7443 2.8 GHz GPU, 8 CPUs, and 16 GB of memory. For each experiment, we report the best overall Fréchet inception distance (FID) score [32], the best average FID score amongst all trials and its variance, and the average epoch the best FID score occurs and its variance. The FID score for each epoch was computed over 10,000 images. For each metric, the lowest numerical value corresponds to the model with the best metric (indicated in bold in the tables). We also report how many trials we include in our summary statistics, as it is possible for a trial to collapse and not train for the full number of epochs. The neural network architectures used in our experiments are presented in Appendix A. The training algorithms are presented in Appendix B.

4.2. Experimental Results

We report the FID metrics for Experiment 1 in Tables 2–4 and for Experiment 2 in Tables 5–7. We report only on those experiments that produced meaningful results. Models that utilize a simplified gradient penalty have the suffix "-GP". For (α_D, α_G)-GANs, we display the output of the best-performing systems in Figure 1 and plot the trajectories of the FID scores throughout the training epochs in Figure 2. Similarly for SLKGANs, outputs of the best-performing systems and FID scores vs. epochs trajectories are provided in Figures 3 and 4, respectively.

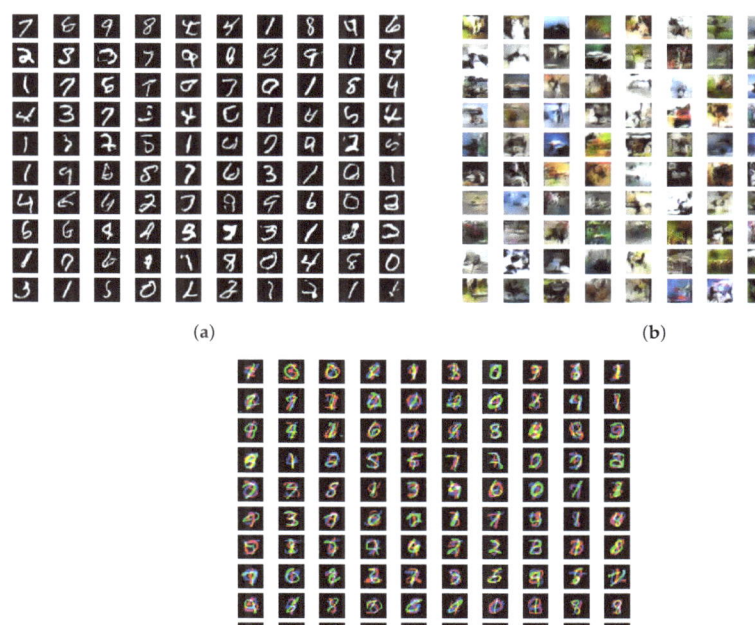

Figure 1. Generated images for the best-performing (α_D, α_G)-GANs. (**a**) (α_D, α_G)-GAN for MNIST, $\alpha_D = 1.0$, $\alpha_G = 5.0$, FID: 1.125. (**b**) (α_D, α_G)-GAN-GP for CIFAR-10, $\alpha_D = 1.0$, $\alpha_G = 20.0$, FID = 8.466. (**c**) (α_D, α_G)-GAN-GP for Stacked MNIST, $\alpha_D = 1.0$, $\alpha_G = 0.5$, FID = 4.833.

Table 2. (α_D, α_G)-GAN results for MNIST.

(α_D, α_G)-GAN	Best FID Score	Average Best FID Score	Best FID Score Variance	Average Epochs	Epoch Variance	Number of Successful Trials (/10)
(1,0.5)-GAN	1.264	1.288	2.979×10^{-4}	227.25	420.25	4
(0.5,0.5)-GAN	1.209	1.265	0.001	234.5	156.7	6
(1,5)-GAN	**1.125**	1.17	8.195×10^{-4}	230.3	617.344	10
(1,10)-GAN	1.147	**1.165**	7.984×10^{-4}	225.6	253.156	10
(10,10)-GAN	36.506	39.361	16.312	1.5	0.5	2
(1,20)-GAN	1.135	1.174	0.001	237.5	274.278	10
(20,20)-GAN	33.23	33.23	**0.0**	**1.0**	**0.0**	1
DCGAN	1.154	1.208	0.001	231.3	357.122	10

Table 3. (α_D, α_G)-GAN results for CIFAR-10.

(α_D, α_G)-GAN	Best FID Score	Average Best FID Score	Best FID Score Variance	Average Epochs	Epoch Variance	Number of Successful Trials (/5)
(1,0.5)-GAN-GP	10.551	14.938	12.272	326.2	1808.7	5
(0.5,0.5)-GAN-GP	13.734	14.93	0.517	223.6	11,378.3	5
(1,5)-GAN-GP	10.772	11.635	0.381	132.0	1233.5	5
(5,5)-GAN-GP	20.79	21.72	0.771	**84.8**	1527.2	5
(1,10)-GAN-GP	9.465	**10.187**	0.199	182.6	**1096.3**	5
(10,10)-GAN-GP	19.99	21.095	0.434	131.8	13,374.7	5
(1,20)-GAN-GP	**8.466**	10.217	1.479	216.2	6479.7	5
(20,20)-GAN-GP	19.378	21.216	2.315	138.2	29,824.2	5
DCGAN-GP	25.731	28.378	3.398	158.0	2510.5	5

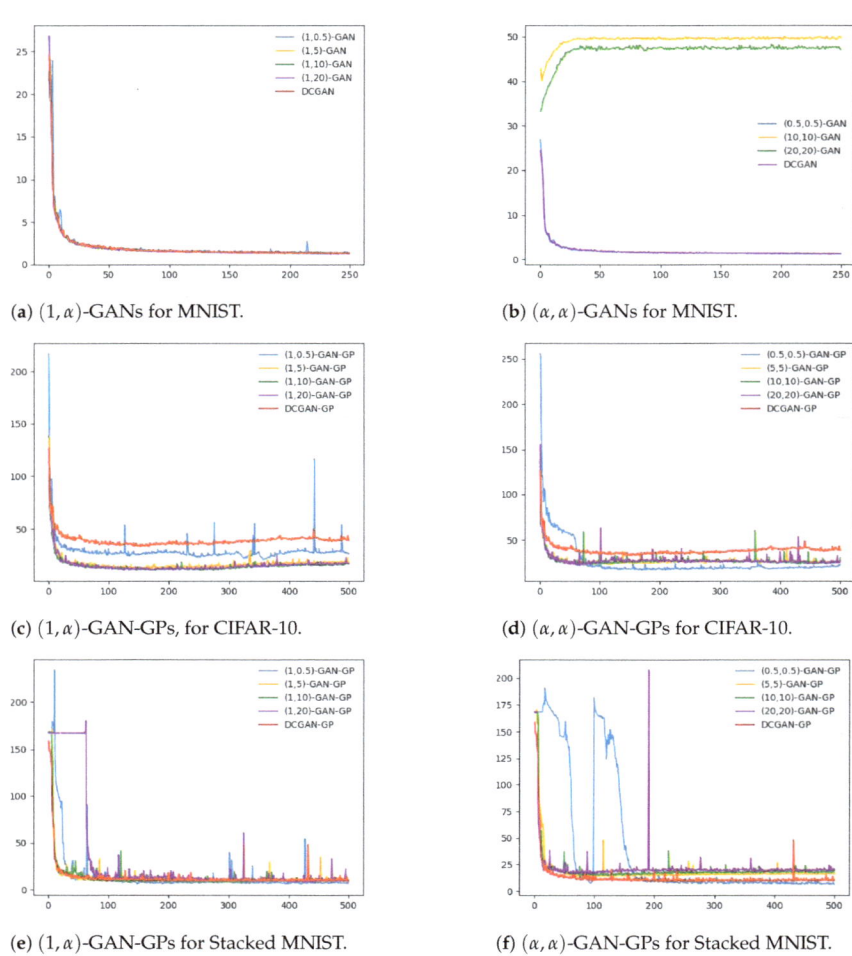

Figure 2. Average FID scores vs. epochs for various (α_D, α_G)-GANs.

Table 4. (α_D, α_G)-GAN results for Stacked MNIST.

(α_D, α_G)-GAN	Best FID Score	Average Best FID Score	Best FID Score Variance	Average Epochs	Epoch Variance	Number of Successful Trials (/5)
(1,0.5)-GAN-GP	**4.833**	**4.997**	0.054	311.5	23,112.5	2
(0.5,0.5)-GAN-GP	6.418	6.418	0.0	479.0	0.0	1
(1,5)-GAN-GP	7.98	7.988	1.357×10^{-4}	379.5	11,704.5	2
(5,5)-GAN-GP	12.236	12.836	0.301	**91.5**	387.0	4
(1,10)-GAN-GP	7.502	7.528	0.001	326.5	14,280.5	2
(10,10)-GAN-GP	14.22	14.573	0.249	95.0	450.0	2
(1,20)-GAN-GP	8.379	8.379	0.0	427.0	0.0	1
(20,20)-GAN-GP	16.584	16.584	0.0	94.0	0.0	1
DCGAN-GP	7.507	7.774	0.064	303.4	11,870.8	5

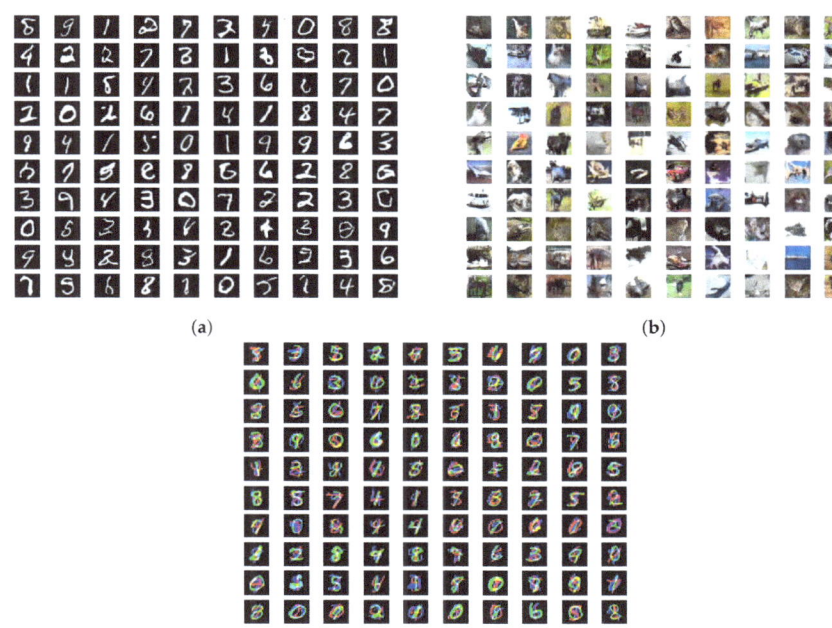

Figure 3. Generated images for best-performing SL*k*GANs. (**a**) Vanilla-SL*k*GAN-0.25 for MNIST, FID = 1.112. (**b**) Vanilla-SL*k*GAN-2.0 for CIFAR-10, FID = 4.58. (**c**) Vanilla-SL*k*GAN-15.0-GP for Stacked MNIST, FID = 3.836.

Table 5. SL*k*GAN results for MNIST.

Variant-SL*k*GAN-*k*	Best FID Score	Average Best FID Score	Best FID Score Variance	Average Epochs	Epoch Variance	Number of Successful Trials (/10)
L*k*-SL*k*GAN-0.25	1.15	1.174	6.298×10^{-4}	224.3	940.9	10
Vanilla-SL*k*GAN-0.25	**1.112**	**1.162**	0.001	237.0	**124.0**	10
L*k*-SL*k*GAN-1.0	1.122	1.167	8.857×10^{-4}	233.0	124.0	10
Vanilla-SL*k*GAN-1.0	1.126	1.17	9.218×10^{-4}	226.2	1182.844	10
L*k*-SL*k*GAN-2.0	1.148	1.198	5.248×10^{-4}	237.2	288.4	10
Vanilla-SL*k*GAN-2.0	1.124	1.184	8.933×10^{-4}	237.8	138.4	10
L*k*-SL*k*GAN-7.5	1.455	1.498	4.422×10^{-4}	229.0	322.222	10
Vanilla-SL*k*GAN-7.5	1.439	1.511	0.001	212.2	1995.067	10
L*k*-SL*k*GAN-15.0	1.733	1.872	0.005	198.8	1885.733	10
Vanilla-SL*k*GAN-15.0	1.773	1.876	0.005	**171.6**	3122.267	10
DCGAN	1.154	1.208	0.001	231.3	357.122	10

Table 6. SL*k*GAN results for CIFAR-10.

Variant-SL*k*GAN-*k*	Best FID Score	Average Best FID Score	Best FID Score Variance	Average Epochs	Epoch Variance	Number of Successful Trials (/5)
L*k*-SL*k*GAN-1.0	4.727	118.242	10,914.643	**60.8**	1897.2	5
Vanilla-SL*k*GAN-1.0	4.821	5.159	**0.092**	88.0	506.5	5
L*k*-SL*k*GAN-2.0	4.723	145.565	7492.26	73.2	3904.2	5
Vanilla-SL*k*GAN-2.0	**4.58**	**5.1**	0.261	105.4	740.8	5
L*k*-SL*k*GAN-7.5	6.556	155.497	7116.521	254.6	18,605.3	5
Vanilla-SL*k*GAN-7.5	6.384	48.905	8698.195	72.2	1711.7	5
L*k*-SL*k*GAN-15.0	8.576	145.774	5945.097	263.0	36,463.0	5
Vanilla-SL*k*GAN-15.0	7.431	50.868	8753.002	82.6	3106.8	5
DCGAN	4.753	5.194	0.117	88.6	**462.8**	5

Table 6. *Cont.*

Variant-SL*k*GAN-*k*	Best FID Score	Average Best FID Score	Best FID Score Variance	Average Epochs	Epoch Variance	Number of Successful Trials (/5)
L*k*-SL*k*GAN-0.25-GP	17.366	18.974	2.627	87.8	1897.2	5
Vanilla-SL*k*GAN-0.25-GP	16.013	17.912	1.961	189.0	9487.5	5
L*k*-SL*k*GAN-1.0-GP	10.771	12.567	1.083	77.8	**239.2**	5
Vanilla-SL*k*GAN-1.0-GP	8.569	9.588	**0.749**	197.6	2690.3	5
L*k*-SL*k*GAN-2.0-GP	23.11	25.013	1.924	**75.4**	658.8	5
Vanilla-SL*k*GAN-2.0-GP	28.215	29.69	1.242	232.0	20,438.5	5
L*k*-SL*k*GAN-7.5-GP	33.304	41.48	49.187	82.8	1081.2	5
Vanilla-SL*k*GAN-7.5-GP	33.085	34.799	1.597	290.8	12,714.7	5
L*k*-SL*k*GAN-15.0-GP	9.157	12.504	3.839	310.4	6976.8	5
Vanilla-SL*k*GAN-15.0-GP	**7.283**	**8.568**	1.535	185.6	5978.3	5
DCGAN-GP	25.731	28.378	3.398	158.0	2510.5	5

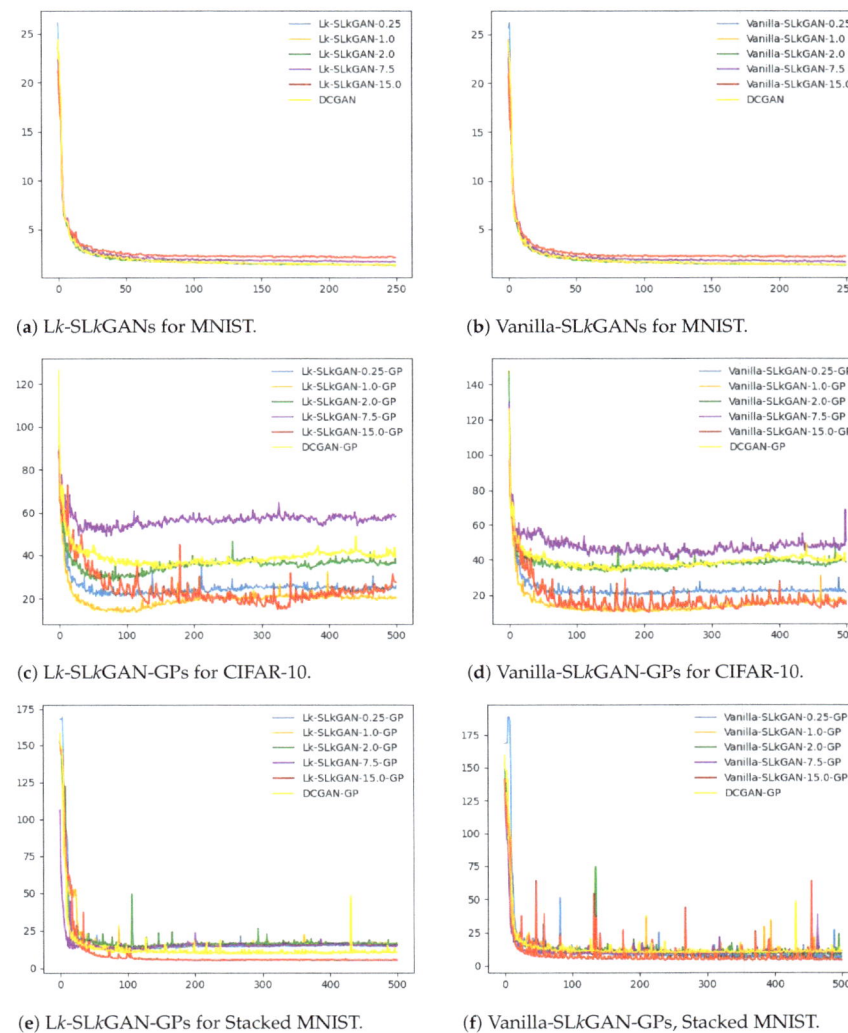

Figure 4. FID scores vs. epochs for various SLkGANs.

Table 7. SLkGAN results for Stacked MNIST.

Variant-SLkGAN-k	Best FID Score	Average Best FID Score	Best FID Score Variance	Average Epochs	Epoch Variance	Number of Successful Trials (/5)
Lk-SLkGAN-0.25-GP	10.541	11.824	0.678	113.6	356.3	5
Vanilla-SLkGAN-0.25-GP	5.197	5.197	0.0	496.0	0.0	1
Lk-SLkGAN-1.0-GP	11.545	12.046	0.291	**89.0**	238.5	5
Vanilla-SLkGAN-1.0-GP	7.475	7.626	0.045	177.0	3528.0	2
Lk-SLkGAN-2.0-GP	10.682	12.782	2.12	180.2	28,484.7	5
Vanilla-SLkGAN-2.0-GP	6.023	7.096	0.991	416.667	12,244.333	3
Lk-SLkGAN-7.5-GP	8.912	9.906	0.577	239.0	35,663.5	5
Vanilla-SLkGAN-7.5-GP	6.074	6.43	0.164	238.0	21,729.5	5
Lk-SLkGAN-15.0-GP	4.458	4.74	0.029	253.4	11,512.3	5
Vanilla-SLkGAN-15.0-GP	**3.836**	**3.873**	0.002	485.0	354.667	4
DCGAN-GP	7.507	7.774	0.064	303.4	11,870.8	5

4.3. Discussion

4.3.1. Experiment 1

From Table 2, we note that 37 of the 90 trials collapse before 250 epochs have passed without a gradient penalty. The (5,5)-GAN collapses for all five trials, and hence, it is not displayed in Table 2. This behavior is expected, as (α,α)-GAN is more sensitive to exploding gradients when α does not tend to 0 or $+\infty$ [8]. The addition of a gradient penalty could mitigate the discriminator's gradients diverging in the (5,5)-GAN by encouraging gradients to have a unit norm. Using a VanillaGAN discriminator with an α-GAN generator (i.e., (1,α)-GAN) produces better quality images for all tested values of α compared to when both networks utilize an α-GAN loss function. The (1,10)-GAN achieves excellent stability, converging in all 10 trials, and also achieves the lowest average FID score. The (1,5)-GAN achieves the lowest FID score overall, marginally outperforming DCGAN. Note that when the average best FID score is very close to the best FID score, the resulting best FID score variance is quite small (of the order of 10^{-3}), indicating little statistical variability over the trials.

Likewise, for the CIFAR-10 and Stacked MNIST datasets, (1,α)-GAN produces lower FID scores than (α, α)-GAN (see Tables 3 and 4). However, both models are more stable with the CIFAR-10 dataset. With the exception of DCGAN, no model converged to its best FID score for all five trials with the Stacked MNIST dataset. Comparing the trials that did converge, both (α, α)-GAN and $(1, \alpha)$-GAN performed better on the Stacked MNIST dataset than the CIFAR-10 dataset. For CIFAR-10, the (1,10)- and (1,20)-GANs produced the best overall FID score and the best average FID score, respectively. On the other hand, the (1,0.5)-GAN produced the best overall FID score and the best average FID score for the Stacked MNIST dataset. We also observe a tradeoff between speed and performance for the CIFAR-10 and Stacked MNIST datasets: the $(1, \alpha)$-GANs arrive at their lowest FID scores later than their respective (α, α)-GANs but achieve lower FID scores overall.

Comparing Figure 2c and Figure 2d, we observe that (α, α)-GAN-GP provides more stability than $(1, \alpha)$-GAN for lower values of α (i.e., $\alpha = 0.5$), while $(1, \alpha)$-GAN-GP exhibits more stability for higher α values ($\alpha = 10$ and $\alpha = 20$). Figure 2e,f show that the two α-GANs trained on the Stacked MNIST dataset exhibit unstable behavior earlier into training when $\alpha = 0.5$ or $\alpha = 20$. However, both systems stabilize and converge to their lowest FID scores as training progresses. The (0.5,0.5)-GAN-GP system in particular exhibits wildly erratic behavior for the first 200 epochs then finishes training with a stable trajectory that outperforms DCGAN-GP.

A future direction is to explore how the complexity of an image dataset influences the best choice of α. For example, the Stacked MNIST dataset might be considered to be less complex than CIFAR-10, as images in the Stacked MNIST dataset only contain four unique colors (black, red, green, and blue), while the CIFAR-10 dataset utilizes significantly more colors.

4.3.2. Experiment 2

We see from Table 5 that all Lk-LkGANs and Vanilla-SLkGANs have FID scores comparable to the DCGAN. When $k = 15$, Vanilla-SLkGAN and Lk-SLkGAN arrive at their lowest FID scores slightly earlier than DCGAN and other SLkGANs.

The addition of a simplified gradient penalty is necessary for Lk-SLkGAN to achieve overall good performance on the CIFAR-10 dataset (see Table 6). Interestingly, Vanilla-SLkGAN achieves lower FID scores without a gradient penalty for lower k values ($k = 1, 2$) and with a gradient penalty for higher k values ($k = 7.5, 15$). When $k = 0.25$, both SLkGANs collapsed for all five trials without a gradient penalty.

Table 7 shows that Vanilla-SLkGANs achieve better FID scores than their respective Lk-LkGAN counterparts. However, Lk-LkGANs are more stable, as no single trial collapsed, while 10 of the 25 Vanilla-SLkGAN trials collapsed before 500 epochs had passed. While all Vanilla-SLkGANs outperform the DCGAN with a gradient penalty, Lk-SLkGAN-GP only outperforms DCGAN-GP when $k = 15$. Except for when $k = 7.5$, we observe that the Lk-

SLkGAN system takes fewer epochs to arrive at its lowest FID score. Comparing Figure 4e and Figure 4f, we observe that Lk-SLkGANs exhibit more stable FID score trajectories than their respective Vanilla-SLkGANs. This makes sense, as the LkGAN loss function aims to increase the GAN's stability compared to DCGAN [6].

5. Conclusions

We introduced a parameterized CPE-based generator loss function for a dual-objective GAN termed $\mathcal{L}_\alpha$-GAN that, when used in tandem with a canonical discriminator loss function that achieves its optimum in (11), minimizes a Jensen-f_α-divergence. We showed that this system can recover VanillaGAN, $(1, \alpha)$-GAN, and LkGAN as special cases. We conducted experiments with the three aforementioned $\mathcal{L}_\alpha$-GANs on three image datasets. The experiments indicate that $(1, \alpha)$-GAN exhibits better performance than (α, α)-GAN with $\alpha > 1$. They also show that the devised SLkGAN system achieves lower FID scores with a VanillaGAN discriminator compared with an LkGAN discriminator.

Future work consists of unveiling more examples of existing GANs that fall under our result as well as applying $\mathcal{L}_\alpha$-GAN to novel, judiciously designed CPE losses $\mathcal{L}_\alpha$ and evaluating the performance (in terms of both quality and diversity of generated samples) and the computational efficiency of the resulting models. Another interesting and related direction is to study $\mathcal{L}_\alpha$-GAN within the context of f-GANs, given that the Jensen-f-divergence is itself an f-divergence (see Remark 1), by systematically analyzing different Jensen-f-divergences and the role they play in improving GAN performance and stability. Other worthwhile directions include incorporating the proposed $\mathcal{L}_\alpha$ loss into state-of-the-art GAN models, such as, among others, BigGAN [33], StyleGAN [34], and CycleGAN [35], for high-resolution data generation and image-to-image translation applications and conducting a meticulous analysis of the sensitivity of the models' performance to different values of the α parameter and providing guidelines on how best to tune α for different types of datasets.

Author Contributions: Conceptualization, investigation and manuscript preparation, all authors; formal analysis, all authors; software development and simulation, J.V. All authors have read and agreed to the published version of the manuscript.

Funding: This work was supported in part by the Natural Sciences and Engineering Research Council (NSERC) of Canada.

Data Availability Statement: All codes used in our experiments can be found at this https://github.com/justin-veiner/MASc, accessed on 20 February 2024.

Conflicts of Interest: The authors declare no conflicts of interest.

Appendix A. Neural Network Architectures

We outline the architectures used for the generator and discriminator. For the MNIST dataset, we use the architectures of [6]. For the CIFAR-10 and Stacked MNIST datasets, we base the architectures on [5]. We summarize some aliases for the architectures in Table A1. For all models, we use a batch size of 100 and a noise size of 784 for the generator input.

Table A1. Summary of aliases used to describe neural network architectures.

Alias	Definition
FC	Fully Connected
UpConv2D	Deconvolutional Layer
Conv2D	Convolutional Layer
BN	Batch Normalization
LeakyReLU	Leaky Rectified Linear Unit

We omit the bias in the convolutional and deconvolutional layers to decrease the number of parameters being trained, which in turn decreases computation times. We initialize our kernels using a normal distribution with zero mean and variance 0.01. We present the MNIST architectures in Tables A2 and A3 and the CIFAR-10 and Stacked MNIST architectures in Tables A4 and A5.

Table A2. Discriminator architecture for the MNIST dataset.

Layer	Output Size	Kernel	Stride	BN	Activation
Input	$28 \times 28 \times 1$			No	
Conv2D	$14 \times 14 \times 64$	5×5	2	No	LeakyReLU (0.3)
Dropout (0.3)				No	
Conv2D	$7 \times 7 \times 128$	5×5	2	No	LeakyReLU (0.3)
Dropout(0.3)				No	
FC	1			No	Sigmoid

Table A3. Generator architecture for the MNIST dataset.

Layer	Output Size	Kernel	Stride	BN	Activation
Input	784				
FC	$7 \times 7 \times 256$				
UpConv2D	$7 \times 7 \times 128$	5×5	1	Yes	LeakyReLU (0.3)
UpConv2D	$14 \times 14 \times 64$	5×5	2	Yes	LeakyReLU (0.3)
UpConv2D	$28 \times 28 \times 1$	5×5	2	No	Tanh

Table A4. Discriminator architecture for the CIFAR-10 and Stacked MNIST datasets.

Layer	Output Size	Kernel	Stride	BN	Activation
Input	$32 \times 32 \times 3$				
Conv2D	$16 \times 16 \times 128$	3×3	2	No	LeakyReLU (0.2)
Conv2D	$8 \times 8 \times 128$	3×3	2	No	LeakyReLU (0.2)
Conv2D	$4 \times 4 \times 256$	3×3	2	No	LeakyReLU (0.2)
Dropout (0.4)				No	
FC	1				Sigmoid

Table A5. Generator architecture for the CIFAR-10 and Stacked MNIST datasets.

Layer	Output Size	Kernel	Stride	BN	Activation
Input	784				
FC	$4 \times 4 \times 256$				
UpConv2D	$8 \times 8 \times 128$	4×4	2	Yes	LeakyReLU (0.2)
UpConv2D	$16 \times 16 \times 128$	4×4	2	Yes	LeakyReLU (0.2)
UpConv2D	$32 \times 32 \times 128$	4×4	2	Yes	LeakyReLU (0.2)
Conv2D	$32 \times 32 \times 3$	3×3	1	No	Tanh

Appendix B. Algorithms

We outline the algorithms used to train our models in Algorithms A1–A3.

Algorithm A1 Overview of (α_D, α_G)-GAN training

Require α_D, α_G, number of epochs n_e, batch size B, learning rate η
Initialize generator G with parameters θ_G, discriminator D with parameters θ_D.
for $i = 1$ to n_e **do**
    Sample batch of real data $\mathbf{x} = \{\mathbf{x}_1, \ldots, \mathbf{x}_B\}$ from dataset
    Sample batch of Gaussian noise vectors $\mathbf{z} = \{\mathbf{z}_1, \ldots, \mathbf{z}_B\} \sim \mathcal{N}(\mathbf{0}, \mathbf{I})$
    Update the discriminator's parameters using an Adam optimizer with learning rate η by descending the gradient:

$$\nabla_{\theta_D}\left(-\frac{1}{B}\sum_{i=1}^{B}(-\ell_\alpha(1, D(\mathbf{x}_i)) - \ell_\alpha(0, D(G(\mathbf{z}_i))))\right)$$

or **update** the discriminator's parameters with a simplified GP:

$$\nabla_{\theta_D}\left(-\frac{1}{B}\sum_{i=1}^{B}(-\ell_\alpha(1, D(\mathbf{x}_i)) - \ell_\alpha(0, D(G(\mathbf{z}_i))))\right.$$
$$\left. +5\left(\sum_{i=1}^{B}\left\|\nabla_{\mathbf{x}}\log\left(\frac{D(\mathbf{x})}{1-D(\mathbf{x})}\right)\right\|_2^2\right)\right)$$

Update the generator's parameters using an Adam optimizer with learning rate η and descending the gradient:

$$\nabla_{\theta_G}\left(\frac{1}{B}\sum_{i=1}^{B}\ell_\alpha(0, D(G(\mathbf{z}_i)))\right)$$

end for

Algorithm A2 Overview of Lk-SLkGAN training

Require k, number of epochs n_e, batch size B, learning rate η
Initialize generator G with parameters θ_G, discriminator D with parameters θ_D.
for $i = 1$ to n_e **do**
    Sample batch of real data $\mathbf{x} = \{\mathbf{x}_1, \ldots, \mathbf{x}_B\}$ from dataset
    Sample batch of Gaussian noise vectors $\mathbf{z} = \{\mathbf{z}_1, \ldots, \mathbf{z}_B\} \sim \mathcal{N}(\mathbf{0}, \mathbf{I})$
    Update the discriminator's parameters using an Adam optimizer with learning rate η by descending the gradient:

$$\nabla_{\theta_D}\left(\frac{1}{B}\sum_{i=1}^{B}\left(\frac{1}{2}(D(\mathbf{x}_i)-1)^2 + \frac{1}{2}(D(G(\mathbf{z}_i)))^2\right)\right)$$

or **update** the discriminator's parameters with a simplified GP:

$$\nabla_{\theta_D}\left(\frac{1}{B}\sum_{i=1}^{B}\left(\frac{1}{2}(D(\mathbf{x}_i)-1)^2 + \frac{1}{2}(D(G(\mathbf{z}_i)))^2\right)\right.$$
$$\left. +5\left(\sum_{i=1}^{B}\left\|\nabla_{\mathbf{x}}\log\left(\frac{D(\mathbf{x})}{1-D(\mathbf{x})}\right)\right\|_2^2\right)\right)$$

Update the generator's parameters using an Adam optimizer with learning rate η and descending the gradient:

$$\nabla_{\theta_G}\left(\frac{1}{B}\sum_{i=1}^{B}\frac{1}{2}(|1-D(G(\mathbf{z}_i))|^k - 1)\right)$$

end for

Algorithm A3 Overview of Vanilla-SLkGAN training

Require k, number of epochs n_e, batch size B, learning rate η
Initialize generator G with parameters $\boldsymbol{\theta}_G$, discriminator D with parameters $\boldsymbol{\theta}_D$.
for $i = 1$ to n_e **do**
  Sample batch of real data $\mathbf{x} = \{\mathbf{x}_1, \ldots, \mathbf{x}_B\}$ from dataset
  Sample batch of noise vectors $\mathbf{z} = \{\mathbf{z}_1, \ldots, \mathbf{z}_B\} \sim \mathcal{N}(\mathbf{0}, \mathbf{I})$
  Update the discriminator's parameters using an Adam optimizer with learning rate η by descending the gradient:

$$\nabla_{\boldsymbol{\theta}_D} \left(-\frac{1}{B} \sum_{i=1}^{B} (\log(D(\mathbf{x}_i)) + \log(1 - D(G(\mathbf{z}_i)))) \right)$$

  or **update** the discriminator's parameters with a simplified (GP):

$$\nabla_{\boldsymbol{\theta}_D} \left(-\frac{1}{B} \sum_{i=1}^{B} (\log(D(\mathbf{x}_i)) + \log(1 - D(G(\mathbf{z}_i)))) \right.$$
$$\left. + 5 \left(\sum_{i=1}^{B} \left\| \nabla_{\mathbf{x}} \log\left(\frac{D(\mathbf{x})}{1 - D(\mathbf{x})} \right) \right\|_2^2 \right) \right)$$

  Update the generator's parameters using an Adam optimizer with learning rate η and descending the gradient:

$$\nabla_{\boldsymbol{\theta}_G} \left(\frac{1}{B} \sum_{i=1}^{B} \frac{1}{2} (|1 - D(G(\mathbf{z}_i))|^k - 1) \right)$$

end for

References

1. Goodfellow, I.; Pouget-Abadie, J.; Mirza, M.; Xu, B.; Warde-Farley, D.; Ozair, S.; Courville, A.; Bengio, Y. Generative adversarial nets. In Proceedings of the Advances in Neural Information Processing Systems, Montreal, QC, Canada, 8–13 December 2014; Ghahramani, Z., Welling, M., Cortes, C., Lawrence, N., Weinberger, K., Eds.; Curran Associates, Inc.: Red Hook, NY, USA, 2014; Volume 27, pp. 2672–2680.
2. Kwon, Y.H.; Park, M.G. Predicting future frames using retrospective cycle GAN. In Proceedings of the IEEE/CVF Conference on Computer Vision and Pattern Recognition (CVPR), Long Beach, CA, USA, 16–20 June 2019.
3. Pan, X.; Zhan, X.; Dai, B.; Lin, D.; Loy, C.C.; Luo, P. Exploiting deep generative prior for versatile image restoration and manipulation. *IEEE Trans. Pattern Anal. Mach. Intell.* **2021**, *44*, 7474–7489. [CrossRef] [PubMed]
4. Jordon, J.; Yoon, J.; Van Der Schaar, M. PATE-GAN: Generating synthetic data with differential privacy guarantees. In Proceedings of the International Conference on Learning Representations, Vancouver, BC, Canada, 30 April–3 May 2018.
5. Radford, A.; Metz, L.; Chintala, S. Unsupervised representation learning with deep convolutional generative adversarial networks. In Proceedings of the 9th International Conference on Image and Graphics, Shanghai, China, 13–15 September 2017; pp. 97–108.
6. Bhatia, H.; Paul, W.; Alajaji, F.; Gharesifard, B.; Burlina, P. Least kth-order and Rényi generative adversarial networks. *Neural Comput.* **2021**, *33*, 2473–2510. [CrossRef] [PubMed]
7. Nowozin, S.; Cseke, B.; Tomioka, R. f-GAN: Training generative neural samplers using variational divergence minimization. In *Advances in Neural Information Processing Systems*; MIT Press: Cambridge, MA, USA, 2016; Volume 29.
8. Kurri, G.R.; Sypherd, T.; Sankar, L. Realizing GANs via a tunable loss function. In Proceedings of the IEEE Information Theory Workshop (ITW), Virtual, 17–21 October 2021; pp. 1–6.
9. Kurri, G.R.; Welfert, M.; Sypherd, T.; Sankar, L. α-GAN: Convergence and estimation guarantees. In Proceedings of the IEEE International Symposium on Information Theory (ISIT), Espoo, Finland, 26 June–1 July 2022; pp. 276–281.
10. Welfert, M.; Otstot, K.; Kurri, G.R.; Sankar, L. (α_D, α_G)-GANs: Addressing GAN training instabilities via dual objectives. In Proceedings of the IEEE International Symposium on Information Theory (ISIT), Taipei, Taiwan, 25–30 June 2023.
11. Welfert, M.; Kurri, G.R.; Otstot, K.; Sankar, L. Addressing GAN training instabilities via tunable classification losses. *arXiv* **2023**, arXiv:2310.18291.
12. Csiszar, I. Eine Informationstheoretische Ungleichung und ihre Anwendung auf den Bewis der Ergodizitat on Markhoffschen Ketten. *Publ. Math. Inst. Hung. Acad. Sci. Ser. A* **1963**, *8*, 85–108.
13. Csiszár, I. Information-type measures of difference of probability distributions and indirect observations. *Stud. Sci. Math. Hung.* **1967**, *2*, 299–318.

14. Ali, S.M.; Silvey, S.D. A general class of coefficients of divergence of one distribution from another. *J. R. Stat. Soc. Ser. (Methodol.)* **1966**, *28*, 131–142. [CrossRef]
15. Liese, F.; Vajda, I. On divergences and informations in statistics and information theory. *IEEE Trans. Inf. Theory* **2006**, *52*, 4394–4412. [CrossRef]
16. Kullback, S.; Leibler, R.A. On information and sufficiency. *Ann. Math. Stat.* **1951**, *22*, 79–86. [CrossRef]
17. Nielsen, F. On a generalization of the Jensen–Shannon divergence and the Jensen–Shannon centroid. *Entropy* **2020**, *22*, 221. [CrossRef] [PubMed]
18. Nielsen, F.; Nock, R. On the chi square and higher-order chi distances for approximating f-divergences. *IEEE Signal Process. Lett.* **2013**, *21*, 10–13. [CrossRef]
19. Arimoto, S. Information-theoretical considerations on estimation problems. *Inf. Control.* **1971**, *19*, 181–194. [CrossRef]
20. Österreicher, F. On a class of perimeter-type distances of probability distributions. *Kybernetika* **1996**, *32*, 389–393.
21. Hellinger, E. Neue Begründung der Theorie quadratischer Formen von unendlichvielen Veränderlichen. *J. Reine Angew. Math.* **1909**, *1909*, 210–271. [CrossRef]
22. Sason, I. On f-divergences: Integral representations, local behavior, and inequalities. *Entropy* **2018**, *20*, 383. [CrossRef] [PubMed]
23. Rényi, A. On measures of entropy and information. In *Proceedings of the Fourth Berkeley Symposium on Mathematical Statistics and Probability, Volume 1: Contributions to the Theory of Statistics*; University of California Press: Berkeley, CA, USA, 1961; Volume 4, pp. 547–562.
24. Van Erven, T.; Harremos, P. Rényi divergence and Kullback-Leibler divergence. *IEEE Trans. Inf. Theory* **2014**, *60*, 3797–3820. [CrossRef]
25. Arjovsky, M.; Chintala, S.; Bottou, L. Wasserstein generative adversarial networks. In Proceedings of the International Conference on Machine Learning, PMLR, Sydney, Australia, 6–11 August 2017; pp. 214–223.
26. Mao, X.; Li, Q.; Xie, H.; Lau, R.Y.; Wang, Z.; Paul Smolley, S. Least squares generative adversarial networks. In Proceedings of the IEEE International Conference on Computer Vision (ICCV), Venice, Italy, 22–29 October 2017.
27. Deng, L. The MNIST database of handwritten digit images for machine learning research. *IEEE Signal Process. Mag.* **2012**, *29*, 141–142. [CrossRef]
28. Krizhevsky, A.; Hinton, G. Learning Multiple Layers of Features from Tiny Images 2009. Available online: https://www.cs.toronto.edu/~kriz/learning-features-2009-TR.pdf (accessed on 22 February 2024).
29. Lin, Z.; Khetan, A.; Fanti, G.; Oh, S. PacGAN: The power of two samples in generative adversarial networks. In *Advances in Neural Information Processing Systems*; MIT Press: Cambridge, MA, USA, 2018; Volume 31, pp. 1–10.
30. Kingma, D.; Ba, J. Adam: A method for stochastic optimization. In Proceedings of the International Conference on Learning Representations, Banff, AB, Canada, 14–16 April 2014.
31. Gulrajani, I.; Ahmed, F.; Arjovsky, M.; Dumoulin, V.; Courville, A.C. Improved training of Wasserstein GANs. In *Advances in Neural Information Processing Systems*; MIT Press: Cambridge, MA, USA, 2017; Volume 30, pp. 1–11.
32. Heusel, M.; Ramsauer, H.; Unterthiner, T.; Nessler, B.; Hochreiter, S. GANs trained by a two time-scale update rule converge to a local Nash equilibrium. In *Advances in Neural Information Processing Systems*; MIT Press: Cambridge, MA, USA, 2017; Volume 30, pp. 6626–6637.
33. Brock, A.; Donahue, J.; Simonyan, K. Large scale GAN training for high fidelity natural image synthesis. *arXiv* **2018**, arXiv:1809.11096.
34. Karras, T.; Laine, S.; Aila, T. A style-based generator architecture for generative adversarial networks. In Proceedings of the IEEE/CVF Conference on Computer Vision and Pattern Recognition, Long Beach, CA, USA, 15–20 June 2019; pp. 4401–4410.
35. Almahairi, A.; Rajeshwar, S.; Sordoni, A.; Bachman, P.; Courville, A. Augmented CycleGAN: Learning many-to-many mappings from unpaired data. In Proceedings of the International Conference on Machine Learning, PMLR, Stockholm, Sweden, 10–15 July 2018; pp. 195–204.

Disclaimer/Publisher's Note: The statements, opinions and data contained in all publications are solely those of the individual author(s) and contributor(s) and not of MDPI and/or the editor(s). MDPI and/or the editor(s) disclaim responsibility for any injury to people or property resulting from any ideas, methods, instructions or products referred to in the content.

Article

Multivariate Time Series Information Bottleneck

Denis Ullmann, Olga Taran and Slava Voloshynovskiy *

Faculty of Science, University of Geneva, CUI, 1227 Carouge, Switzerland; denis.ullmann@unige.ch (D.U.)
* Correspondence: svolos@unige.ch

Abstract: Time series (TS) and multiple time series (MTS) predictions have historically paved the way for distinct families of deep learning models. The temporal dimension, distinguished by its evolutionary sequential aspect, is usually modeled by decomposition into the trio of "trend, seasonality, noise", by attempts to copy the functioning of human synapses, and more recently, by transformer models with self-attention on the temporal dimension. These models may find applications in finance and e-commerce, where any increase in performance of less than 1% has large monetary repercussions, they also have potential applications in natural language processing (NLP), medicine, and physics. To the best of our knowledge, the information bottleneck (IB) framework has not received significant attention in the context of TS or MTS analyses. One can demonstrate that a compression of the temporal dimension is key in the context of MTS. We propose a new approach with partial convolution, where a time sequence is encoded into a two-dimensional representation resembling images. Accordingly, we use the recent advances made in image extension to predict an unseen part of an image from a given one. We show that our model compares well with traditional TS models, has information–theoretical foundations, and can be easily extended to more dimensions than only time and space. An evaluation of our multiple time series–information bottleneck (MTS-IB) model proves its efficiency in electricity production, road traffic, and astronomical data representing solar activity, as recorded by NASA's interface region imaging spectrograph (IRIS) satellite.

Keywords: multiple time series; forecasting method; information bottleneck; entropy; KL-divergence; mutual information; deep models; RNN; U-Net; partial convolutions

Citation: Ullmann, D.; Taran, O.; Voloshynovskiy, S. Multivariate Time Series Information Bottleneck. *Entropy* **2023**, *25*, 831. https://doi.org/10.3390/e25050831

Academic Editors: Shuangming Yang, Shujian Yu, Luis Gonzalo Sánchez Giraldo and Badong Chen

Received: 22 February 2023
Revised: 10 May 2023
Accepted: 17 May 2023
Published: 22 May 2023

Copyright: © 2023 by the authors. Licensee MDPI, Basel, Switzerland. This article is an open access article distributed under the terms and conditions of the Creative Commons Attribution (CC BY) license (https://creativecommons.org/licenses/by/4.0/).

1. Introduction

The scope of this work lies at the intersection of several domains, offering contributions to information theory (IT) applied to machine learning (ML), applied astrophysics, and computer vision (CV). Recently, non-recurrent models, such as transformers [1], among others [2,3], have been used to accurately predict forecasts for multivariate time series (MTS). The training of these models is guided by a proposed information–theoretical approach. This study supports the validity of some of these models with an IT approach describing the IB in the context of time series (TS). A CV-based model using partial convolution [4] with an MTS forecasting goal is presented and the link with the IB principle is proved. The approach was tested on astrophysical production, electricity production, and road traffic data. MTS, CV, and IT metrics show the empirical effectiveness of the proposed idea.

TS and MTS predictions are among the key applications of ML. They enable models to forecast the future evolution of data over time, where the time flow is represented as a single scalar for TS and a multi-dimensional vector for MTS. Meteorology, finance, online purchases, epidemic spread, and space weather forecasting are all examples of areas with great interest. Even a marginal improvement, as small as a tenth of a percent, can have a significant monetary or scientific impact. TS and MTS predictions are domains where models, such as recurrent neural networks (RNNs) [5] and long-short-term-memory (LSTM) [6], were historically developed to comply with the specificities of the temporal dimension. Although these models have similarities with classical CV models, they are part of a separate group of models that aim to mimic human memory and attention mechanisms.

Historically, one-step-forward models were formalized before multi-step-forward models. For the former, the model predicts one step of time after a known time series. Before the rise of deep models, time series decompositions, regressions [7–10], moving averages [11], exponential smoothing techniques [12], and ARIMA [13] models were designed to forecast the most probable outcome of a time step following the given time steps in a series. Later, deep models advocated for learning a larger number of regression parameters through gradient descent [14]. RNNs face a vanishing gradient problem when they consist of more than three layers. LSTMs, a family of RNNs, aim to mimic the memory and synaptic functioning of human brains, as well as solve the vanishing gradient issue, at the cost of a possible explosion of the gradients. Finally, the more recent gated recurrent unit (GRU) [15] is an intermediate version of RNNs that works efficiently in more cases compared to classical RNNs and LSTMs.

The most recent challenges of forecasting with deep models include (a) achieving high-efficiency prediction in the context of MTS, where each time step consists of a multi-dimensional vector, with multi-step-ahead forecasts, where the model predicts multiple time steps ahead in one run, (b) interpretability, and (c) predicting the errors at each forecasted time step. The error prediction is often performed by integrating them as a joint time series that the model has to predict in parallel to the targeted time series [2]. Another option relies on stochastic predictions, where the possible forecast at each time is modeled by probabilistic distributions whose parameters are predicted by the model [2]. Interpretability is often obtained by explicit time representations or decompositions [16–18], as well as hierarchically built models that are supposed to learn classical time series decompositions by trend and seasonality [3]. To our knowledge, the most significant recent performance gains have been obtained by models that first construct a joint embedding representation of the time and space dimensions, along with compression and decompression techniques [2,3,17–20], which are afterward fed into a version of RNN, graph neural networks (GNNs) [21] or self-attention network-like transformers [17], at very high memory costs [18,20].

On the other hand, from the CV family of deep models, the objectives of *image inpainting* [4,22–24] is very similar to TS forecasting. Both attempt to recover some missing data from the information provided by two correlated known dimensions: pixel coordinates for CV and temporal–spatial for MTS. For TS and MTS, the observed temporal evolution of some data provides information to the model to forecast how these data will evolve in the future [25,26]. For image inpainting, the given parts of the image serve as prior information that aids the model in reconstructing the missing parts [24].

Recent works on images denoising [27] and inpainting [4] have shown a high capability to capture prior distributions of images and restore masked or noisy images with high accuracy. They measure accuracy in various ways, including classical Manhattan or Frobenius norms, more advanced styles [28], perceptual losses [29], and human assessments such as the mean opinion score (MOS) [30]. All of these methods use the U-Net architecture [31], with partial convolutions [4], which are particularly efficient for learning outputs that are close to the inputs in terms of similar pixels.

U-Net is a deep convolutional network that was originally designed for image segmentation [31]. It can be sketched by the following Markov chain:

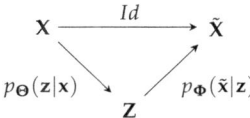

where $\mathbf{Z}$ is a latent representation, $p_{\Theta}(\mathbf{z}|\mathbf{x})$ is an encoding part modeled by reducing the time dimension through successive strided convolution layers, and $p_{\Phi}(\tilde{\mathbf{x}}|\mathbf{x})$ is a decoding part performed by an architecture symmetric to $p_{\Theta}(\mathbf{z}|\mathbf{x})$, such that the posterior $\tilde{\mathbf{X}}$ has the same shape as the prior $\mathbf{X}$. U-Net also allows a direct flow of information with an identity mapper Id between $\mathbf{X}$ and $\tilde{\mathbf{X}}$, also referred to as the skipping layer. This direct flow of information between the prior and the posterior allows for easy reconstruction of the prior image while the information flow through the latent $\mathbf{Z}$ is responsible for the image segmentation objective. Skipping layers are also present between symmetrical hidden layers of the encoder and the decoder. Without the skipping layers, the U-Net is reduced to an autoencoder (AE) structure [32] sketched by the Markov chain $\mathbf{X} \to \mathbf{Z} \to \tilde{\mathbf{X}}$ acting as a principal component analysis dimensional reduction of $\mathbf{X}$ in $\mathbf{Z}$.

Considering the spectral time sequences as images, one can demonstrate that image processing based on generative machine learning techniques can capture the temporal patterns of the physics or logic behind the spatial data, enabling the prediction of short-term evolution. Therefore, our objective is to predict time sequences efficiently with the support of the IB principle rather than classical time sequence modelings, such as LSTM or RNN. The problem with time sequence prediction is, in this way, very similar to *image inpainting* or an *extension* problem [4,22,23].

Recently, IT approaches have formalized deep models through IB [33]. This shows that deep models are guided to find the most informative yet compressed representations for given tasks. Deep models must compress the input information into a format that ideally contains only sufficient statistics to recover posterior targeted data. To our knowledge, very few past works [34–37] have attempted to describe the IB principle in the TS and MTS contexts, whereas an extensive body of literature exists that focuses on deriving the IB principle in CV models [33,38–42].

Very few past works have used IT to design or explain the TS and MTS forecasting models that they proposed. Some attempted to estimate the entropy of TS or MTS in order to quantify their variability [34,35,37]. More interestingly, the IB principle was formulated in the RNN context but without compression of the time dimension, such that only the information present at each time step was compressed and decompressed [36]. Their work claims that each time step can be formulated by its own IB principle and that a time series with N time steps can be modeled by N IB steps. In our work, we claim that the compression of time is key for efficient forecasting and most of the existing models are realizations of a single IB principle with the compression of time and spatial dimensions.

From an information–theoretical point of view, Tishby [33] proposed the information bottleneck principle (IB), which aims to compress the input $\mathbf{X}$ and filter out all task-irrelevant information while preserving sufficient statistics in the bottleneck $\mathbf{Z}$; this was in order to decode the compressed representation into the task-specific representation, denoted as $\tilde{\mathbf{X}}$ in this context. The goal of the model is to find the parameters of the compression encoder $\boldsymbol{\Theta}$ and the decoding $\boldsymbol{\Phi}$ by solving the following optimization problem:

$$(\hat{\boldsymbol{\Theta}}, \hat{\boldsymbol{\Phi}}) = \underset{\substack{(\boldsymbol{\Theta}, \boldsymbol{\Phi}) \\ I_{\boldsymbol{\Phi}}(\mathbf{Z}; \tilde{\mathbf{X}}) \geq \alpha}}{\operatorname{argmin}} I_{\boldsymbol{\Theta}}(\mathbf{X}; \mathbf{Z}), \tag{1}$$

where $I_{\boldsymbol{\Theta}}(\mathbf{X}; \mathbf{Z})$ represents Shannon's mutual information between $\mathbf{X}$ and $\mathbf{Z}$, which is parameterized by the parameters $\boldsymbol{\Theta}$ of the network $f_{\boldsymbol{\Theta}}(\cdot)$ mapping $\mathbf{X}$ to $\mathbf{Z}$, defined by:

$$I_{\boldsymbol{\Theta}}(\mathbf{X}; \mathbf{Z}) = \mathbb{E}_{p(\mathbf{X}, \mathbf{Z})} \left[\log_2 \frac{p(\mathbf{X}, \mathbf{Z})}{p(\mathbf{X}), p(\mathbf{Z})} \right], \quad \text{where} \quad \mathbf{z} \sim p_{\boldsymbol{\Theta}}(\mathbf{z}|\mathbf{x}) \text{ for all } \mathbf{x} \sim \mathbf{X}. \tag{2}$$

α represents the lower bound on the mutual information between the genuine $\tilde{\mathbf{X}}$ and the compressed $\mathbf{Z}$. This lower bound ensures sufficient statistics of the genuine in the compressed $\mathbf{Z}$ in order to allow the decoder to decode $\tilde{\mathbf{X}}$. Equation (1) can also be refined with a Lagrange multiplier β, such that the parameters of the compression and decompression are solutions of:

$$(\hat{\boldsymbol{\Theta}}, \hat{\boldsymbol{\Phi}}) = \underset{(\boldsymbol{\Theta}, \boldsymbol{\Phi})}{\operatorname{argmin}} \underbrace{I_{\boldsymbol{\Theta}}(\mathbf{X}; \mathbf{Z}) - \beta I_{\boldsymbol{\Phi}}(\mathbf{Z}; \tilde{\mathbf{X}})}_{\mathcal{L}(\boldsymbol{\Theta}, \boldsymbol{\Phi})}. \tag{3}$$

Past works [43–46] have studied the IB of AEs, often by empirically estimating the information plane (IP), i.e., the temporal graph of the training relation between mutual information, $I(\mathbf{X}; \mathbf{Z})$ and $I(\mathbf{Z}; \tilde{\mathbf{X}})$. For all studies, the estimation of mutual information is not exact and requires the tuning of some hyperparameters. In [43,46], the authors studied the IP at training times for different types of AEs. They show that sparse autoencoders (SAEs) significantly compress the information of MNIST data in the bottleneck, unlike the other AE, such as the variational autoencoder (VAE), for which the compression is not clear for the data (even though the VAE provides high constraints on the distribution of the bottleneck). More details about the variational decomposition of the IB and its variational approximations are provided in [47]. In [44], the authors studied the IP of vanilla AE on MNIST with different hyperparameters for mutual information estimation. Their work shows the compression of information at each hidden layer, extending from the input to the bottleneck layer. It also provides an interpretation of the link between the dimensions of the bottleneck and the compression of information. It shows that when the bottleneck dimensions are relatively small, compared to the entropy of the source, further compression is forced due to the limitation imposed by the bottleneck dimension. When the bottleneck dimensions are relatively large, there are no such limitations. Our broad interpretation of this outcome is that the AE training follows Shannon's separation theorem from the joint source and channel coding theory [48] because of the large capacity of the channel formed by the AE. In [45], the authors studied the rate-distortion performance of an AE where the IB was used as the dimensionality reduction with a fixed number of noisy information channels; they applied this AE strategy to efficiently store analog data on an array of phase-change memory (PCM) devices. The IB of AEs showed efficient rate-distortion results in this context; the authors provided theoretical insights by utilizing Shannon's separation theorem from the joint source and channel coding theory [48].

We propose a general formulation of the IB principle for MTS forecasting. We show that the U-Net architecture with source masking and an approximation of the IB loss can be regarded as a particular instance of the formulated IB principle for MTS. We provide an extensive evaluation of the proposed model on some astrophysical data of interest, and we compare the model to concurrent ones with MTS, CV, and astrophysical metrics. Interestingly, without fine-tuning, and with an approximation of the IB loss, our models based on the IB principle formulation can achieve top results on different datasets involving astrophysics solar activity prediction, electricity production, and road traffic.

One important direction of this work is the application of the IB principle to astrophysical data. The accurate prediction of solar activity, solar flares, in particular, is still an open issue. Solar flares occur as a result of the reconfiguration of magnetic fields in the corona. These energetic events accelerate highly energetic particles into space and toward the solar surface, where they cause heat and emissions in a broad range of wavelengths. Solar flares are major protagonists in space weather and can cause adverse effects, such as disruptions in communications, power grid failures on Earth, and damage to satellites and other critical infrastructures. Many attempts to predict flares exist [49–53], as well as works on flare detection [54] and analyses [55–58].

2. Methods

Forecasting models take TS data as input, noted as $X_{1:T} = [X_1 : X_T]$, or MTS data, noted $\mathbf{X}_{1:T} = [\mathbf{X}_1 : \mathbf{X}_T]$, both of length T. For TS, each time step X_t, ($t \in [1, \ldots, T]$) is scalar, whereas for MTS, each time step $\mathbf{X}_t = [X_t^1, \ldots, X_t^M]$, ($t \in [1, \ldots, T]$) is a vector of length M. As a consequence, $\mathbf{X}_{1:T}$ represents a two-dimensional tensor, with the first dimension being *temporal* of length T, and the second typically referred to as the *spatial* dimension of length M.

The goal of the forecasting models is to predict the time continuation of the input data by forecasting one step ahead or multiple steps ahead; this is denoted as $X_{T+1:T+F} = [X_{T+1}, \ldots, X_{T+F}]$ for TS, and $\mathbf{X}_{T+1:T+F} = [\mathbf{X}_{T+1}, \ldots, \mathbf{X}_{T+F}]$ for MTS, where F refers to the number of steps ahead to forecast.

In this paper, the input series $X_{1:T}$ or $\mathbf{X}_{1:T}$ is referred to as the *prior*, the true forecast $X_{T+1:T+F}$ (or $\mathbf{X}_{T+1:T+F}$) is referred to as *genuine*, and the forecast predicted by the model $\tilde{X}_{T+1:T+F}$ or $\tilde{\mathbf{X}}_{T+1:T+F}$ is referred to as *posterior*. $\mathcal{D}$ refers to the training dataset, which is also denoted as $\{\mathbf{X}_{1:T+F}\}_\mathcal{D}$ or $\{(\mathbf{X}_{1:T+F}, K)\}_\mathcal{D}$ when the data are labeled; K denotes the label, or it can be represented as $\mathbf{K}$ in the case of categorical vectors. Table A1 recalls most of the notations used in the paper.

2.1. IB-Based Optimal Compression for Time Series Forecasts

The general IB principle proposes to compress the input into a latent representation while ensuring the preservation of sufficient statistics, which are crucial for the downstream task. In the context of TS forecasting, this implies that the effective compression of the time dimension needs to be employed in order to achieve accurate forecasting. Using our notations, and according to the IB formulation of Equation (3), the goal of a model is to find the parameters of the compression encoder Θ and of decoding Φ by solving the following optimization problem:

$$(\hat{\Theta}, \hat{\Phi}) = \underset{(\Theta, \Phi)}{\mathrm{argmin}} \underbrace{I_\Theta(\mathbf{X}_{1:T}; \mathbf{Z}_{ib\_tr}) - \beta I_\Phi(\mathbf{Z}_{ib\_tr}; \mathbf{X}_{T+1:T+F})}_{\mathcal{L}(\Theta, \Phi)}, \qquad (4)$$

where the input $\mathbf{X}_{1:T}$ represents the previous T time steps of values, and the output $\mathbf{X}_{T+1:T+F}$ represents the subsequent F time steps. As a consequence, the bottleneck variable $\mathbf{Z}_{ib\_tr}$ should then hold the necessary part of information of prior time steps $1:T$ for the model to be able to forecast the time steps $T+1:T+F$. The index ib_tr explicitly reflects the nature of the MTS bottleneck task as an IB learning statistics of transitions $1:T \to T+1:T+F$. Taking inspiration from works [39], Proof of Equation (5) in the Appendix A shows that an upper bound $\tilde{\mathcal{L}}(\Theta, \Phi)$ on the loss $\mathcal{L}(\Theta, \Phi)$ of Equation (3) can be reduced as follows:

$$\tilde{\mathcal{L}}(\Theta, \Phi) = H_{p_\Theta}(\mathbf{Z}_{ib\_tr}) - H_{p_\Theta}(\mathbf{Z}_{ib\_tr}|\mathbf{X}_{1:T}) + \beta H_{p_{\Theta, \Phi}}(\mathbf{X}_{T+1:T+F}|\mathbf{Z}_{ib\_tr}), \qquad (5)$$

where $p_\Theta(\mathbf{Z}_{ib\_tr}) = \mathbb{E}_{p_\mathcal{D}}[p_\Theta(\mathbf{Z}_{ib\_tr}|\mathbf{X}_{1:T})]$, where $\mathcal{D}$ represents the training data consisting of pairs of priors and their corresponding known forecasts: $\mathcal{D} = \{(\mathbf{x}_{1:T}, \mathbf{x}_{T+1:T+F}) \sim \mathbf{X}_{1:T+F}\}$ and $H(.)$ stands for Shannon's entropy, such that the upper bound on $\mathcal{L}(\Theta, \Phi)$ is composed by these three components:

$$\begin{aligned}
\mathcal{L}_1(\Theta) &= H_{p_\Theta}(\mathbf{Z}_{ib\_tr}) \\
&= -\mathbb{E}_{p_\Theta(\mathbf{Z}_{ib\_tr})}[\log_2 p_\Theta(\mathbf{Z}_{ib\_tr})], \\
\mathcal{L}_2(\Theta) &= -H_{p_\Theta}(\mathbf{Z}_{ib\_tr}|\mathbf{X}_{1:T}) \\
&= \mathbb{E}_{p_\Theta(\mathbf{X}_{1:T}, \mathbf{Z}_{ib\_tr})}[\log_2 p_\Theta(\mathbf{Z}_{ib\_tr}|\mathbf{X}_{1:T})], \\
\mathcal{L}_3(\Theta, \Phi) &= H_{p_{\Theta, \Phi}}(\mathbf{X}_{T+1:T+F}|\mathbf{Z}_{ib\_tr}) \\
&= -\mathbb{E}_{p_\mathcal{D}(\mathbf{X}_{1:T+F})}\left[\mathbb{E}_{p_\Theta(\mathbf{Z}_{ib\_tr}|\mathbf{X}_{1:T})}[\log_2 p_\Phi(\mathbf{X}_{T+1:T+F}|\mathbf{Z}_{ib\_tr})]\right].
\end{aligned} \qquad (6)$$

$\mathcal{L}_3(\Theta, \Phi)$ is the average cross-entropy $H(p_\Theta(\mathbf{Z}_{ib\_tr}|\mathbf{X}_{1:T}), p_\Phi(\mathbf{X}_{T+1:T+F}|\mathbf{Z}_{ib\_tr}))$. Moreover, if the decoding distribution $p_\Phi(\mathbf{X}_{T+1:T+F}|\mathbf{Z}_{ib\_tr})$ is assumed to follow the Laplacian distribution, ref. [39] shows that the loss $\mathcal{L}_3(\Theta, \Phi)$ can be reduced into the average Manhattan distance, which is also referred to as the mean average error loss (MAE) between the genuine and the model estimation:

$$\mathcal{L}_3^{Lap}(\Theta, \Phi) = \mathbb{E}_{p_\mathcal{D}(\mathbf{X}_{1:T+F})}\left[\mathbb{E}_{p_\Theta(\mathbf{Z}_{ib\_tr}|\mathbf{X}_{1:T})}[\|\mathbf{X}_{T+1:T+F} - g_\Phi(\mathbf{Z}_{ib\_tr})\|_1]\right]. \qquad (7)$$

Throughout the years, different forecasting models have been proposed; the MAE of $\mathcal{L}_3^{Lap}(\Theta, \Phi)$ has been used for training the initial models and for evaluating the performances of the forecasting models. We show in Figure 1 how existing models design a bottleneck **Z** that compresses the time dimension, similar to $\mathbf{Z}_{ib\_tr}$ in Equation (4). The following paragraphs briefly explain the time compression and a few differences between the models selected in Figure 1.

LSTM [6], GRU [15], and DEEP-AR [2] operate with an RNN [5] over the time dimension, which is compressed in the hidden memory channel **Z**. The constituting cell operates only on one time step and predicts another unique time step ($T = 1$ and $F = 1$). DEEP-AR predicts the mean and standard deviations of the forecast value, enabling the model to exhibit stochastic behavior and to learn the uncertainty on the forecast.

NBeats [3] directly operates on all prior times $\mathbf{X}_{1:T}$ and uses a hierarchical RNN structure to capture trends, seasonality, and repetitions, resulting in a hidden representation **Z**. From this time compression, the model can reproduce the prior TS and forecast multiple time steps ahead $\mathbf{X}_{T+1:T+F}$. The hierarchical structure allows for interpreting the time series.

Transformers [19] encode the given TS with multiple self-attention layers in order to capture repetitions and logic between time steps. Each time step is input into its own self-attention layer. Once the time dimension is effectively compressed into **Z**, the model decodes the compressed representation to generate one (or multiple) time step forecast(s) $\mathbf{X}_{T+1:T+F}$, depending on the model.

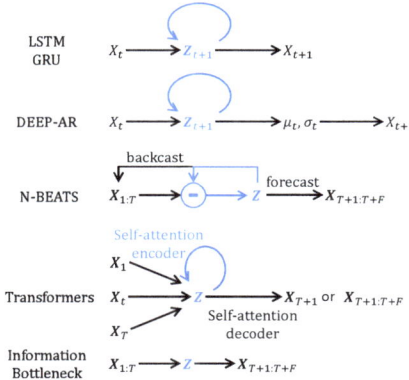

Figure 1. Comparison of Markov chains for a selection of deep TS predictors: the blue parts correspond to the compressed representations of the time dimension. Some of these may accept additional inputs (correlated context) but we did not include them in these diagrams because that would overload the global understanding, and the time dimension is compressed in the same way. A bold **X** is used when the model accepts vectors as input.

2.2. Compression by Source Masking

According to Tishby's original IB formulation, the downstream task was a classification. The form of information minimization in the IB is not necessary via the dimension reduction or the addition of noise, but it can be via any lossy operation, such as lossy compression or masking. We propose to address the IB principle for MTS via source masking, dimension reduction, and prediction of the masked parts. Using masks, Equation (4) can be rewritten as:

$$\mathcal{L}(\Theta, \Phi) = I_\Theta(\mathbf{X}_{1:T+F} \odot \mathbf{M}_{1:T}; \mathbf{Z}_{ib\_tr}) - \beta I_\Phi(\mathbf{Z}_{ib\_tr}; \mathbf{X}_{1:T+F} \odot \mathbf{M}_{T+1:T+F}), \qquad (8)$$

where $\odot$ is the element-wise product, also known as the Hadamard dot product, where $\mathbf{M}_{1:T}$ and $\mathbf{M}_{T+1:T+F}$ are binary time masks that have ones at the indexed time positions, $1:T$ or $T+1:T+F$, and zeros at the other time positions. Note that Equation (8) is very close to the formulation of IB for AEs in Equation (1) but with additional masks. Without masks, the bottleneck not only holds statistics for the transitions $1{:}T \to T+1{:}T+F$, but also contains all statistics for the reconstruction of the entire sequence $1{:}T+F$. In that case, the bottleneck is reduced to an AE bottleneck $\mathbf{Z}_{ib\_ae}$ with dimension reduction purposes only. In contrast, with masking, the bottleneck $\mathbf{Z}_{ib\_tr}$ is designed to learn transition statistics $1{:}T \to T+1{:}T+F$.

2.3. Compressing Multi-Dimensional Data by Extreme Spatiotemporal Dimension Reduction

Previous subsections have not specifically taken into account the multi-dimensional aspects of MTS. Instead of scalar values X_t for TS, each time step is a vector $\mathbf{X}_t = [X_t^1, \ldots, X_t^M]$ or tensor for MTS, usually referred to as the *spatial dimension*. Previous works [59] show that models designed for TS usually fail to capture the dependencies between spatial and temporal dimensions. This difficulty has been addressed in two ways: at each time step, adding a model for the spatial interdependencies [60], or designing the spatiotemporal interdependencies jointly [18]. The first proposition models the joint spatial distributions $p(X_t^1, \ldots, X_t^M)$ for each t, either explicitly with GNN [21] or implicitly with the spatial compression [1]. The second proposition models the spatiotemporal joint distribution $p(X_1^1, \ldots, X_1^M, \ldots, X_T^1, \ldots, X_T^M)$ with joint spatiotemporal attention [18], as well as an encoder–decoder structure made of attention layers for each spatiotemporal scalar variable. The latter performs better than the first one because the spatiotemporal dependencies $X_{t'}^{m'} | X_t^m$ are explicitly designed, whereas the first type decomposes spatiotemporal dependencies in two steps: spatial plus temporal $X_t^m \to X_t^{m'} \to X_{t'}^{m'}$ or temporal plus spatial $X_t^m \to X_{t'}^m \to X_{t'}^{m'}$.

We propose to handle the spatiotemporal compression of the masked MTS data $\mathbf{X}_{1:T+F} \odot \mathbf{M}_{1:T}$ present in Equation (8) using successive two-dimensional (temporal and spatial)-strided partial convolutions $PConv$ [4]. When the stride is 2, each $PConv$ layer divides the 2 spatiotemporal dimensions by 2, such that, with an adequate number of hidden $PConv$ layers, the spatiotemporal dimensions of the bottleneck $\mathbf{Z}_{ib\_tr}$ are reduced to 1×1, and the resulting mask $\mathbf{M}_{ib\_tr}$ is a 1×1 unit matrix. This means that $\mathbf{Z}_{ib\_tr} \odot \mathbf{M}_{ib\_tr} = \mathbf{Z}_{ib\_tr}$ and the posterior $\mathbf{X}_{1:T+F} \odot \mathbf{M}_{T+1:T+F} = \mathbf{X}_{T+1:T+F}$ can be decoded from $\mathbf{Z}_{ib\_tr}$ without any masking considerations. Finally, our approach proposes to assimilate the MTS forecasting problem as an image extension problem, where MTS, being two-dimensional, can be visualized as pseudo-images and processed with classical CV layers as convolutions.

Convolutions also present non-negligible advantages because they locally model spatiotemporal dependencies present in these MTS pseudo-images. Moreover, because of the spatiotemporal compression structure, each successive strided $PConv$ hidden layer creates a more global model of the spatiotemporal dependencies, such that, in the end, the bottleneck, $\mathbf{Z}_{ib\_tr}$ fully models the global spatiotemporal dependencies.

2.4. Performing the Forecast

2.4.1. Decoder

Section 2.3 shows that the IB for MTS forecasting is equivalent to a pseudo-image extension problem, where the masked source can be compressed with successive $PConv$ layers. A very efficient image inpainting model that also uses masks and $PConv$ layers is proposed in [4]. Instead of simply decoding the masked posterior from the bottleneck, it proposes to use a U-Net structure with partial convolution in order to output the full image with the unmasked parts reconstructed and the masked parts predicted. We propose designing the decoder in the same way, i.e., using skipping layers and a structure similar to the encoder, consisting of $PConv$ hidden layers, such that the global model is a U-Net architecture with successive $PConv$ layers that extends to the bottleneck, followed by successive partial deconvolution layers $PDConv$ [4]. The information flow of such a model is sketched by the following Markov chain:

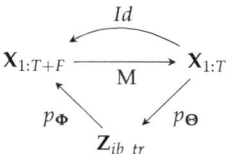

For this configuration, and under a Laplacian assumption for the distribution $p_\Phi(\mathbf{X}_{T+1:T+F}|\mathbf{Z}_{ib\_tr})$, the third term of the IB loss $\mathcal{L}_3(\Theta, \Phi)$ in Equation (8) becomes equivalent to:

$$\mathcal{L}_3^{Lap,UNet}(\Theta, \Phi) = \mathbb{E}_{p_\mathcal{D}(\mathbf{X}_{1:T+F})}\left[\mathbb{E}_{p_\Theta(\mathbf{Z}_{ib\_tr}|\mathbf{X}_{1:T+F}\odot\mathbf{M}_{1:T})}\left[\|\mathbf{X}_{1:T+F} - \tilde{\mathbf{X}}_{1:T+F}\|_1\right]\right], \quad (9)$$

where $\tilde{\mathbf{X}}_{1:T+F}$ is the output of the U-Net. This equivalence and more details are given in Proof of Equation (A13) and Remark A1 of the Appendix A.

2.4.2. Partial IB Loss with U-Net

In Section 2.1, we show that for MTS, the IB principle imposes the three losses defined in Equation (6). Moreover, if one assumes a Laplacian distribution for $p_\Phi(\mathbf{X}_{T+1:T+F}|\mathbf{Z}_{ib\_tr})$, Equation (9) shows that the cross-entropy $H(p_\Theta, p_\Phi)$, which is the third part, $\mathcal{L}_3$, of the upper bound on the IB loss, can be reduced to $\mathcal{L}_3^{Lap,UNet}$, an average Manhattan distance, which is also referred to as MAE between the output $\tilde{\mathbf{X}}_{T+1:T+F}$ and the genuine $\mathbf{X}_{T+1:T+F}$, when one samples $\mathbf{Z}_{ib\_tr}$ from the prior samples $\mathbf{X}_{1:T}$ of the training data, assuming that the Laplacian distribution of $p_\Phi(\mathbf{X}_{T+1:T+F}|\mathbf{Z}_{ib\_tr})$ is too restrictive for real MTS datasets, and a simple MAE cannot provide the best forecasting performance.

Image extension and inpainting processing works [4,23,61] use the same design for their models. They develop powerful image inpainting models, which involve recovering masked or missing parts of images, not only in central regions but also on the borders. These models use U-Net [31] with gated, partial, or dilated convolutions and complex losses based on the Manhattan distance MAE, such as style loss by the Gram matrix computation [62], perceptual loss by the VGG-16 hidden layer value computation [29], and/or adversarial loss [63]. One of the most efficient of these works [4] decomposes the loss into six partial losses, each of which is responsible for optimizing specific errors between the global genuine $\mathbf{X}_{1:T+F}$ and the output $\tilde{\mathbf{X}}_{1:T+F}$. The rest of this section will provide interpretations of these losses in the context of MTS. The first partial loss, $\mathcal{L}_{valid}$, is related to the *valid* or *prior* parts of the pseudo-images that can be easily reconstructed with the skipping layers:

$$\mathcal{L}_{valid} = \frac{1}{N_{pi}}\|\mathbf{M}_{1:T} \odot (\tilde{\mathbf{X}}_{1:T+F} - \mathbf{X}_{1:T+F})\|_1 = \frac{1}{N_{pi}}\|\tilde{\mathbf{X}}_{1:T} - \mathbf{X}_{1:T}\|_1, \quad (10)$$

where $N_{pi} = M \times (T+F)$ is the size of the MTS pseudo-image $\mathbf{X}_{1:T+F}$ or the number of pixels. As explained in Section 2.4.1 and Proof of Equation (A13) from the Appendix A, this part of the loss is responsible for the equivalence between the partial IB loss $\mathcal{L}_3$ defined in Equation (6) and $\mathcal{L}_3^{Lap,UNet}$, which is the Manhattan distance MAE between the U-Net output $\tilde{\mathbf{X}}_{1:T+F}$ and the genuine $\mathbf{X}_{1:T+F}$ due to the presence of the skipping layers. It ensures an easy reconstruction of the known parts, and forces the bottleneck $\mathbf{Z}_{ib\_tr}$ to learn the transition statistics $1:T \to T+1:T+F$ but not the reconstruction statistics $1:T \to 1:T$. As a consequence, in some way, it also softly minimizes $\mathcal{L}_1(\Theta) = H_{p_\Theta}(\mathbf{Z}_{ib\_tr})$, but without forcing this loss to reach a local minimum. The second loss is noted $\mathcal{L}_{hole}$ for the masked parts of the pseud-images that need to be forecasted:

$$\mathcal{L}_{hole} = \frac{1}{N_{pi}}\|(1 - \mathbf{M}_{1:T}) \odot (\tilde{\mathbf{X}}_{1:T+F} - \mathbf{X}_{1:T+F})\|_1 = \frac{1}{N_{pi}}\|\tilde{\mathbf{X}}_{T+1:T+F} - \mathbf{X}_{T+1:T+F}\|_1. \quad (11)$$

This loss is exactly the IB partial loss $\mathcal{L}_3 = \mathcal{L}_{hole}$ of Equation (6) if we assume $p_\Phi(\mathbf{X}_{T+1:T+F}|\mathbf{Z}_{ib\_tr})$ to follow a Laplacian distribution. Under this assumption, this loss forces the encoder to actually let $\mathbf{Z}_{ib\_tr}$ represent the transition statistics between the prior and the posterior; this loss also lets the decoder generate well the posterior from this bottleneck representation. It is interesting to note the $\mathcal{L}_{valid} + \mathcal{L}_{hole} = \mathcal{L}_3^{Lap,UNet} = \mathcal{L}_3$ under the Laplacian assumption of $p_\Phi(\mathbf{X}_{T+1:T+F}|\mathbf{Z}_{ib\_tr})$ and for the U-Net flow of information. The three next losses are also MAE, but instead of being directly computed on the genuine $\mathbf{X}$ and prior $\tilde{\mathbf{X}}$, they are computed on deep representations of these variables. These three losses are referred to as *perceptual* and *style* losses:

$$\begin{aligned}
\mathcal{L}_{perceptual} &= 2 \sum_{p \in H_{VGG}} \frac{\|\boldsymbol{\Psi}_p(\tilde{\mathbf{X}}_{T+1:T+F}) - \boldsymbol{\Psi}_p(\mathbf{X}_{T+1:T+F})\|_1}{N_{\boldsymbol{\Psi}_p(\mathbf{X}_{1:T+F})}} \\
&+ \sum_{p \in H_{VGG}} \frac{\|\boldsymbol{\Psi}_p(\tilde{\mathbf{X}}_{1:T}) - \boldsymbol{\Psi}_p(\mathbf{X}_{1:T})\|_1}{N_{\boldsymbol{\Psi}_p(\mathbf{X}_{1:T+F})}}, \\
\mathcal{L}_{style_{out}} &= \sum_{p \in H_{VGG}} \frac{\|\boldsymbol{\Gamma}_p(\tilde{\mathbf{X}}_{1:T+F}) - \boldsymbol{\Gamma}_p(\mathbf{X}_{1:T+F})\|_1}{N_{\boldsymbol{\Psi}_p(\mathbf{X}_{1:T+F})}}, \\
\mathcal{L}_{style_{comp}} &= \sum_{p \in H_{VGG}} \frac{\|\boldsymbol{\Gamma}_p([\mathbf{X}_{1:T}, \tilde{\mathbf{X}}_{T+1:T+F}]) - \boldsymbol{\Gamma}_p(\mathbf{X}_{1:T+F})\|_1}{N_{\boldsymbol{\Psi}_p(\mathbf{X}_{1:T+F})}},
\end{aligned} \quad (12)$$

where $\boldsymbol{\Psi}_p$ are selected hidden layers of a pre-trained VGG-16 [64] deep image model classifier, where H_{VGG} is the set of selected hidden layer indices, and $\boldsymbol{\Gamma}_p(\mathbf{X})$ are Gram operators on the hidden layers of VGG [29], as defined by $flatten[\boldsymbol{\Psi}_p(\mathbf{X})] \cdot flatten[\boldsymbol{\Psi}_p(\mathbf{X})]^T$. While the MAE of $\mathcal{L}_3^{Lap,Unet}$ is equivalent to the IB partial loss $\mathcal{L}_3$ from Equation (6) with the Laplacian assumption of $p_\Phi(\mathbf{X}_{T+1:T+F}|\mathbf{Z}_{ib\_tr})$, for these losses, MAE is applied to deep hidden representations of $\mathbf{X}$ and $\tilde{\mathbf{X}}$. In a similar manner to the normalizing flow [65], where each hidden layer of a deep network modifies the distribution, hidden layers of the VGG and Gram operators are deterministic mappers that modify the distribution of $\mathbf{X}_{T+1:T+F}$. As a consequence, we assume that the MAEs of $\mathcal{L}_{perceptual}$ and $\mathcal{L}_{style}$ can provide equivalents to the IB partial loss $\mathcal{L}_3$ from Equation (6) for other distributions $p_\Phi(\mathbf{X}_{T+1:T+F}|\mathbf{Z}_{ib\_tr})$ than the simple Laplacian. Hidden layers of the VGG-16 model capture the statistics related to the prediction of the humanly recognizable class to which an image may belong. The losses using MAE on these hidden layers are assumed to measure human perceptual features, and Gram operators are known to capture styles in an image [62]. Finally, a combination of $\mathcal{L}_{valid}$, $\mathcal{L}_{hole}$, $\mathcal{L}_{perceptual}$, $\mathcal{L}_{style_{out}}$, and $\mathcal{L}_{style_{comp}}$ provides an equivalent to the IB partial loss $\mathcal{L}_3$ for a less restrictive assumption than the simple Laplacian distribution of $p_\Phi(\mathbf{X}_{T+1:T+F}|\mathbf{Z}_{ib\_tr})$. The last loss is referred to as *total variation*:

$$\mathcal{L}_{tv} = \|\mathbf{X}_T - \tilde{\mathbf{X}}_{T+1}\|_1. \quad (13)$$

In image extension or inpainting problems, this loss forces the borders of the predicted holes to be smooth, which is a valid assumption for large images with high definition. In the context of MTS, this loss forces the first forecasted time step $T+1$ to be similar to the last known time step T. This smoothness assumption is also valid for the majority of real-world observations, where most of the functions are continuous.

The U-Net structure does not impose specific distributions for $p(\mathbf{Z}_{ib\_tr})$ and $p(\mathbf{Z}_{ib\_tr}|\mathbf{X}_{1:T})$, such that the partial IB losses $\mathcal{L}_1$ and $\mathcal{L}_2$ are intractable, but U-Net imposes an extreme spatiotemporal compression in the bottleneck $\mathbf{Z}_{ib\_tr}$. The source masking, combined with U-Net's skipping layers, allows for a limitation of $\mathcal{L}_1$, as the transition statistics $1:T \to T+1:T+F$ rather than the reconstruction ones $1:T \to 1:T$ are learned. For these reasons, the loss used for the model in the experiments is the following partial IB loss:

$$\mathcal{L}_{total} = \mathcal{L}_{valid} + a_1 \mathcal{L}_{hole} + a_2 \mathcal{L}_{perceptual} + a_3(\mathcal{L}_{style_{out}} + \mathcal{L}_{style_{comp}}) + a_4 \mathcal{L}_{tv}, \quad (14)$$

where a_1, a_2, a_3, and a_4 are empirically defined hyperparameters. In practice, we use $a_1 = 6$, $a_2 = 0.05$, $a_3 = 120$, and $a_4 = 0.1$, and only the hidden layer activations Ψ_p with indices $p = 3$, 6, and 10 of the VGG-16 [64] are used to compute $\mathcal{L}_{style_{out}}$, $\mathcal{L}_{style_{comp}}$, and $\mathcal{L}_{perceptual}$, such that $H_{VGG} = \{3, 6, 10\}$, such as in [4]. These parameters were fine-tuned in [4] for image datasets, where pixels take values between 0 and 1. The pseudo-images created from the IRIS, AL, and PB datasets also have pixels ranging from 0 to 1. Because of the good results we achieved with these parameters, we assumed that it was enough to prove the efficiency and adaptability of the described method on different types of MTS data, and we did not attempt to further fine-tune these hyperparameters for each dataset evaluated.

2.4.3. IB Interpretation with the Partial Loss

The encoder has a mapping form that consists of two parts. The first encoding corresponds to the masking, i.e., vector $X_{1:T+F}$, only $X_{1:T}$ is retained as the input to the second part. Thus, in principle, the masking part can be any stochastic map that masks the parts to be predicted. This technique is similar to recent methods referred to as *masked image modeling* (MIM) [66,67] and it is often used in the pretraining of image autoencoders or transformers [66,68]. The second encoding part is a nonlinear embedding implemented as a deterministic encoder, which is the compression part of the U-Net, along with its connecting layers. This second compression is guided by successive masked convolutions with strides of the order of 2 to obtain a bottleneck by the dimension reduction of shape $1 \times 1 \times K$, i.e., where the spatial and temporal dimensions are reduced to 1. This compressed representation is noted as $\mathbf{Z}_{ib\_tr}$ and referred to as the bottleneck in the paper. The masking, together with the deterministic nonlinear embedding, form a stochastic mapping, and can be considered as the equivalent part of the stochastic encoder in the IB framework.

In the end, a nonlinear decompression implemented in a form of a deterministic decoder predicts $\mathbf{X}_{1:T+F}$ from this bottleneck representation $\mathbf{Z}_{ib\_tr}$ and from the skipping layers that map the prior $\mathbf{X}_{1:T}$ information between the input and output. Theoretically, in Section 2.3, we show that the bottleneck should only retain the necessary information of the transition statistics $1 : T \to T + 1 : T + F$ between the prior and the posterior, and not the statistics of the reconstruction of the prior $\mathbf{X}_{1:T}$. This is because all of the information from the prior $\mathbf{X}_{1:T}$ is transmitted to the output via the skipping layers. This shortcut flow of information is specific to the structure of U-Net, is performed without compression, and preserves the spatiotemporal positions of the prior information. As such, theoretically, only the statistics of the transitions $1 : T \to T + 1 : T + F$ are retained in the bottleneck $\mathbf{Z}_{ib\_tr}$ and the following Markov chain holds:

$$\mathbf{X}_{1:T} \to \mathbf{Z}_{ib\_tr} \to \mathbf{X}_{T+1:T+F}. \tag{15}$$

Moreover, to better understand the role of the bottleneck, we can consider these two thought experiments:

- If we remove the skipping layers, the bottleneck should not only retain the statistics of the transitions from the prior to the posterior but also the reconstruction statistics of the prior.
- If we also remove the source masking of the posterior in $\mathbf{X}_{1:T+F}$, the model is reduced to an autoencoder (AE) and the bottleneck is supposed to perform a dimension reduction of the MTS. Because of the curse of dimensionality, this technique is commonly used to further perform better classifications on the bottleneck representation than on the raw high-dimensional MTS data.

In our case, instead of imposing a distribution of the latent space, such as for VAE, we apply special masking jointly with a dimensionality reduction. This framework can be considered as the lossy part of the information encoding.

2.5. Proposed Model

The model designed in Section 2.4 corresponds to a traditional U-Net complemented with masks and partial convolutions [4,31]. Multidimensional successive $PConv$ and $PDConv$ layers with a stride of 2 are used when the data are MTS ($M > 1$). The bottleneck must have a 1×1 spatiotemporal shape; because of stride 2, the input pseudo-images must be zero-padded to become squares with a power of 2. As a consequence, if $2^l \times 2^l$ is the spatiotemporal shape of the pseudo-image, the designed U-Net must have l successive $PConv$ followed by l successive $PDConv$. Training is performed with 100 epochs and the Adam optimization of gradient descent with a 2×10^{-4} learning rate for the loss defined in Equation (14). The model could be generalized to N-dimensional $PConv$ and $PDConv$ layers when several dimensions are necessary to model each time step. For instance, in videos, each time step is an image with horizontal and vertical spatial dependencies.

Example of architecture when $128 < \max(M, T+F) \leq 256$: The maximum spatiotemporal size is $\max(M, T+F)$, which can also be interpreted as the maximum width or height of the pseudo-images. In this situation, input pseudo-images are zero-padded to obtain a square shape 256×256, and the investigated model is sketched in Figure 2; it uses the classical image extension architecture, U-Net [31], which has a symmetrical structure made of an encoder and a decoder, both with 8 layers. Implementation details of the architecture are given in the Appendix B, Table A2. The encoded representation $\mathbf{Z}_{ib\_tr}$ has a size of $1 \times 1 \times 512$. Each layer of the encoding part divides the width and height with strides of a factor of 2, and increases the number of channels up to 512. The decoder has a symmetrical structure, but the inputs of each layer are concatenations of upsampled versions of the previous layer's outputs with the output of the symmetrical encoding layer. It is combined with partial convolutions (PCs) that were proposed in [4] to handle the masked data. These convolutions are applied at each hidden step and are designed to not take into account the missing data, such that $\mathbf{X}_{T+1:T+F}$ from $\mathbf{X}_{1:T+F}$ at the input layer. At each step of the encoding, the proportion of the masked part is reduced. Each PC is followed by a batch normalization and a ReLU activation, but for the last output layer, the activation is a sigmoid. For the training, we used input images of size 240×240, which were center-padded by zeros to make an image of size 256×256 for fitting the U-Net input size. Because of the 2 strides at the encoding steps and the 1×1 size of the latent representation, a U-Net with 8 encoding layers requires input sizes of $2^8 = 256$.

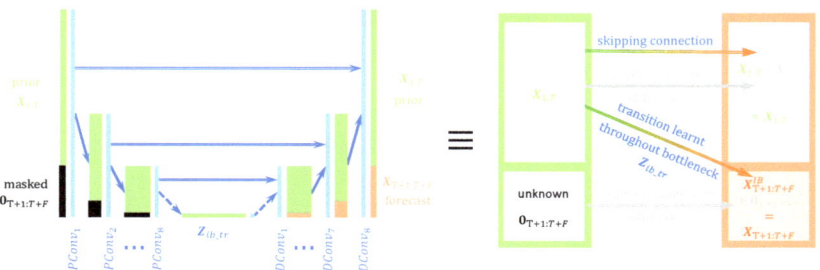

Figure 2. Schematic analogy between the IB principle and image extension: (**Left**) schematically shows the time prediction under the IB principle, with compression and decoding, using $PConv$ and $DPConv$ and skipping connections to form a variant of U-Net. (**Right**) is an equivalent representation seen as the image extension, where the skipping layers connect $\mathbf{X}_{1:T}$ from the input to the output, and the bottleneck principle allows predicting $\mathbf{X}_{T+1:T+F}$ from $\mathbf{X}_{1:T}$.

When the input of the maximum spatiotemporal size $\max(M, T+F)$ is smaller than 128, the model needs less than 8 $PConv$ and $PDConv$ layers for the encoder and decoder parts of the U-Net. In general, the number of layers must be $\log_2(\max(M, T+F))$ to ensure a 1×1 spatiotemporal size in the bottleneck $\mathbf{Z}_{ib\_tr}$.

In [4], they specify that because of the masks, batch normalization prevents training from converging. This is because the mean and standard deviation values of batch normalization layers for each sample are biased by the masks. As a consequence, they train the first half of epochs with trainable batch normalization layers, and they freeze the batch normalization layers for the second half of epochs. This is done in TensorFlow by setting the layer parameter *trainable = False* during training. In our case, all sample masks have the same size and spatiotemporal positions. As a consequence, the mean and standard variations of the samples are not very biased by those masks. Actually, the experimentation showed that freezing the batch normalization for the last epochs did not lead to improved performance.

2.6. IRIS Dataset

IRIS is NASA's interface region imaging spectrograph satellite [69]. IRIS observes regions of the atmosphere of the Sun with many different settings of possible observations recorded in a specified cadence. A time sequence is encoded into a two-dimensional representation in the form of images. We used the designed model to predict time sequence data provided by the IRIS mission. The basis of the IRIS satellite data retrieval is shown in Figure 3. Each observed event is composed of a maximum of four videos of a selected region on the surface of the Sun, together with spectral videos, where a slit is positioned to perform the diffraction [70].

In this work, only the spectral data from *MgII h&k* lines, between 2793.8401Å and 2806.02Å, were considered. This wavelength's range is represented by a vector of size 240. According to modern solar physics theories, spectral data are supposed to contain most of the information on the physics of the Sun, and *MgII h&k* lines are considered some of the best lines to recover information from the chromosphere [71]. The predictions of solar spectral data are crucial for different reasons, including the solar flares forecasting and solar activity in general.

IRIS data are publicly available (iris.lmsal.com/data.html) (accessed on 20 February 2023) but only part of the data is labeled [72]. Only three types of solar activities were considered for this study: quiet Sun (QS), where nothing special appears, active region (AR), where some activity is observed, such as solar prominence, filaments, jets, and flaring profile (FL), when a flare appears during the observed event. Each event is assigned a hierarchical label, such that an event is labeled FL even when it includes AR time steps. The data are normalized at each time step by its maximum value, such that the maximum value at each time step, or the *intensity* of the signal, is reduced to one. This allows for an easier comparison of spectral profiles at each time step, and simplifies the process in terms of the ML.

2.6.1. Problem Formulation

The IRIS restrictions of online observations: Figure 3 explains the IRIS observations in the atmosphere of the Sun with images of given wavelengths and spectra of given positions. Despite the very high precision of IRIS and its capacity to observe a very wide range of astrophysical parameters in time and space, significant difficulties inherent to online observations remain. Spectral observations are limited in time and space as they only correspond to the position of the slit at a given time, which may vary, and the satellite has to store the data before sending them to Earth-based stations [70]. IRIS observations are, therefore, very sparse in all of the potential observable parameters and they may lack a lot of data from other spatial positions. We may also be interested in further observations after the termination of the acquisition/recording session limited by the IRIS storage memory capacity.

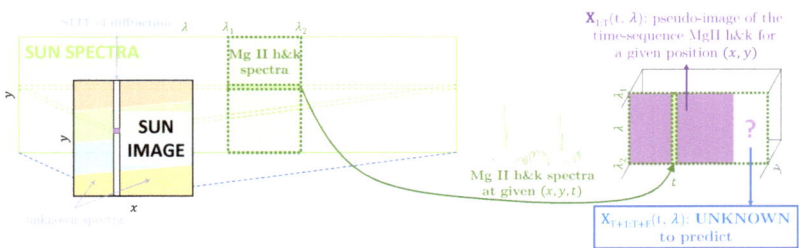

Figure 3. Problem formulation: (x,y) represent the spatial coordinates, λ and t, respectively, represent the spectral and time coordinates. NASA's IRIS satellite integrates a mirror from which the *Sun image* or videos are captured by a sensor paired with a wavelength filter chosen among 1330 Å, 1400 Å, 2796 Å, and 2832 Å. This mirror holds a vertical slit from which the diffraction occurs. The x position of the slit can vary in time and is chosen before the observation. A sensor behind the mirror captures the *Sun spectra* for each vertical position y of the *Sun's image*, but only at the x position of the slit. We only consider the MgIIh/k data, which are between $\lambda_1 = 2793.8401$ Å and $\lambda_2 = 2806.02$ Å, and we consider all available time sequences.

Spectral time sequence forecasting represents a significant step forward in flare forecasting and assists in planning satellite observations. Figure 3 presents the solar–physical interpretation of the spectral time sequence data, represented as images $\mathbf{X}_{1:T+F}^{1:M}$ of physical dimensions *time × wavelength* with $1 \leq time\ t \leq T+F$, $1 \leq wavelength\ \lambda \leq M$; the left part $\mathbf{X}_{1:T}^{1:M}$ ($1 \leq t \leq T$, $1 \leq \lambda \leq M$) corresponds to the known prior sequence, and the right part, $\mathbf{X}_{T+1:T+F}^{1:M}$ ($T+1 \leq t \leq T+F$, $1 \leq \lambda \leq M$), masked, predicted, or genuine, is the sequence that has to be predicted by the model.

Non-homogeneous cadences of the data time series modeling are usually performed by RNNs [73] or LSTMs [6], as briefly summarized in Figure 1. These models are designed for time series with fixed given cadences; Figure 4 shows the wide variety of our data cadences, making the use of RNN or LSTM difficult. To represent the time sequences $\mathbf{X}_{1:T+F}$ of the data under a common cadence, one should represent them by a cadence equal to the greatest common divisor of all of the cadences, which would obviously make those time sequences $\mathbf{X}_{1:T+F}$ highly sparse and penalize the learning of transitions between time steps.

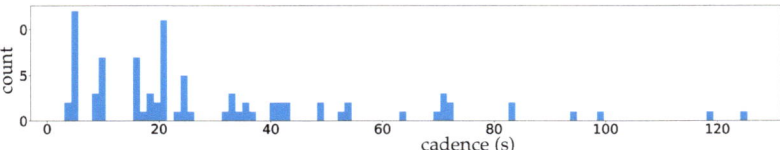

Figure 4. Histogram of the cadences in seconds/time steps.

Clustering spectral data: The 53 clusters of MgIIh/k lines found in [55] allow interpreting the physics on the surface of the Sun. We can compare the original and predicted time sequences through their clustered time sequences in order to prove the utility of our forecasting model in solar–physics by conserving the types of activities.

Astrophysical features: In [72], the authors defined ten solar spectra features to be used as dimensional reductions of spectral data for activity classification purposes. We studied the conservation of these features in the forecasted sequences to show the applicability to astrophysics.

2.6.2. Proposed Approach

As described in Section 2.6.1, a solar spectral time sequence is represented by an image $\mathbf{X}_{1:T}$ and the model has to predict the continuation, which is the time sequence equivalent to the image $\mathbf{X}_{T+1:T+F}$. $\mathbf{X}_{T+1:T+F}$ should be the right extension of the image $\mathbf{X}_{1:T}$, where each column of the image represents a spectrum at a growing time step from the left to the right. Because of the architecture of the image extension models, the input and output images have the same dimensions. The targeted output image $\mathbf{X}_{T+1:T+F}$ is the concatenation of $\mathbf{X}_{1:T}$ with $\mathbf{X}_{T+1:T+F}$ on the right of it, whereas the input image $Concat([\mathbf{X}_{1:T}, \mathbf{0}_{T+1:T:F}])$, has a blank image $\mathbf{0}_{mask}$ of the same shape as $\mathbf{X}_{T+1:T+F}$ on the right of $\mathbf{X}_{1:T}$.

For both recurrent and image extension models, the input has the same information, organized differently, and the output of the image extension models differs by the left concatenation of the input. Figure 2 shows the skipping layers in the image extension models that help the transition of $\mathbf{X}_{1:T}$ from the input to the output.

2.7. Other MTS Dataset

Two other datasets are used to provide a baseline evaluation between our IB-designed models and concurrent ones.

- **AL dataset:** The solar power dataset for the year 2006 in Alabama is publicly available (www.nrel.gov/grid/solar-power-data.html, accessed on 20 February 2023). It contains solar power data for 137 solar photovoltaic power plants. Power was sampled every 5 min in the year 2006. Preprocessing was conducted to only extract daily events by ignoring nights when data were zero. At each 5-min interval, the data consisted of vectors with 137 dimensions, and these vectors were normalized by their maximum coordinates. For example, in the case of IRIS data, the maximum value at each time was always set to 1.
- **PB dataset:** PeMS-BAY data [74] are publicly available (https://zenodo.org/record/5146275#.Y5hF7nbMI2w, accessed on 20 February 2023) and were selected from 325 sensors in the Bay Area of San Francisco by the California State Transportation Agency's Performance Measurement System [75]. The data represent 6 months of traffic speeds ranging from January 1 to May 31 2017. At each 5-minute interval, the data consist of vectors with 325 dimensions, and these vectors are normalized by their maximum coordinates. For example, in the case of IRIS data, the maximum value at each time was always set to 1.

2.8. Complementary Classifiers to Show Consistency with Applied Sciences

The experimental proof was conducted on IRIS-labeled data to show that the proposed model is not simply capable of predicting possible images but also capable of predicting the information logic behind them. It is common for MTS data (that are to be forecasted) to be classified based on types of activity. There are multiple examples of MTS types of activity, including displacement, boom, euphoria, profit-taking, and panic classifications. In astrophysics, when dealing with solar observations, the types of activity can be categorized as quiet, active, and flaring.

We implemented a classifier composed of eight strided convolutional layers, with dense ending layers, which allowed it to output a vector of size corresponding to the number of classes. This classifier was trained on labeled MTS data $\{(\mathbf{X}_{1:T+F}, \mathbf{K})\}_{\mathcal{D}}$, where $\mathbf{K}$ stands for the categorical one-hot vector representing the class activity for the series $\mathbf{X}_{1:T}$. Once trained, the classifier was used to classify the prior, the genuine, and the predicted forecasts. The classification accuracy between the genuine and the predicted forecasts was evaluated together with the true skill statistic (TSS), which is also known as the Hansen and Kuiper skill score [76], and the Heidke skill score (HSS) [77], which is also known as *kappa* [78]. These two scores were evaluated globally and for each class of prediction. For one class, these scores are defined as follows:

$$TSS = \frac{tP \times tN - fP \times fN}{gP \times gN}, \quad \text{and} \quad HSS = 2\frac{tP \times tN - fP \times fN}{gP \times pN + gN \times tP}, \tag{16}$$

where t stands for *true*, f is *false*, g is *genuine*, p is *predicted*, P represents *positives*, and N represents *negatives*. In a classification with more than two classes, [79] shows that these scores can be defined by generalization, as follows:

$$TSS = \frac{trace(CM - ICM)}{trace(CM^* - ICM^*)}, \quad \text{and} \quad HSS = 2\frac{trace(CM - ICM)}{trace(CM^* - ICM)}, \quad (17)$$

where $trace(.)$ is the diagonal sum operator for a matrix of dimension $m \times m$, which is eventually larger than 2×2. $CM = \left(Count_{g_i, p_j}\right)_{i,j}$ is the confusion matrix holding the joint counts of genuine classification cases g_i (rows) versus forecast classification cases p_j (columns), and $ICM = \left(\dfrac{Count_{g_i} \times Count_{p_j}}{total\ count}\right)_{i,j}$ is the confusion matrix expected when the genuine and forecast classifications are independent events. $CM^* = diag(Count_{g_i})$ is the expected diagonal confusion matrix when the classifications are ideal (an ideal classification is defined by $Count_{g_i, p_j} = 0$ for all $i \neq j$, such that the confusion matrix CM is diagonal); ICM^* is the corresponding expected confusion matrix when genuine and forecast classifications are independent events.

2.9. Comparison with Other Models

To our knowledge, for almost all MTS datasets, current state-of-the-art (SOTA) datasets are achieved by TS decomposition networks, such as NBeats [3] and SCINet [80], and by pre-trained models designed as graph neural networks [60,81] or transformers [17]. We compare our proposed IB-MTS model with three types of models:

- Multiple successive IBs, where each time step is an instance of the IB formulation. This includes multidimensional RNN, LSTM, and GRU models [5,6,15].
- Composition of two successive IBs: A spatial IB is followed by a temporal IB. For example, this would involve encoder–decoder models using successive RNN, LSTM, or GRU recurrent models at each layer of compression and decoding [82,83].
- Unique joint spatiotemporal IB: The encoder jointly compresses spatial and temporal dimensions of the prior into a bottleneck with an extreme spatiotemporal dimensional reduction; this is our proposed IB-MTS formulation.
- MTS decomposition model, such as NBeats [3].

Names and details of the concurrent evaluated models are listed below:

- **LSTM** model: An LSTM cell [6] performs the one-step-ahead forecast and is trained to predict $\mathbf{X}_{t+1}$ from $\mathbf{X}_t$. It incorporates one layer with M LSTM units. For instance, for the 240×240 spatiotemporal dimensions of IRIS data, the 180 first time steps are the prior data, and the 60 last time steps are the posterior data to forecast. This model is designed with 240 spatial LSTM/GRU units looped 180 times and all of the cell outputs are returned by the model using TensorFlow option $return\_sequences = True$. This layer returns a 180×240 output and only the last 60 time steps are kept. Moreover, a source masking of the posterior is applied to the input and an identity skipping layer is added to transmit the prior $\mathbf{X}_{1:T}$ to the output at the same temporal positions in $\mathbf{X}_{1:T+F}$, such that the LSTM layer only accounts for predicting the posterior part $\mathbf{X}_{T+1:T+F}$. The number of units is directly determined by the shape of the input and output data. Details of the architecture are given in the Appendix B, Table A3.
- **GRU** model: A GRU [15] cell is trained to predict $\mathbf{X}_{t+F}$ from $\mathbf{X}_t$. The structure and number of units are the same, similar to the LSTM models, but GRU cells are used instead of LSTM ones. Details of the architecture are given in the Appendix B, Table A3.
- **ED-LSTM** model: A version using LSTM cells with an encoder and a decoder was implemented as described in Figure 5. Because of the encoder and decoder structures, we name it ED-LSTM. This model conducts multiple step-ahead forecasts and can forecast $\mathbf{X}_{T+1:T+F}$ from $\mathbf{X}_{1:T}$. The model incorporates LSTM cells organized into four

layers: two layers of encoding into a bottleneck and two layers of decoding from the bottleneck. The first encoding layer is composed of 100 spatial units looped 180 times on the prior IRIS data and all of the cell outputs are returned by the model using TensorFlow option $return\_sequences = True$, returning a 180×100 spatiotemporal output accounting for a spatial compression. The second encoding layer is composed of 100 spatial units looped 180 times and only the last cell outputs of the recurrences are returned, returning a 100-dimensional bottleneck that accounts for a spatial compression followed by a temporal compression. This bottleneck representation is repeated 60 times for IRIS data in order to model the decoding of 60 posterior time steps to forecast. After this repetition, the data are 60×100 and fed to the first decoding layer with 100 spatial units looped 60 times and initialized with the states obtained from the second encoding layer; indeed, the structure is symmetrical, such that the first and second decoding layers are, respectively, the images of the second and the first encoding layers. All cell outputs are returned by the model using TensorFlow option $return\_sequences = True$, such that a 60×100 spatiotemporal output is returned. The second layer of the decoder is designed with 100 spatial units looped 60 times and initialized with the states obtained from the first encoding layer, such that a 60×100 output is returned. In the end, a time-distributed dense layer is used to map the 60×100 output data into a 60×180 MTS data format. For these models, the input and output shapes are determined by the data and one can only change the number of spatial cells n_1 and n_2 used, respectively, in the first and second layers of the encoding part. n_2 determines the dimension of the bottleneck and on the IRIS data, $180 > n_1 \geq n_2 \geq 1$. Our experiments show that the results of these models do not depend much on the values of n_1 and n_2, but significantly drop when n_2 is very small, close to 1. Details of the architecture are given in the Appendix B, Table A4.

- **ED-GRU** model: This model follows the same structure as the ED-LSTM but with GRU cells instead of LSTM cells. The structure and number of units are the same as with ED-LSTM models, but GRU cells are used instead of LSTM ones. Details of the architecture are given in the Appendix B, Table A4.
- **NBeats** model: We use the code given in the original paper [3]. This model can forecast $\mathbf{X}_{T+1:T+F}$ from $\mathbf{X}_{1:T}$. The model is used in its generic architecture as described in [3], with 2 blocks per stack, theta dimensions of $(4,4)$, shared weights in stacks, and 100 hidden layers units. For IRIS data, the prior is 180×240, the forecast posterior is 60×240, and the backcast posterior is 180×240, but we also use a skipping layer to connect the input to the backcast posterior, such that the model is forced to learn the transition between the prior and the forecast posterior. we attempted NBeats with other settings and other numbers of stacks without the gain of performance, and when the number of stacks became greater than 4, the model failed to initialize on our machines.

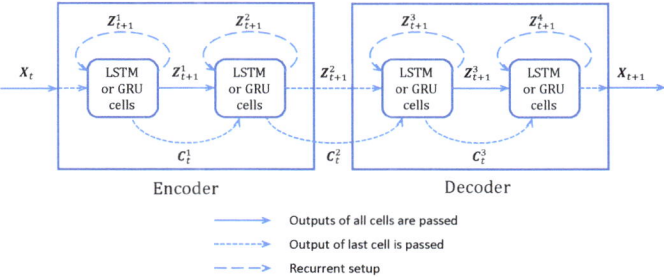

Figure 5. Structure of the ED-LSTM and ED-GRU models used for comparison. $\mathbf{C}_t^i$ represents the hidden state vectors for GRU cells, combined with cell state vectors for LSTM cells.

Table 1 provides the number of parameters for each model. The evident drawback of our proposed IB-MTS is the high amount of parameters inherent to U-Net structures with several levels of deepness. The number of parameters for the concurrent evaluated models is determined by the shape of the input data or by hardware constraints for NBeats. We believe that our model also integrates more parameters because it is based on a jointly spatiotemporal compression whereas the others are based either on a temporal succession of spatial IB or on a combination of a spatial followed by a temporal IB. In theory, the number of parameters for our proposed model should be the square of the number of parameters of the models based on the N successive spatial IB. In practice, it is less than the square, and still able to model a joint distribution, which is not the case for the other ones.

Table 1. Parameters and trained steps of the evaluated models.

	IB-MTS	LSTM	ED-LSTM	GRU	ED-GRU	N-BEATS
Parameters	65,714,097	461,760	401,840	347,040	308,640	100,800
Trained step (ms/sample)	91	83	98	87	98	424

Moreover, a remarkable thing is that our proposed IB-MTS model needs less time to be trained than the others, except for simple RNNs. The differences in duration are even more significant compared to NBeats. NBeats has a very small amount of parameters but is very slow to train compared to the other models. From our experience, instantiating the NBeats model can be quite slow, and in practice, it is impossible to instantiate with much more layers and parameters than the vanilla one. For instance, 120 GB of RAM was not enough when we attempted to set the NBeats model with millions of parameters.

3. Results

Considering that our work may be of interest to readers from various backgrounds, be it MTS prediction, information theory, ML in general, or applied physics, several types of evaluations performed on our model and concurrent ones are listed below; Figure 6 explains the last three listed evaluations.

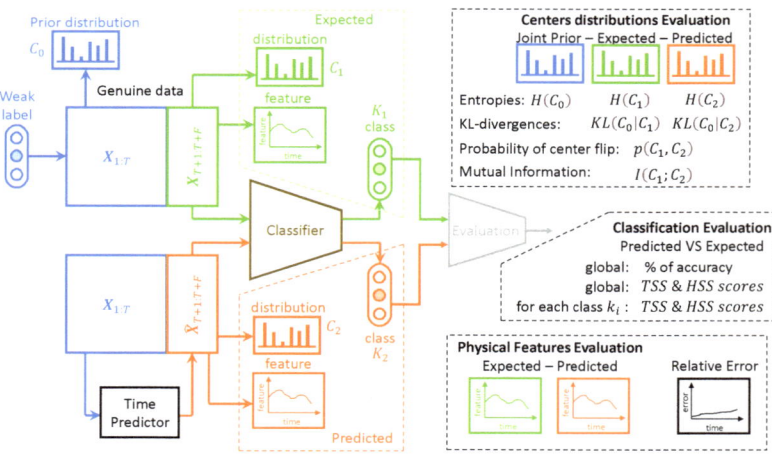

Figure 6. Evaluations performed on the proposed time predictor: center assignments, activity classification, and physical features. Classical MTS and CV evaluations were also performed without appearing in this diagram for readability concerns.

- **MTS metrics:** MAE, MAPE, and RMSE evaluation. These metrics are defined at each time step as the means of $|\mathbf{X}_t - \hat{\mathbf{X}}_t|$ for MAE, $|\mathbf{X}_t - \hat{\mathbf{X}}_t|/|\mathbf{X}_t|$ for MAPE, and the square root of the mean of $(\mathbf{X}_t - \hat{\mathbf{X}}_t)^2$ for RMSE.
- **CV metrics:** PSNR and SSIM evaluation. The PSNR_t is defined at each time step t as $-10 \log_{10}(\text{MSE}_t)$, with MSE_t being the mean of $(\mathbf{X}_t - \hat{\mathbf{X}}_t)^2$. The larger the PSNR, the better the prediction. The SSIM is defined at each time step by [84]:

$$SSIM_t = \frac{(2\mu_t \hat{\mu}_t + (0.01L)^2)(2\sigma_t \hat{\sigma}_t + (0.03L)^2)(cov_t + (0.0212L)^2)}{(\mu_t^2 + \hat{\mu}_t^2 + (0.01L)^2)(\sigma_t^2 + \hat{\sigma}_t^2 + (0.03L)^2)(\sigma_t \hat{\sigma}_t + (0.0212L)^2)}, \quad (18)$$

where L is the dynamic range of the pixel values, usually $L = 255$; μ_t and σ_t are the mean and standard deviations of all possible windows of length 7 in the time step data $\mathbf{X}_t$, which are similar for $\hat{\mu}_t$ and $\hat{\sigma}_t$ for the predicted time step data $\hat{\mathbf{X}}_t$. cov_t is the covariance between all corresponding windows of length 7 on $\mathbf{X}_t$ and $\hat{\mathbf{X}}_t$. The SSIM has a maximum of 1 when $\mathbf{X}_t = \hat{\mathbf{X}}_t$ and quantifies the visual structure present in the one-dimensional graph [84].
- **Astrophysical features** evaluation: Twelve features defined in [72] are evaluated for IRIS data. For these data, each time step corresponds to an observed spectral line in a particular region of the Sun. The intensity, triplet intensity, line center, line width, line asymmetry, total continuum, triplet emission, k/h ratio integrated, k/h ratio max, k-height, peak ratio, and peak separation are the twelve measures on these spectral lines. These features provide insight into the nature of physics occurring at the observed region of the Sun. These metrics are evaluated at each time to show that the IB principle and a powerful CV metric are sufficient to provide reliable predictions in terms of physics.
- **The IB evaluation** is performed on centroid distributions in the prior $\mathbf{X}_{1:T}$, genuine $\mathbf{X}_{T+1:T+F}$, and predicted forecasts $\hat{\mathbf{X}}_{T+1:T+F}$. A k-means was performed in [55] for the spectral lines $\mathbf{X}_t$ that are to be predicted over time. The corresponding centroids C are used in this work to evaluate information theory measurements on the quantized data. Entropies for the prior $H(c_0)$, genuine $H(c_1)$, and predicted $H(c_2)$ distributions were averaged on the test data, and a comparison of the distributions between the prediction and the genuine was evaluated by computing the mutual information $I(c_1; c_2)$.
- The **classification accuracy** between the genuine and the forecast classifications was also evaluated. In the context of the IRIS data, three classes of solar activity are considered: QS, AR, and FL. Classifications are compared between the genuine target $\mathbf{X}_{T+1:T+F}$ and predicted forecast $\hat{\mathbf{X}}_{T+1:T+F}$, to assert whether the forecast activity complies with the targeted activity. TSS [76] and HSS [77] are evaluated globally and for each prediction class. These scores are defined in Section 2.8.

3.1. Evaluations of Predictions on IRIS Data

The model was trained on 240×240-sized images $\mathbf{X}_{1:240}$ representing MTS with 240 time steps and 240 features at each time step, and the last 25% $\mathbf{X}_{180:240}$ was masked at the input and predicted at the output. Each feature corresponds to a specific wavelength.

The data contain events of various durations. They were firstly partitioned into *training*, *validation*, and *testing* events; the model was tested on events that were not even partially seen at training time. All of the events were selected among those that last more than 240 time steps. Each event was divided into several 240×240 sized images $\mathbf{X}_{1:240}$ and paired with the corresponding 240×240 masks.

The model was trained on 12,738 images of size 240×240; 25% of the right part of each image was used as the target for prediction. In the image, each spectrum (column) was normalized, such that the maximum value was 1; this is compliant with [55], where the 53 clusters were obtained after the normalization of the spectra. We directly applied the trained model in order to predict the time sequence with the half-duration continuation of the input; this is the *direct prediction* procedure. It was tested on 4490 *direct images*. To predict a longer continuation of the input, we adopted a straightforward common procedure and used a sliding 240 × 240 prediction window; this is the *iterated prediction* procedure. It was tested on 1962 *iterated images*. The evaluation was made by PSNR, SSIM, and the Hamming distance between the original and predicted corresponding cluster sequences. For this last metric, we adopted four different options. The cluster assignments are determined using a k-nearest-neighbor search at each time step, where the accuracy is measured by comparing if the data points have a common nearest centroid. NN_1 refers to $k = 1$ and NN_4 refers to $k = 4$.

Figure 7 presents the forecast by the proposed IB-MTS model and its evaluations for one flaring (FL) sample. The first row of results shows that the genuine and predicted sequences look very similar, with a high PSNR of 35.65 dB. Although, some magnified differences can be naturally observed.

The second row shows results for the prior, genuine, and predicted sequences, in terms of the assignment at each time step to the NN centroid obtained from a k-mean procedure described in [55]. Although the prior distribution differs from the genuine sequence to be predicted, the model was able to generate a sequence that exhibited a similar physical pattern to the genuine one. This shows that the model seems to be able to predict astrophysical patterns even with a CV-based loss that does not specifically measure astrophysical features.

The third row of results evaluates the usual MTS metrics for this specific FL sequence prediction. The three metrics (MAE, MAPE, and RMSE) have small averages over the forecasted times. Interestingly, the MTS errors are very small and below the averages for the first ten predicted time steps. This could be attributed to the temporal proximity with the prior information, as well as the combination of convolutions with the $\mathcal{L}_{tv}$ component of the loss defined in Equation (13), which softens the transition between the prior and the predicted data.

The last twelve plots show the time evolution of the astrophysical features extracted from the genuine (in blue) and predicted (in green) sequences. They show that the genuine features are predicted with more or less errors over time, but the predictions tend to follow the patterns of the genuine sequences. As these features were not considered in the loss used, this shows a non-negligible correlation between astrophysical features and CV metrics that were used to train the model.

Longer Predictions

For longer predictions, a standard well-known method performs recursive forecasts on data forecasted by the model. Under this setup, the prior MTS is a previously performed forecast, and one can legitimately expect an accumulation of errors. This is historically justified by the usage of one-step-forward models, such as the LSTM.

Figure 8 presents the short and long forecasts performed on a normalized IRIS quiet Sun (QS) sample. We can visually see that our approach is able to predict direct predictions as well as correct patters when we iterate the predictions on already predicted data.

3.2. MTS Metrics Evaluation

Table 2 presents the results of the evaluations of MAE, MAPE, and RMSE on IRIS, AR, and PB data. These metrics are averaged over all of the spectral and spatial dimensions, and all of the predicted time steps; for IRIS data, these metrics are also averaged over all types of solar activities. The model was trained and evaluated on each individual dataset. For all three metrics, our model outperforms the concurrent ones on the three datasets.

The descriptive temporal evolutions of these metrics are given in Figure 9 for the prediction errors under the *direct* setup, and in Figure 10 for the prediction errors under the *iterated* setup.

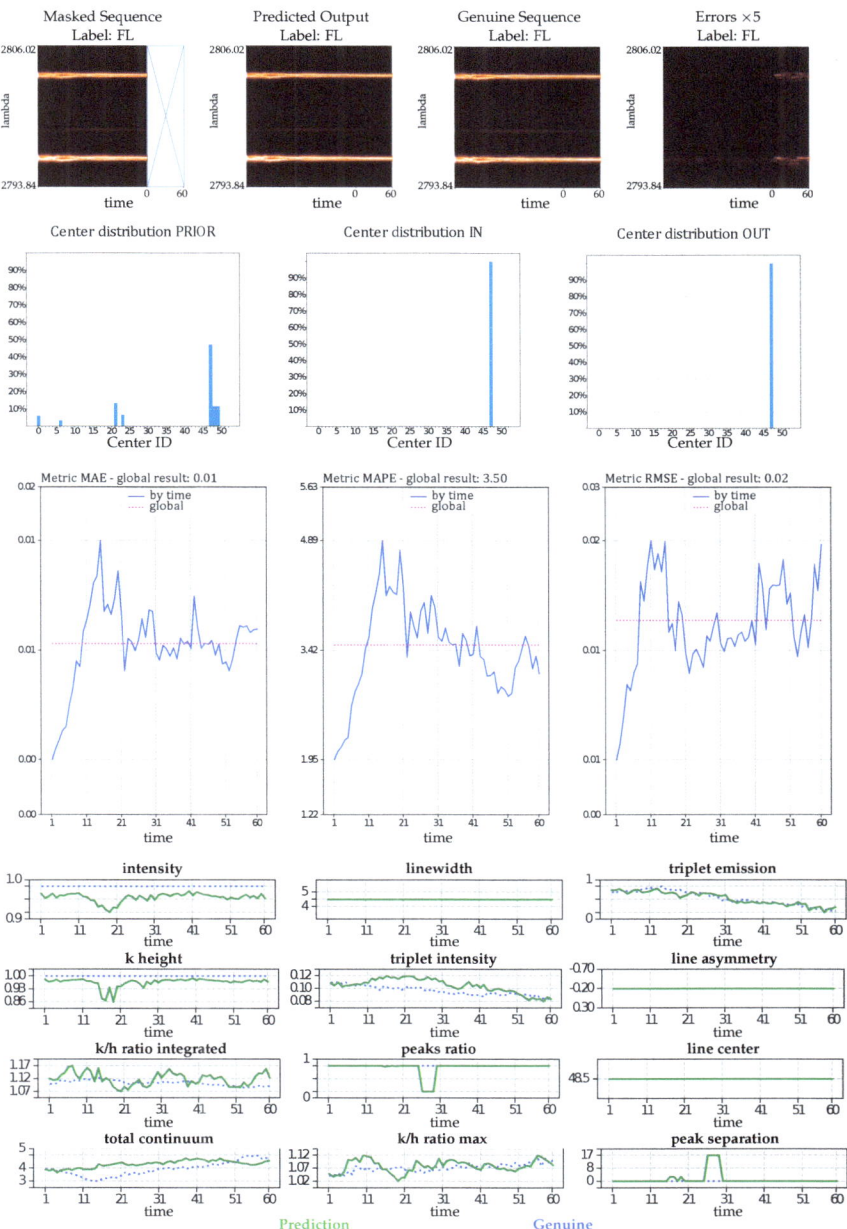

Figure 7. Evaluation of predictions for one flaring (FL) sample performed by the proposed IB-MTS model. The **first row** contains, respectively, the masked input, the predicted output, the genuine data, and the magnified pixel-wise error between the predicted and genuine. **Second row**: Spectral center distribution for the prior, the predicted, and the genuine MTS. **Third row**: MTS evaluation on the prediction. **Last twelve plots**: astrophysical features evaluations; the dotted blues represent the genuine and the green lines represent the prediction.

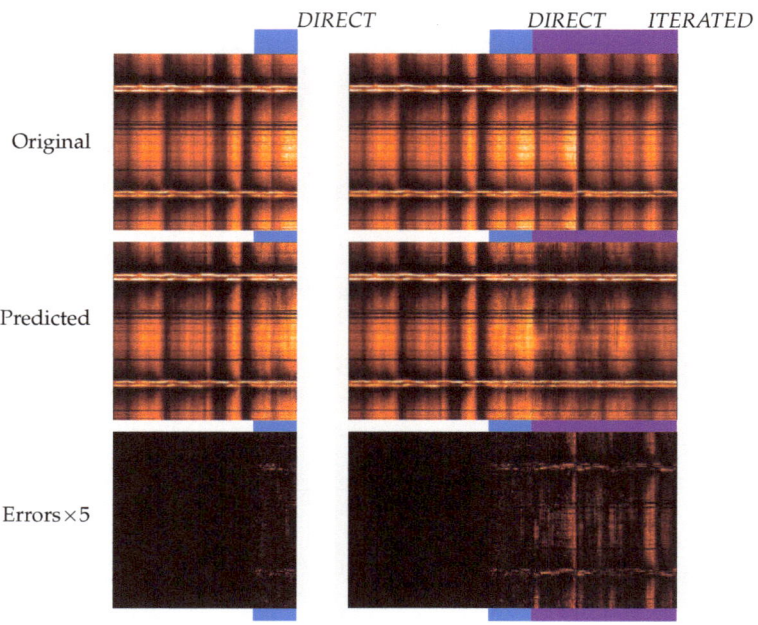

Figure 8. Prediction results: The first column presents the results of the direct predictions (blue part) and the second column presents the iterated predictions (violet part). A masked sample is given from the original sequence (**first row**); the prediction (**second row**) and the magnified (×5) differences (**third row**) are shown.

Table 2. MTS metric results.

Data		Model	IB-MTS	LSTM	ED-LSTM	GRU	ED-GRU	NBeats
IRIS	direct	MAE	**0.04**	0.05	0.05	0.05	**0.04**	0.10
		MAPE	**2.76**	13.13	4.71	26.84	3.16	4.75
		RMSE	**0.07**	0.08	0.08	0.08	**0.07**	0.19
	iterated	MAE	0.05	0.06	**0.05**	0.06	**0.05**	0.13
		MAPE	**2.94**	12.35	3.53	26.32	3.22	6.47
		RMSE	**0.08**	0.09	0.09	0.10	**0.08**	0.22
AL	direct	MAE	**0.08**	0.10	**0.08**	0.10	0.09	0.11
		MAPE	**3.71**	5.27	4.58	5.50	5.20	6.56
		RMSE	0.15	0.16	**0.14**	0.16	0.16	0.18
	iterated	MAE	**0.08**	0.19	0.16	0.23	0.16	0.11
		MAPE	**4.00**	11.37	9.10	12.94	9.28	6.23
		RMSE	**0.15**	0.26	0.23	0.30	0.23	0.18
PB	direct	MAE	**0.19**	0.46	0.46	0.50	0.46	0.22
		MAPE	**4.47**	10.15	10.03	10.76	10.14	5.19
		RMSE	**0.24**	0.54	0.51	0.60	0.52	0.28
	iterated	MAE	0.24	0.45	0.45	0.45	0.45	**0.23**
		MAPE	**4.23**	10.00	9.98	10.01	9.98	5.51
		RMSE	0.30	0.51	0.500	0.51	0.50	**0.28**

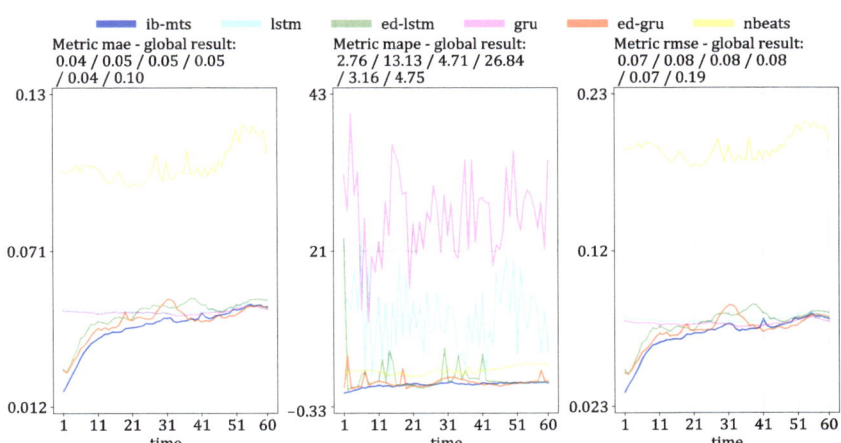

Figure 9. MTS metrics evaluation averaged on the test set for the direct prediction setups on QS, AR, and FL IRIS data.

For the *direct* setup of Figure 9, our proposed model performs better than all of the concurrent ones in more than half of the time steps, and there is even a gap in the performance for the first 30 time steps. The traditional LSTM and GRU have very bad performances in the first 20 time steps compared to the other models. The three models with IB formulations, which propose compressions of the time dimension similar to ED-LSTM and ED-GRU, demonstrate similar performances with a performance gap in the first 20 time steps compared to the proposed IB-MTS. However, ED-GRU manages to recover this gap and even performs slightly better in the last 20 time steps in terms of MAE and RMSE. NBeats does not perform well on the IRIS dataset; the results for MAE and RMSE are among the worst, whereas the MAPE results are average. This means that NBeats produces predictions with significant errors for high values, but it is highly accurate for small values. One reason for this could be the small number of trainable parameters for NBeats, compared with the complexity of the IRIS dataset. In simpler datasets, such as AL and PB, NBeats can achieve the second-best results after IB-MTS and the best results on iterated predictions on the PB dataset. One possible explanation for the weak performances of NBeats on IRIS datasets could be the complexity and the strong spatiotemporal dependencies of spectral data, where the spatiotemporal dependencies are less clear on AL and PB data, with sensors being sorted by their latitudes, ignoring their longitudes. For the MAPE metric, the proposed IB-MTS still performs better than the other ones, even with the last time steps. One interesting fact is that even if the performances are quite far in the first part of the time steps, the classical LSTM and GRU seem to have fewer error variabilities than the ED-LSTM and ED-GRU for MAE and RMSE metrics. This could be explained by the specific designs of NBeats for long-term predictions, suggesting that other currently designed IB models may close the performance gap over the long term while still providing comparable results. In contrast to these conclusions, concerning the MAPE metric, the classical LSTM and GRU models have a lot of error variability and perform worse than the IB-designed models. The variability could be due to larger errors for small values because these types of errors have significant impacts on the MAPE metric.

Concerning the last 20 time steps, Figure A1 from Appendix C can provide some explanation for the gain of performance in terms of the MAE and RMSE of the ED-GRU. This figure provides details of evaluations on the three different types of data included in the training and test data, i.e., QS, AR, and FL data, representing, respectively, 45.6%, 26.2%, and 28.2% of the (short) data. The figure shows that our proposed IB-MTS performs better than all of the others in all of the time steps for QS data, and is the most represented class in the trained and tested data. The other IB models still perform worse than IB-MTS for the first 30 time steps but they perform better in terms of MAE and RMSE in AR and FL data for the last 20 time steps.

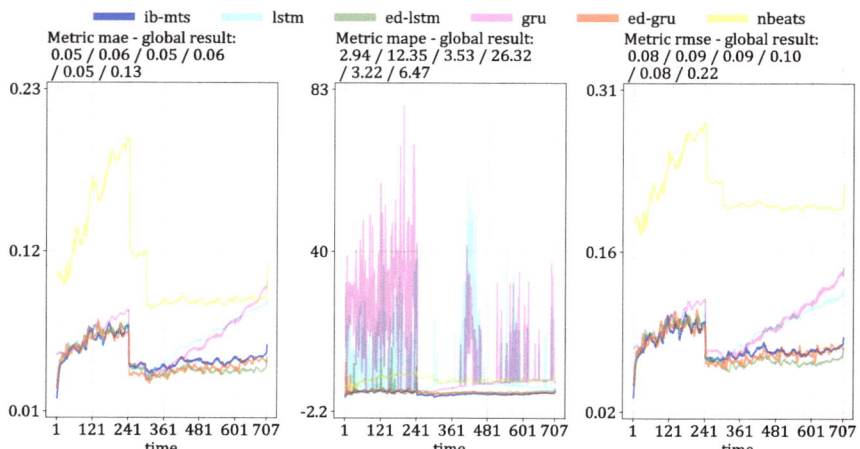

Figure 10. MTS metrics evaluation averaged on the test set for the iterated prediction setups on QS, AR, and FL IRIS data.

Figure 10 presents the evaluations of the MTS metrics in the *iterated* setup, where the model predicts 60 time steps ahead on data that have already been predicted. For this procedure, the proposed IB-MTS does not show a specific improvement in performance, except for the MAPE metric and the first 20 time steps, where the first *direct* prediction is performed. It is also important to note that the traditional LSTM and GRU models have high accumulated errors over time and perform much worse than the others in the last 200 time steps. The specific drop in the curves at 241 time steps is directly related to the variation in the length of the MTS within the testing set.

Figure 11 shows a histogram of the number of QS, AR, and FL data present in the test data by the number of total time steps; the majority of FL data have predicted durations greater than 700 time steps. On the contrary, the majority of QS and AR data have predicted durations smaller than 300 time steps.

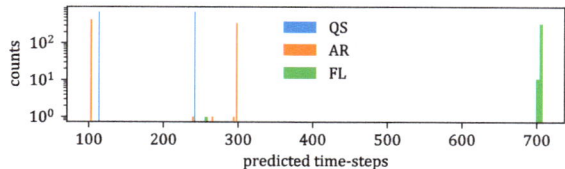

Figure 11. Histogram of the event durations from IRIS data.

Figure A2 from Appendix C presents a detailed comparison of the MTS evaluations for each class of *iterated* data. These graphs firstly explain the specific shapes present in Figure 10 by the fact that no QS data are present after 242 predicted time steps and no AR data are present after 298 predicted time steps. The proposed IB-MTS still performs very well on *iterated* QS data for all of the metrics, as well as for the MAPE metric on all types of data. ED-LSTM and ED-GRU perform better than IB-MTS after 120 time steps for MAE and RMSE metrics. One interpretation of this could be that the proposed IB-MTS is not designed to handle predictions on predictions, and does not include a state channel, such as in LSTM of GRU. Moreover, many variabilities are present for LSTM and GRU on the MAPE metric, whereas the IB-MTS model remains consistently stable and outperforms the other models in all scenarios. This could be attributed to the errors present for small values because they impact a lot of the results of the MAPE. In fact, an error of 0.1 for a value of 0.2 has a MAPE of $100 \times 0.1/0.2 = 50$, whereas the same error of 0.1 for a value of 0.8 has a MAPE of $100 \times 0.1/0.8 = 12.5$.

3.3. Computer Vision Metrics Evaluation

For the two procedures, *direct* and *iterated*, as described in Section 3.1, Table 3 provides the results of the evaluations in terms of PSNR and SSIM averaged on the test data. The proposed IB-MTS performs better than the concurrent models on IRIS data for both procedures. The gain of performance is very sensible for *direct* predictions. For *iterated* predictions, the results are more grouped and the ED-GRU performs similar to IB-MTS. On AL data, IB-MTS also outperforms concurrent models, except for the PSNR on *direct* data, where ED-LSTM performs a bit better.

Table 3. Accuracy in terms of average PSNR and SSIM for *direct* and *iterated* predictions.

Dataset		Metric	IB-MTS	LSTM	ED-LSTM	GRU	ED-GRU	NBeats
IRIS	direct	PSNR	**27.2**	25.6	26.3	25.9	26.7	14.6
		SSIM	**0.897**	0.869	0.887	0.864	0.891	0.673
	iterated	PSNR	**23.8**	23.0	23.4	22.8	**23.8**	13.4
		SSIM	**0.868**	0.821	0.864	0.809	**0.868**	0.586
AL	direct	PSNR	17.2	16.0	**17.4**	15.9	16.4	15.7
		SSIM	**0.518**	0.400	0.488	0.377	0.401	0.346
	iterated	PSNR	**16.7**	11.8	13.0	10.6	13.1	15.2
		SSIM	**0.516**	0.046	0.198	0.023	0.166	0.361
PB	direct	PSNR	**12.5**	5.4	6.0	4.5	5.7	11.4
		SSIM	0.361	0.013	0.000	0.004	0.000	**0.470**
	iterated	PSNR	10.5	5.9	6.0	5.9	6.0	**11.0**
		SSIM	0.235	0.003	0.003	0.003	0.004	**0.472**

NBeats still fails on IRIS data for the CV metric evaluation but performs well on the simpler datasets (AL and PB). NBeats can even achieve the highest SSIM on PB data. Yet our proposed IB-MTS model is the most stable in terms of the results on various datasets and it outperforms the concurrent ones on almost all metrics and datasets. NBeats also performs the best for the *iterated* procedure on PB data. Our proposed IB-MTS model was designed to predict multiple steps ahead in a *direct* fashion and does not generally extend very well for the *iterated* procedure.

The first row of Figure 12 provides detailed time evolutions of these metrics on IRIS *direct* data. They show a sensible gain of performance for the first 20 time steps, whereas the classical LSTM and GRU models do not have specific time evolutions in terms of performance and they perform worse than the others.

The second row of Figure 12 provides detailed time evolutions of the PSNR and SSIM metrics on the IRIS *iterated* data. ED-LSTM and ED-GRU perform a bit better than IB-MTS under the *iterated* setup for more than 300 time steps whereas the classical LSTM and GRU models perform worse. The specific variation of the curve at 300 time steps is explained by the diversity of the MTS durations evoked in Figure 11.

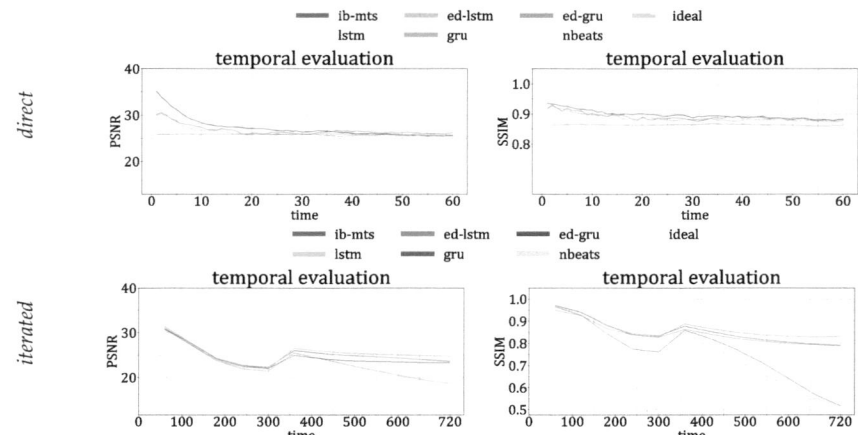

Figure 12. CV evaluation (over time) of the forecast for the direct and iterated predictions on IRIS data.

3.3.1. Information Bottleneck Evaluation on IRIS Data

This subsection evaluates IT-related measures on IRIS prior $\mathbf{X}_{1:180}$, genuine $\mathbf{X}_{181:240}$, and predicted $\hat{\mathbf{X}}_{181:240}$ data, as explained in Figure 6. Entropies $H(\cdot)$, KL-divergences $KL(\cdot||\cdot)$, and mutual information $I(\cdot,\cdot)$ are estimated by using the centroids obtained by a version of the k-means process performed in [55]. The dictionary of these 53 centroids is publicly available (i4ds.github.io/IRISreader/html/centroid_data.html, accessed on 20 February 2023). Each prior sequence $\mathbf{X}_{1:180}$ contains 180 centroids, one for each time step, with repetitions because the dictionary of centroids only has 53 centroids. In the same manner, each genuine $\mathbf{X}_{181:240}$ and predicted $\hat{\mathbf{X}}_{181:240}$ sequence contains 60 centroids, with repetitions.

Figure 13 shows the average distributions for prior, genuine, and predicted data. As expected, the average prior and genuine distributions of centroids are very similar and correspond to averages of the observed data. The average distribution of the predicted data remains close to that of the observed data, with only a few deviations in means and standard deviations. In particularly, centroid numbers 42 and 49 are a bit over-represented in the predictions whereas centroid numbers 20 and 44 are a bit under-represented. More details are given in Appendix C with the joint probabilities $p(c_1, c_2)$ of the centers present in the genuine c_1 and pred c_2 forecasts. Figure A3 presents the direct setup of IRIS data and Figure A4 presents the iterated setup. High probabilities on the diagonal $c_1 = c_2$ indicate a high accuracy of the prediction in terms of centroids. These figures show that our proposed IB-MTS ensures the high conservation of the physics behind the spectra, whereas NBeats totally fails in this task.

Table 4 presents the average IT measurements estimated on the prior, genuine, and predicted data. c_0 stands for the centroids present in prior data, c_1 and c_2 are the ones present in genuine and predicted data. Ideally, $KL(c_0||c_2) = KL(c_0||c_1)$, and $H(c_2) = H(c_1) = I(c_1, c_2)$. The higher the $I(c_1; c_2)$, the better. The results show that IB-MTS predicts the best c_2 centroids. This is confirmed by the highest value of mutual information $I(c_1; c_2)$ between the genuine and prediction data. Moreover, the KL-divergence $KL(c0||c_2)$ between the prior and the prediction data is the closest to $KL(c0||c_1)$ between the prior and the genuine data for IB-MTS on *direct* data. The interpretation of a high $I(c1; c2)$ is that the IB-MTS model is the best at predicting the information present in the prediction, even without the need for a lot of extra information beyond what is given in the prior, because $KL(c_0||c_2)$ is the lowest and closest to $KL(c_0||c_1)$. As a consequence, it seems that IB-MTS is the model that best adheres to the IB principles. NBeats failed to predict the correct centroids. The KL-divergence $KL(c0||c_2)$ between the prior and the prediction is the closest to $KL(c0||c_1)$ but equal to 0; the mutual information $I(c_1;c_2)$ between the genuine and the prediction is 0, which means that, on average, it could not predict the information of the target. One reason for this could be that the intensity information is very important for the NBeats process on IRIS data. The fact that we removed this information from the dataset by normalizing each time step by the maximum values may penalize NBeats on the IRIS data, which is not the case with AL and PB data, where NBeats performs fine.

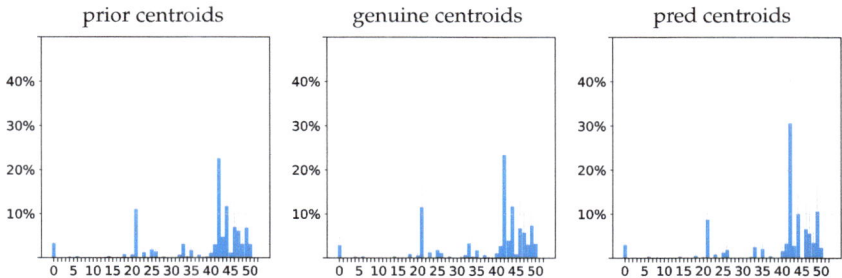

Figure 13. Average distributions of centroids with their standard deviations as vertical gray error bars. The first graph is for the average prior central data, the middle graph is for the average genuine target, and the right graph is the average distribution of predictions performed with IB-MTS.

Table 4. Information comparison between the prior centroids $c0$, the genuine centroids $c1$, and the predicted centroids $c2$ for the IRIS dataset. The results on H, KL, and I are averaged over all testing samples. $H(c_0)$, $KL(c_0||c_1)$, and $H(c_1)$, being statistics on the prior and the genuine, do not depend on the method.

Dataset		Metric	IB-MTS	LSTM	ED-LSTM	GRU	ED-GRU	NBeats
IRIS	direct	$H(c_0)$	3.922	3.922	3.922	3.922	3.922	3.922
		$KL(c_0||c_1)$	0.005	0.005	0.005	0.005	0.005	0.005
		$KL(c_0||c_2)$	0.111	0.311	0.111	0.344	0.198	0.000
		$H(c_1)$	3.890	3.890	3.890	3.890	3.890	3.890
		$H(c_2)$	3.567	3.382	3.579	3.280	3.465	0.000
		$I(c_1;c_2)$	**1.753**	1.607	1.613	1.597	1.681	0.000
	iterated	$H(c_0)$	3.968	3.968	3.968	3.968	3.968	3.968
		$KL(c_0||c_1)$	0.003	0.003	0.003	0.003	0.003	0.003
		$KL(c_0||c_2)$	**0.288**	0.575	0.308	0.416	0.486	0.000
		$H(c_1)$	3.957	3.957	3.957	3.957	3.957	3.957
		$H(c_2)$	3.487	3.325	3.385	3.301	3.229	0.000
		$I(c_1;c_2)$	**1.352**	1.276	1.319	1.219	1.314	0.000

Concerning the *iterated* data, the highest values of mutual information $I(c1;c_2)$ are still obtained by the IB models. IB-MTS can achieve the highest mutual information $I(c_1,c_2)$ with the lowest $KL(c_0||c_1)$.

3.3.2. Astrophysical Evaluations

A public dictionary of 53 centroids obtained by a version of k-means was performed on IRIS Mgh&k data [55]. Moreover, astrophysical features defined in [72] allow interpretability of Mghk spectra. This part evaluates the correspondence between centroid assignments for each genuine and predicted time step, and also evaluates the relative time evolution of the error between the genuine and predicted time steps. A k-NN search was performed between the genuine spectra at a given time step and the dictionary consisting of 53 centroids. The same search was performed for the same time step between the predicted spectra and the dictionary, and two sets of k centroids were compared. The considered time steps are successful k-NN assignments when they have at least one center in common.

For the two procedures (*direct* and *iterated*) described in Section 3.1, Table 5 provides the results of the prediction in terms of k-NN metrics averaged on the test data. For comparison, in the third column, we provide the accuracies of a theoretical worst model, which randomly assigns the k-nearest-neighbors among the 53 found in [55]. The most pessimistic accuracy for random classifications is obtained by the following combinatorial calculation:

$$\text{Random}_{k\text{-NN}} = \frac{\binom{53}{k} - \binom{53-k}{k}}{\binom{53}{k}}. \tag{19}$$

For $k = 2$, the proposed IB-MTS model can already predict the sequence of clusters with 82% of accuracy, and even 99% for $k = 5$, whereas a random assignment would give corresponding accuracies of 7.5% and 40%. The NBeats model fails on IRIS data, performing accuracies lower than the random assignments and not being able to predict spectra with the same centroid assignment as the genuine. Figure 14 presents the time evolution of the average k-NN accuracy for the *direct* procedure. There is a clear gain in performance for IB-MTS in the first 20 time steps for 1-NN and 2-NN accuracies. When k is greater than 4, the accounted performances are very similar for all time steps.

Figure 15 presents the time evolution of the average k-NN accuracy for the *iterated* procedure. Similar to the other metrics, the IB-MTS model shows an average performance for the *iterated* procedure, while the other IB models and NBeats perform better when predictions are made iteratively on predicted data.

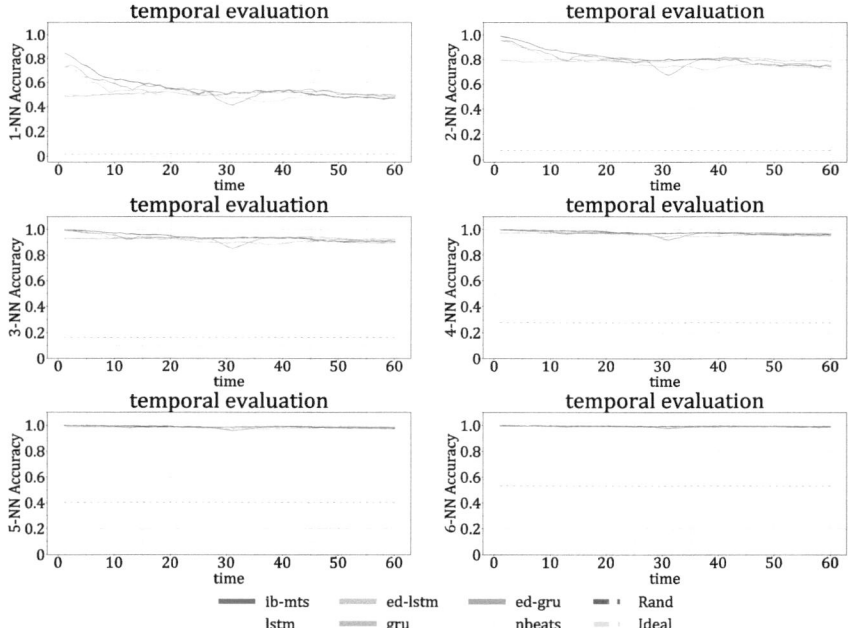

Figure 14. IRIS center assignment evaluation (over time) of the forecasts for direct predictions.

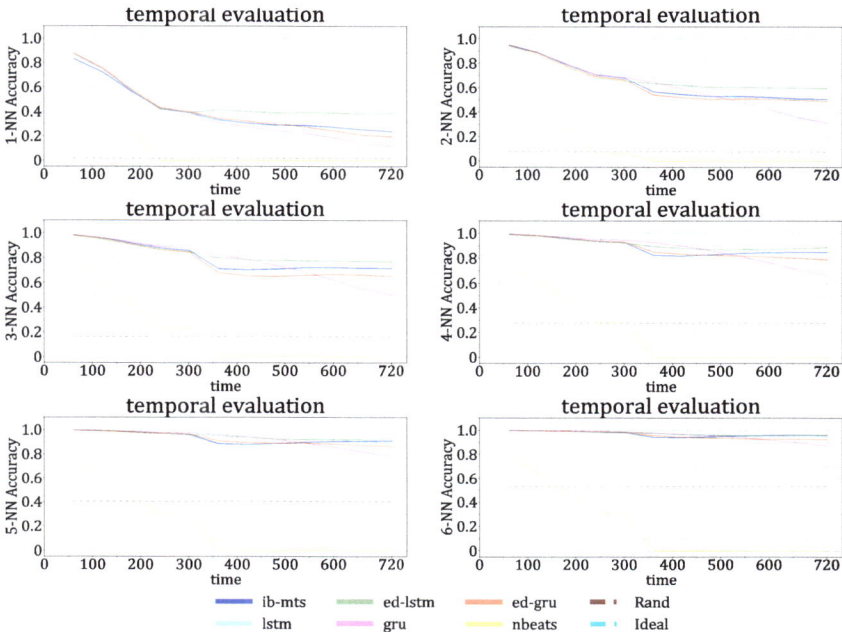

Figure 15. IRIS center assignment evaluation (over time) of the forecasts for iterated predictions.

Table 5. Evaluation on IRIS data: Percentage accuracies in terms of k-NN for *direct* prediction of the sizes of the training data and *iterated* prediction using a basic sliding window approach. The random k-NN cluster assignment accuracy is given for comparison and corresponds to the worst that can be expected for each k-NN assignment.

	Metric	Rand$_{k\text{-NN}}$	IB-MTS	LSTM	ED-LSTM	GRU	ED-GRU	NBeats
direct	1-NN	1.9	**55.7**	50.5	51.4	50.8	54.1	0.0
	2-NN	7.5	**81.9**	79.5	77.8	79.4	80.5	3.8
	3-NN	16.3	**94.3**	93.0	91.8	93.2	93.1	15.8
	4-NN	27.6	**97.7**	97.3	96.3	97.4	97.0	19.0
	5-NN	40.3	**98.9**	98.8	98.2	**98.9**	98.6	19.7
	6-NN	53.2	**99.6**	99.5	99.1	99.5	99.4	21.1
iterated	1-NN	1.9	**45.8**	42.6	43.6	43.4	45.0	0.0
	2-NN	7.5	**73.8**	72.1	70.1	72.0	72.4	3.9
	3-NN	16.3	**89.4**	88.9	87.0	88.3	87.8	16.1
	4-NN	27.6	95.1	**95.2**	93.7	94.5	94.4	19.4
	5-NN	40.3	97.6	**97.8**	96.8	97.3	97.2	20.2
	6-NN	53.2	98.9	**99.0**	98.5	98.6	98.7	21.8

Table 6 provides detailed data on 1-NN center assignment accuracy, as well as HSS and TSS metrics, broken down by label and aggregated for all the data. Concerning the *direct* procedure, IB-MTS performs the best on each label, as well as overall, and ED-GRU obtains comparable results on AR data only. The results for the *iterated* procedure show that IB-MTS performs less favorably compared to other IB models.

The time evolutions of the average relative errors for the astrophysical features are given in Figure 16. Given that each feature of a spectrum is a scalar output of a deterministic function $f_k(\cdot)$, these relative errors are defined at each time step by:

$$ref_{k,t} = \frac{|f_k(\mathbf{X}_t) - f_k(\tilde{\mathbf{X}}_t)|}{f_k(\mathbf{X}_t)}, \tag{20}$$

where $\tilde{\mathbf{X}}_t$ is the time step t estimation of $\mathbf{X}$ by the model. IB-MTS is able to predict the physical features relatively well, with a significant gain of performance in the first 20 time steps in almost all time steps. This is an important result because features, such as the line center, k/h ratios, k-height, and peak separation are related to the positions of specific local maximums on the spectra, and the corresponding functions are not differentiable. We provide experimental proof that IB-MTS is able to predict features that are not easy to integrate in the loss of a deep model. NBeats have high errors in predicting intensities. This is coherent with the comments formulated in Section 3.3.1. It seems that NBeats cannot function without intensity information on IRIS data, which could be the reason for its failure on these data.

Figure 17 shows the time estimations for the relative errors of features under the *iterated* setup. IB-MTS has an average performance under this setup, other IB models perform better, and classical LSTM and GRU performing worse.

Table 6. Evaluation of 1-NN centroid assignment accuracy for the *direct* and *iterated* predictions.

Model	Metric	IB-MTS	LSTM	ED-LSTM	GRU	ED-GRU	N-BEATS
				direct			
	% Accuracy	**55.7**	50.5	51.4	50.8	54.1	0.0
Global	TSS	**0.49**	0.43	0.45	0.43	0.47	0.00
	HSS	**0.50**	0.44	0.45	0.44	0.48	0.00
	% Accuracy	**52.5**	47.6	47.7	48.6	49.0	0.0
QS	TSS	**0.26**	0.18	0.21	0.19	0.22	0.00
	HSS	**0.28**	0.20	0.22	0.20	0.22	0.00
	% Accuracy	49.5	44.8	45.7	46.0	**49.9**	0.0
AR	TSS	**0.43**	0.37	0.39	0.39	**0.43**	0.00
	HSS	**0.43**	0.37	0.39	0.39	**0.43**	0.00
	% Accuracy	**63.7**	57.3	60.3	56.3	63.5	0.0
FL	TSS	**0.58**	0.51	0.53	0.49	0.57	0.00
	HSS	**0.58**	0.51	0.53	0.49	0.57	0.00
				iterated			
	% Accuracy	40.4	36.4	**41.8**	37.4	40.0	0.0
Global	TSS	0.33	0.29	**0.35**	0.30	0.32	0.00
	HSS	0.34	0.29	**0.35**	0.30	0.32	0.00
	% Accuracy	**46.3**	43.4	42.7	44.7	43.9	0.0
QS	TSS	**0.15**	0.10	0.12	0.10	0.12	0.00
	HSS	**0.17**	0.11	0.13	0.12	0.14	0.00
	% Accuracy	37.2	38.2	34.8	39.0	**41.3**	0.0
AR	TSS	0.30	0.30	0.26	0.31	**0.33**	0.00
	HSS	0.30	0.30	0.26	0.31	**0.33**	0.00
	% Accuracy	33.0	24.8	**42.6**	26.3	31.8	0.0
FL	TSS	0.24	0.18	**0.33**	0.18	0.22	0.00
	HSS	0.24	0.17	**0.33**	0.17	0.22	0.00

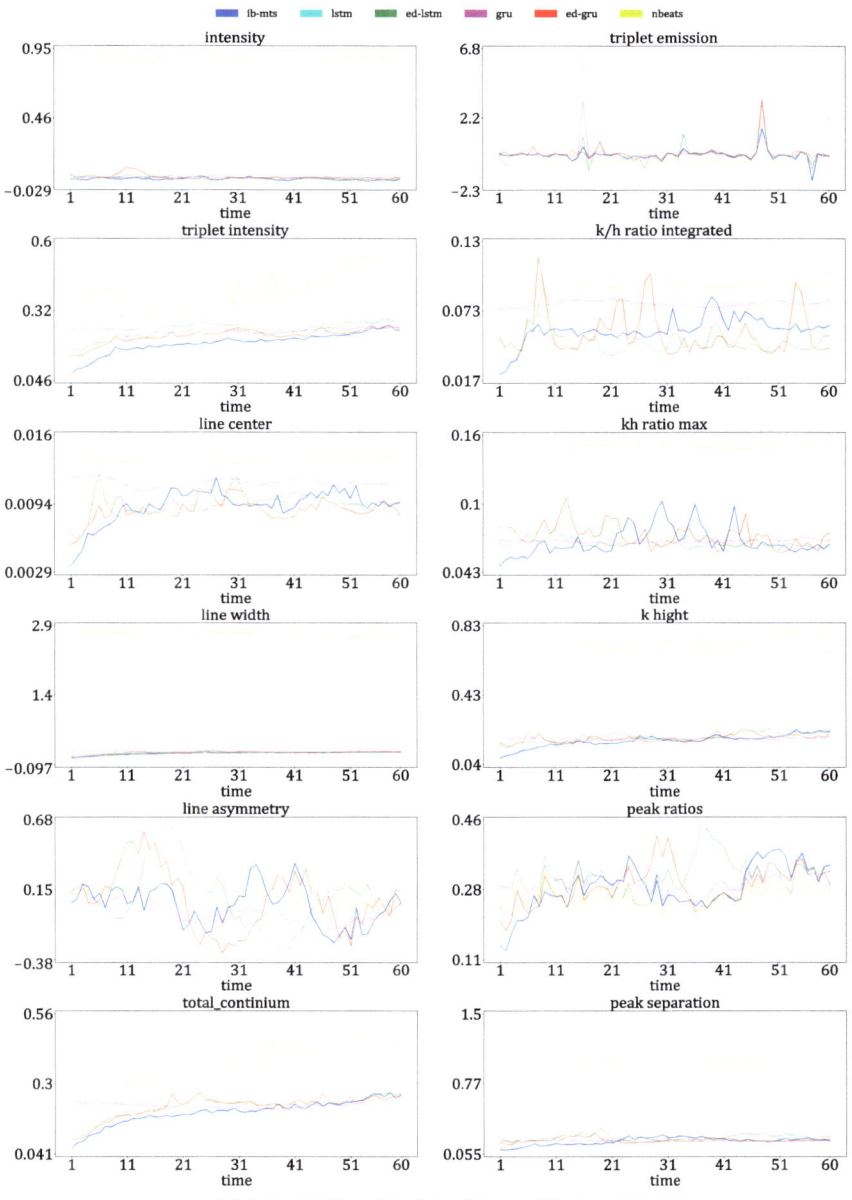

Figure 16. Evaluation of the relative prediction errors for physical features over time of the forecasts for IRIS data and the *direct* setup. The lower the better.

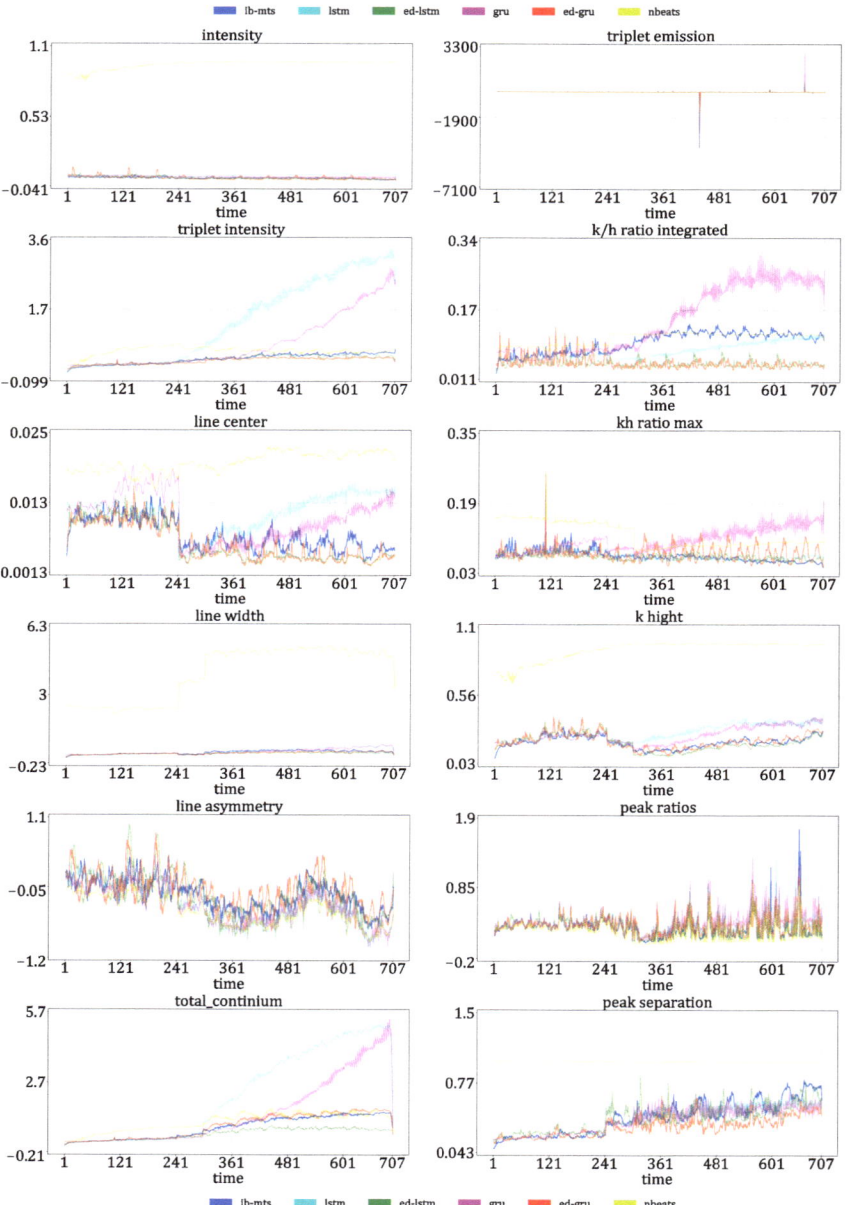

Figure 17. Evaluation of the relative prediction errors for physical features over time of the forecasts for IRIS data and the *iterated* setup.

3.3.3. Solar Activity Classification

This section investigates the solar activity classifications of test data. Part of the IRIS Mghk data were labeled by the type of activity, such as QS, AR, and FL. The labeling was performed globally for each time sequence and not at each time step, such that if an event presents a flaring FL episode between time steps t_0 and t_1, the sample $\mathbf{X}_{1:T+F}$ will be labeled as FL ($1 < t_0 < t_1 < T + F$).

A previously trained classifier was used to classify the genuine and predicted sequences, $\mathbf{X}_{T+1:T+F}$ and $\tilde{\mathbf{X}}_{T+1:T+F}$. This classifier outputs a vector of size 3 with a categorical assignment. The assigned class corresponds to the minimum of the cosine pseudo-distance between the output of the classifier and the one-hot encoded version of the class. The classification is considered successful when they match. For the *iterated* procedure, the classification is estimated by the minimum cosine pseudo-distance with the average of the categorical outputs obtained by the classifier at each iteration. Table 7 shows the results of the classification in terms of percentage accuracy, HSS, and TSS metrics. For the short and long procedures, there are no specific performance gains for IB-MTS compared to the concurrent models. All models show high activity classification performances, except NBeats; previous results sections showed that the model failed to predict on the IRIS normalized data. IB-MTS has slightly higher TSS and HSS scores than other models.

Table 7. Accuracy of solar activity classifications for the predicted versus genuine MTS with the *direct* and *iterated* prediction setups.

Model (Count)	Metric	IB-MTS	LSTM	ED-LSTM	GRU	ED-GRU	N-BEATS
				direct			
Global (8000)	% Acc	**95**	**95**	**95**	**95**	**95**	88
	TSS	**0.911**	**0.911**	0.906	0.910	0.909	0.805
	HSS	**0.915**	0.906	0.911	0.905	0.914	0.785
QS (3680)	% Acc	**97**	96	96	96	96	94
	TSS	**0.938**	0.911	0.916	0.910	0.918	0.876
	HSS	**0.936**	0.911	0.915	0.910	0.917	0.874
AR (536)	% Acc	96	96	**97**	96	**97**	91
	TSS	**0.613**	0.401	0.327	0.400	0.311	0.000
	HSS	**0.640**	0.371	0.366	0.362	0.349	0.000
FL (3784)	% Acc	98	**99**	98	**99**	**99**	92
	TSS	0.958	0.971	0.965	**0.972**	**0.972**	0.838
	HSS	0.959	0.971	0.965	**0.972**	**0.972**	0.843
				iterated			
Global (8000)	% Acc	94	94	93	94	**95**	86
	TSS	**0.979**	0.899	0.870	0.896	0.895	0.768
	HSS	0.889	0.891	0.869	0.889	**0.901**	0.738
QS (3680)	% Acc	**96**	95	95	95	95	88
	TSS	**0.914**	0.903	0.891	0.892	0.907	0.777
	HSS	**0.915**	0.903	0.893	0.891	0.908	0.767
AR (536)	% Acc	94	95	95	**96**	**96**	92
	TSS	**0.544**	0.387	0.188	0.399	0.277	0.168
	HSS	**0.594**	0.331	0.185	0.346	0.311	0.113
FL (3784)	% Acc	**98**	**98**	97	**98**	**98**	91
	TSS	0.948	0.955	0.930	**0.960**	0.957	0.932
	HSS	0.949	0.957	0.930	**0.962**	0.957	0.920

4. Discussion

4.1. Conclusions

Our proposed model is not perfectly fine-tuned but it already shows very competitive results. Moreover, the integration of the total loss of $\mathcal{L}_1$ and $\mathcal{L}_2$ from Equation (6) will allow for better optimization of the full IB loss from Equation (4). The main goal of this paper was to provide a new theoretical formulation of the IB in the context of MTS, i.e., to bring theoretical and empirical proofs that are not only problems of multiple successive IBs, but unique, joint spatiotemporal IBs. As a consequence, these results and comparisons are convincing and support the presented IB formulation for MTS forecasting. Moreover, we show that IB models, which utilize compression through encoding and decoding of the time dimension, also perform better than classical recurrent models.

The gain of performance is also very significant for the first 20 time steps across almost all evaluated metrics. This may be due to the combination of convolutions and the transition term $\mathcal{L}_{tv}$ present in the loss in Equation (13), which smooths out the predictions at the border for the first predicted time steps.

4.2. Spatial Sorting of MTS Data

Spatial dimensions in AL and PB are sorted by increasing latitudes, while the IRIS spatial dimension is sorted by increasing the wavelength. Other possible orderings for AL and PB datasets involve increasing longitudes or distances from a specific coordinate. The spatial relationship of the time series in the AL dataset is closely associated with the spatial correlation of the weather and sunshine levels. The spatial relation of the time series in the PB dataset is linked to the connection with the road networks around San Francisco.

Other works [1,17,18,60] highlight the limitations of the models that only consider spatial and temporal dependencies separately. Spatiotemporal dependencies are locally modeled with convolutions on spatiotemporal pseudo-images. Moreover, the spatiotemporal dimensions are compressed by applying successive convolutions with a stride of 2 in the first half of the U-Net architecture. Because of this spatiotemporal compression structure, each hidden layer of the encoding part of the U-Net creates a more global model of the spatiotemporal dependencies, such that, in the end, the bottleneck models the global spatiotemporal dependencies. We did not test the results of permuting the natural spatial ordering of the datasets as it was not part of our research questions. However, we believe that such permutation would likely penalize the training of all models except for the simple LSTM and GRU models.

The bottleneck of our proposed model has 1×1 spatiotemporal dimensions. This extreme shrinking of spatiotemporal dimensions is crucial in our model. Firstly, it allows one to always obtain unmasked data in the bottleneck and predict by decoding the posterior that is masked at the source. Secondly, as explained above, it allows for the global modeling of the spatiotemporal dependencies of MTS.

4.3. Non-Homogeneous Cadences of IRIS Data

The proposed model achieves an extreme reduction of the spatiotemporal dimensions to 1×1 and C channels. We believe that this extreme spatiotemporal reduction helps to tackle the problem of the non-homogeneous cadences of the temporal dimension presented in Figure 4 because it is compressed into a unique spatiotemporal dimension in the bottleneck.

The exact theoretical explanation as to why the model performs well with non-homogeneous data still remains open and is the subject of investigation. Synthetic periodic data with non-homogeneous frequencies may help test the robustness of all models. In our paper, the convincing results on IRIS data show that our proposed model is robust to non-homogeneous data. We did not extend the study of this question to other datasets as we could not find any other MTS dataset with non-homogeneous cadences of observations. Usually, physical observations are designed with a fixed cadence to keep the analysis simple. As a consequence, we do not believe that the elaboration of synthetic non-homogeneous data is a priority for this work and we just showed the good performance of the proposed model on IRIS data.

In addition, the non-homogeneous cadences of observations in the IRIS data may contribute to the poor forecasting performance of NBeats for this dataset. NBeats is based on the decomposition of MTS data into interpretable MTS signals that compose the observations, similar to the trend and seasonality decomposition. It is very challenging and perhaps impossible to find the trend and seasonality of MTS observations with non-homogeneous cadences. In AL and PB data, the cadences were the same for all of the data, and NBeats performs much better; however, the best results are given by our proposed model for these data.

4.4. Pros

Interestingly, while the model is trained on a CV loss that is not designed to measure accuracies in activity classifications or astrophysical information, the model is still able to predict the information with significant accuracy. This is in favor of interpretability and we believe that this is a great plus.

Unlike most recent studies in MTS forecasting, where spatiotemporal embeddings are designed prior to being fed to the models, our model jointly works straight on spatiotemporal dimensions seen together as images. Because of the fully masked convolutional structure, we believe that such simplicity is the advantage of our model, which can be easily applied to data, and generalized to more dimensions, such as for videos where the spatial information is composed of two joint dimensions.

4.5. Cons and Possible Extensions

Because of the activations used, the models were tested on normalized data, where each time step had a maximum of one. While this is suitable for many applications where only the spatial distribution of the data is important at each time step, such as the shape of a spectral line, in some applications, it is also important to know the real maximum value or *intensity* of the data at each time step. We believe that in this case, intensity forecasting is a simpler issue than the one solved in our work; one can train a classical RNN model to predict the intensities in parallel to the spatiotemporal MTS.

Our model has much more parameters to train than classical RNNs, but still less than the most recent transformers. Without significant difficulties, we could train our model on data with 240×240 dimensions. Moreover, the performant CV loss used to train the model comes at the expense of memory comes at the expense of to save the parameters of the VGG-16 used in the loss.

We believe that the model could be further improved by integrating more interpretability and prediction of the forecast errors. These features were not targeted in this step and are not in the scope of this work.

4.6. Future Research Directions

Recent understandings and implementations of the IB principle could also further improve the performance of our presented IB-MTS. For instance, [39] showed that the general IB principle is equivalent to several adversarial and CV losses present at the output and at the compressed bottleneck levels, where we only considered the particular case with the CV loss at the output. In particular, introducing a loss at the bottleneck should help the compression and enhance data representations at the bottleneck, leading to increased interpretability. This approach would certainly bring new improvements, following the ones achieved by this work, showing the importance of the IB formulation in the context of MTS forecasting. Moreover, for a better estimation of the forecasting error, one could attempt to amend the output of the network and predict the means and standard deviations of Gaussian distributions for each predicted pixel instead of a singular value. This would make the model stochastic and facilitate the confidence estimation in the forecasted outputs.

Author Contributions: Conceptualization, S.V. and D.U.; methodology, D.U.; software, D.U.; validation, S.V. and D.U.; formal analysis, D.U.; investigation, D.U.; resources, D.U.; data curation, D.U.; writing—original draft preparation, S.V., D.U. and O.T.; writing—review and editing, S.V., D.U. and O.T.; visualization, D.U.; supervision, S.V.; project administration, D.U.; funding acquisition, S.V. All authors have read and agreed to the published version of the manuscript.

Funding: This research was funded by the Swiss National Science Foundation SNSF, NRP75 project no. 407540_167158, SNSF Sinergia project no. 193826, and the University of Geneva.

Institutional Review Board Statement: Not applicable.

Data Availability Statement: Publicly available datasets were analyzed in this study. The code used in this work and selected classified IRIS data can be found at github.com/DenisUllmann/IB-MTS, accessed on 20 February 2023. [IRIS] Author: NASA; IRIS is a NASA small explorer mission developed and operated by LMSA. LMission operations are conducted at the NASA Ames Research Center, and significant contributions to downlink communications are funded by the ESA and the Norwegian Space Centre. For more information, please visit iris.lmsal.com/search/, accessed on 20 February 2023. [AL] Author: The National Renewable Energy Laboratory, U.S. Department of Energy, Office of Energy Efficiency and Renewable Energy, operated by the Alliance for Sustainable Energy LLC; Solar Power Data for the year 2006 in Alabama at www.nrel.gov/grid/solar-power-data.html, accessed on 20 February 2023. [PB] Author: California State Transportation Agency (CalSTA) Performance Measurement System (PeMS) and Yaguang Li; PeMS-BAY traffic data [74] at dx.doi.org/10.5281/zenodo.5146275, accessed on 20 February 2023.

Acknowledgments: We would like to acknowledge Lucia Kleint, Brandon Panos, and Cedric Huwyler for their assistance in providing access to IRIS satellite data, as well as for their valuable explanations and labeling of the data. Additionally, we utilized the Python library https://github.com/i4Ds/IRISreader, accessed on 20 February 2023 to work with the IRIS data and accomplish the objectives of this work.

Conflicts of Interest: The authors declare no conflict of interest. The funders had no role in the design of the study; in the collection, analyses, or interpretation of data; in the writing of the manuscript; or in the decision to publish the results.

Abbreviations

The following abbreviations are used in this manuscript:

AL	solar power dataset for the year 2006 in Alabama
AR	solar active region
ARIMA	autoregressive integrated moving average model
CV	computer vision
DNN	deep neural network
FL	solar flare
GNN	graph neural network
GRU	gated recurrent unit
HSS	Heidke skill score
IB	information bottleneck
IRIS	NASA's interface region imaging spectrograph satellite
IT	information theory
LSTM	long short-term memory model
MAE	mean absolute error
MAPE	mean absolute percentage error
ML	machine learning
MOS	mean opinion score
MSE	mean square error
MTS	multiple time series
NLP	natural language processing
NN	neural network
PB	PeMS-BAY dataset
PC	partial convolution
PSNR	peak signal-to-noise ratio
QS	quiet Sun
RAM	random access memory
RGB	red–green–blue
RMSE	root mean square error
RNN	recurrent neural network
SSIM	structural similarity
TS	time series
TSS	true skill statistic

Appendix A. Theory

Table A1. Summary table of the notations.

Random Variables	
$\mathbf{X}$	generic spatiotemporal data
$\tilde{\mathbf{X}}$	estimation of $\mathbf{X}$
T	scalar duration of the prior sequence
F	scalar duration of the posterior sequence
M	spatial size of spatiotemporal data
$\mathbf{X}_t$	multidimensional data at time step t
X_t^m	scalar value at time step t and spatial index m
$\mathbf{X}_{1:T} = \mathbf{X}_{1:T}^{1:M}$	prior sequence
$\tilde{\mathbf{X}}_{1:T}$	prior sequence estimation
$\mathbf{X}_{T+1:T+F} = \mathbf{X}_{T+1:T+F}^{1:M}$	posterior genuine sequence
$\tilde{\mathbf{X}}_{T+1:T+F}$	posterior genuine sequence estimation
$\mathbf{X}_{1:T+F} = \mathbf{X}_{1:T+F}^{1:M}$	full sequence
$\tilde{\mathbf{X}}_{1:T+F}$	full sequence estimation
$\mathbf{Z}$	bottleneck
$1:T \to T+1:T+F$	transition from prior to posterior
$\mathbf{Z}_{ib\_tr}$	IB bottleneck for transition $1:T \to T+1:T+F$ learning
$\mathbf{Z}_{ib\_ae}$	IB bottleneck of AE
$\mathbf{M}$	generic mask for spatiotemporal data
$\mathbf{M}_{1:T}$	prior mask
$\mathbf{M}_{T+1:T+F}$	posterior mask
$\mathbf{M}_{1:T+F}$	full mask
$\mathbf{M}_{ib\_tr}$	mask at the IB bottleneck for transition $1:T \to T+1:T+F$ learning
$\mathbf{1}$ & $\mathbf{1}_{len}$ & $\mathbf{1}_{row \times col}$	vectors and matrices of ones, eventually with specified length len or row and col sizes.
$\mathbf{0}$ & $\mathbf{0}_{len}$ & $\mathbf{0}_{row \times col}$	vectors and matrices of zeros, eventually with specified length len or row and col sizes.
K & $\mathbf{K}$	scalar & categorical labels
c_0, c_1 & c_2	prior, genuine, and predicted centroid assignments
Information Theory	
$p_\mathcal{D}$	data distribution
p_Θ & p_Φ	(encoding/decoding) distribution with parameter (Θ/Φ)
$\mathbb{E}_{p_\mathcal{D}}[\cdot]$	mean by sampling from $p_\mathcal{D}$
$\mathbb{E}_{p_\Theta}[\cdot]$	mean by sampling from $p_\Theta(\mathbf{Z}|\mathbf{X})$
$H(\cdot)$ & $H(\cdot,\cdot)$	generic entropy and cross-entropy
H_{p_Θ}	entropy parametrized by the encoder
H_{p_Θ, p_Φ}	cross-entropy parametrized by the encoder and the decoder
$KL(\cdot||\cdot)$ & $I(\cdot;\cdot)$	KL-divergence & mutual information
I_Θ & I_Φ	Encoding and decoding mutual information
Layers & mappers	
Id	Identity mapper
$Concat$	Concatenation of tensors
$(-/B/P)Conv$	(-/Binary/Partial) Convolutional layer
$(-/B/P)DConv$	(-/Binary/Partial) Deconvolutional layer
Losses & metrics	
$\mathcal{L}$	generic loss
$\tilde{\mathcal{L}} = \mathcal{L}_1 + \mathcal{L}_2 + \mathcal{L}_3$	upper bound on the loss $\mathcal{L}$
$\mathcal{L}_3^{Lap}$	$\mathcal{L}_3$ with Laplacian assumption of $p_\Phi(\mathbf{X}_{T+1:T+F}|\mathbf{Z}_{ib\_tr})$
$\mathcal{L}_3^{Lap,UNet}$	$\mathcal{L}_3^{Lap}$ for a U-Net architecture
$ref_{k,t}$	relative error for feature k at time step t

Proof of Equation (5). This proof is highly inspired by [39] but without variational approximation considerations. Let us consider the loss defined in Equation (4) and let us simplify the TS notations that are not relevant to this proof:

$$\mathcal{L}(\Theta, \Phi) = I_\Theta(\mathbf{X}_{1:T}; \mathbf{Z}_{ib\_tr}) - \beta I_\Phi(\mathbf{Z}_{ib\_tr}; \mathbf{X}_{T+1:T+F}) = I_\Theta(\mathbf{X}; \mathbf{Z}) - \beta I_\Phi(\mathbf{Z}; \mathbf{Y}). \tag{A1}$$

The first term is mutual information that is parameterized by Θ, which represents the parameters of the encoding part. This term can be decomposed:

$$\begin{aligned} I_\Theta(\mathbf{X}; \mathbf{Z}) &= \mathbb{E}_{p_\Theta(\mathbf{x},\mathbf{z})} \left[\log \frac{p_\Theta(\mathbf{z}|\mathbf{x}) p_\mathcal{D}(\mathbf{x})}{p_\Theta(\mathbf{z}) p_\mathcal{D}(\mathbf{x})} \right] \\ &= \mathbb{E}_{p_\Theta(\mathbf{z})}[\log p_\Theta(\mathbf{z})] - \mathbb{E}_{p_\Theta(\mathbf{x},\mathbf{z})}[\log p_\Theta(\mathbf{z}|\mathbf{x})] \\ &= H_{p_\Theta}(\mathbf{Z}) - H_{p_\Theta}(\mathbf{Z}|\mathbf{X}). \end{aligned} \tag{A2}$$

The second term of (A1) is the mutual information parametrized by Φ, which represents the parameters of decoding, and can be decomposed:

$$\begin{aligned} I_\Phi(\mathbf{Z}; \mathbf{Y}) &= \mathbb{E}_{p_\Phi(\mathbf{z},\mathbf{y})} \left[\log \frac{p_\mathcal{D}(\mathbf{y}|\mathbf{z}) p_\Phi(\mathbf{z})}{p_\mathcal{D}(\mathbf{y}) p_\Phi(\mathbf{z})} \right] \\ &= \mathbb{E}_{p_\mathcal{D}(\mathbf{y})}[\log p_\mathcal{D}(\mathbf{y})] - \mathbb{E}_{p_\Phi(\mathbf{z},\mathbf{y})}[\log p_\mathcal{D}(\mathbf{y}|\mathbf{z})] \\ &= H_{p_\mathcal{D}}(\mathbf{Y}) - \mathbb{E}_{p_\Phi(\mathbf{z},\mathbf{y})} \left[\log p_\mathcal{D}(\mathbf{y}|\mathbf{z}) \frac{p_\Phi(\mathbf{y}|\mathbf{z})}{p_\Phi(\mathbf{y}|\mathbf{z})} \right] \\ &= H_{p_\mathcal{D}}(\mathbf{Y}) - \mathbb{E}_{p_\mathcal{D}(\mathbf{x},\mathbf{y})} \left[\mathbb{E}_{p_\Theta(\mathbf{z}|\mathbf{x})}[\log p_\Phi(\mathbf{y}|\mathbf{z})] \right] + \mathbb{E}_{p_\Phi(\mathbf{z},\mathbf{y})} \left[\log \frac{p_\Phi(\mathbf{y}|\mathbf{z})}{p_\mathcal{D}(\mathbf{y}|\mathbf{z})} \right] \\ &= H_{p_\mathcal{D}}(\mathbf{Y}) - H_{p_{\Theta,\Phi}}(\mathbf{Y}|\mathbf{Z}) + KL(p_\Phi(\mathbf{y}|\mathbf{z})||p_\mathcal{D}(\mathbf{y}|\mathbf{z})) \\ &\geq H_{p_\mathcal{D}}(\mathbf{Y}) - H_{p_{\Theta,\Phi}}(\mathbf{Y}|\mathbf{Z}), \end{aligned} \tag{A3}$$

because the Kullback–Leibler divergence $KL(p_\Phi(\mathbf{y}|\mathbf{z})||p_\mathcal{D}(\mathbf{y}|\mathbf{z}))$ is positive.

As a consequence, by putting the results of Equations (A2) and (A3) in Equation (A1), one can obtain the following upper bound on the loss:

$$\mathcal{L}(\Theta, \Phi) \leq H_{p_\Theta}(\mathbf{Z}) - H_{p_\Theta}(\mathbf{Z}|\mathbf{X}) + \beta H_{p_{\Theta,\Phi}}(\mathbf{Y}|\mathbf{Z}) - \beta H_{p_\mathcal{D}}(\mathbf{Y}), \tag{A4}$$

and $H_{p_\mathcal{D}}(\mathbf{Y})$ being fixed by the data, the upper bound on the loss can be reduced to:

$$\tilde{\mathcal{L}}(\Theta, \Phi) = H_{p_\Theta}(\mathbf{Z}) - H_{p_\Theta}(\mathbf{Z}|\mathbf{X}) + \beta H_{p_{\Theta,\Phi}}(\mathbf{Y}|\mathbf{Z}), \tag{A5}$$

□

Remark A1 (Details on *PConv* and *PDeconv* for MTS). *With T representing the time steps of prior values and F representing the time steps of forecasted values, let us recall Equation (4):*

$$\mathcal{L}(\Theta, \Phi) = I_\Theta(\mathbf{X}_{1:T}; \mathbf{Z}_{ib\_tr}) - \beta I_\Phi(\mathbf{Z}_{ib\_tr}; \mathbf{X}_{T+1:T+F}). \tag{A6}$$

This corresponds to the general formulation of the IB principle with the MTS notation. The bottleneck variable $\mathbf{Z}_{ib\_tr}$ should then hold part of the information of prior time steps $1:T$ and forecast time steps $T+1:T+F$ in order to learn the time transition. Equation (A6) can be rewritten using temporal masks on the source $\mathbf{X}_{1:T+F} = Concat[\mathbf{X}_{1:T}, \mathbf{X}_{T+1:T+F}]$:

$$\mathcal{L}(\Theta, \Phi) = \underbrace{I_\Theta([\mathbf{X}_{1:T}, \mathbf{X}_{T+1:T+F}] \odot \mathbf{M}_{1:T}; \mathbf{Z}_{ib\_tr} \odot \mathbf{M}_{ib\_tr})}_{A} \\ - \beta \underbrace{I_\Phi(\mathbf{Z}_{ib\_tr} \odot \mathbf{M}_{ib\_tr}; [\mathbf{X}_{1:T}, \mathbf{X}_{T+1:T+F}] \odot \mathbf{M}_{T+1:T+F})}_{B}, \tag{A7}$$

where $\odot$ is the element-wise product, also known as the Hadamard dot product, with $\mathbf{M}_{1:T}$ and $\mathbf{M}_{T+1:T+F}$ representing binary time masks having ones at the indexed time positions, $1:T$ or $T+1:T+F$, and zeros at the other time positions. Binary masks $\mathbf{M}_{1:T}$ and $\mathbf{M}_{T+1:T+F}$ lie in the same manifold, such as the MTS $\mathbf{X}_{1:T+F} = Concat[\mathbf{X}_{1:T}, \mathbf{X}_{T+F}]$, and $\mathbf{M}_{ib\_tr}$ in the same manifold, such as the compressed variable $\mathbf{Z}_{ib\_tr}$, such that $\mathbf{M}_{1:T}, \mathbf{M}_{T+1:T+F} \in \mathbb{R}^{(T+F) \times M}$, $\mathbf{M}_{1:T} = Concat[\mathbf{1}_{T \times M}, \mathbf{0}_{F \times M}]$, $\mathbf{M}_{T+1:T+F} = Concat[\mathbf{0}_{T \times M}, \mathbf{1}_{F \times M}]$; $\mathbf{M}_{ib\_tr}$ is a binary mask for the compressed manifold of $\mathbf{Z}_{ib\_tr}$, and is filled only by ones: $\mathbf{Z}_{ib\_tr} \odot \mathbf{M}_{ib\_tr} = \mathbf{Z}_{ib\_tr}$.

A straightforward approach to designing the compression, described in part A of Equation (A7) for pseudo-images $\mathbf{X}_{1:T}$, consists of a convolution Conv and binary convolution BConv, both with strides larger than 2 for spatiotemporal dimension reduction. Without a loss of generality for the explanation of Conv and BConv layers, let us consider the example with one prior time step $T=1$, $\mathbf{X}_{1:T} = \mathbf{X}_1$, one posterior time step to forecast $F=1$, $\mathbf{X}_{T+1:T+F} = \mathbf{X}_2$, and 2 spatial dimensions $M=2$, such that $\mathbf{X}_{1:2} \in \mathbb{R}^{2 \times 2}$; the bottleneck $\mathbf{Z}_{ib\_tr} = \mathbf{Z}_{1 \to 2}$ learns the transition $1 \to 2$:

$$\mathbf{Z}_{1 \to 2} = Conv_{\Theta}([\mathbf{X}_1, \mathbf{X}_2] \odot \mathbf{M}_1) \in \mathbb{R}^{1 \times 1 \times C} \quad and \quad \mathbf{M}_{1 \to 2} = BConv(\mathbf{M}_1) = [1], \quad (A8)$$

where C is the number of channels for $Conv_{\Theta}$. Proof of Equation (A8) is given in Appendix A. The combination of $Conv_{\Theta}$, BConv with corresponding masks $\mathbf{M}_1$ and $\mathbf{M}_{1 \to 2}$ is usually referred to as partial convolution $PConv_{\Theta}$ [4], such that:

$$PConv_{\Theta}(\mathbf{X}_{1:2}, \mathbf{M}_1) = (\mathbf{Z}_{1 \to 2}, \mathbf{M}_{1 \to 2}). \quad (A9)$$

In a symmetrical approach, still considering the example when $T=1, F=1, M=2$, the decoding described in part B of Equation (A7) can be designed by a deconvolution DConv and a binary deconvolution BDConv, both with strides of 2, but in this case, the decoder performs as well as a backcast of the prior $\mathbf{X}_1$ because the deconvolution of $\mathbf{M}_{1 \to 2}$ returns $\mathbf{M}_{1:2}$ instead of $\mathbf{M}_2$ of B:

$$DConv_{\Phi}(\mathbf{Z}_{1 \to 2} \odot \mathbf{M}_{1 \to 2}) = [\tilde{\mathbf{X}}_1, \tilde{\mathbf{X}}_2] \in \mathbb{R}^2 \quad and \quad BDConv(\mathbf{M}_{1 \to 2}) = \mathbf{M}_{1:2} = \mathbf{1}_{2 \times 2}, \quad (A10)$$

and Proof of Equation (A10) is given in Appendix A. The combination of $DConv_{\Phi}$, BDConv with corresponding masks $\mathbf{M}_{1 \to 2}$ and $\mathbf{M}_{1:2}$ is usually referred to as partial deconvolution $PDConv_{\Phi}$, such that:

$$PDConv_{\Phi}(\mathbf{Z}_{ib\_tr}, \mathbf{M}_{ib\_tr}) = (\tilde{\mathbf{X}}_{1:2}, \mathbf{M}_{1:2}). \quad (A11)$$

When $T+F$ and M are larger than 2, pseudo-images $\mathbf{X}_{1:T}$ and masks $\mathbf{M}_{1:T}$ must be zero-padded to a square pseudo-image, whose size is a power of 2, and successive PConv and PDConv layers must be used to obtain a $1 \times 1 \times C$ bottleneck. For instance, when the padded input image is 254×256, 8 successive PConv and 8 successive PDConv layers must be used, and the model is deep. This forecast model design finally makes use of more traditional CV layers, such as convolutions, compared to classical TS deep models, such as LSTMs; however, the model is directly justified by the IB formulation of the time dimension compression.

A drawback of this design is that the binary deconvolution decoder outputs $\mathbf{M}_{1:T+F} = \mathbf{1}_{(T+F) \times M}$ instead of $\mathbf{M}_{T+1:T+F} = Concat[\mathbf{0}_{T \times M}, \mathbf{1}_{F \times M}]$ from part B of the IB Equation (A7). As a consequence, only with these PConv and PDConv layers would it have to perform a backcast and output an estimation of the prior $\tilde{\mathbf{X}}_{1:T}$ in addition to the estimated forecast $\tilde{\mathbf{X}}_{T+1:T+F}$, which means that the bottleneck does not only learn the transition statistics $1:T \to T+1:T+F$ but also the reconstruction of $1:T$. This is not the right formulation of the IB bottleneck for MTS forecasting. As a consequence, a skipping connection between the masked input $\mathbf{X}_{1:T+F} \odot \mathbf{M}_{1:T}$ and the output is then added to the model in order to let all of the information about the prior $\mathbf{X}_{1:T}$ pass without any parameter learning, bypassing the bottleneck $\mathbf{Z}_{ib\_tr}$. Complemented by these skipping layers, the bottleneck of the network only learns the statistics of the transition between the prior and the forecast. The resulting output for the designed model is then given by:

$$\begin{aligned} UNet_{\Phi,\Theta}(\mathbf{X}_{1:T+F}, \mathbf{M}_{1:T}) &= \left[\mathbf{X}_{1:T}^{IB}, \mathbf{X}_{T+1:T+F}^{IB}\right] \odot \mathbf{M}_{1:T+F} + \mathbf{X}_{1:T+F} \odot \mathbf{M}_{1:T} \\ &= \left[\mathbf{X}_{1:T}^{IB} + \mathbf{X}_{1:T}, \mathbf{X}_{T+1:T+F}^{IB}\right], \end{aligned} \quad (A12)$$

where $UNet_{\Phi,\Theta}$ is the network with the PConv, PDConv, and skipping layers. $\mathbf{X}_{1:T}^{IB}$ is the estimation of the prior $\mathbf{X}_{1:T}$ performed through the bottleneck $\mathbf{Z}_{ib\_tr}$, whereas $\mathbf{X}_{1:T+F} \odot \mathbf{M}_{1:T} = \mathbf{X}_{1:T}$ is the prior input directly connected to the output by the skipping layer. The output of the network is still not $[\mathbf{X}_{1:T}, \mathbf{X}_{T+1:T+F}] \odot \mathbf{M}_{T+1:T+F} = [0, \mathbf{X}_{T+1:T+F}] = \mathbf{X}_{T+1:T+F}$ from part B of the IB loss in Equation (A7), but we will now show the equivalence. With the described design of the prior compression, bottleneck decoding, and prior connection to the output, the upper bound $\mathcal{L}_3$ loss defined in Equation (7) then becomes equivalent to the following loss on the model estimation output from Equation (A12):

$$\mathcal{L}_3^{Lap,UNet}(\Theta, \Phi) \equiv \mathbb{E}_{p_\mathcal{D}(\mathbf{X}_{1:T+F})}\left[\mathbb{E}_{p_\Theta(\mathbf{Z}_{ib\_tr}|\mathbf{X}_{1:T})}\left[\|\mathbf{X}_{1:T+F} - UNet_{\Phi,\Theta}(\mathbf{X}_{1:T+F}, \mathbf{M}_{1:T})\|_1\right]\right]. \quad (A13)$$

This equivalence and more details are given in Proof of Equation (A13) of this Appendix A.

Proof of Equation (A8).

$$\begin{aligned}
\mathbf{Z}_{1\rightarrow 2} &= Conv_\Theta([\mathbf{X}_1, \mathbf{X}_2] \odot \mathbf{M}_1) \\
&= Conv_\Theta([\mathbf{X}_1, \mathbf{X}_2] \odot [\mathbf{1}_M, \mathbf{0}_M]) \\
&= Conv_\Theta([\mathbf{X}_1, \mathbf{0}_M]) \\
&= \sigma(\Theta_1 \times \mathbf{X}_1 + \Theta_2 \times \mathbf{0}_M) \in \mathbb{R},
\end{aligned} \quad (A14)$$

where σ is a nonlinear activation and $Conv$ is a one-dimensional convolution with parameter $\Theta = [\Theta_1, \Theta_2]$, and:

$$\mathbf{M}_{1\rightarrow 2} = BConv(\mathbf{M}_1) = BConv([1, 0]) = [1], \quad (A15)$$

where $BConv$ is a one-dimensional binary convolution defined by:

$$BConv(\mathbf{M}) = Binary(Conv_{[1,1]}(\mathbf{M})) \quad \text{and} \quad Binary(m) = \begin{cases} 1, & \text{if } m > 0 \\ 0, & \text{otherwise} \end{cases} \quad (A16)$$

□

Proof of Equation (A10).

$$\begin{aligned}
DConv_\Phi(\mathbf{Z}_{1\rightarrow 2} \odot \mathbf{M}_{1\rightarrow 2}) &= DConv_\Phi(\mathbf{Z}_{1\rightarrow 2} \odot \mathbf{1}) = DConv_\Phi(\mathbf{Z}_{1\rightarrow 2}) \\
&= \sigma([\Phi_1 \times \mathbf{Z}_{1\rightarrow 2}, \Phi_2 \times \mathbf{Z}_{1\rightarrow 2}]) = [\tilde{\mathbf{X}}_1, \tilde{\mathbf{X}}_2] \in \mathbb{R}^2,
\end{aligned} \quad (A17)$$

where σ is a nonlinear activation and $DConv$ is a one-dimensional deconvolution of stride 2 with parameter $\Phi = [\Phi_1, \Phi_2]$, and:

$$BDConv(\mathbf{M}_{1\rightarrow 2}) = BDConv([\mathbf{1}]) = [\mathbf{1}, \mathbf{1}], \quad (A18)$$

where $BConv$ is a one-dimensional binary convolution of stride 2, defined by:

$$BDConv(\mathbf{M}) = Binary(DConv(\mathbf{M})). \quad (A19)$$

□

Proof of Equation (A13). $\mathcal{L}_3^{Lap}(\Theta, \Phi)$ is the third component of the upper bound on the IB loss from Equation (6), where $p_\Phi(\mathbf{X}_{T+1:T+F}|\mathbf{Z}_{ib\_tr})$ is assumed to be Laplacian, and $\mathcal{L}_3^{Lap,UNet}(\Theta, \Phi)$ is the theoretical loss for our proposed model designed with U-Net and a Laplacian assumption of $p_\Phi(\mathbf{X}_{T+1:T+F}|\mathbf{Z}_{ib\_tr})$:

$$\begin{aligned}
\mathcal{L}_3^{Lap}(\Theta, \Phi) &= \mathbb{E}_{p_\mathcal{D}(\mathbf{X}_{1:T+F})}\left[\mathbb{E}_{p_\Theta(\mathbf{Z}_{ib\_tr}|\mathbf{X}_{1:T})}\left[\|\mathbf{X}_{T+1:T+F} - g_\Phi(\mathbf{Z}_{ib\_tr})\|_1\right]\right] \\
&= \mathbb{E}_{p_\mathcal{D}(\mathbf{X}_{1:T+F})}\left[\mathbb{E}_{p_\Theta(\mathbf{Z}_{ib\_tr}|\mathbf{X}_{1:T})}\left[\left\|\mathbf{X}_{T+1:T+F} - \mathbf{X}_{T+1:T+F}^{IB}\right\|_1\right]\right],
\end{aligned} \quad (A20)$$

$$\mathcal{L}_3^{Lap,UNet}(\boldsymbol{\Theta},\boldsymbol{\Phi}) = \mathbb{E}_{p_{\mathcal{D}}(\mathbf{X}_{1:T+F})}\left[\mathbb{E}_{p_{\boldsymbol{\Theta}}(\mathbf{Z}_{ib\_tr}|\mathbf{X}_{1:T})}\left[\|\mathbf{X}_{1:T+F} - UNet_{\boldsymbol{\Theta},\boldsymbol{\Phi}}(\mathbf{X}_{1:T+F},\mathbf{M}_{1:T})\|_1\right]\right]$$
$$= \mathbb{E}_{p_{\mathcal{D}}(\mathbf{X}_{1:T+F})}\left[\mathbb{E}_{p_{\boldsymbol{\Theta}}(\mathbf{Z}_{ib\_tr}|\mathbf{X}_{1:T})}\left[\left\|\mathbf{X}_{1:T+F} - \left[\mathbf{X}_{1:T} + \mathbf{X}_{1:T}^{IB}, \mathbf{X}_{T+1:T+F}^{IB}\right]\right\|_1\right]\right], \quad (A21)$$

where $\mathbf{X}_{1:T}$ and $\mathbf{X}_{T+1:T+F}$ are the prior and genuine forecasts given in the training dataset, and $\mathbf{X}_{1:T}^{IB}$ and $\mathbf{X}_{T+1:T+F}^{IB}$ are the predicted prior and forecast after the compression and decompression using the bottleneck $\mathbf{Z}_{ib\_tr}$. Starting with the norm in Equation (A21), we can prove:

$$\left\|\mathbf{X}_{1:T+F} - \left[\mathbf{X}_{1:T} + \mathbf{X}_{1:T}^{IB}, \mathbf{X}_{T+1:T+F}^{IB}\right]\right\|_1 = \left\|\left[\mathbf{X}_{1:T}^{IB}, \mathbf{X}_{T+1:T+F} - \mathbf{X}_{T+1:T+F}^{IB}\right]\right\|_1$$
$$= \left\|\mathbf{X}_{1:T}^{IB}\right\|_1 + \left\|\mathbf{X}_{T+1:T+F} - \mathbf{X}_{T+1:T+F}^{IB}\right\|_1, \quad (A22)$$

and by the linearity of the expected value function:

$$\mathcal{L}_3^{Lap,UNet}(\boldsymbol{\Theta},\boldsymbol{\Phi}) + \mathbb{E}_{p_{\mathcal{D}}(\mathbf{X}_{1:T+F})}\left[\mathbb{E}_{p_{\boldsymbol{\Theta}}(\mathbf{Z}_{ib\_tr}|\mathbf{X}_{1:T})}\left[\left\|\mathbf{X}_{1:T}^{IB}\right\|_1\right]\right] = \mathcal{L}_3^{Lap}(\boldsymbol{\Theta},\boldsymbol{\Phi}), \quad (A23)$$

such that $\mathcal{L}_3^{Lap}(\boldsymbol{\Theta},\boldsymbol{\Phi}) \leq \mathcal{L}_3^{Lap,UNet}(\boldsymbol{\Theta},\boldsymbol{\Phi})$, because the norm is positive. Moreover, the minimum of $\mathbb{E}_{p_{\mathcal{D}}(\mathbf{X}_{1:T+F})}\left[\mathbb{E}_{p_{\boldsymbol{\Theta}}(\mathbf{Z}_{ib\_tr}|\mathbf{X}_{1:T})}\left[\left\|\mathbf{X}_{1:T}^{IB}\right\|_1\right]\right]$ is 0, obtained when $\mathbf{X}_{1:T}^{IB} = 0$ for all $\mathbf{X}_{1:T} \sim p_{\mathcal{D}}(\mathbf{X}_{1:T})$. The two losses, $\mathcal{L}_3^{Lap,UNet}(\boldsymbol{\Theta},\boldsymbol{\Phi})$ and $\mathcal{L}_3^{Lap}(\boldsymbol{\Theta},\boldsymbol{\Phi})$, share the same minimum. In fact, minimizing $\mathcal{L}_3^{Lap,UNet}(\boldsymbol{\Theta},\boldsymbol{\Phi})$ is equivalent to minimizing $\mathcal{L}_3^{Lap}(\boldsymbol{\Theta},\boldsymbol{\Phi})$ while forcing the model to not learn a backcast $\mathbf{X}_{1:T}^{IB}$; instead, the bottleneck $\mathbf{Z}_{ib\_tr}$ only learns the sufficient statistics of transitioning from the prior $\mathbf{X}_{1:T}$ to the forecast $\mathbf{X}_{T+1:T+F}$. □

Appendix B. Models

Table A2. Model summary of IB-MTS for IRIS data. The encoding part has 7 successive repetitions indexed by $i \in [0:7]$ of *PConv* and *BatchNormalization* layers followed by *ReLu* activations, except when $i = 0$, no *BatchNormalization* layer is included. The decoding part has 7 successive repetitions indexed by $i \in [0:7]$ of *UpSampling*, *Concatenation*, *PConv*, and *BatchNormalization* layers followed by *ReLu* activations, except when $i = 7$, no *BatchNormalization* layer is included. EncPConv2D$_0$ is connected to [zero_pad2d$_1$, zero_pad2d$_2$]. DecUpImg$_0$ is connected to [EncReLu$_7$]. DecUpMsk$_0$ is connected to [EncPConv2D$_7$[1]]. DecConcatImg$_7$ is connected to [zero_pad2d$_1$[1], DecUpImg$_7$]. DecConcatMsk$_7$ is connected to [zero_pad2d$_2$[1], DecUpMsk$_7$].

Model: IB-MTS for IRIS Data				
Layer (Type)	Output Shape	Kernel	Param #	Connected to
inputs_img (InputLayer)	[(240, 240, 1)]	–	0	[]
inputs_mask (InputLayer)	[(240, 240, 1)]	–	0	[]
zero_pad2d$_1$ (ZeroPad2D)	(256, 256, 1)	–	0	[inputs_img]
zero_pad2d$_2$ (ZeroPad2D)	(256, 256, 1)	–	0	[inputs_mask]

Table A2. Cont.

Model: IB-MTS for IRIS Data

Layer (Type)	Output Shape	Kernel	Param #	Connected to
EncPConv2D$_i$ (PConv2D)	$i = 0$ (128,128,64)	7	18880	[EncReLu$_{i-1}$, EncPConv2D$_{i-1}$[1]]
	$i = 1$ (64, 64, 128)	5	410240	
	$i = 2$ (32, 32, 256)	5	1639168	
EncBN$_{i \neq 0}$ (BatchNorm)	$i = 3$ (16, 16, 512)	3	2361856	[EncPConv2D$_i$[0]]
	$i = 4$ (8, 8, 512)	3	4721152	
	$i = 5$ (4, 4, 512)	3	4721152	
EncReLu$_i$ (Activation)	$i = 6$ (2, 2, 512)	3	4721152	[EncBN$_i$]
	$i = 7$ (1, 1, 512)	3	4721152	
DecUpImg$_i$ (UpSampling2D)				[DecLReLU$_{i-1}$]
DecUpMsk$_i$ (UpSampling2D)	$i = 0$ (2, 2, 512)	3	9439744	[DecPConv2D$_{i-1}$[1]]
	$i = 1$ (4, 4, 512)	3	9439744	
DecConcatImg$_i$ (Concatenate)	$i = 2$ (16, 16, 512)	3	9439744	[EncReLu$_{6-i}$, DecUpImg$_i$]
	$i = 3$ (32, 32, 512)	3	9439744	
DecConcatMsk$_i$ (Concatenate)	$i = 4$ (64, 64, 256)	3	3540224	[EncPConv2D$_{6-i}$[1], DecUpMsk$_i$]
	$i = 5$ (128, 128, 128)	3	885376	
	$i = 6$ (256, 256, 64)	3	221504	
DecPConv2D$_i$ (PConv2D)	$i = 7$ (256, 256, 3)	3	3621	[DecConcatImg$_i$, DecConcatMsk$_i$]
DecBN$_{i \neq 7}$ (BatchNorm)				[DecPConv2D$_i$[0]]
DecLReLU$_i$ (LeakyReLU)				[DecBN$_i$]
outputs_img (Conv2D)	(256, 256, 1)	1	4	[DecLReLU7]
OutCrop (Cropping2D)	(240, 240, 1)	–	0	[outputs_img]
Total params: 65,724,969				

Table A3. Model summary of LSTM for the IRIS data. The ED-GRU model replaces the LSTM layer with a GRU layer consisting of 240 units and has a total of 347,040 parameters.

Model: LSTM for IRIS Data

Layer (Type)	Output Shape	Units	Param #	Connected to
inputs_seq (InputLayer)	[(240, 240)]	–	0	[]
slice$_0$ (SlicingOp)	(180, 240)	–	0	[inputs_seq]
lstm (LSTM)	(180, 240)	240	461760	[slice$_0$]
slice$_1$ (SlicingOp)	(60, 240)	–	0	[lstm]
concat (TFOp)	(240, 240)	–	0	[slice$_0$, slice$_1$]
Total params: 461,760				

Table A4. Model summary for ED-LSTM for the IRIS data. The ED-GRU model replaces the LSTM layers with GRU layers, each consisting of 100 units. The total number of parameters in the model is 164,100.

Model: ED-LSTM for IRIS Data				
Layer (Type)	Output Shape	Units	Param #	Connected to
inputs_seq (InputLayer)	[(240, 240)]	–	0	[]
slice (SlicingOp)	(180, 240)	–	0	[inputs_seq]
lstm$_0$ (LSTM)	[(180, 100), (100)]	100	136400	[slice]
lstm$_1$ (LSTM)	[(100), (100)]	100	80400	[lstm$_0$[0]]
repeat_vector (RepeatVector)	(60, 100)	–	0	[lstm$_1$[0]]
lstm$_2$ (LSTM)	(60, 100)	100	80400	[repeat_vector, lstm$_0$[0][2]]
lstm$_3$ (LSTM)	(60, 100)	100	80400	[lstm$_2$[0], lstm$_1$[1]]
time_distributed (TimeDistributed)	(60, 240)	240	24240	[lstm$_3$]
concat (TFOp)	(240, 240)	–	0	[slice, time_distributed]
Total params: 401,840				

Appendix C. Results

IRIS QS Data

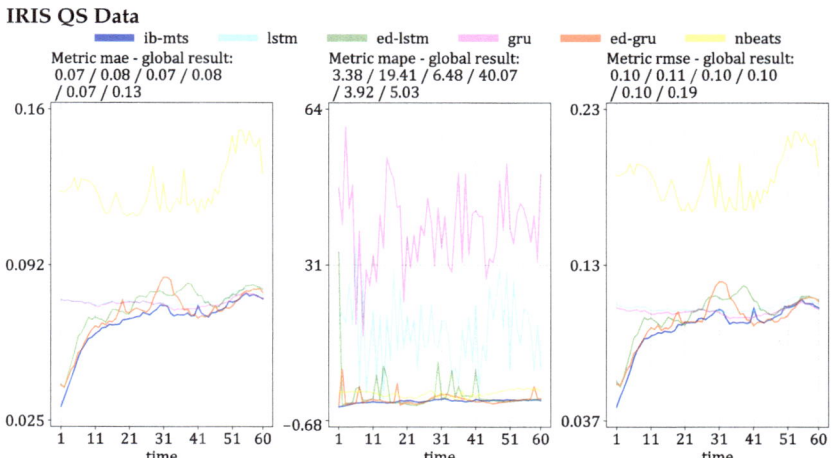

Figure A1. *Cont.*

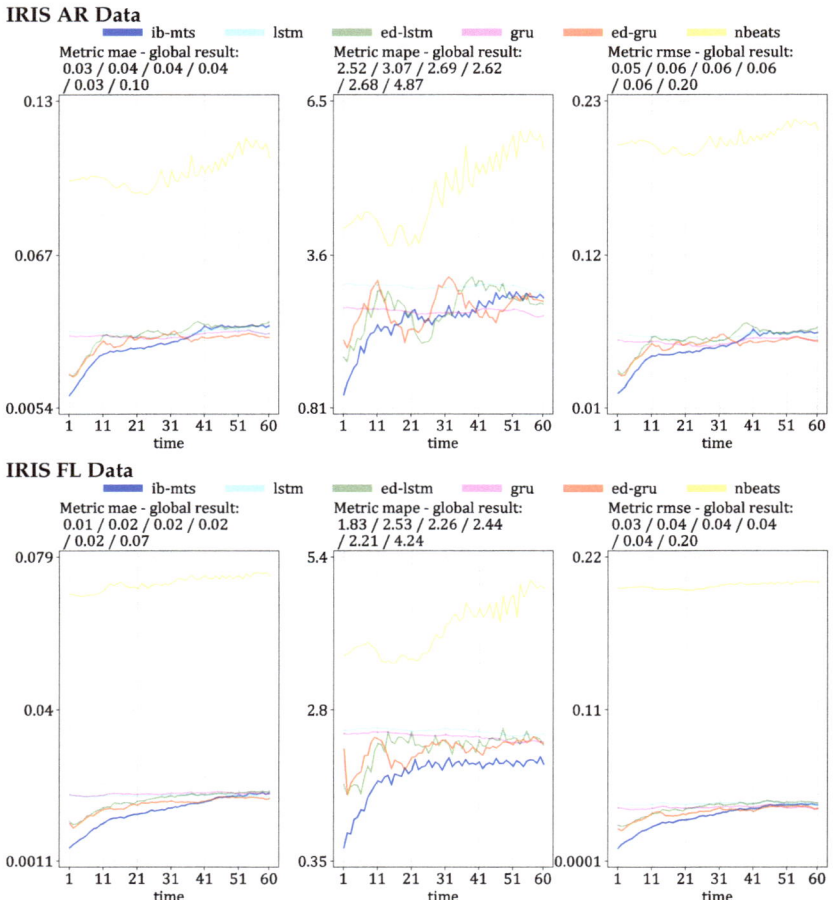

Figure A1. Detailed MTS metrics evaluation on the test set for the direct prediction setup. The evaluations are given for each solar activity: the first row of results is for QS activity, the second row is for AR, and the last row is for FL.

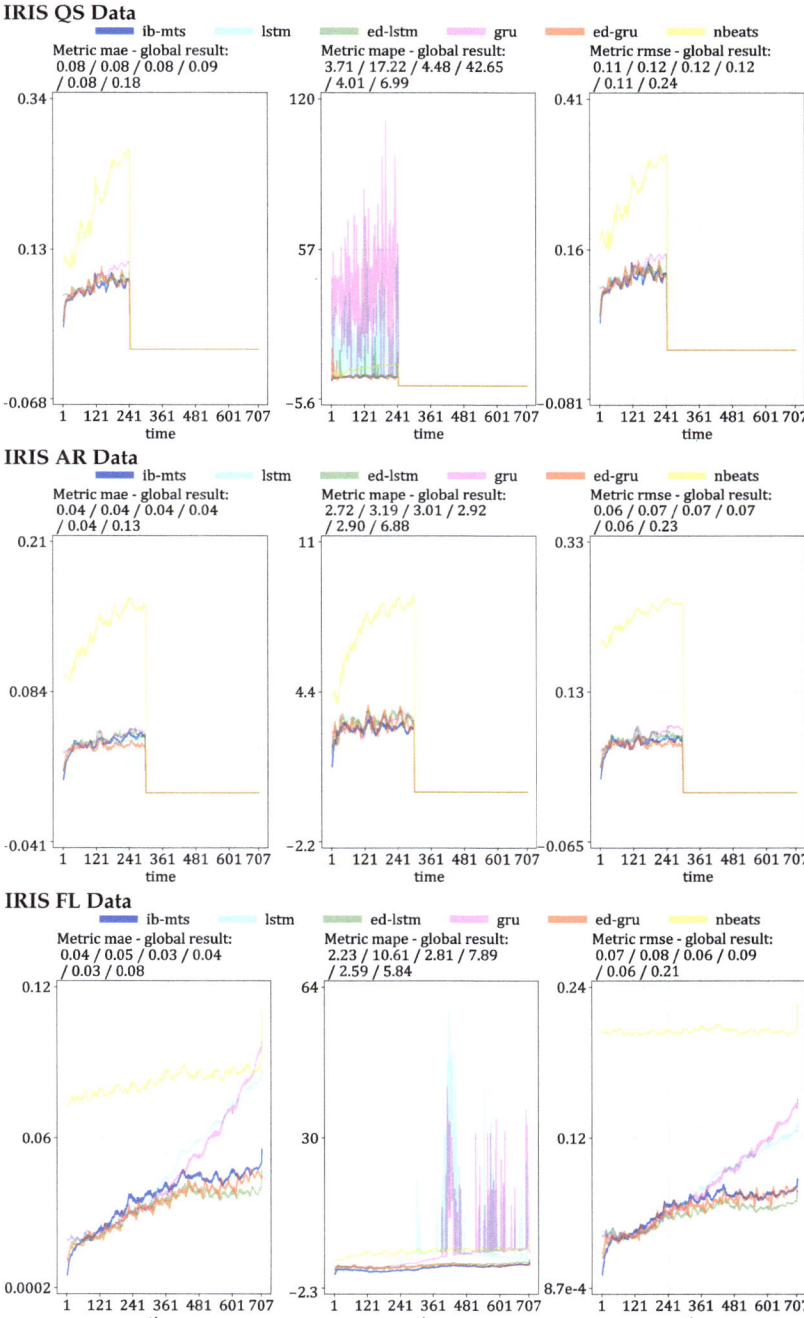

Figure A2. Detailed MTS metrics evaluation on the test set for the iterated prediction setup. The evaluations are given for each solar activity: the first row of results is for QS activity, the second row is for AR, and the last row is for FL.

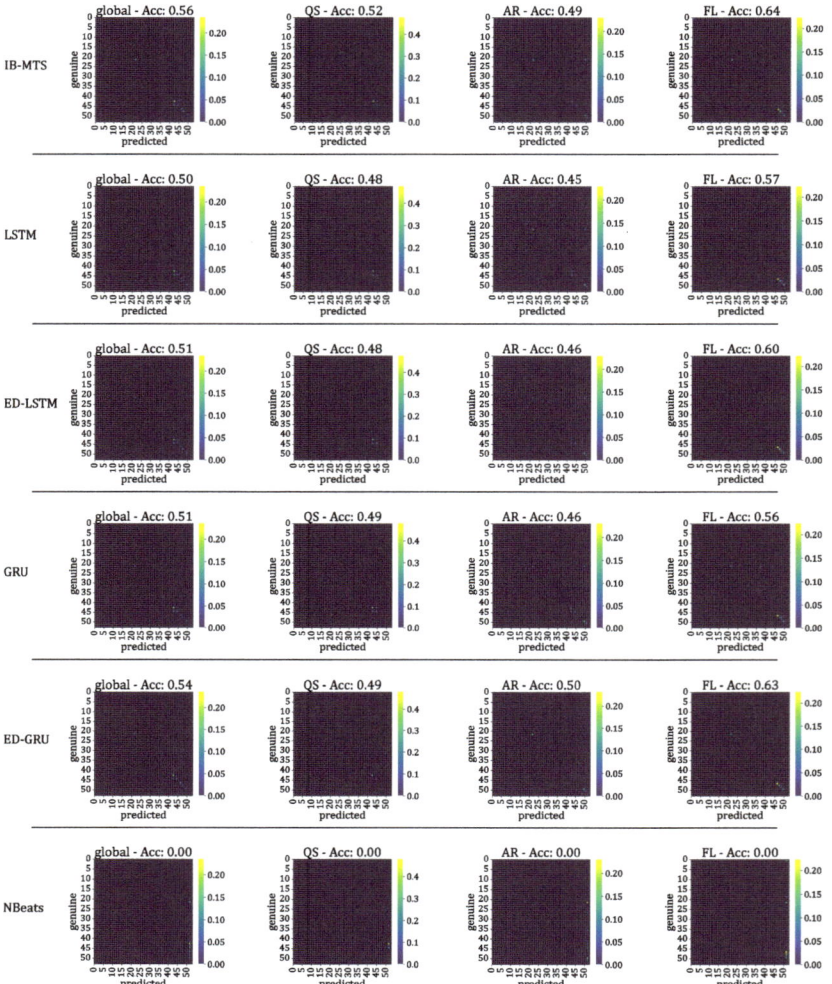

Figure A3. Confusion matrices for the prediction of centroids on IRIS data, for the direct procedure. We used the 53 centroids from [55]. Each row of results corresponds to a model. Columns are organized by data labels: *global* aggregate results for QS, AR, and FL data; other columns present the result for of each label, taken separately. Each confusion matrix gives results in terms of join probability distribution values between the genuine and the predicted. Probability values are displayed with color maps, where violet is the lowest probability and yellow is the highest.

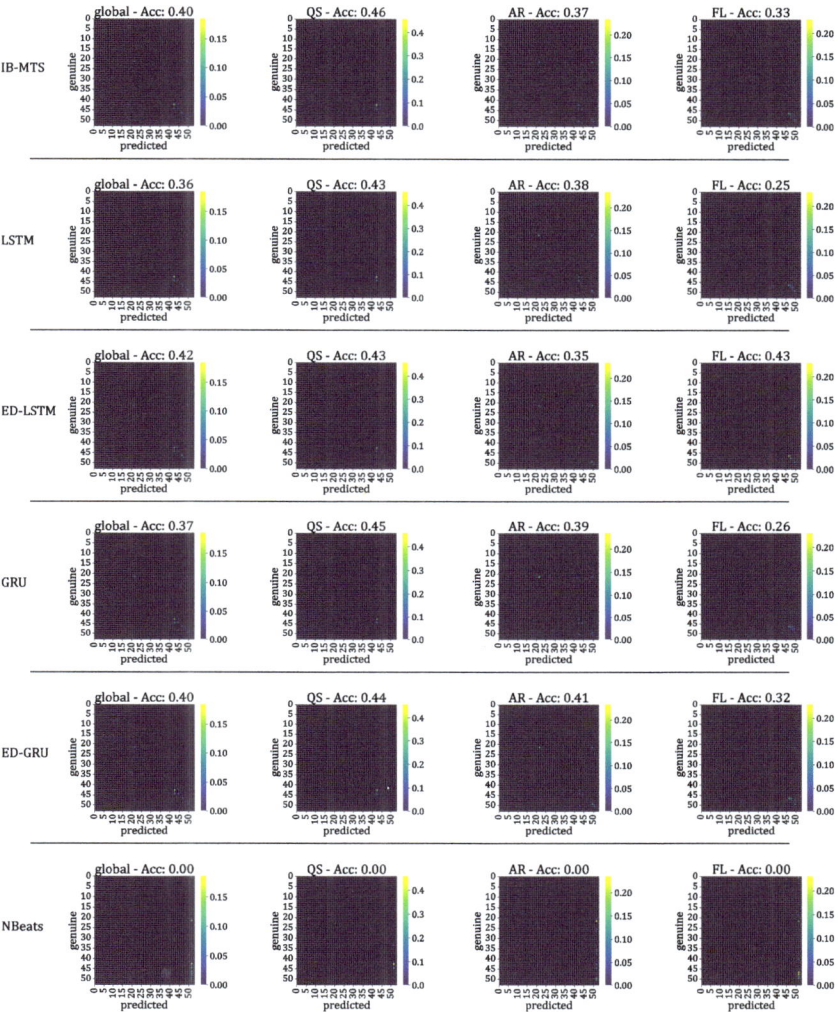

Figure A4. Confusion matrices for the prediction of centroids on IRIS data, for the iterated procedure. We used the 53 centroids from [55]. Each row of results corresponds to a model. Columns are organized by data labels: *global* aggregate results for QS, AR, and FL data; other columns present the results for of each label, taken separately. Each confusion matrix provides results in terms of join probability distribution values, between the genuine and the predicted. Probability values are displayed with color maps, where violet is the lowest probability and yellow is the highest.

References

1. Gangopadhyay, T.; Tan, S.Y.; Jiang, Z.; Meng, R.; Sarkar, S. Spatiotemporal Attention for Multivariate Time Series Prediction and Interpretation. *arXiv* **2020**, arXiv:2008.04882.
2. Flunkert, V.; Salinas, D.; Gasthaus, J. DeepAR: Probabilistic Forecasting with Autoregressive Recurrent Networks. *arXiv* **2017**, arXiv:1704.04110.
3. Oreshkin, B.N.; Carpov, D.; Chapados, N.; Bengio, Y. N-BEATS: Neural basis expansion analysis for interpretable time series forecasting. *arXiv* **2019**, arXiv:1905.10437.
4. Liu, G.; Reda, F.A.; Shih, K.J.; Wang, T.; Tao, A.; Catanzaro, B. Image Inpainting for Irregular Holes Using Partial Convolutions. *arXiv* **2018**, arXiv:1804.07723.

5. Rumelhart, D.E.; McClelland, J.L. Learning Internal Representations by Error Propagation. In *Parallel Distributed Processing: Explorations in the Microstructure of Cognition: Foundations*; The MIT Press: Cambridge, MA, USA, 1987; Volume 1, pp. 318–362.
6. Hochreiter, S.; Schmidhuber, J. Long Short-Term Memory. *Neural Comput.* **1997**, *9*, 1735–1780. [CrossRef]
7. Dobson, A. *The Oxford Dictionary of Statistical Terms*; Oxford University Press: Oxford, UK, 2003; p. 506.
8. Kendall, M. *Time Series*; Charles Griffin and Co Ltd.: London, UK; High Wycombe, UK, 1976.
9. West, M. Time Series Decomposition. *Biometrika* **1997**, *84*, 489–494. [CrossRef]
10. Sheather, S. *A Modern Approach to Regression with R*; Springer: New York, NY, USA, 2009. [CrossRef]
11. Molugaram, K.; Rao, G.S. Chapter 12—Analysis of Time Series. In *Statistical Techniques for Transportation Engineering*; Molugaram, K., Rao, G.S., Eds.; Butterworth-Heinemann: Oxford, UK, 2017; pp. 463–489. [CrossRef]
12. Gardner, E.S. Exponential smoothing: The state of the art. *J. Forecast.* **1985**, *4*, 1–28. [CrossRef]
13. Box, G.; Jenkins, G.M. *Time Series Analysis: Forecasting and Control*; Holden-Day: Cleveland, Australia, 1976.
14. Curry, H.B. The method of steepest descent for nonlinear minimization problems. *Quart. Appl. Math.* **1944**, *2*, 258–261. [CrossRef]
15. Cho, K.; van Merrienboer, B.; Bahdanau, D.; Bengio, Y. On the Properties of Neural Machine Translation: Encoder-Decoder Approaches. *arXiv* **2014**, arXiv:1409.1259.
16. Kazemi, S.M.; Goel, R.; Eghbali, S.; Ramanan, J.; Sahota, J.; Thakur, S.; Wu, S.; Smyth, C.; Poupart, P.; Brubaker, M. Time2Vec: Learning a Vector Representation of Time. *arXiv* **2019**, arXiv:1907.05321.
17. Lim, B.; Arik, S.O.; Loeff, N.; Pfister, T. Temporal Fusion Transformers for Interpretable Multi-horizon Time Series Forecasting. *arXiv* **2019**, arXiv:1912.09363.
18. Grigsby, J.; Wang, Z.; Qi, Y. Long-Range Transformers for Dynamic Spatiotemporal Forecasting. *arXiv* **2021**, arXiv:2109.12218.
19. Vaswani, A.; Shazeer, N.; Parmar, N.; Uszkoreit, J.; Jones, L.; Gomez, A.N.; Kaiser, L.; Polosukhin, I. Attention Is All You Need. *arXiv* **2021**, arXiv:1706.03762.
20. Zhou, H.; Zhang, S.; Peng, J.; Zhang, S.; Li, J.; Xiong, H.; Zhang, W. Informer: Beyond Efficient Transformer for Long Sequence Time-Series Forecasting. *arXiv* **2020**, arXiv:2012.07436.
21. Scarselli, F.; Gori, M.; Tsoi, A.C.; Hagenbuchner, M.; Monfardini, G. The Graph Neural Network Model. *IEEE Trans. Neural Netw.* **2009**, *20*, 61–80. [CrossRef] [PubMed]
22. Bertalmio, M.; Sapiro, G.; Caselles, V.; Ballester, C. Image Inpainting. In Proceedings of the 27th Annual Conference on Computer Graphics and Interactive Techniques, New Orleans, LA, USA, 23–28 July 2000; ACM Press/Addison-Wesley Publishing Co.: Boston, MA, USA, 2000; SIGGRAPH '00; pp. 417–424. [CrossRef]
23. Teterwak, P.; Sarna, A.; Krishnan, D.; Maschinot, A.; Belanger, D.; Liu, C.; Freeman, W.T. Boundless: Generative Adversarial Networks for Image Extension. *arXiv* **2019**, arXiv:1908.07007 2019.
24. Ulyanov, D.; Vedaldi, A.; Lempitsky, V. Deep Image Prior. *Int. J. Comput. Vis.* **2020**, *128*, 1867–1888. [CrossRef]
25. Dama, F.; Sinoquet, C. Time Series Analysis and Modeling to Forecast: A Survey. *arXiv* **2021**, arXiv:2104.00164.
26. Tessoni, V.; Amoretti, M. Advanced statistical and machine learning methods for multi-step multivariate time series forecasting in predictive maintenance. *Procedia Comput. Sci.* **2022**, *200*, 748–757. [CrossRef]
27. Lehtinen, J.; Munkberg, J.; Hasselgren, J.; Laine, S.; Karras, T.; Aittala, M.; Aila, T. Noise2Noise: Learning Image Restoration without Clean Data. *arXiv* **2018**, arXiv:1803.04189.
28. Gatys, L.A.; Ecker, A.S.; Bethge, M. Image Style Transfer Using Convolutional Neural Networks. In Proceedings of the 2016 IEEE Conference on Computer Vision and Pattern Recognition (CVPR), Las Vegas, NV, USA, 27–30 June 2016; pp. 2414–2423.
29. Johnson, J.; Alahi, A.; Fei-Fei, L. Perceptual Losses for Real-Time Style Transfer and Super-Resolution. *arXiv* **2016**, arXiv:1603.08155.
30. Ledig, C.; Theis, L.; Huszar, F.; Caballero, J.; Cunningham, A.; Acosta, A.; Aitken, A.; Tejani, A.; Totz, J.; Wang, Z.; et al. Photo-Realistic Single Image Super-Resolution Using a Generative Adversarial Network. *arXiv* **2016**, arXiv:1609.04802.
31. Ronneberger, O.; Fischer, P.; Brox, T. U-Net: Convolutional Networks for Biomedical Image Segmentation. *arXiv* **2015**, arXiv:1505.04597.
32. Kramer, M.A. Nonlinear principal component analysis using autoassociative neural networks. *AIChE J.* **1991**, *37*, 233–243. [CrossRef]
33. Tishby, N.; Zaslavsky, N. Deep Learning and the Information Bottleneck Principle. *arXiv* **2015**, arXiv:1503.02406.
34. Costa, J.; Costa, A.; Kenda, K.; Costa, J.P. Entropy for Time Series Forecasting. In Proceedings of the Slovenian KDD Conference, Ljubljana, Slovenia, 4 October 2021. Available online: https://ailab.ijs.si/dunja/SiKDD2021/Papers/Costaetal_2.pdf (accessed on 20 February 2023).
35. Zapart, C.A. Forecasting with Entropy. In Proceedings of the Econophysics Colloquium, Taipei, Taiwan, 4–6 November 2010. Available online: https://www.phys.sinica.edu.tw/~socioecono/econophysics2010/pdfs/ZapartPaper.pdf (accessed on 20 February 2023).
36. Xu, D.; Fekri, F. Time Series Prediction Via Recurrent Neural Networks with the Information Bottleneck Principle. In Proceedings of the 2018 IEEE 19th International Workshop on Signal Processing Advances in Wireless Communications (SPAWC), Kalamata, Greece, 25–28 June 2018; pp. 1–5. [CrossRef]
37. Ponce-Flores, M.; Frausto-Solís, J.; Santamaría-Bonfil, G.; Pérez-Ortega, J.; González-Barbosa, J.J. Time Series Complexities and Their Relationship to Forecasting Performance. *Entropy* **2020**, *22*, 89. [CrossRef] [PubMed]

38. Zaidi, A.; Estella-Aguerri, I.; Shamai (Shitz), S. On the Information Bottleneck Problems: Models, Connections, Applications and Information Theoretic Views. *Entropy* **2020**, *22*, 151. [CrossRef] [PubMed]
39. Voloshynovskiy, S.; Kondah, M.; Rezaeifar, S.; Taran, O.; Holotyak, T.; Rezende, D.J. Information bottleneck through variational glasses. *arXiv* **2019**, arXiv:1912.00830.
40. Alemi, A.A.; Fischer, I.; Dillon, J.V.; Murphy, K. Deep Variational Information Bottleneck. *arXiv* **2016**, arXiv:1612.00410.
41. Ullmann, D.; Rezaeifar, S.; Taran, O.; Holotyak, T.; Panos, B.; Voloshynovskiy, S. Information Bottleneck Classification in Extremely Distributed Systems. *Entropy* **2020**, *22*, 237. [CrossRef]
42. Geiger, B.C.; Kubin, G. Information Bottleneck: Theory and Applications in Deep Learning. *Entropy* **2020**, *22*, 1408. [CrossRef] [PubMed]
43. Lee, S.; Jo, J. Information Flows of Diverse Autoencoders. *Entropy* **2021**, *23*, 862. [CrossRef]
44. Tapia, N.I.; Estévez, P.A. On the Information Plane of Autoencoders. In Proceedings of the 2020 International Joint Conference on Neural Networks (IJCNN), Glasgow, UK, 19–24 July 2020; pp. 1–8. [CrossRef]
45. Zarcone, R.; Paiton, D.; Anderson, A.; Engel, J.; Wong, H.P.; Olshausen, B. Joint Source-Channel Coding with Neural Networks for Analog Data Compression and Storage. In Proceedings of the 2018 Data Compression Conference, Snowbird, UT, USA, 27–30 March 2018; pp. 147–156. [CrossRef]
46. Boquet, G.; Macias, E.; Morell, A.; Serrano, J.; Vicario, J.L. Theoretical Tuning of the Autoencoder Bottleneck Layer Dimension: A Mutual Information-based Algorithm. In Proceedings of the 2020 28th European Signal Processing Conference (EUSIPCO), Amsterdam, The Netherlands, 18–21 January 2021; pp. 1512–1516. [CrossRef]
47. Voloshynovskiy, S.; Taran, O.; Kondah, M.; Holotyak, T.; Rezende, D. Variational Information Bottleneck for Semi-Supervised Classification. *Entropy* **2020**, *22*, 943. [CrossRef]
48. Shannon, C.E. A mathematical theory of communication. *Bell Syst. Tech. J.* **1948**, *27*, 379–423. [CrossRef]
49. Barnes, G.; Leka, K.D.; Schrijver, C.J.; Colak, T.; Qahwaji, R.; Ashamari, O.W.; Yuan, Y.; Zhang, J.; McAteer, R.T.J.; Bloomfield, D.S.; et al. A comparison of flare forecasting methods. *Astrophys. J.* **2016**, *829*, 89. [CrossRef]
50. Guennou, C.; Pariat, E.; Leake, J.E.; Vilmer, N. Testing predictors of eruptivity using parametric flux emergence simulations. *J. Space Weather Space Clim.* **2017**, *7*, A17. [CrossRef]
51. Benvenuto, F.; Piana, M.; Campi, C.; Massone, A.M. A Hybrid Supervised/Unsupervised Machine Learning Approach to Solar Flare Prediction. *Astrophys. J.* **2018**, *853*, 90. [CrossRef]
52. Florios, K.; Kontogiannis, I.; Park, S.H.; Guerra, J.A.; Benvenuto, F.; Bloomfield, D.S.; Georgoulis, M.K. Forecasting Solar Flares Using Magnetogram-based Predictors and Machine Learning. *Sol. Phys.* **2018**, *293*, 28. [CrossRef]
53. Kontogiannis, I.; Georgoulis, M.K.; Park, S.H.; Guerra, J.A. Testing and Improving a Set of Morphological Predictors of Flaring Activity. *Sol. Phys.* **2018**, *293*, 96. [CrossRef]
54. Ullmann, D.; Voloshynovskiy, S.; Kleint, L.; Krucker, S.; Melchior, M.; Huwyler, C.; Panos, B. DCT-Tensor-Net for Solar Flares Detection on IRIS Data. In Proceedings of the 2018 7th European Workshop on Visual Information Processing (EUVIP), Tampere, Finland, 26–28 November 2018; pp. 1–6. [CrossRef]
55. Panos, B.; Kleint, L.; Huwyler, C.; Krucker, S.; Melchior, M.; Ullmann, D.; Voloshynovskiy, S. Identifying Typical Mg ii Flare Spectra Using Machine Learning. *Astrophys. J.* **2018**, *861*, 62. [CrossRef]
56. Murray, S.A.; Bingham, S.; Sharpe, M.; Jackson, D.R. Flare forecasting at the Met Office Space Weather Operations Centre. *Space Weather* **2017**, *15*, 577–588.
57. Sharpe, M.A.; Murray, S.A. Verification of Space Weather Forecasts Issued by the Met Office Space Weather Operations Centre. *Space Weather* **2017**, *15*, 1383–1395.
58. Chen, Y.; Manchester, W.B.; Hero, A.O.; Toth, G.; DuFumier, B.; Zhou, T.; Wang, X.; Zhu, H.; Sun, Z.; Gombosi, T.I. Identifying Solar Flare Precursors Using Time Series of SDO/HMI Images and SHARP Parameters. *arXiv* **2019**, arXiv:1904.00125.
59. Li, Y.; Yu, R.; Shahabi, C.; Liu, Y. Graph Convolutional Recurrent Neural Network: Data-Driven Traffic Forecasting. *arXiv* **2017**, arXiv:1707.01926.
60. Yu, B.; Yin, H.; Zhu, Z. Spatio-temporal Graph Convolutional Neural Network: A Deep Learning Framework for Traffic Forecasting. *arXiv* **2017**, arXiv:1709.04875.
61. Yu, J.; Lin, Z.; Yang, J.; Shen, X.; Lu, X.; Huang, T.S. Free-Form Image Inpainting with Gated Convolution. *arXiv* **2018**, arXiv:1806.03589.
62. Gatys, L.A.; Ecker, A.S.; Bethge, M. A Neural Algorithm of Artistic Style. *arXiv* **2015**, arXiv:1508.06576.
63. Wang, C.; Xu, C.; Wang, C.; Tao, D. Perceptual Adversarial Networks for Image-to-Image Transformation. *IEEE Trans. Image Process.* **2018**, *27*, 4066–4079. [CrossRef] [PubMed]
64. Simonyan, K.; Zisserman, A. Very Deep Convolutional Networks for Large-Scale Image Recognition. *arXiv* **2014**, arXiv:1409.1556.
65. Kobyzev, I.; Prince, S.J.; Brubaker, M.A. Normalizing Flows: An Introduction and Review of Current Methods. *IEEE Trans. Pattern Anal. Mach. Intell.* **2021**, *43*, 3964–3979. [CrossRef] [PubMed]
66. Bao, H.; Dong, L.; Piao, S.; Wei, F. BEiT: BERT Pre-Training of Image Transformers. *arXiv* **2022**, arXiv:2106.08254.
67. Xie, Z.; Zhang, Z.; Cao, Y.; Lin, Y.; Bao, J.; Yao, Z.; Dai, Q.; Hu, H. SimMIM: A Simple Framework for Masked Image Modeling. *arXiv* **2022**, arXiv:111.09886.
68. He, K.; Chen, X.; Xie, S.; Li, Y.; Dollár, P.; Girshick, R. Masked Autoencoders Are Scalable Vision Learners. *arXiv* **2021**, arXiv:2111.06377.

69. Pontieu, B.D.; Lemen, J. *IRIS Technical Note 1: IRIS Operations*; Version 17; LMSAL, NASA: Washington, DC, USA, 2013.
70. LMSAL. *A User's Guide to IRIS Data Retrieval, Reduction & Analysis*; Release 1.0; LMSAL, NASA: Washington, DC, USA, 2019.
71. Gošic, M.; Dalda, A.S.; Chintzoglou, G. *Optically Thick Diagnostics*; Release 1.0 ed.; LMSAL, NASA: Washington, DC, USA, 2018.
72. Panos, B.; Kleint, L. Real-time Flare Prediction Based on Distinctions between Flaring and Non-flaring Active Region Spectra. *Astrophys. J.* **2020**, *891*, 17. [CrossRef]
73. Gherrity, M. A learning algorithm for analog, fully recurrent neural networks. In Proceedings of the International 1989 Joint Conference on Neural Networks, Washington, DC, USA, 16–18 October 1989; Volume 1, pp. 643–644.
74. Li, Y.; Yu, R.; Shahabi, C.; Liu, Y. Diffusion Convolutional Recurrent Neural Network: Data-Driven Traffic Forecasting. In Proceedings of the International Conference on Learning Representations (ICLR '18), Vancouver, BC, Canada, 30 April–3 May 2018.
75. California, S.o. Performance Measurement System (PeMS) Data Source. Available online: https://pems.dot.ca.gov/ (accessed on 20 February 2023).
76. Hanssen, A.; Kuipers, W. On the relationship between the frequency of rain and various meteorological parameters. *Meded. En Verh.* **1965**, *81*, 3–15. Available online: https://cdn.knmi.nl/knmi/pdf/bibliotheek/knmipubmetnummer/knmipub102-81.pdf (accessed on 20 February 2023).
77. Heidke, P. Berechnung des Erfolges und der Gute der Windstarkevorhersagen im Sturmwarnungsdienst (Measures of success and goodness of wind force forecasts by the gale-warning service). *Geogr. Ann.* **1926**, *8*, 301–349.
78. Cohen, J. A coefficient of agreement for nominal scales. *Educ. Psychol. Meas.* **1960**, *20*, 213–220. [CrossRef]
79. Allouche, O.; Tsoar, A.; Kadmon, R. Assessing the accuracy of species distribution models: Prevalence, kappa and the true skill statistic (TSS). *J. Appl. Ecol.* **2006**, *43*, 1223–1232. .: 10.1111/j.1365-2664.2006.01214.x. [CrossRef]
80. Liu, M.; Zeng, A.; Chen, M.; Xu, Z.; Lai, Q.; Ma, L.; Xu, Q. SCINet: Time Series Modeling and Forecasting with Sample Convolution and Interaction. *arXiv* **2022**, arXiv:2106.09305.
81. Shao, Z.; Zhang, Z.; Wang, F.; Xu, Y. Pre-Training Enhanced Spatial-Temporal Graph Neural Network for Multivariate Time Series Forecasting. In Proceedings of the 28th ACM SIGKDD Conference on Knowledge Discovery and Data Mining, Washington, DC, USA, 14–18 August 2022; Association for Computing Machinery: New York, NY, USA, 2022; KDD '22; pp. 1567–1577. [CrossRef]
82. Cho, K.; van Merrienboer, B.; Gulcehre, C.; Bahdanau, D.; Bougares, F.; Schwenk, H.; Bengio, Y. Learning Phrase Representations using RNN Encoder-Decoder for Statistical Machine Translation. *arXiv* **2014**, arXiv:1406.1078.
83. Sutskever, I.; Vinyals, O.; Le, Q.V. Sequence to Sequence Learning with Neural Networks. *arXiv* **2014**, arXiv:1409.3215.
84. Wang, Z.; Bovik, A.; Sheikh, H.; Simoncelli, E. Image quality assessment: From error visibility to structural similarity. *IEEE Trans. Image Process.* **2004**, *13*, 600–612. [CrossRef] [PubMed]

Disclaimer/Publisher's Note: The statements, opinions and data contained in all publications are solely those of the individual author(s) and contributor(s) and not of MDPI and/or the editor(s). MDPI and/or the editor(s) disclaim responsibility for any injury to people or property resulting from any ideas, methods, instructions or products referred to in the content.

Article

Deep Individual Active Learning: Safeguarding against Out-of-Distribution Challenges in Neural Networks

Shachar Shayovitz *,†, **Koby Bibas** † and **Meir Feder**

School of Electrical Engineering, Tel Aviv University, Tel Aviv 6997801, Israel; kobybibas@gmail.com (K.B.); meir@tauex.tau.ac.il (M.F.)
* Correspondence: shachar.shay@gmail.com
† These authors contributed equally to this work.

Abstract: Active learning (AL) is a paradigm focused on purposefully selecting training data to enhance a model's performance by minimizing the need for annotated samples. Typically, strategies assume that the training pool shares the same distribution as the test set, which is not always valid in privacy-sensitive applications where annotating user data is challenging. In this study, we operate within an individual setting and leverage an active learning criterion which selects data points for labeling based on minimizing the min-max regret on a small unlabeled test set sample. Our key contribution lies in the development of an efficient algorithm, addressing the challenging computational complexity associated with approximating this criterion for neural networks. Notably, our results show that, especially in the presence of out-of-distribution data, the proposed algorithm substantially reduces the required training set size by up to 15.4%, 11%, and 35.1% for CIFAR10, EMNIST, and MNIST datasets, respectively.

Keywords: active learning; universal prediction; deep active learning; individual sequences; normalized maximum likelihood; out-of-distribution

Citation: Shayovitz, S.; Bibas, K.; Feder, M. Deep Individual Active Learning: Safeguarding against Out-of-Distribution Challenges in Neural Networks. *Entropy* **2024**, *26*, 129. https://doi.org/10.3390/e26020129

Academic Editors: Badong Chen, Luis Gonzalo Sánchez Giraldo, Shuangming Yang and Shujian Yu

Received: 27 December 2023
Revised: 28 January 2024
Accepted: 30 January 2024
Published: 31 January 2024

Copyright: © 2024 by the authors. Licensee MDPI, Basel, Switzerland. This article is an open access article distributed under the terms and conditions of the Creative Commons Attribution (CC BY) license (https://creativecommons.org/licenses/by/4.0/).

1. Introduction

In supervised learning, a training set is provided to a learner, which can then be used to choose parameters for a model that minimize the error on this set. The process of creating this training set requires annotation, where an expert labels the data points. This is a time-consuming and costly process and results in only a small subset of the data being labeled, which may not represent the true underlying model [1]. Active learning, where the training data are actively and purposely chosen, allows the learner to interact with a labeling expert by sequentially selecting samples for the expert to label based on previously observed data, thereby reducing the number of examples needed to achieve a given accuracy level [2].

Recent research has focused on obtaining a diverse set of samples for training deep learning models with reduced sampling bias. The strategies in [3–6] aim to quantify the uncertainties of samples from the unlabeled pool and utilize them to select a sample for annotation. A widely used criterion for active learning is Bayesian Active Learning by Disagreement (BALD), which was originally proposed by Houlsby et al. [3]. This method finds the unlabeled sample $\hat{x}_i$ that maximizes the mutual information between the model parameters θ and the candidate label random variable Y_i given the candidate x_i and training set $z^{n-1} = \{(x_i, y_i)\}_{i=1}^{n-1}$:

$$\hat{x}_i = \underset{x_i}{\operatorname{argmax}}\, I(\theta; Y_i | x_i, z^{n-1}) \qquad (1)$$

where $I(X; Y|z)$ denotes the mutual information between the random variables X and Y conditioned on a realization z. The idea in BALD's core is to minimize the uncertainty about model parameters using Shannon's entropy. This criterion also appears as an upper bound on information-based complexity of stochastic optimization [7] and also for experimental design [8,9]. There is an issue of postulating a reasonable prior for this Bayesian approach. Empirically, this approach was investigated by Gal et al. [4], where a heuristic Bayesian method for deep learning was proposed, leading to several heuristic active learning acquisition functions that were explored within this framework.

However, BALD has a fundamental disadvantage if the test distribution differs from the training set distribution, since what is maximally informative for model estimation may not be maximally informative for test time prediction. In a previous work, Shayovitz and Feder [6] derived a criterion named Universal Active Learning (UAL) that takes into account the unlabeled test set when optimizing the training set:

$$\hat{x}_i = \underset{x_i}{\arg\min}\ I(\theta; Y|X, x_i, Y_i, z^{n-1}) \qquad (2)$$

where X and Y are the test feature and label random variables. UAL is derived from a capacity–redundancy theorem [10] and implicitly optimizes an exploration–exploitation trade-off in feature selection. In addition, in the derivation of [10], the prior on θ is expressed as the capacity-maximizing distribution for $I(\theta; Y|X, x_i, Y_i, z^{n-1})$. It should be noted that Smith et al. [11] have recently proposed a criterion denoted Expected Predictive Information Gain (EPIG) which also takes into account the unlabelled test set and focuses on prediction and not model estimation (In Appendix A, it is proven that EPIG is equivalent to UAL, but unlike EPIG, which does not optimize the model prior, UAL provides an expression for the optimal model prior.):

$$\hat{x}_i = \underset{x_i}{\arg\max}\ I(Y; Y_i|X, x_i, z^{n-1}) \qquad (3)$$

However, the above-mentioned AL schemes assume that both training and test data follow a conditional distribution which belongs to a given parametric hypothesis class, $\{p(y|x,\theta)\}$. This assumption cannot be verified on real-world data, particularly in privacy-sensitive applications where real user data cannot be annotated [12] and the unlabeled pool may contain irrelevant information. In such cases, choosing samples from the unlabeled pool may not necessarily improve model performance on the test set. As an alternative to making distributional assumptions, we build upon the *individual setting* [13]. This setting does not assume any probabilistic connection between the training and test data. Moreover, the relationship between labels and data can even be determined by an adversary. The generalization error in this setting is known as the *regret* [14], which is defined as the log-loss difference between a learner and a *genie*: a learner that knows the specific test label but is constrained to use an explanation from a set of hypotheses. The predictive Normalized Maximum Likelihood (pNML) learner [14] was proposed as the min-max solution of the regret, where the minimum is over the learner choice and the maximum is for any possible test label value. The pNML was previously developed for linear regression [15] and was evaluated empirically for DNN [16].

The setting considered in this work, i.e., active learning with no distributional assumption, is related to the active online learning literature [17,18], which deals primarily with task-agnostic learning that does not assume a connection between the training and test tasks. The research in Yoo and Kweon [17] proposed an active learning method that works efficiently with deep networks. A small parametric module, named "loss prediction module", is attached to a target network, and learns it to predict target losses of unlabeled inputs. Then, this module can suggest data for which the target model is likely to produce a wrong prediction. This method is task-agnostic, as networks are learned from a single loss regardless of target tasks. The research in Sinha et al. [18] suggested a pool-based semi-supervised active learning algorithm that implicitly learns a sampling mechanism in an adversarial manner. Unlike conventional active learning algorithms, this approach is task-agnostic, i.e., it does not depend on the performance of the task for which we are trying to acquire labeled data. This method learns a latent space using a variational autoencoder

(VAE) and an adversarial network trained to discriminate between unlabeled and labeled data. The minimax game between the VAE and the adversarial network is played such that while the VAE tries to trick the adversarial network into predicting that all data points are from the labeled pool, the adversarial network learns how to discriminate between dissimilarities in the latent space.

Moreover, as an additional incentive for the individual setting, in scenarios involving Out-Of-Distribution (OOD) data, the application of uncertainty-based Active Learning (AL) without meticulous consideration may increase the likelihood of selecting OOD samples for labeling, surpassing the selection of in-distribution (IND) data. OOD data typically demonstrate high uncertainty, leading the AL algorithm to preferentially choose such samples for labeling, thereby inefficiently utilizing the labeling budget. Consequently, there is an urgent need for active learning methods resilient to such scenarios.

While empirical evidence has demonstrated the real-life impact of the OOD problem on AL [19], there is a scarcity of research addressing this crucial issue. The research in Kothawade et al. [20] approached OOD as a sub-task, and its sub-modular mutual information-based sampling scheme is marked by both time and memory consumption. In contrast, Du et al. [21] mandated the pre-training of additional self-supervised models like SimCLR [22], introducing hyperparameters to balance semantic and distinctive scores. The values of these hyperparameters exert a significant influence on the final performance, thereby limiting the broader applicability of the proposed approach.

In addition to the challenges highlighted in the aforementioned context, another promising avenue of research explores counterfactual training [23] to enhance OOD generalization. This approach involves learning model parameters by comparing pairs of factual samples and counterfactual samples, illustrating how changes in features lead to changes in labels. Notably, modifications to causal features and labels disrupt spurious correlations, as non-causal features are present in both factual and counterfactual samples with distinct classes [24]. Through counterfactual training, the model avoids relying on spurious correlations for predictions, enhancing its ability for OOD generalization [24,25]. This approach effectively breaks the link between non-causal features and labels, contributing to an improved OOD generalization capability. Nevertheless, counterfactual learning may be considered less feasible, as generating meaningful counterfactual samples requires sufficient and representative data, which may be challenging to obtain in some cases, especially if the dataset is limited or biased.

The research in Shayovitz and Feder [26] proposed an active learning criterion for the individual setting that takes into account a trained model, the unlabeled pool, and a small set of unlabeled test features. This criterion, denoted IAL (Individual Active Learning), is designed to select a sample to be labeled in such a way that, when added to the training set with its worst-case label, it attains the minimal pNML regret for the test set. The algorithm proposed by Shayovitz and Feder [26] for Gaussian Process Classification is based on an Expectation Propagation approximation of the model posterior. This approximation is both computationally expensive for large-scale deep neural networks (DNNs) and does not provide good enough performance in empirical tests. The computational complexity associated with the re-training for each candidate sample is extremely demanding.

Main Contributions

Our contributions can be succinctly outlined as follows:

- In this investigation, we address AL in the presence of OOD challenges by utilizing a small unlabeled sample from the test distribution. We focus on the individual data setting and leverage an existing active learning criterion [26]. However, the computation of this criterion is deemed impractical for DNNs.
- Our primary contribution lies in the development of an efficient algorithm aimed at mitigating the challenging computational complexity associated with approximating the mentioned criterion for neural networks. Termed DIAL (Deep Individual Ac-

tive Learning), this algorithm facilitates faster and more practical implementation of Individual Active Learning (IAL) for DNNs.
- We demonstrate that, in the presence of OOD samples, our algorithm requires only 66.2%, 91.9%, and 77.2% of labeled samples compared to recent leading methods for CIFAR10 [27], EMNIST [28], and MNIST [29] datasets, respectively, for the same accuracy level. When considering only IND samples, our approach necessitates 64.9%, 99.0%, and 64.9% labeled samples on the aforementioned datasets.
- In OOD scenarios, DIAL does not rely on the annotator to provide semantic information or counterfactual examples. The criterion is universally applicable across various datasets and can be implemented immediately.

This paper is organized as follows. In Section 2, the individual learning setting is introduced and the pNML is reviewed. In Section 3, IAL is presented and motivated by the minimax regret problem discussed in the previous section. In Section 4, IAL is applied to the DNN hypothesis class and a novel low-complexity algorithm denoted as DIAL is presented. In Section 5, the performance of DIAL is analyzed in comparison with state-of-the-art deep active learning algorithms. Throughout this paper, a sequence of samples will be denoted $x^n = (x_1, x_2, \ldots, x_n)$. The variables $x \in \mathbb{X}$ and $y \in \mathbb{Y}$ will represent the features and labels, respectively, with $\mathbb{X}$ and $\mathbb{Y}$ being the sets containing the features' and labels' alphabets, respectively.

2. The Individual Data Setting

In the supervised learning framework, a training set consisting of n pairs of examples is provided to the learner:

$$z^n = \{(x_i, y_i)\}_{i=1}^n \quad (4)$$

where x_i is the i-th data point and y_i is its corresponding label. The goal of a learner is to predict an unknown test label y given its test data, x, by assigning a probability distribution $q(\cdot|x, z^n)$ for each training set z^n.

In the commonly used stochastic setting as defined in [13], the data follow a distribution assumed to be part of some parametric family of hypotheses. A more general framework, named *individual setting* [13], does not assume that there exists some probabilistic relation between a feature x and a label y, and so the sequence $z^n = \{x^n, y^n\}$ is an individual sequence where the relation can even be set by an adversary. Since there is no distribution over the data, finding the optimal learner, $q(\cdot|x, z^n)$, is an ill-posed problem. In order to mitigate this problem, an alternative objective is proposed: find a learner $q(\cdot|x, z^n)$ which performs as well as a reference learner on the test set.

Denote Θ as a general index set. Let P_Θ be a set of conditional probability distributions:

$$P_\Theta = \{p(y|x, \theta) | \theta \in \Theta\} \quad (5)$$

It is assumed that the reference learner knows the test label value y but is restricted to using a model from the given hypothesis set P_Θ. This reference learner then chooses a model, $\hat{\theta}(x, y, z^n)$, that attains the minimum loss over the training set and the test sample:

$$\hat{\theta} = \arg\max_{\theta \in \Theta}[p(y|x, \theta)w(\theta)\Pi_{i=1}^n p(y_i|x_i, \theta)] \quad (6)$$

where performance is evaluated using the log-loss function, i.e., $-\log(q(\cdot|x, z^n))$.

Note that, in this work, we extended the individual setting of [30] and allowed the usage of some prior $w(\theta)$ over the parameter space, which may be useful for regularization purposes. The learning problem is defined as the log-loss difference between a learner q and the reference learner (genie):

$$R_n(q, y; x) = \log \frac{p(y|x, \hat{\theta})}{q(y|x, z^n)}. \quad (7)$$

An important result for this setting is provided in Fogel and Feder [14] and provides a closed-form expression for the minimax regret along with the optimal learner, q_{pNML}:

Theorem 1 (Fogel and Feder [14]). *The universal learner, denoted as the pNML, minimizes the worst case regret:*

$$R_n(x) = \min_q \max_{y \in \mathbb{Y}} \log\left(\frac{p(y|x,\hat{\theta})}{q(y|x,z^n)}\right)$$

The pNML probability assignment and regret are:

$$q_{pNML}(y|x,z^n) = \frac{p(y|x,\hat{\theta})}{\sum_y p(y|x,\hat{\theta})}$$

$$R_n(x) = \log \sum_{y \in \mathbb{Y}} p(y|x,\hat{\theta})$$

Since the main contribution of this work relies on this theorem, we provide a short proof here:

Proof. We note that the regret, $R_n(x)$, is equal for all choices of y. Now, if we consider a different probability assignment, then it would assign a smaller probability for at least one of the possible outcomes. In this case, choosing one of those outcomes will lead to a higher regret and then the maximal regret will be higher, leading to a contradiction. □

The pNML regret is associated with the *stochastic complexity* of a hypothesis class, as discussed by Rosas et al. [31] and Zhou and Levine [16]. It is clear that for pNML, a model that fits almost every data pattern would be much more complex than a model that provides a relatively good fit to a small set of data. Thus, high pNML regret indicates that the model class may be too expressive and overfit. The pNML learner is the min-max solution for supervised batch learning in the individual setting [14]. For sequential prediction it is termed the conditional normalized maximum likelihood [32,33].

Several methods deal with obtaining the pNML learner for different hypothesis sets. The research in Bibas et al. [15] and Bibas and Feder [34] showed the pNML solution for linear regression. The research in Rosas et al. [35] proposed an NML-based decision strategy for supervised classification problems and showed that it attains heuristic PAC learning. The research in Fu and Levine [36] used the pNML for model optimization based on learning a density function by discretizing the space and fitting a distinct model for each value. For the DNN hypothesis set, Bibas et al. [37] estimated the pNML distribution with DNN by fine-tuning the last layers of the network for every test input and label combination. This approach is computationally expensive since training is needed for every test input. The research in Zhou and Levine [16] suggested a way to accelerate the pNML computation in DNN by using approximate Bayesian inference techniques to produce a tractable approximation to the pNML.

3. Active Learning for Individual Data

In active learning, the learner sequentially selects data instances x_i based on some criterion and produces n training examples: z^n. The objective is to select a subset of the unlabelled pool and derive a probabilistic learner $q(y|x,z^n)$ that attains the minimal prediction error (on the test set) among all training sets of the same size. Most selection criteria are based on uncertainty quantification of data instances to quantify their informativeness. However, in the individual setting, there is no natural uncertainty measure, since there is no distribution governing the data.

As proposed in [26], the min-max regret R_n as defined in Theorem 1 is used as an active learning criterion, which essentially quantifies the prediction performance of the training set z^n for a given unlabeled test feature x. A "good" z^n minimizes the min-max regret for any test feature and thus provides good test set performance. Since R_n is a point-wise quantity, the average over all test data is taken:

$$C_n = \min_{x^n} \max_{y^n} \sum_x \log\left(\sum_y p(y|x,\hat{\theta})\right) \tag{8}$$

where $\hat{\theta} = \hat{\theta}(x, y, z^n)$ is the Maximum Likelihood estimator, as defined in (6).

The idea is to find a set of training points, x^n, that minimizes the averaged log normalization factor (across unlabeled test points) for the worst possible labels y^n. This criterion looks for the worst-case scenario since there is no assumption on the data distribution. Since (8) selects a batch of points x^n, it is computationally prohibitive to solve for a general hypothesis class. In order to reduce complexity, a greedy approach denoted Individual Active Learning (IAL) is proposed in [26] which performs well empirically:

$$C_{n|n-1} = \min_{x_n} \max_{y_n} \sum_x \log\left(\sum_y p(y|x,\hat{\theta})\right) \tag{9}$$

Note that when computing (9), the previously labeled training set, z^{n-1}, is assumed to be available for the learner and $\hat{\theta} = \hat{\theta}(x, y, x_n, y_n, z^{n-1})$. The objective in (9) is to find a single point x_n from the unlabelled pool as opposed to the objective in (8) that tries to find an optimal batch x^n.

4. Deep Individual Active Learning

The DNN (deep neural network) hypothesis class poses a challenging problem for information-theoretic active learning since its parameter space is of very high dimension and the weights' posterior distribution (assuming a Bayesian setting) is analytically intractable. Moreover, direct application of deep active learning schemes is unfeasible for real-world large-scale data, since it requires training the entire model for each possible training point. To make matters worse, for IAL, the network also needs to be trained for every test point and every possible corresponding label.

In this section, we derive an approximation of IAL for DNNs which is based on variational inference algorithms [4,38,39]. We define the hypothesis class in this case as follows:

$$p(y|x,\theta) = softmax(f_\theta(x)) \tag{10}$$

where θ represents all the weights and biases of the network and $f_\theta(x)$ is the model output before the last softmax layer. Note that x, y, and $p(\theta)$ reresent the test feature, test label, and prior on the weights, respectively.

The MAP estimation for θ is:

$$\hat{\theta} = \arg\max_\theta p(y^n, y|x^n, x, \theta) p(\theta), \tag{11}$$

where the prior $p(\theta)$ acts as a regularizer over the latent vector θ. It is common practice to use some regularization mechanism to control the training error for DNNs. In order to embed the regularization mechanism into the MAP, we introduced this prior $p(\theta)$.

Given a training set x^n, y^n and test couple x, y, the maximization in (11) is performed by training the DNN with all the data and converging to a steady-state maximum. Note that x^{n-1}, y^{n-1} are assumed to be known, while x_n, y_n, x and y are not known, and all the different possibilities need to be considered, resulting in multiple training sessions of the network. In order to avoid re-training the entire network for all possible values of x, y, x_n, and y_n, we utilize the independence between soft-max scores in the MAP estimation. Using Bayes, we observe that (11) can be re-written as:

$$\hat{\theta} = \arg\max_\theta p(y|x,\theta) p(y_n|x_n,\theta) p\left(\theta|y^{n-1}, x^{n-1}\right) \tag{12}$$

where $p(\theta|y^{n-1}, x^{n-1})$ is the posterior of θ given the available data $z^{n-1} = (x^{n-1}, y^{n-1})$.

The posterior $p(\theta|z^{n-1})$ is not dependent on the test data (x, y) and the evaluated labeling candidate (x_n, y_n), and thus can be computed once per selection iteration and then used throughout the IAL selection process. This is a very important point which needs to be highlighted; there is no need to re-train the network for every (x, y) and (x_n, y_n). We only need to train the network using x^{n-1}, y^{n-1} and then, during the IAL selection process, run forward passes on different θ with high $p(\theta|z^{n-1})$ values, to compute $p(y|x, \theta)$ and $p(y_n|x_n, \theta)$. This fact represents a significant computational complexity reduction since the number of possible points x_n can be significant and we wish to avoid re-training the network for each point.

In order to acquire the weight posterior for a DNN, some advanced techniques are required [40–42]; these involve multiple training passes over the network. For a DNN, the posterior, $p(\theta|y^{n-1}, x^{n-1})$, is multi-modal and intractable to compute directly. Therefore, we propose approximating it by some simpler distribution, which will allow easier computation of the maximum likelihood $\hat{\theta}$.

4.1. Variational Inference

Variational inference is a technique used in probabilistic modeling to approximate complex probability distributions that are difficult or impossible to calculate exactly [42–44]. Variational inference has been used in a wide range of applications, including in Bayesian neural networks, latent Dirichlet allocation, and Gaussian processes. The goal of variational inference is to find an approximation, $q^*(\theta)$ from a parametric family $\mathbb{Q}$, to the true distribution, $p(\theta|z^{n-1})$, that is as close as possible to the true distribution, but is also computationally tractable. This goal is formulated as minimizing the Kullback–Leibler (KL) divergence between the two distributions (also called information projection):

$$q^*(\theta) = \underset{q \in \mathbb{Q}}{\operatorname{argmin}} D_{KL}\Big(q(\theta) || p(\theta|z^{n-1})\Big)$$

There are different algorithms for implementing variational inference; most involve optimizing a lower bound on the log-likelihood of the data under the true distribution (called evidence). The lower bound is defined as the difference between the true distribution's data log-likelihood and the Kullback–Leibler (KL) divergence between the true distribution and the approximation. The KL divergence measures the distance between the two distributions, and so optimizing the lower bound is equivalent to minimizing the distance between the true distribution and the approximation.

One common algorithm for implementing variational inference is called mean field variational inference [45]. In this approach, the approximation to the true distribution is factorized into simpler distributions that are easier to work with, such as Gaussians or Bernoullis. The parameters of these simpler distributions are then optimized to minimize the KL divergence between the true distribution and the approximation. Another algorithm for variational inference is called stochastic variational inference [46]. In this approach, the optimization is performed using stochastic gradient descent, with a random subset of the data used in each iteration. This allows the algorithm to scale to large datasets and complex models.

4.2. Deep Individual Active Learning (DIAL)

In this work, we opted to use the method in Gal and Ghahramani [41], denoted as MC dropout (Monte Carlo dropout), due to its computational simplicity and favorable performance. MC dropout represents a sophisticated extension of the conventional dropout regularization technique within the domain of machine learning, and it is particularly associated with improving the robustness and uncertainty quantification of neural networks. This concept finds its roots in the broader effort to address the challenge of overfitting, a common concern in training deep learning models where the network becomes excessively attuned to the training data, hindering its generalization to new, unseen data.

Traditional dropout involves randomly deactivating, or "dropping out", a fraction of the neurons during the training phase. This stochastic process introduces a level of noise, preventing the neural network from relying too heavily on specific features, thus enhancing its ability to generalize to diverse datasets. However, dropout is typically applied solely during the training phase, and the model's predictions during the inference phase are based on a single deterministic forward pass through the network.

Monte Carlo dropout introduces a novel approach to the inference phase by extending the dropout mechanism beyond training. In this context, during inference, the model performs multiple forward passes with different dropout masks applied each time. This process generates a set of predictions, and the final output is obtained by averaging or aggregating these predictions. The rationale behind this technique lies in its ability to capture and quantify uncertainty associated with the model's predictions.

By leveraging Monte Carlo dropout during inference, practitioners can gain valuable insights into the uncertainty inherent in the model's predictions. This uncertainty is crucial in real-world applications where understanding the model's confidence level is essential. For instance, in autonomous vehicles, medical diagnostics, or financial predictions, knowing the uncertainty associated with a model's output can inform decision making and improve overall system reliability.

In Gal and Ghahramani [41], the authors argued that performing dropout during training on DNNs, with dropout applied before every weight layer, is mathematically equivalent to minimizing the KL divergence between the weight posterior of the full network and a parametric distribution which is controlled by a set of Bernoulli random variables defined by the dropout probability. Therefore, $p(\theta|y^{n-1}, x^{n-1})$ can be approximated in KL-sense by a distribution which is controlled by the dropout parameter. We can use this idea in order to approximate (12) and find an approximated weight distribution, $q(\theta)$. Therefore, we can re-write (12) using the variational approximation $q(\theta)$:

$$\hat{\theta} \approx \arg\max_{\theta} p(y|x,\theta) p(y_n|x_n,\theta) q(\theta) \tag{13}$$

However, $q(\theta)$ as described in Gal and Ghahramani [41] is still complex to analytically compute. In fact, in Gal and Ghahramani [41], the authors do not explicitly sample from this distribution but compute integral quantities on this distribution (such as expectation and variance) using averaging of multiple independent realizations and the Law of Large Numbers (LLN). Since we focus on point-wise samples from $q(\theta)$, we cannot use the same approach as in Gal and Ghahramani [41].

In this work, we propose to sample M weights from $q(\theta)$ and find $\hat{\theta}$ among all the different samples. Since the weights are embedded in a high-dimensional space, the probability of the sampled weights can be assumed to be relatively uniform. Therefore, we propose approximating (13) as:

$$\hat{\theta} \approx \arg\max_{\{\theta_m\}_{m=1}^{M}} p(y|x,\theta_m) p(y_n|x_n,\theta_m) \tag{14}$$

As observed by Gal and Ghahramani [41], (14) can be computed by running multiple forward passes on the network trained using dropout with z^{n-1} during inference with x and x_n. The resulting algorithm, denoted Deep Individual Active Learning (DIAL), is shown in Algorithm 1 and follows these steps:

1. Train a model on the labeled training set z^{n-1} with dropout.
2. For each pair of x and x_n, run M forward passes with different dropout masks and compute the product of the softmax outputs.
3. Find the weight that maximizes DNN prediction of the test input and the unlabeled candidate input as in (12).
4. Accumulate the pNML regret of the test point given these estimations.
5. Find the unlabeled candidate for which the worst-case averaged regret of the test set is minimal, as in (9).

For step 2, since the variational posterior associated with MC dropout is difficult to evaluate, we assume that it is uniform for all the sampled weights.

We emphasize the significant complexity reduction provided by our approximation; a naïve implementation of pNML computation would require training the network over all possible training points x_n and test points x with all possibilities of their respective labels y_n, y. This would render our criterion unfeasible for real-world applications. Our proposed approach, DIAL, only requires performing training with dropout on z^{n-1} only once per selection iteration and then performing forward passes (considerably faster than training passes) to obtain multiple samples of the weights.

Algorithm 1: DIAL: Deep Individual Active Learning

Input Training set z^{n-1}, unlabeled pool and test samples $\{x_i\}_{i=1}^{N}$ and $\{x_k\}_{k=1}^{K}$.
Output Next data point for labeling $\hat{x}_i$
Run MC-Dropout using z^{n-1} to get $\{\theta_m\}_{m=1}^{M}$
$\mathbf{S} = zeros(N, |\mathbb{Y}|)$
for $i \leftarrow 1$ to N do
  for $y_i \in \mathbb{Y}$ do
    for $k \leftarrow 1$ to K do
      $\Gamma = 0$
      for $y_k \in \mathbb{Y}$ do
        $\hat{\theta} = \operatorname{argmax}_{\theta_m} p(y_k|x_k, \theta_m) p(y_i|x_i, \theta_m)$
        $\Gamma = \Gamma + p(y_k|x_k, \hat{\theta})$
      end for
      $\mathbf{S}(i, y_i) = \mathbf{S}(i, y_i) + \log \Gamma$
    end for
  end for
end for
$\hat{x}_i = \operatorname{argmin}_{x_i} \max_{y_i} \mathbf{S}$

---

5. Experiments

In this section, we analyze the performance of DIAL and compare its performance to state-of-the-art active learning criteria. We tested the proposed DIAL strategy in two scenarios:

- The initial training, unlabeled pool, and test data come from the same distribution (IND scenario).
- There are OOD samples present in the unlabeled pool (OOD scenario).

The reason for using the individual setting and DIAL as its associated strategy in the presence of OOD samples is that it does not make any assumptions about the data generation process, making the results applicable to a wide range of scenarios, including PAC [47], stochastic [13], adversarial settings, as well as samples from unknown distributions.

We considered the following datasets for training and evaluation of the different active learning methods:

- **The MNIST dataset** [29] consists of 28×28 grayscale images of handwritten digits, with 60 K images for training and 10 K images for testing.
- **The EMNIST dataset** [28] is a variant of the MNIST dataset that includes a larger variety of images (upper and lower case letters, digits, and symbols). It consists of 240 K images with 47 different labels.
- **The CIFAR10 dataset** [27] consists of 60 K 32×32 color images in 10 classes. The classes include objects such as airplanes, cars, birds, and ships.
- **Fashion MNIST** [48] is a dataset of images of clothing and accessories, consisting of 70 K images. Each image is 28×28 grayscale pixels.

- **The SVHN dataset** [49] contains 600 K real-world images with digits and numbers in natural scene images collected from Google Street View.

We built upon Huang [50] and Smith et al. [11] open-source implementations of the following methods:

The Random sampling algorithm is the most basic approach in learning. It selects samples to label randomly, without considering any other criteria. This method can be useful when the data are relatively homogeneous and easy to classify, but it can be less efficient when the data are more complex or when there is a high degree of uncertainty.

The Bayesian Active Learning by Disagreement (BALD) method [4] utilizes an acquisition function that calculates the mutual information between the model's predictions and the model's parameters. This function measures how closely the predictions for a specific data point are linked to the model's parameters, indicating that determining the true label of samples with high mutual information would also provide insight into the true model parameters.

The Core-set algorithm [5] aims to find a small subset from a large labeled dataset such that a model learned from this subset will perform well on the entire dataset. The associated active learning algorithm chooses a subset that minimizes this bound, which is equivalent to the k-center problem.

The Expected Predictive Information Gain (EPIG) method [11] was motivated by BALD's weakness in prediction-oriented settings. This acquisition function directly targets a reduction in predictive uncertainty on inputs of interest by utilizing the unlabelled test set. It is shown in Appendix A that this approach is similar to UAL [6], where the main difference is that UAL assumes the stochastic setting, where the data follow some parametric distribution.

5.1. Experimental Setup

The first setting we consider consists of an initial training set, an unlabeled pool (from which the training examples are selected), and an unlabeled test set, all drawn from the **same distribution**. The experiment includes the following four steps:

1. A model is trained on the small labeled dataset (initial training set).
2. One of the active learning strategies is utilized to select a small number of the most informative examples from the unlabeled pool.
3. The labels of the selected samples are queried and added to the labeled dataset.
4. The model is retrained using the new training set.

Steps 2–4 are repeated multiple times, with the model becoming more accurate with each iteration, as it is trained on a larger labeled dataset.

In addition to the standard setting, we evaluate the performance in **the presence of OOD samples**. In this scenario, the initial training and test sets are drawn from the same distribution, but the unlabeled pool contains a mix of OOD samples. When an OOD unlabeled sample is selected for annotation, it is not used in training of the next iteration of the model. Across all x-axis values in the subsequent test accuracy figures, the presented metric is the count of Oracle calls, reflecting the instances when a selection strategy chose a sample, whether it be IND or OOD. It is crucial to differentiate this metric from the training set size, as the selection of an OOD sample leads to an increase in the number of Oracle calls, while the training set size remains unaffected. An effective strategy would recognize that OOD samples do not improve performance on the test set and avoid selecting them.

A visual representation of the scenario with OOD samples is illustrated in Figure 1a–c. These figures show the unlabeled pool, which contains a mixture of both IND and OOD samples. Figure 1d–f show the test set, which contains only IND samples. We argue that this is a representative setting for active learning in real life. In the real world, unlabelled pools are collected from many data sources and will most certainly contain OOD data. The process of pruning the unlabelled pool is a costly process and involves human inspection and labeling, which needs to be minimized. This is exactly the goal of active learning and finding a criterion which implicitly filters OOD data is of significant interest.

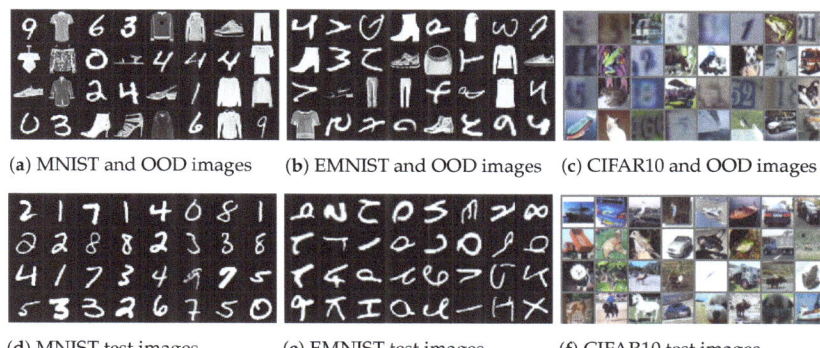

(a) MNIST and OOD images (b) EMNIST and OOD images (c) CIFAR10 and OOD images

(d) MNIST test images (e) EMNIST test images (f) CIFAR10 test images

Figure 1. Datasets that contain a mix of images with OOD samples. (Top) Unlabeled pool contains OOD samples (Bottom). Test set includes only valid data.

5.2. MNIST Experimental Results

Following Gal et al. [4], we considered a model consisting of two blocks of convolution, dropout, max-pooling, and ReLu, with 32 and 64 5 × 5 convolution filters. These blocks are followed by two fully connected layers that include dropout between them. The layers have 128 and 10 hidden units, respectively. The dropout probability was set to 0.5 in all three locations. In each active learning round, a single sample was selected. We executed all active learning methods six times with different random seeds. For BALD, EPIG, and DIAL, we used 100 dropout iterations and employed the criterion on 512 random samples from the unlabeled pool. MNIST results are shown in Figure 2a. The largest efficiency is at a number of Oracle calls of 71, where DIAL attains an accuracy rate of 0.9, while EPIG and BALD achieve an accuracy rate of 0.86.

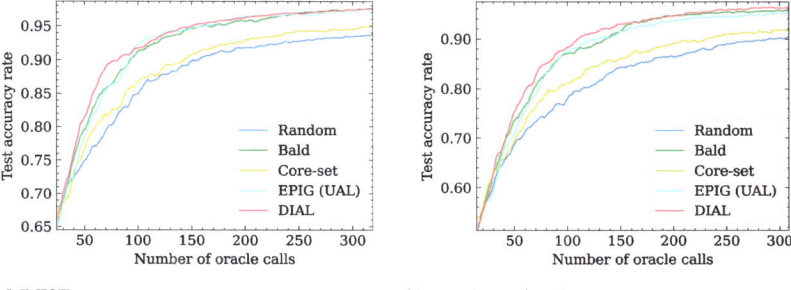

(a) MNIST (b) MNIST with OOD

Figure 2. Accuracy as function of number of Oracle calls on MNIST dataset. DIAL outperforms the baselines for the two setups.

To simulate the presence of OOD samples, we added the Fashion MNIST to the unlabeled pool such that the ratio of Fashion MNIST to MNIST was 1:1. In this setting, DIAL outperforms all other baselines, as shown in Figure 2b. DIAL is the top-performing method and has better accuracy than EPIG, BALD, Core-set, and Random. The largest efficiency is an accuracy rate of 0.95, where DIAL uses 240 Oracle calls, while BALD needs 307 (−35.1%). EPIG never reaches this accuracy level. The number of Oracle calls for additional accuracy rates is shown in Table 1.

Table 1. MNIST with OOD number of Oracle calls at x% accuracy.

Methods	85% Acc.	75% Acc.	65% Acc.
Random	145	73	36
Core-set	117	61	33
BALD	83	51	32
EPIG	84	56	35
DIAL	73 (−12.1%)	48 (−5.9%)	30 (−6.2%)

5.3. EMNIST Experimental Results

We followed the same setting as the MNIST experiment with a slightly larger model than MNIST consisting of three blocks of convolution, dropout, max-pooling, and ReLu. The experimental results, shown in Figure 3a, indicate that DIAL is the top-performing method. For an accuracy rate of 0.56, it requires 8.3% less Oracle calls when compared to the second best method.

In the presence of OOD samples, the DIAL method outperforms all other baselines, as shown in Figure 3b and Table 2. For 300 Oracle calls, DIAL achieves a test set accuracy rate of 0.52, while BALD, EPIG, Core-set, and Random attain 0.51, 0.5, 0.42, and 0.40, respectively. For an accuracy rate of 0.53, DIAL needs 308 Oracle calls, while BALD and EPIG require 346 and 342, respectively (−11%). Moreover, Core-set and Random do not achieve this accuracy.

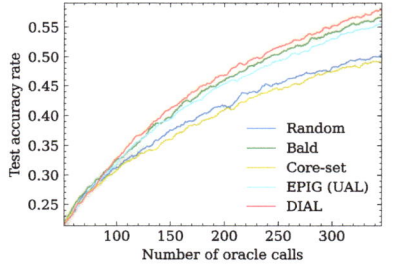
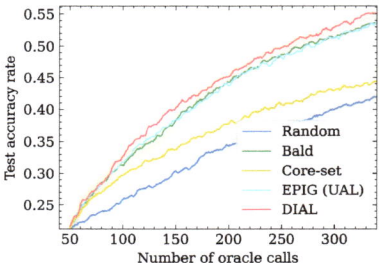

(a) EMNIST (b) EMNIST with OOD

Figure 3. Active learning performance on the EMNIST dataset. DIAL is more efficient than tested baselines in the number of Oracle calls.

Table 2. EMNIST with OOD number of Oracle calls at x% accuracy.

Methods	40% Acc.	30% Acc.	25% Acc.
Random	281	140	80
Core-set	221	96	62
BALD	154	85	**59**
EPIG	157	84	59
DIAL	138 (−10.4%)	84 (−1.2%)	59 (0%)

5.4. Cifar10 Experimental Results

For the CIFAR10 dataset, we utilized ResNet-18 [51] with an acquisition size of 16 samples. We used 1K initial training set size and measured the performance of the active learning strategies up to a training set size of 3K. The CIFAR10 results are shown in Figure 4a. Overall, DIAL and Random perform the same and have a better test set accuracy than the other baselines for Oracle calls greater than 2100.

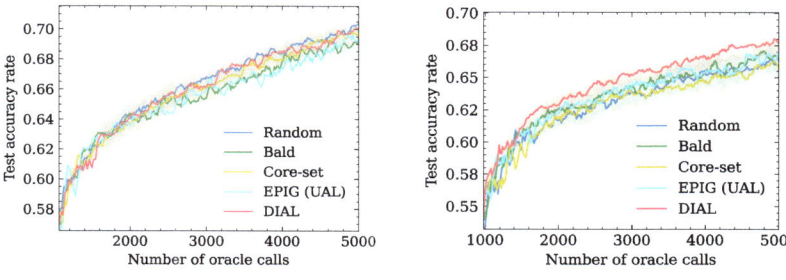

(a) CIFAR10 (b) CIFAR10 with OOD

Figure 4. The left figure illustrates the performance of CIFAR10 using only IND samples. The DIAL method performs similarly to the Random method. The figure on the right shows the performance of a combination of OOD samples, where DIAL outperforms all other methods.

When the presence of OOD samples in the unlabeled pool is considered, as shown in Figure 4b, DIAL outperforms the other methods. Table 3 shows the number of Oracle calls required for different accuracy levels. For the same accuracy rate of 0.65, DIAL needs up to 15.4% less Oracle calls than the second best method. This can be explained by Figure 5, which shows the ratio of OOD samples to the number of Oracle calls. The figure suggests that DIAL outperforms other criteria by selecting fewer OOD samples, contributing to its commendable performance. It is noteworthy that in all OOD scenarios, DIAL demonstrated superior ability to identify in-distribution samples without explicit knowledge of the distribution and solely utilizing unlabeled test features. This underscores the universality of DIAL, showcasing its adaptability to various distribution shifts. Additionally, the second-best performer, EPIG, also considers the unlabeled test set and performs better than other baseline methods but falls short of DIAL. Notably, BALD and Core-set exhibit similar behavior, possibly attributed to their emphasis on model estimation rather than leveraging the test set for predictive focus.

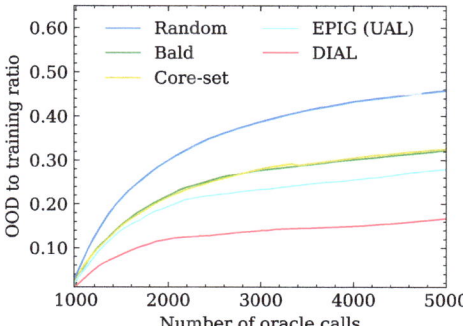

Figure 5. The amount of chosen OOD samples for CIFAR10 with the presence of OOD samples.

Table 3. CIFAR10: the presence of OOD samples: Number of Oracle calls at specific accuracy rate values.

Methods	66% Acc.	62% Acc.	58% Acc.
Random	3956	1828	1220
Core-set	4468	1844	1412
BALD	4020	1636	1202
EPIG	3636	1700	1108
DIAL	3076 (−15.4%)	1556 (−4.9%)	1060 (−4.3%)

6. Limitations

The proposed DIAL algorithm is a min-max strategy for the individual settings. However, DIAL may not be the most beneficial approach in scenarios where the unlabeled pool is very similar to the test set, where different selection strategies may perform similarly and with smaller complexity. This limitation of DIAL is supported by the experimental results of Section 5.4, where the DIAL algorithm performed similarly to random selection for the CIFAR10 dataset (but better than all the other baselines).

Another limitation of DIAL is that it has a higher overhead computation compared to other active learning methods such as BALD. This is because DIAL involves computing the regret on the test set, which requires additional computations and could become significant when the unlabeled pool or the test set are very large.

7. Conclusions

In this study, we propose a min-max active learning criterion for the individual setting, which does not rely on any distributional assumptions. We have also developed an efficient method for computing this criterion for DNNs. Our experimental results demonstrate that the proposed strategy, referred to as DIAL, is particularly effective in the presence of OOD samples in the unlabeled pool. Specifically, our results show that DIAL requires 12%, 10.4%, and 15.4% fewer Oracle calls than the next best method to achieve a certain level of accuracy on the MNIST, EMNIST, and CIFAR10 datasets, respectively.

As future work, we plan to investigate batch acquisition criteria that take into account batch selection. This will allow us to consider the relationship between the selected samples and the overall composition of the batch, which may lead to even further improvements in performance.

Author Contributions: K.B., coding, visualization, writing—review and editing; S.S., conceptualization, formal analysis, writing—review and editing; M.F., writing—review and editing. All authors have read and agreed to the published version of the manuscript.

Funding: This research received no external funding.

Institutional Review Board Statement: Not applicable.

Informed Consent Statement: Not applicable.

Data Availability Statement: The paper itself contains all the information required to assess the conclusions. Additional data related to this paper may be requested from the corresponding author.

Conflicts of Interest: The authors declare no conflicts of interest.

Appendix A. Equivalence between EPIG and UAL

In this section, we will prove that the criterion proposed by Smith et al. [11] is equivalent to the criterion in Shayovitz and Feder [6].

Proof. Assuming some prior $\pi(\theta)$, the UAL criterion is:

$$\hat{x}_n = \underset{x_n}{\operatorname{argmin}} I(\theta; Y | X, x_n, Y_n, z^{n-1})$$

where X and Y are the test feature and label random variables.

The EPIG criterion [11] is:

$$\hat{x}_n = \underset{x_n}{\operatorname{argmax}} I(Y; Y_n | X, x_n, z^{n-1})$$

In order to show the equivalence between the two acquisition functions (UAL and EPIG), we can write the following mutual information equality using the mutual information chain rule:

$$I(Y; Y_n, \theta | X, x_n, z^{n-1}) = I(Y; Y_n | X, x_n, z^{n-1}) + I(Y; \theta | X, Y_n, x_n, z^{n-1})$$

The same mutual information $I(Y; Y_n, \theta | X, x_n, z^{n-1})$ can also be expressed by the chain rule using a different conditioning:

$$I(Y; Y_n, \theta | X, x_n, z^{n-1}) = I(Y; \theta | X, x_n, z^{n-1}) + I(Y; Y_n | X, x_n, \theta, z^{n-1})$$

Therefore,

$$I(Y; Y_n | X, x_n, z^{n-1}) + I(Y; \theta | X, Y_n, x_n, z^{n-1}) = I(Y; \theta | X, x_n, z^{n-1}) + I(Y; Y_i | X, x_n, \theta, z^{n-1}) \tag{A1}$$

Given θ, the test and train are independent; therefore, $I(Y; Y_n | X, x_n, \theta, z^{n-1}) = 0$ and (A1) becomes:

$$I(Y; \theta | X, Y_n, x_n, z^{n-1}) = I(Y; \theta | X, x_n, z^{n-1}) + I(Y; Y_n | X, x_n, \theta, z^{n-1}) \tag{A2}$$

It is assumed that θ is independent of x_n ($p(\theta | x_n) = p(\theta)$ and that $p(z^{n-1} | x_n) = p(z^{n-1})$. These assumptions, coupled with Bayes, lead to the following conditional independence: $p(\theta | x_n, z^{n-1}) = p(\theta | z^{n-1})$. We can now remove the conditioning on x_n and obtain $I(Y; \theta | X, x_n, z^{n-1}) = I(Y; \theta | X, z^{n-1})$. We note that $I(Y; \theta | X, z^{n-1})$ is not dependent on x_n and is a fixed quantity. Therefore, we can re-write (A3):

$$I(Y; \theta | X, z^{n-1}) = I(Y; \theta | X, Y_n, x_n, z^{n-1}) - I(Y; Y_n | X, x_n, \theta, z^{n-1}) \tag{A3}$$

It is now clear that if we find x_n which minimizes $I(\theta; Y | X, x_n, Y_n, z^{n-1})$ (UAL), it will simultaneously maximize $I(Y; Y_n | X, x_n, z^{n-1})$ (EPIG), since their difference is a constant. □

References

1. Ren, P.; Xiao, Y.; Chang, X.; Huang, P.Y.; Li, Z.; Gupta, B.B.; Chen, X.; Wang, X. A survey of deep active learning. *ACM Comput. Surv. (CSUR)* **2021**, *54*, 1–40. [CrossRef]
2. Wang, K.; Zhang, D.; Li, Y.; Zhang, R.; Lin, L. Cost-effective active learning for deep image classification. *IEEE Trans. Circuits Syst. Video Technol.* **2016**, *27*, 2591–2600. [CrossRef]
3. Houlsby, N.; Huszár, F.; Ghahramani, Z.; Lengyel, M. Bayesian active learning for classification and preference learning. *arXiv* **2011**, arXiv:1112.5745.
4. Gal, Y.; Islam, R.; Ghahramani, Z. Deep bayesian active learning with image data. In Proceedings of the International Conference on Machine Learning, Sydney, Australia, 6–11 August 2017.
5. Sener, O.; Savarese, S. Active Learning for Convolutional Neural Networks: A Core-Set Approach. In Proceedings of the International Conferenc on Learning Representations, Vancouver, BC, Canada, 30 April–3 May 2018.
6. Shayovitz, S.; Feder, M. Universal Active Learning via Conditional Mutual Information Minimization. *IEEE J. Sel. Areas Inf. Theory* **2021**, *2*, 720–734. [CrossRef]
7. Raginsky, M.; Rakhlin, A. Information-based complexity, feedback and dynamics in convex programming. *IEEE Trans. Inf. Theory* **2011**, *57*, 7036–7056. [CrossRef]
8. MacKay, D.J. Information-based objective functions for active data selection. *Neural Comput.* **1992**, *4*, 590–604. [CrossRef]
9. Fedorov, V.V. *Theory of Optimal Experiments*; Elsevier: Amsterdam, The Netherlands, 2013.
10. Shayovitz, S.; Feder, M. Minimax Active Learning Via Minimal Model Capacity. In Proceedings of the 29th IEEE International Workshop on Machine Learning for Signal Processing, MLSP 2019, Pittsburgh, PA, USA, 13–16 October 2019.
11. Smith, F.B.; Kirsch, A.; Farquhar, S.; Gal, Y.; Foster, A.; Rainforth, T. Prediction-Oriented Bayesian Active Learning. In Proceedings of the International Conference on Artificial Intelligence and Statistics, Valencia, Spain, 25–27 April 2023.
12. Alabduljabbar, A.; Abusnaina, A.; Meteriz-Yildiran, Ü.; Mohaisen, D. TLDR: Deep Learning-Based Automated Privacy Policy Annotation with Key Policy Highlights. In Proceedings of the 20th Workshop on Workshop on Privacy in the Electronic Society, Seoul, Republic of Korea, 15 November 2021.
13. Merhav, N.; Feder, M. Universal prediction. *IEEE Trans. Inf. Theory* **1998**, *44*, 2124–2147. [CrossRef]

14. Fogel, Y.; Feder, M. Universal batch learning with log-loss. In Proceedings of the International Symposium on Information Theory, Vail, CO, USA, 17–22 June 2018; IEEE: Piscataway, NJ, USA, 2018.
15. Bibas, K.; Fogel, Y.; Feder, M. A New Look at an Old Problem: A Universal Learning Approach to Linear Regression. In Proceedings of the 2019 IEEE International Symposium on Information Theory (ISIT), Paris, France, 7–12 July 2019.
16. Zhou, A.; Levine, S. Amortized Conditional Normalized Maximum Likelihood: Reliable Out of Distribution Uncertainty Estimation. In Proceedings of the International Conference on Machine Learning, Virtual, 18–24 July 2021.
17. Yoo, D.; Kweon, I.S. Learning loss for active learning. In Proceedings of the IEEE/CVF Conference on Computer Vision and Pattern Recognition, Long Beach, CA, USA, 15–20 June 2019.
18. Sinha, S.; Ebrahimi, S.; Darrell, T. Variational adversarial active learning. In Proceedings of the IEEE/CVF International Conference on Computer Vision, Seoul, Republic of Korea, 27 October–2 November 2019.
19. Karamcheti, S.; Krishna, R.; Fei-Fei, L.; Manning, C.D. Mind your outliers! investigating the negative impact of outliers on active learning for visual question answering. *arXiv* **2021**, arXiv:2107.02331.
20. Kothawade, S.; Beck, N.; Killamsetty, K.; Iyer, R. Similar: Submodular information measures based active learning in realistic scenarios. *Adv. Neural Inf. Process. Syst.* **2021**, *34*, 18685–18697.
21. Du, P.; Zhao, S.; Chen, H.; Chai, S.; Chen, H.; Li, C. Contrastive coding for active learning under class distribution mismatch. In Proceedings of the IEEE/CVF International Conference on Computer Vision, Montreal, BC, Canada, 11–17 October 2021; pp. 8927–8936.
22. Chen, T.; Kornblith, S.; Norouzi, M.; Hinton, G. A simple framework for contrastive learning of visual representations. In Proceedings of the International Conference on Machine Learning, Virtual, 26–28 August 2020; pp. 1597–1607.
23. Teney, D.; Abbasnejad, E.; van den Hengel, A. Learning what makes a difference from counterfactual examples and gradient supervision. In Proceedings of the Computer Vision—ECCV 2020: 16th European Conference, Glasgow, UK, 23–28 August 2020; Proceedings, Part X 16. Springer: Berlin/Heidelberg, Germany, 2020; pp. 580–599.
24. Kaushik, D.; Hovy, E.; Lipton, Z.C. Learning the difference that makes a difference with counterfactually-augmented data. *arXiv* **2019**, arXiv:1909.12434.
25. Nie, Y.; Williams, A.; Dinan, E.; Bansal, M.; Weston, J.; Kiela, D. Adversarial NLI: A new benchmark for natural language understanding. *arXiv* **2019**, arXiv:1910.14599.
26. Shayovitz, S.; Feder, M. Active Learning for Individual Data via Minimal Stochastic Complexity. In Proceedings of the 2022 58th Annual Allerton Conference on Communication, Control, and Computing (Allerton), Monticello, NY, USA, 27–30 September 2022; IEEE: Piscataway, NJ, USA, 2022; pp. 1–5.
27. Krizhevsky, A.; Nair, V.; Hinton, G. The CIFAR-10 Dataset. 2014. Available online: http://www.cs.toronto.edu/kriz/cifar.html (accessed on 29 January 2024).
28. Cohen, G.; Afshar, S.; Tapson, J.; Van Schaik, A. EMNIST: Extending MNIST to handwritten letters. In Proceedings of the 2017 International Joint Conference on Neural Networks (IJCNN), Anchorage, AK, USA, 14–19 May 2017; IEEE: Piscataway, NJ, USA, 2017.
29. Deng, L. The mnist database of handwritten digit images for machine learning research [best of the web]. *IEEE Signal Process. Mag.* **2012**, *29*, 141–142. [CrossRef]
30. Bibas, K.; Feder, M. Distribution Free Uncertainty for the Minimum Norm Solution of Over-parameterized Linear Regression. *arXiv* **2021**, arXiv:2102.07181.
31. Rosas, F.E.; Mediano, P.A.; Gastpar, M. Learning, compression, and leakage: Minimising classification error via meta-universal compression principles. In Proceedings of the 2020 IEEE Information Theory Workshop (ITW), Virtual, 11–15 April 2020; IEEE: Piscataway, NJ, USA, 2021.
32. Rissanen, J.; Roos, T. Conditional NML universal models. In Proceedings of the 2007 Information Theory and Applications Workshop, San Diego, CA, USA, 18–23 February 2007; IEEE: Piscataway, NJ, USA, 2007.
33. Roos, T.; Rissanen, J. On sequentially normalized maximum likelihood models. *Compare* **2008**, *27*, 256.
34. Bibas, K.; Feder, M. The Predictive Normalized Maximum Likelihood for Over-parameterized Linear Regression with Norm Constraint: Regret and Double Descent. *arXiv* **2021**, arXiv:2102.07181.
35. Rosas, F.E.; Mediano, P.A.; Gastpar, M. Learning, compression, and leakage: Minimizing classification error via meta-universal compression principles. *arXiv* **2020**, arXiv:2010.07382.
36. Fu, J.; Levine, S. Offline Model-Based Optimization via Normalized Maximum Likelihood Estimation. In Proceedings of the International Conference on Learning Representations, Virtual, 3–7 May 2021.
37. Bibas, K.; Fogel, Y.; Feder, M. Deep pnml: Predictive normalized maximum likelihood for deep neural networks. *arXiv* **2019**, arXiv:1904.12286.
38. Karzand, M.; Nowak, R.D. Maximin active learning in overparameterized model classes. *IEEE J. Sel. Areas Inf. Theory* **2020**, *1*, 167–177. [CrossRef]
39. Kirsch, A.; van Amersfoort, J.; Gal, Y. BatchBALD: Efficient and Diverse Batch Acquisition for Deep Bayesian Active Learning. In Proceedings of the Advances in Neural Information Processing Systems 32 (NeurIPS 2019), Vancouver, BC, Canada, 8–14 December 2019.
40. Maddox, W.J.; Izmailov, P.; Garipov, T.; Vetrov, D.P.; Wilson, A.G. A simple baseline for bayesian uncertainty in deep learning. *Adv. Neural Inf. Process. Syst.* **2019**, *32*.

41. Gal, Y.; Ghahramani, Z. Dropout as a bayesian approximation: Representing model uncertainty in deep learning. In Proceedings of the International Conference Machine Learning, New York, NY, USA, 19–24 June 2016.
42. Daxberger, E.; Kristiadi, A.; Immer, A.; Eschenhagen, R.; Bauer, M.; Hennig, P. Laplace redux-effortless bayesian deep learning. *Adv. Neural Inf. Process. Syst.* **2021**, *34*, 20089–20103.
43. Wilson, A.G.; Hu, Z.; Salakhutdinov, R.R.; Xing, E.P. Stochastic variational deep kernel learning. *Adv. Neural Inf. Process. Syst.* **2016**, *29*.
44. Zhang, C.; Bütepage, J.; Kjellström, H.; Mandt, S. Advances in variational inference. *IEEE Trans. Pattern Anal. Mach. Intell.* **2018**, *41*, 2008–2026. [CrossRef] [PubMed]
45. Blei, D.M.; Kucukelbir, A.; McAuliffe, J.D. Variational inference: A review for statisticians. *J. Am. Stat. Assoc.* **2017**, *112*, 859–877. [CrossRef]
46. Hoffman, M.D.; Blei, D.M.; Wang, C.; Paisley, J. Stochastic variational inference. *J. Mach. Learn. Res.* **2013**, *14*, 1303–1347.
47. Simon, H.U. An almost optimal PAC algorithm. In Proceedings of the Conference on Learning Theory, Paris, France, 3–6 July 2015.
48. Xiao, H.; Rasul, K.; Vollgraf, R. Fashion-mnist: A novel image dataset for benchmarking machine learning algorithms. *arXiv* **2017**, arXiv:1708.07747.
49. Sermanet, P.; Chintala, S.; LeCun, Y. Convolutional neural networks applied to house numbers digit classification. In Proceedings of the 21st International Conference on Pattern Recognition (ICPR2012), Tsukuba, Japan, 11–15 November 2012; IEEE: Piscataway, NJ, USA, 2012.
50. Huang, K.H. DeepAL: Deep Active Learning in Python. *arXiv* **2021**, arXiv:2111.15258.
51. He, K.; Zhang, X.; Ren, S.; Sun, J. Deep residual learning for image recognition. In Proceedings of the IEEE Conference on Computer Vision and Pattern Recognition, Las Vegas, NV, USA, 27–30 June 2016.

Disclaimer/Publisher's Note: The statements, opinions and data contained in all publications are solely those of the individual author(s) and contributor(s) and not of MDPI and/or the editor(s). MDPI and/or the editor(s) disclaim responsibility for any injury to people or property resulting from any ideas, methods, instructions or products referred to in the content.

Article

Analysis of Deep Convolutional Neural Networks Using Tensor Kernels and Matrix-Based Entropy

Kristoffer K. Wickstrøm [1,*], Sigurd Løkse [1], Michael C. Kampffmeyer [1,2], Shujian Yu [1,3,4], José C. Príncipe [3] and Robert Jenssen [1,2,5]

[1] Machine Learning Group, Department of Physics and Technology, UiT The Arctic University of Norway, NO-9037 Tromsø, Norway; sigurd.lokse@uit.no (S.L.); michael.c.kampffmeyer@uit.no (M.C.K.); s.yu3@vu.nl (S.Y.); robert.jenssen@uit.no (R.J.)
[2] Norwegian Computing Center, Department of Statistical Analysis and Machine Learning, 114 Blindern, NO-0314 Oslo, Norway
[3] Computational NeuroEngineering Laboratory, Department of Electrical and Computer Engineering, University of Florida, Gainesville, FL 32611, USA; principe@cnel.ufl.edu
[4] Department of Computer Science, Vrije Universiteit Amsterdam, 1081 HV Amsterdam, The Netherlands
[5] Department of Computer Science, University of Copenhagen, Universitetsparken 1, 2100 Copenhagen, Denmark
* Correspondence: kristoffer.k.wickstrom@uit.no

Citation: Wickstrøm, K.K.; Løkse, S.; Kampffmeyer, M.C.; Yu, S.; Príncipe, J.C.; Jenssen, R. Analysis of Deep Convolutional Neural Networks Using Tensor Kernels and Matrix-Based Entropy. *Entropy* 2023, 25, 899. https://doi.org/10.3390/e25060899

Academic Editor: Jerry D. Gibson

Received: 25 April 2023
Revised: 31 May 2023
Accepted: 2 June 2023
Published: 3 June 2023

Copyright: © 2023 by the authors. Licensee MDPI, Basel, Switzerland. This article is an open access article distributed under the terms and conditions of the Creative Commons Attribution (CC BY) license (https://creativecommons.org/licenses/by/4.0/).

Abstract: Analyzing deep neural networks (DNNs) via information plane (IP) theory has gained tremendous attention recently to gain insight into, among others, DNNs' generalization ability. However, it is by no means obvious how to estimate the mutual information (MI) between each hidden layer and the input/desired output to construct the IP. For instance, hidden layers with many neurons require MI estimators with robustness toward the high dimensionality associated with such layers. MI estimators should also be able to handle convolutional layers while at the same time being computationally tractable to scale to large networks. Existing IP methods have not been able to study truly deep convolutional neural networks (CNNs). We propose an IP analysis using the new matrix-based Rényi's entropy coupled with tensor kernels, leveraging the power of kernel methods to represent properties of the probability distribution independently of the dimensionality of the data. Our results shed new light on previous studies concerning small-scale DNNs using a completely new approach. We provide a comprehensive IP analysis of large-scale CNNs, investigating the different training phases and providing new insights into the training dynamics of large-scale neural networks.

Keywords: information theory; deep learning; information plane; kernels methods

1. Introduction

Although deep neural networks (DNNs) are at the core of most state-of-the art systems in computer vision, the theoretical understanding of such networks is still not at a satisfactory level [1]. In order to provide insight into the inner workings of DNNs, the prospect of utilizing the mutual information (MI), a measure of dependency between two random variables, has recently garnered a significant amount of attention [1–8]. Given the input variable X and the desired output Y for a supervised learning task, a DNN is viewed as a transformation of X into a representation that is favorable for obtaining a good prediction of Y. By treating the output of each hidden layer as a random variable T, one can model the MI $I(X;T)$ between X and T. Likewise, the MI $I(T;Y)$ between T and Y can be modeled. The quantities $I(X;T)$ and $I(T;Y)$ span what is referred to as the information plane (IP). Several works have unveiled interesting properties of the training dynamics through IP analysis of DNNs [4,7,9–11]. Figure 1, produced using our proposed measure, illustrates one such insight that is similar to the observations of [1], where training can be separated into two distinct phases: the fitting phase and the compression phase.

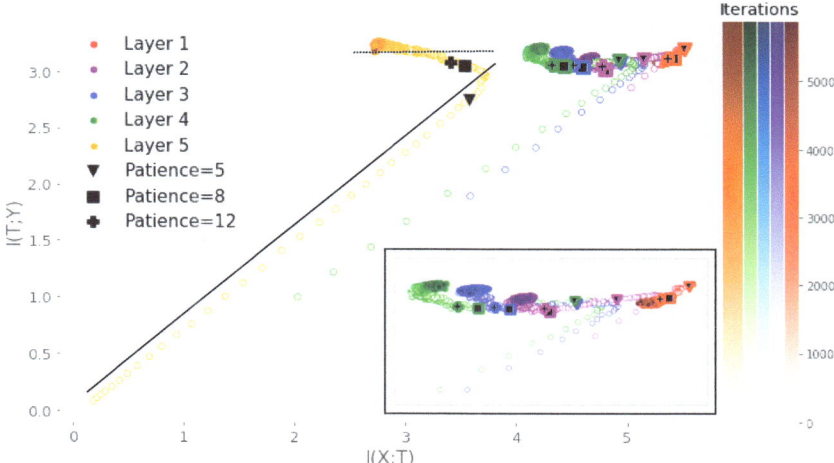

Figure 1. IP obtained using our proposed measure for a small DNN averaged over 5 training runs. The solid black line illustrates the fitting phase while the dotted black line illustrates the compression phase. The iterations at which early stopping would be performed assuming a given patience parameter are highlighted. Patience denotes the number of iterations that need to pass without progress on a validation set before training is stopped to avoid overfitting. For low patience values, training will stop before the compression phase. For the benefit of the reader, a magnified version of the first four layers is also displayed.

The claim of a fitting and compression phase has been highly debated as subsequent research has linked the compression phase to the saturation of neurons [5] or clustering of the hidden representations [9]. Recent studies [1,5,7,9] have been focused on small-scale networks or non-convolutional networks, as the current MI estimators cannot tackle the tensor representations produced by convolutional layers or do not scale well to convolutional layers with many filters [6]. This severely limits the scope of IP analysis, as most real-world applications rely on large-scale CNNs. In this work, we continue the IP line of research through a new matrix-based entropy functional [6,7,12]. We provide insights on this functional by linking the functional to well-understood measures from the kernel literature and propose a new kernel tensor-based approach to the matrix-based entropy functional. Furthermore, we give a new formulation of the matrix-based entropy that is closely connected to measures from quantum information theory. Using the proposed estimator, we provide an analysis of large-scale DNNs and give a new information theoretic understanding of the training procedure of DNNs. Using the proposed measure, we investigate the claim of [3] that the entropy $H(X) \approx I(T;X)$ and $H(Y) \approx I(T;Y)$ in high dimensions (in which case MI-based analysis would be meaningless). The contributions of this work can be summarized as:

- We propose a kernel tensor-based approach to the matrix-based entropy functional that is designed for measuring MI in large-scale convolutional neural networks (CNNs).
- We provide new insights on the matrix-based entropy functional by showing its connection to well-known quantities in the kernel literature such as the kernel mean embedding and maximum mean discrepancy. Furthermore, we show that the matrix-based entropy functional is closely linked with the von Neuman entropy from quantum information theory.
- Our results indicate that the compression phase is apparent mostly for the training data and less so for the test data, particularly for more challenging datasets. When using a technique such as early stopping to avoid overfitting, training tends to stop before the compression phase occurs (see Figure 1).

2. Related Work

Analyzing DNNs in the IP was first proposed by [13] and later demonstrated by [1]. Among other results, the authors studied the evolution of the IP during the training process of DNNs and noted that the process was composed of two different phases. First, there is an initial fitting phase where $I(T;Y)$ increases, which is followed by a phase of compression where $I(X;T)$ decreases. These results were later questioned by [5], who argued that the compression phase is not a general property of the DNN training process but rather an effect of different activation functions. However, a recent study by [4] seems to support the claim of a compression phase regardless of the activation function. The authors argue that the base estimator of MI utilized by [5] might not be accurate enough and demonstrate that a compression phase does occur, but the amount of compression can vary between different activation functions. Another recent study by [10] also reported a compression phase but highlighted the importance of adaptive MI estimators. They also showed that when L2 regularization was included in the training, compression was observed regardless of the activation function. In addition, some recent studies have discussed the limitations of the IP framework for analysis and optimization for particular types of DNN [14,15]. Furthermore, ref. [16] investigated similarities between hidden layers and between hidden layers of different networks, but they did so only for the representation obtained after the networks were fully trained. The dynamics of large-scale DNNs was investigated [17] using MINE [18]. A number of information plane-related studies have also been discussed in [19].

On a different note, Ref. [3] proposed an evaluation framework for DNNs based on the IP and demonstrated that MI can be used to infer the capability of DNNs to recognize objects for an image classification task. Furthermore, the authors argue that when the number of neurons in a hidden layer grows large, $I(T;X)$ and $I(Y;T)$ barely change and are, using [3] terminology, approximately deterministic, i.e., $I(T;X) \approx H(X)$ and $I(T;Y) \approx H(Y)$. Therefore, they only model the MI between X and the last hidden layer—that is, the output of the network—and the last hidden layer and Y.

Ref. [7] investigated a matrix-based measure of MI for analyzing different data processing inequalities in feed-forward stacked autoencoders (SAEs), concluding that the compression phase in the IP of SAEs is determined by the values of the SAE bottleneck layer size and the intrinsic dimensionality of the given data. In follow-up work, a simplistic analysis of small convolutional neural networks (CNNs) was provided in [6]; however, it was based on a multivariate extension [20] of matrix-based Renyi entropy that does not scale well numerically or computationally in the number of feature maps. The interested reader can find additional information on the multivariate extension by [20] in Appendix A.

Recently, the information plane of quantized neural networks was modeled [8], which allowed for an exact analysis of its dynamics. In addition, log-determinant entropy has been used for information plane analysis [11]. Lastly, information plane analysis has also been used to improve the understanding of graph convolutional neural networks [21].

In this paper, we continue the recent trend of leveraging the new matrix-based measures of entropy. We contribute both new insight to the definition of these measures (see Section 3.2.1), and importantly, we extend matrix-based measures of entropy to exploit tensor kernels to enable the first IP analysis of large-scale CNNs by treating feature maps as tensors (Section 3.3).

3. Materials and Methods

3.1. Preliminaries on Matrix-Based Information Measures

For the benefit of the reader, we review in this section first the theory underlying the recent matrix-based measures of entropy and mutual information. Thereafter, we contribute a new special case interpretation of the definition of matrix-based Renyi entropy (Section 3.2.1) and give new insights on the link to other measures in the kernel literature before presenting our new tensor-based approach.

3.1.1. Matrix-Based Entropy and Mutual Information

The matrix-based measure of entropy, originally proposed by [12], is built on kernel matrices obtained from raw data, involving no explicit density estimation or binning procedure:

Definition 1 ([12]). *Let $x_i \in \mathcal{X}$, $i = 1, 2, \ldots, N$ denote data points and let $\kappa : \mathcal{X} \times \mathcal{X} \mapsto \mathbb{R}$ be an infinitely divisible positive definite kernel [22]. Given the kernel matrix $\mathbf{K} \in \mathbb{R}^{N \times N}$ with elements $(\mathbf{K})_{ij} = \kappa(x_i, x_j)$ and the matrix $\mathbf{A}$, $(\mathbf{A})_{ij} = \frac{1}{N} \frac{(\mathbf{K})_{ij}}{\sqrt{(\mathbf{K})_{ii}(\mathbf{K})_{jj}}}$, the matrix-based Rényi's α-order entropy is given by*

$$S_\alpha(\mathbf{A}) = \frac{1}{1-\alpha} \log_2 \left(\mathrm{tr}(\mathbf{A}^\alpha) \right) \\ = \frac{1}{1-\alpha} \log_2 \left[\sum_{i=1}^{N} \lambda_i(\mathbf{A})^\alpha \right]. \qquad (1)$$

Here, $\lambda_i(\mathbf{A})$ denotes the ith eigenvalue of the matrix $\mathbf{A}$. Equation (1) is a measure of an entropy-like quantity that satisfies Renyi's axiomatic characterization of entropy [23], which is referred to as matrix-based Renyi entropy. In addition to the matrix-based entropy, ref. [12] also defined the matrix-based joint entropy between $\mathbf{x} \in \mathcal{X}$ and $\mathbf{y} \in \mathcal{Y}$ as

$$S_\alpha(\mathbf{A}_\mathcal{X}, \mathbf{A}_\mathcal{Y}) = S_\alpha \left(\frac{\mathbf{A}_\mathcal{X} \circ \mathbf{A}_\mathcal{Y}}{\mathrm{tr}(\mathbf{A}_\mathcal{X} \circ \mathbf{A}_\mathcal{Y})} \right), \qquad (2)$$

where x_i and y_i are two different representations of the same object and $\circ$ denotes the Hadamard product. Finally, the MI is, similar to Shannon's formulation, defined as

$$I_\alpha(\mathbf{A}_\mathcal{X}; \mathbf{A}_\mathcal{Y}) = S_\alpha(\mathbf{A}_\mathcal{X}) + S_\alpha(\mathbf{A}_\mathcal{Y}) - S_\alpha(\mathbf{A}_\mathcal{X}, \mathbf{A}_\mathcal{Y}). \qquad (3)$$

The properties of these quantities were analyzed in detail in [12], but we want to highlight some important properties and provide links with other measures in the kernel literature.

Information theoretic measures are developed in such a way that they satisfy certain axioms. The measures presented above satisfy the axioms put forth by [23] and are closely connected with quantum information theory [24]. In quantum statistical mechanics, the Von Neumann's entropy [24] is defined as

$$S(\rho) = -\mathrm{tr}(\rho \log \rho), \qquad (4)$$

where ρ is a density matrix that described a quantum mechanical system. If ρ is written in terms of its eigenvalues, $\lambda_i(\rho)$, then Equation (4) can also be formulated as

$$S(\rho) = -\sum_{i=1}^{N} \lambda_i(\rho) \log[\lambda_i(\rho)]. \qquad (5)$$

In addition, the quantum extensions of Renyi's entropy [25] that is defined as

$$S_\alpha(\rho) = \frac{1}{1-\alpha} \log[\mathrm{tr}(\rho^\alpha)], \qquad (6)$$

bears a close resemblance to the matrix-based definition of entropy in Equation (1). While some properties of Equations (4) and (6) can also be extended to Equation (1), it is important to note that the two approaches are very different since the matrix-based framework is built around kernel matrices obtained directly from raw data.

3.1.2. Bound on Matrix-Based Entropy Measure

Not all measures of entropy have the same properties. Many of the estimators used and developed for Shannon suffer from the curse of dimensionality [26]. In contrast, Renyi's entropy measures have the same functional form of the statistical quantity in a reproducing kernel Hilbert space (RKHS), thus capturing properties of the data population. Essentially, we are projecting marginal distribution to an RKHS in order to measure entropy and MI. This is similar to the approach of maximum mean discrepancy and the kernel mean embedding [27,28]. The connection with the data population can be shown via the theory of covariance operators. The covariance operator $G : \mathcal{H} \to \mathcal{H}$ is defined through the bilinear form

$$\mathcal{G}(f,g) = \langle f, Gg \rangle = \int_\mathcal{X} \langle f, \psi(\mathbf{x}) \rangle \langle \psi(\mathbf{x}), g \rangle d\mathbb{P}_\mathcal{X}(\mathbf{x}) \quad (7)$$
$$= E_\mathcal{X}\{f(X), g(Y)\}$$

where $\mathbb{P}_\mathcal{X}$ is a probability measure and $f, g \in \mathcal{H}$. Based on the empirical distribution $\mathbb{P}_N = \frac{1}{N}\sum_{i=1}^{N} \delta_{\mathbf{x}_i}(\mathbf{x})$, the empirical version $\hat{G}$ of G obtained from a sample $\mathbf{x}_i$ of size N is given by:

$$\langle f, \hat{G}_N g \rangle = \hat{\mathcal{G}}(f,g) = \int_\mathcal{X} \langle f, \psi(\mathbf{x}) \rangle \langle \psi(\mathbf{x}), g \rangle d\mathbb{P}_\mathcal{X}(\mathbf{x})$$
$$= \frac{1}{N}\sum_{i=1}^{N} \langle f, \psi(\mathbf{x}_i) \rangle \langle \psi(\mathbf{x}_i), g \rangle \quad (8)$$

By analyzing the spectrum of $\hat{G}$ and G, Ref. [12] showed that the difference between $\text{tr}(G)$ and $\text{tr}(\hat{G})$ can be bounded, as stated in the following proposition:

Proposition 2. *Let $\mathbb{P}_N = \frac{1}{N}\sum_{i=1}^{N} \delta_{\mathbf{x}_i}(\mathbf{x})$ be the empirical distribution. Then, as a consequence of Proposition 6.1 in [12], $\text{tr}[\hat{G}_N^\alpha] = \text{tr}\left[\left(\frac{1}{N}\mathbf{K}\right)^\alpha\right]$. The difference between $\text{tr}(G)$ and $\text{tr}(\hat{G})$ can be bounded under the conditions of Theorem 6.2 in [12] and for $\alpha > 1$, with probability 1-δ*

$$\left|\text{tr}(G^\alpha) - \text{tr}(\hat{G}_N^\alpha)\right| \leq \alpha C \sqrt{\frac{2\log\frac{2}{\delta}}{N}} \quad (9)$$

where C is a compact self-adjoint operator.

3.2. Analysis of Matrix-Based Information Measures

In this section, we present new theoretical insights into the Matrix-Based Information Measures.

3.2.1. A New Special-Case Interpretation of the Matrix-Based Renyi Entropy Definition

In previous works, the α in Equation (1) has been ad hoc set to a value of 1.01 in order to approximate Shannon's entropy [6,7]. For $\alpha = 1$, both the denominator and the numerator become zero, so Equation (1) cannot be used directly in this case. However, as a contribution to the matrix-based Renyi entropy theory, we show here that for the case $\alpha \to 1$, Equation (1) can be expressed similarly to the matrix-based Von Neumann's entropy [24], resembling Shannon's definition over probability states and expressed as

$$\lim_{\alpha \to 1} S_\alpha(\mathbf{A}) = -\sum_{i=1}^{N} \lambda_i(\mathbf{A}) \log_2[\lambda_i(\mathbf{A})]. \quad (10)$$

Equation (1) can be proved using L'Hôpital's rule as follows:

Proof.

$$\lim_{\alpha \to 1} S_\alpha(\mathbf{A}) = \lim_{\alpha \to 1} \frac{1}{1-\alpha} \log_2\left(\sum_{i=1}^{n} \lambda_i^\alpha\right) \to \frac{0}{0}, \quad (11)$$

since $\sum_{i=1}^{N} \lambda_i = \text{tr}(\mathbf{A}) = 1$. L'Hôpital's rule yields

$$\begin{aligned}
\lim_{\alpha \to 1} S_\alpha(\mathbf{A}) &= \lim_{\alpha \to 1} \frac{\frac{\partial}{\partial \alpha} \log_2[\sum_{i=1}^{n} \lambda_i(\mathbf{A})^\alpha]}{\frac{\partial}{\partial \alpha}(1-\alpha)} \\
&= -\frac{1}{\ln 2} \lim_{\alpha \to 1} \frac{\sum_{i=1}^{n} \lambda_i(\mathbf{A})^\alpha \ln[\lambda_i(\mathbf{A})]}{|\sum_{i=1}^{n} \lambda_i(\mathbf{A})^\alpha|} \\
&= -\sum_{i=1}^{n} \lambda_i(\mathbf{A}) \log_2[\lambda_i(\mathbf{A})].
\end{aligned} \quad (12)$$

□

3.2.2. Link to Measures in Kernel Literature and Validation on High-Dimensional Synthetic Data

An interesting aspect of the matrix-based measure of entropy is the special case connection with the theory of maximum mean discrepancy and Hilbert–Schmidt norms via covariance operators [29]. Let G be the covariance operator (see [28] for details), then, for the particular case of $\alpha = 2$, the empirical trace of the covariance operator, $\text{tr}(G^2)$, is given by $\text{tr}(\mathbf{A}^2)$. Furthermore,

$$\begin{aligned}
\text{tr}(G^2) &= \left\langle \int_{\mathcal{X}} \kappa(\cdot, \mathbf{x}) d\mathbb{P}_\mathcal{X}(\mathbf{x}), \int_{\mathcal{X}} \kappa(\cdot, \mathbf{y}) d\mathbb{P}_\mathcal{X}(\mathbf{y}), \right\rangle \\
&= \|\mu_\mathcal{X}\|_\mathcal{K}^2,
\end{aligned} \quad (13)$$

where $\mu_\mathcal{X} = \int_{\mathcal{X}} \kappa(\cdot, \mathbf{x}) d\mathbb{P}_\mathcal{X}(\mathbf{x})$ is the *kernel mean map* [30], i.e., an embedding of the probability measure $\mathbb{P}_\mathcal{X}(\mathbf{x})$ in a reproducing kernel Hilbert space (RKHS). Thus, the matrix $\mathbf{A}$ can be related to an empirical covariance operator on embeddings of probability distributions in an RKHS. Moreover, ref. [12] showed that under certain conditions, Equation (1) converges to the trace of the underlying covariance operator, as shown in Proposition 2 in Section 3.1.2. Notice that the dimensionality of the data does not appear in Proposition 2. This means that $S_\alpha(\mathbf{A})$ captures properties of the distribution with a certain robustness with respect to high-dimensional data. This is a beneficial property compared to KNN and KDE-based information measures used in previous works [5,10], which have difficulties handling high-dimensional data [26]. Some measures of entropy developed for measuring the Shannon entropy suffer from the curse of dimensionality [26]. In addition, there is no need for any binning procedure utilized in previous works [1], which are known to struggle with the ReLU activation function commonly used in DNNs [5]. While Equation (13) is not explicitly used in the remainder of our manuscript, we believe that these insights provides a deeper understanding of the inner workings of the matrix-based entropy measure.

To examine the behavior of the matrix-based measures described in Section 3.1, we have conducted a simple experiment on measuring entropy and mutual information in high-dimensional data following a normal distribution with known mean and covariance matrix. In the particular case of the normal distribution, the entropy and mutual information can be calculated analytically. The entropy can be calculated as:

$$H(\mathcal{N}_0) = \frac{1}{2} \log\left((2\pi e)^d \det(\mathbf{\Sigma}_0)\right), \quad (14)$$

where $\mathcal{N}_0$ denotes a normal distribution with mean vector $\boldsymbol{\mu}_0$ covariance matrix $\mathbf{\Sigma}_0$, and dimensionality d. For mutual information, we use the experimental setup considered in [31]. Let Z have a $d+1$ dimensional Gaussian distribution with covariance matrix $\mathbf{\Sigma}_z$. Next, let $X = (Z_1, \ldots, Z_d)$ and $Y = Z_{d+1}$. Then, their mutual information satisfies:

$$I(X, Y) = I(Z_1, \ldots, Z_{d+1}) - I(Z_1, \ldots, Z_d) \quad (15)$$

$$= -\frac{1}{2} \log\left(\frac{\det(\mathbf{\Sigma}_z)}{\det(\mathbf{\Sigma}_x)}\right), \quad (16)$$

where Σ_x is the covariance matrix of X. We consider five cases of $(d+1)$-dimensional Gaussian distributions with mean zero, unit variance, and an increasing amount of dependence. The unit variance covariance matrices for the five cases are given as follows:

$$\begin{cases} \Sigma_A(i,j) = 0.1, & \text{for } i \neq j, \\ \Sigma_B(i,j) = 0.25, & \text{for } i \neq j, \\ \Sigma_C(i,j) = 0.5, & \text{for } i \neq j, \\ \Sigma_D(i,j) = 0.75, & \text{for } i \neq j, \\ \Sigma_E(i,j) = 0.9, & \text{for } i \neq j. \end{cases}$$

The left plot in Figure 2 displays the entropy of a 100-dimensional normal distribution with zero mean and isotropic covariance matrix, which is calculated using Equation (14). The right plot in Figure 2 displays the estimated entropy using Equation (1) on 500 randomly drawn samples from $\mathcal{N}_0$, which are computed on all 500 samples and in batches of 100. The results show how the estimated entropy follows the same trend as the analytically computed entropy. We quantitativly evaluate the correlation between the analytic quantity and the estimated quantity by calculating Pearson's correlation coefficient and find that that both the full data and batch-wise estimation are highly correlated with the analytic calculation (correlation ≈ 0.99, p-value ≤ 0.01). For mutual information, we generate 500 samples from a 100 + 1 dimensional Gaussian distribution and compare the exact and estimated mutual information, which are both based on all 500 samples and in the batch-wise setting. The left plot of Figure 3 shows the mutual information between X and Y calculated using Equation (16) for the five cases described above. The right part of Figure 3 shows the estimated mutual information using Equation (3), which is computed on all 500 samples and in batches of 100. Again, the result shows how the estimated values follow the same trend as the exact mutual information values. Similarly as with the entropy, we quantitativly evaluate the correlation between the analytic quantity and the estimated quantity by calculating Pearson's correlation coefficient and find that that both the full data and batch-wise estimation are highly correlated with the analytic calculation (correlation ≈ 0.99, p-value ≤ 0.01). Note that the exact value of both the entropy and mutual information is different between the exact and estimated quantities. This is expected, as the matrix-based entropy estimators measure information theoretic quantities in RKHS without the need for explicit PDF but with similar properties as common information theoretic measures. The kernel width was selected by taking the median distance between all samples.

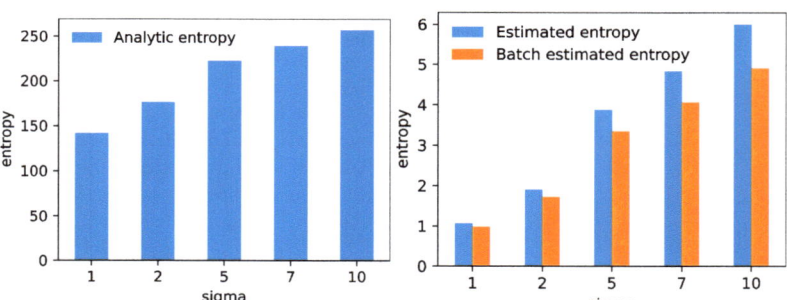

Figure 2. The leftmost plot shows the entropy calculated using Equation (14) of a 100-dimensional normal distribution with zero mean and an isotropic covariance matrix for different variances. The variances are given along the x-axis. The rightmost plot shows the entropy estimated using Equation (1) for the same distribution. The plots illustrated that the analytically computed entropy and the estimated quantity follow the same trend.

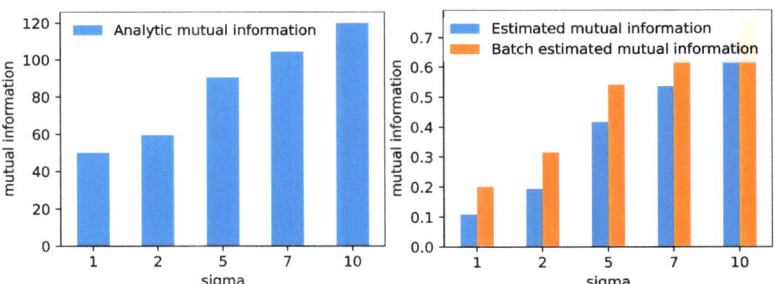

Figure 3. The leftmost plot shows the mutual information calculated using Equation (16) between a standard 100-dimensional normal distribution and a normal distribution with a mean vector of all ones and an isotropic covariance matrix with different variances. The variances are given along the x-axis. The rightmost plot shows the mutual information estimated using Equation (3) for the same distributions. The plots illustrated that the analytically computed mutual information and the estimated quantity follow the same trend.

3.3. Novel Tensor-Based Matrix-Based Renyi Information Measures

To invoke information theoretic quantities of features produced by convolutional layers and to address the limitations discussed above, we introduce in this section our novel tensor-based approach for measuring entropy and MI in DNNs. This enables for the first time an IP analysis of large-scale CNNs.

3.4. Tensor Kernels for Measuring Mutual Information

The output of a convolutional layer is represented as a tensor $\mathbb{X}_i \in \mathbb{R}^C \otimes \mathbb{R}^H \otimes \mathbb{R}^W$ for a data point i. As discussed above, the matrix-based Rényi's α-entropy cannot include tensor data without modifications. To handle the tensor-based nature of convolutional layers, we propose to utilize tensor kernels [32] to produce a kernel matrix for the output of a convolutional layer. A tensor formulation of the radial basis function (RBF) kernel can be stated as

$$\kappa_{\text{ten}}(\mathbb{X}_i, \mathbb{X}_j) = e^{-\frac{1}{\sigma^2}\|\mathbb{X}_i - \mathbb{X}_j\|_F^2}, \tag{17}$$

where $\|\cdot\|_F$ denotes the Hilbert–Frobenius norm [32] and σ is the kernel width parameter. In practice, the tensor kernel in Equation (17) can be computed by reshaping the tensor into a vectorized representation while replacing the Hilbert–Frobenius norm with a Euclidean norm. We compute the MI in Equation (3) by replacing the matrix **A** with

$$\begin{aligned}(\mathbf{A}_{\text{ten}})_{ij} &= \frac{1}{N} \frac{(\mathbf{K}_{\text{ten}})_{ij}}{\sqrt{(\mathbf{K}_{\text{ten}})_{ii}(\mathbf{K}_{\text{ten}})_{jj}}} \\ &= \frac{1}{N} \kappa_{\text{ten}}(\mathbb{X}_i, \mathbb{X}_j).\end{aligned} \tag{18}$$

While Equation (17) provides the simplest and most intuitive approach for using kernels with tensor data, it does have its limitations. Namely, a tensor kernel that simply vectorizes the tensor ignores the inter-component structures within and between the respective tensor [32]. For simple tensor data, such structures might not be present and a tensor kernel as described above can suffice; however, other tensor kernels do exist, such as for instance the matricization-based tensor kernels [32]. In this work, we have chosen the tensor kernel defined in Equation (17) for its simplicity and computational benefits, which come from the fact that the entropy and joint entropy are computed batch-wise by finding the eigenvalues of a kernel matrix, or the eigenvalues of the Hadamard product of two kernel matrices, and utilizing Equation (1). Nevertheless, exploring structure-preserving kernels can be an interesting research path in future works. In Appendix C, we have included a simple example toward this direction, where the tensor kernel described in this paper is compared to a matricization-based tensor kernel.

3.4.1. Choosing the Kernel Width

With methods involving RBF kernels, the choice of the kernel width parameter, σ, is always critical. For supervised learning, one might choose this parameter by cross-validation based on validation accuracy, while in unsupervised problems, one might use a rule of thumb [33–35]. However, in the case of measuring MI in DNNs, the data are often high dimensional, in which case unsupervised rules of thumb often fail [34].

In this work, we choose σ based on an optimality criterion. Intuitively, one can make the following observation: a good kernel matrix should reveal the class structures present in the data. This can be accomplished by maximizing the so-called *kernel alignment* loss [36] between the kernel matrix of a given layer, $\mathbf{K}_\sigma$, and the label kernel matrix, $\mathbf{K}_y$. The kernel alignment loss is defined as

$$A(\mathbf{K}_a, \mathbf{K}_b) = \frac{\langle \mathbf{K}_a, \mathbf{K}_b \rangle_F}{\|\mathbf{K}_a\|_F \|\mathbf{K}_b\|_F}, \tag{19}$$

where $\|\cdot\|_F$ and $\langle \cdot, \cdot \rangle_F$ denote the Frobenius norm and inner product, respectively. Thus, we choose our optimal σ as

$$\sigma^* = \arg\max_\sigma A(\mathbf{K}_\sigma, \mathbf{K}_y).$$

To stabilize the σ values across mini batches, we employ an exponential moving average, such that in layer ℓ at iteration t, we have

$$\sigma_{\ell,t} = \beta \sigma_{\ell,t-1} + (1-\beta) \sigma^*_{\ell,t},$$

where $\beta \in [0,1]$ and $\sigma_{\ell,1} = \sigma^*_{\ell,1}$.

4. Results

We evaluate our approach by comparing it to previous results obtained on small networks by considering the MNIST dataset and a Multilayer Perceptron (MLP) architecture that was inspired by [5]. We further compare to a small CNN architecture similar to that of [4] before considering large networks, namely VGG16, and a more challenging dataset, namely CIFAR-10. Note that unless stated otherwise, we use CNN to denote the small CNN architecture. Details about the MLP and the CNN utilized in these experiments can be found in Appendix D. All MI measures were computed using Equations (2), (3) and (10) and the tensor approach described in Section 4, which amounts to setting $\alpha = 1$. Furthermore, the MI estimates showed in all plots are averages across multiple training runs. Code is available online (https://github.com/Wickstrom/InformationTheoryExperiment, accessed on 1 June 2023).

Since the MI is computed at the mini-batch level, a certain degree of noise is present. To smooth the MI measures, we employ a moving average approach where each sample is averaged over k mini-batches. For the MLP and CNN experiments, we use $k = 10$, and for the VGG16, we use $k = 50$. We use a batch size of 100 samples and determine the kernel width using the kernel alignment loss defined in Equation (19). For each hidden layer, we chose the kernel width that maximizes the kernel alignment loss in the range 0.1 and 10 times the mean distance between the samples in one mini-batch. Initially, we sample 75 equally spaced values for the kernel width in the given range for the MLP and CNN and 300 values for the VGG16 network. During training, we dynamically reduce the number of samples to 50 and 100, respectively, to reduce computational complexity, which is motivated by the fact that the kernel width remains relatively stable during the latter part of training (illustrated in Section 5). We chose the ranges 0.1 and 10 times the mean distance between the samples in one mini-batch to avoid the kernel width becoming too small and to ensure that we cover a wide enough range of possible values. For the input kernel width, we empirically evaluated values in the range 2–16 and found consistent results for values in the range 4–12. All our experiments were conducted with an input kernel width of 8. For the label kernel matrix, we want a kernel width that is as small as possible to approach an ideal kernel matrix while at the same time large enough to avoid numerical instabilities. For all our experiments, we use a value of 0.1 for the kernel width of the label kernel matrix.

Comparison to previous approaches First, we study the IP of the MLP similar to the one examined in previous works on DNN analysis using information theory [4,5]. We utilize stochastic gradient descent, a cross-entropy loss function, and repeat the experiment 5 times. Figure 1 displays the IP of the MLP with a ReLU activation function in each hidden layer. MI was measured using the training data of the MNIST dataset. A similar experiment was performed with the tanh activation function, obtaining similar results. The interested reader can find these results in Appendix E.

From Figure 1, one can clearly observe a fitting phase, where both $I(T;X)$ and $I(Y;T)$ increase rapidly, followed by a compression phase where $I(T;X)$ decrease and $I(Y;T)$ remains unchanged. In addition, note that $I(Y;T)$ for the output layer (layer 5 in Figure 1) stabilizes at an approximate value of $\log_2(10)$. The following analysis shows that this is to be expected. When the network achieves approximately 100% accuracy, $I(Y;\hat{Y}) \approx S(Y)$, where $\hat{Y}$ denotes the output of the network, since Y and $\hat{Y}$ will be approximately identical and the MI between a variable and itself is just the entropy of the variable. The entropy of Y is measured using Equation (10), which requires the computation of the eigenvalues of the label kernel matrix $\frac{1}{N}\mathbf{K}_y$. For the ideal case, where $(\mathbf{K}_y)_{ij} = 1$ if $y_i = y_j$ and zero otherwise, $\mathbf{K}_y$ is a rank K matrix, where K is the number of classes in the data. Thus, $\frac{1}{N}\mathbf{K}_y$ has K non-zero eigenvalues which are given by $\lambda_k(\frac{1}{N}\mathbf{K}_y) = \frac{1}{N}\lambda_k(\mathbf{K}_y) = \frac{N_{c_k}}{N}$, where N_{c_k} is the number of datapoints in class k, $k = 1, 2, \ldots, K$. Furthermore, if the dataset is balanced, we have $N_{c_1} = N_{c_2} = \ldots = N_{c_K} \equiv N_c$. Then, $\lambda_k\left(\frac{1}{N}\mathbf{K}_y\right) = \frac{N_c}{N} = \frac{1}{K}$, which gives us the entropy measure

$$\begin{aligned} S\left(\frac{1}{N}\mathbf{K}_y\right) &= -\sum_{k=1}^{K} \lambda_k\left(\frac{1}{N}\mathbf{K}_y\right) \log_2\left[\lambda_k\left(\frac{1}{N}\mathbf{K}_y\right)\right] \\ &= -\sum_{k=1}^{K} \frac{1}{K} \log_2\left[\frac{1}{K}\right] \\ &= \log_2[K]. \end{aligned} \quad (20)$$

Next, we examine the IP of a CNN, similar to that studied by [4], with a similar experimental setup as for the MLP experiment. Figure 4 displays the IP of the CNN with a ReLU activation function in all hidden layers. A similar experiment was conducted using the tanh activation function and can be found in Appendix F. While the output layer behaves similarly to that of the MLP, the preceding layers show much less movement. In particular, no fitting phase is observed, which we hypothesize is a result of the convolutional layers being able to extract the necessary information in very few iterations. Note that the output layer is again settling at the expected value of $\log_2(10)$, similar to the MLP, as it also achieves close to 100% accuracy.

Increasing DNN size We analyze the IP of the VGG16 network on the CIFAR-10 dataset with the same experimental setup as in the previous experiments. To our knowledge, this is the first time that the full IP has been modeled for such a large-scale network. Figures 5 and 6 show the IP when measuring the MI for the training dataset and the test dataset, respectively. For the training dataset, we can clearly observe the same trend as for the smaller networks, where layers experience a fitting phase during the early stages of training and a compression phase in the later stage. Note that the compression phase is less prominent for the testing dataset. Note also the difference between the final values of $I(Y;T)$ for the output layer measured using the training and test data, which is a result of the different accuracy achieved on the training data (≈100%) and test data (≈90%). Ref. [3] claims that $I(T;X) \approx H(X)$ and $I(Y;T) \approx H(Y)$ for high-dimensional data, and they highlight particular difficulties with measuring the MI between convolutional layers and the input/output. However, this statement is dependent on their particular measure for the MI, and the results presented in Figure 5 and 6 demonstrate that neither $I(T;X)$ nor $I(Y;T)$ is deterministic for our proposed measure. Furthermore, other measures of MI have also demonstrated that both $I(T;X) \approx H(X)$ and $I(Y;T) \approx H(Y)$ evolve during training [4,18].

Another type of widely used DNNs is residual networks [37]. While these networks typically have less parameters than the VGG16, they usually have more layers. This increase in the number of layers is enabled by skip-connections that allow data to flow through the network without loss of information. This complicates the information theoretic analysis, as the dynamics between the layers change and information do not need to decrease in between the layers. While our proposed estimator is computationally capable of handling residual networks, an extensive analysis would be required to understand the added complexity that is introduced by the lossless flow of information in these networks. We consider such an analysis as outside the scope of this paper but an interesting avenue of future research.

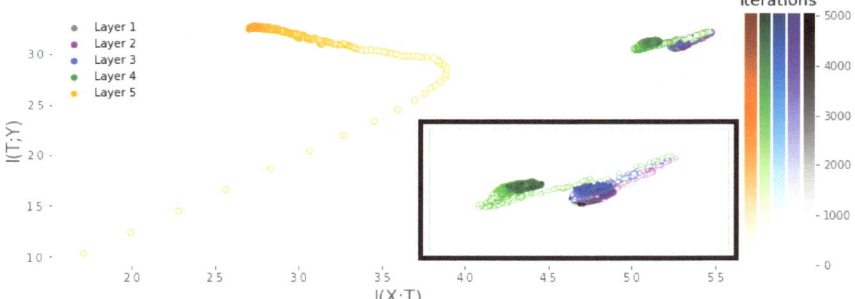

Figure 4. IP of a CNN consisting of three convolutional layers with 4, 8 and 12 filters and one fully connected layer with 256 neurons and a ReLU activation function in each hidden layer. MI was measured using the training data of the MNIST dataset and averaged over 5 runs.

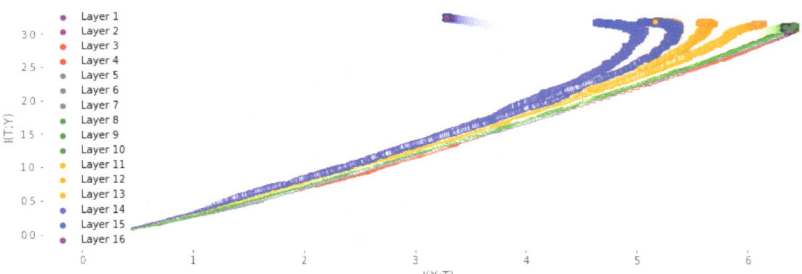

Figure 5. IP of the VGG16 on the CIFAR-10 dataset. MI was measured using the training data and averaged over 2 runs. Color saturation increases as training progresses. Both the fitting phase and the compression phase is clearly visible for several layers.

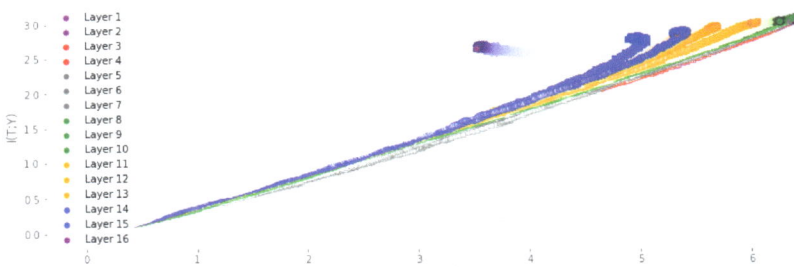

Figure 6. IP of the VGG16 on the CIFAR-10 dataset. MI was measured using the test data and averaged over 2 runs. Color saturation increases as training progresses. The fitting phase is clearly visible, while the compression phase can only be seen in the output layer.

Effect of early stopping We also investigate the effect of using early stopping on the IP described above. Early stopping is a regularization technique where the validation accuracy is monitored and training is stopped if the validation accuracy does not increase for a set number of iterations, which is often referred to as the patience hyperparameter. Figure 1 displays the results of monitoring where the training would stop if the early stopping procedure was applied for different values of patience. For a patience of five iterations, the network training would stop before the compression phase takes place for several of the layers. For larger patience values, the effects of the compression phase can be observed before training is stopped. Early stopping is a procedure intended to prevent the network from overfitting, which may imply that the compression phase observed in the IP of DNNs can be related to overfitting. However, recent research on the so-called double descent phenomenon has shown that longer training might be necessary for good performance for overparameterized DNNs [38,39]. In such settings, early stopping might not be as applicable. We describe the double descent phenomenon and investigate its possible connection with the IP in Appendix H.

Data processing inequality The data processing inequality (DPI) is a concept in information theory which states that the amount of information cannot increase in a chain of transformations. A good information theoretic estimator should tend to uphold the DPI. DNN consists of a chain of mappings from the input through the hidden layers and to the output. One can interpret a DNN as a Markov chain [1,7] that defines an information path [1], which should satisfy the DPI [40]:

$$I(X;T_1) \geq I(X;T_2) \geq \ldots \geq I(X;T_L), \qquad (21)$$

where L is the number of layers in the network. An indication of a good MI measure is that it tends to uphold the DPI. Figure 7 illustrates the mean difference in MI between two subsequent layers in the MLP and VGG16 networks. Positive numbers indicate that MI decreases, thus indicating compliance with the DPI. We observe that our measure complies with the DPI for all layers in the MLP and all except one in the VGG16 network. Furthermore, we also model the DPI for a simple MLP using the EDGE MI estimator, which has shown encouraging results on several MI estimation tasks [4]. The DPI for the EDGE estimator is shown in Figure A4 of Appendix G, which shows that the EDGE estimator also upholds the DPI. This agrees with our results with regard to the information flow in neural networks. However, a limitation of the EDGE estimator is that it is not differentiable, which can be beneficial if MI estimates are to be included in the training [41].

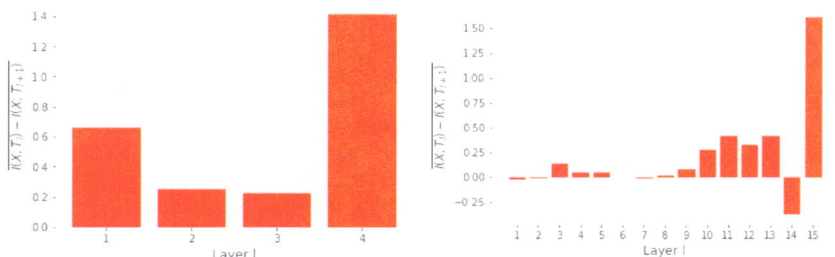

Figure 7. Mean difference in MI of subsequent layers ℓ and $\ell + 1$. Positive numbers indicate compliance with the DPI. MI was measured on the MNIST training set for the MLP and on the CIFAR-10 training set for the VGG16.

5. Kernel Width Sigma

We further evaluate our dynamic approach of finding the kernel width σ. Figure 8 shows the variation of σ in each layer for the MLP, the small CNN and the VGG16 network. We observe that the optimal kernel width for each layer (based on the criterion in Section 3.4.1) stabilizes reasonably quickly and remains relatively constant during training. This illustrates that decreasing the sampling range is a useful approach to decreasing computational complexity.

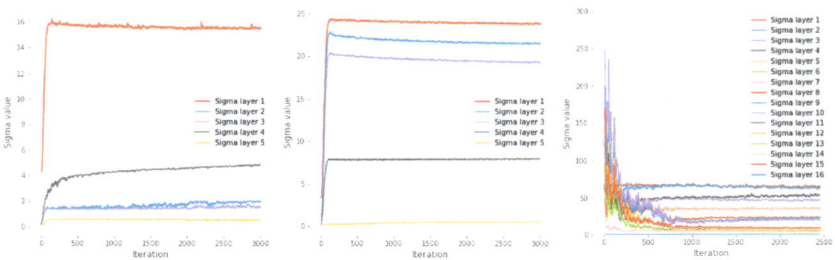

Figure 8. Evolution of kernel width as a function of iteration for the three networks that we considered in this work. From left to right, plots shows the kernel width for the MLP, CNN, and VGG16. The plots demonstrate how the optimal kernel width quickly stabilizes and stays relatively stable throughout the training.

6. Discussion and Conclusions

In this work, we propose a novel framework for analyzing DNNs from an information theoretic perspective using a tensor-based measure of the matrix-based approach of [12]. Our experiments illustrate that the proposed approach scales to large DNNs, which allows us to provide insights into the training dynamics. We observe that the compression phase in neural network training tends to be more prominent when MI is measured on the training set and that commonly used early-stopping criteria tend to stop training before or at the onset of the compression phase. This could imply that the compression phase is linked to overfitting. However, recent research on the double descent phenomenon has shown that a longer training time might be beneficial for generalization [38,39]. In Appendix H, we perform a preliminary study that examines a potential connection between the compression phase and the recent epoch-wise double descent phenomenon. Furthermore, we showed that for our tensor-based approach, the claim that $H(X) \approx I(T;X)$ and $H(Y) \approx I(T;Y)$ does not hold. We believe that our proposed approach can provide new insight and facilitate a more theoretical understanding of DNNs.

Author Contributions: Conceptualization, K.K.W., S.L., M.C.K., S.Y., J.C.P. and R.J.; Formal analysis, K.K.W.; Funding acquisition, R.J.; Investigation, K.K.W., S.L., M.C.K., S.Y., J.C.P. and R.J.; Methodology, K.K.W., S.L., M.C.K., S.Y., J.C.P. and R.J.; Software, K.K.W.; Supervision, M.C.K., J.C.P. and R.J.; Visualization, K.K.W.; Writing—original draft, K.K.W.; Writing—review and editing, K.K.W., S.L., M.C.K., S.Y., J.C.P. and R.J. All authors have read and agreed to the published version of the manuscript.

Funding: This work was supported by The Research Council of Norway (RCN) through its Centre for Research-based Innovation funding scheme (grant number 309439) and Consortium Partners; RCN FRIPRO (grant number 315029); RCN IKTPLUSS (grant number 303514) and the UiT Thematic Initiative.

Data Availability Statement: We used the publicly available MNIST (http://yann.lecun.com/exdb/mnist/, accessed on accessed on 1 January 2023) and CIFAR 10 (https://www.cs.toronto.edu/~kriz/cifar.html, accessed on 1 January 2023) datasets in our analysis.

Conflicts of Interest: The authors declare no conflict of interest.

Appendix A. Preliminaries on Multivariate Matrix-Based Renyi's Alpha-Entropy Functionals

The matrix-based Rényi's α-order entropy functional is not suitable for estimating the amount of information of the features produced by a convolutional layer in a DNN as the output consists of C feature maps, each represented by their own matrix, that characterize different properties of the same sample. Ref. [20] proposed a multivariate extension of the matrix-based Rényi's α-order entropy, which computes the joint entropy among C variables as

$$S_\alpha(\mathbf{A}_1, \ldots, \mathbf{A}_C) = S_\alpha\left(\frac{\mathbf{A}_1 \circ \ldots \circ \mathbf{A}_C}{\text{tr}(\mathbf{A}_1 \circ \ldots \circ \mathbf{A}_C)}\right), \tag{A1}$$

where

$$(\mathbf{A}_1)_{ij} = \kappa_1(\mathbf{x}_i^{(1)}, \mathbf{x}_j^{(1)}), \ldots, (\mathbf{A}_C)_{ij} = \kappa_C(\mathbf{x}_i^{(C)}, \mathbf{x}_j^{(C)}). \tag{A2}$$

Ref. [6] also demonstrated how Equation (A1) could be utilized for analyzing the synergy and redundancy of convolutional layers in DNN, but they noted that this formulation can encounter difficulties when the number of feature maps increases, such as in more complex CNNs. Difficulties arise due to the Hadamard products in Equation (A1), given that each element of $\mathbf{A}_c$, $c \in \{1, 2, \ldots, C\}$ takes on a value between 0 and $\frac{1}{N}$, and the product of C such elements thus tends toward 0 as C grows.

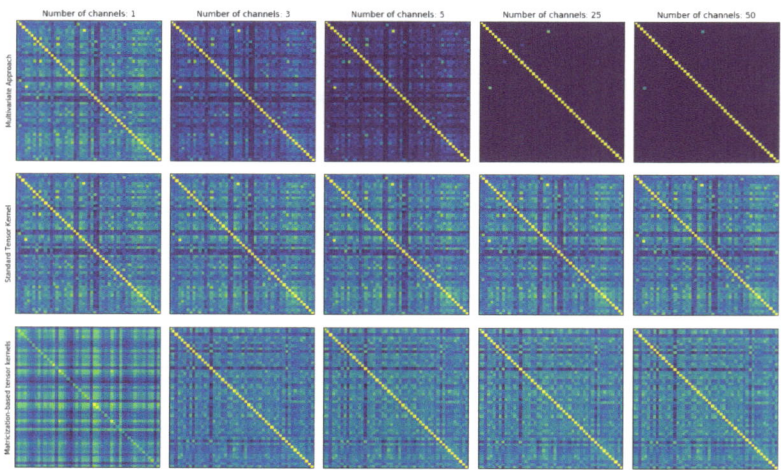

Figure A1. Different approaches for calculating kernels based on tensor data. The first row shows results when using the multivariate approach of [20], the second row depicts the tensor kernel approach used in this paper, and the third row displays the kernel obtained using matricization-based tensor kernels [32] that preserve the structure between channels. Bright colors indicate high values, while dark values indicate low values in all the kernel matrices.

Appendix B. Tensor-Based Approach Contains Multivariate Approach as Special Case

Let $\mathbf{x}_i(\ell) \in \mathbb{R}^{HWC}$ denote the vector representation of data point i in layer ℓ and let $\mathbf{x}_i^{(c)}(\ell) \in \mathbb{R}^{HW}$ denote its representation produced by filter c. In the following, we omit the layer index for ease of notation but assume it is fixed. Consider the case when $\kappa_c(\cdot, \cdot)$ is an RBF kernel with kernel width parameter σ_c. That is, $\kappa_c(\mathbf{x}_i^{(c)}, \mathbf{x}_j^{(c)}) = e^{-\frac{1}{\sigma_c^2}\|\mathbf{x}_i^{(c)} - \mathbf{x}_j^{(c)}\|^2}$. In this case, $\mathbf{A}_c = \frac{1}{N}\mathbf{K}_c$ and

$$\frac{\mathbf{A}_1 \circ \ldots \circ \mathbf{A}_C}{\operatorname{tr}(\mathbf{A}_1 \circ \ldots \circ \mathbf{A}_C)} = \frac{\frac{1}{N}\mathbf{K}_1 \circ \ldots \circ \frac{1}{N}\mathbf{K}_C}{\operatorname{tr}(\frac{1}{N}\mathbf{K}_1 \circ \ldots \circ \frac{1}{N}\mathbf{K}_C)} \quad (A3)$$
$$= \frac{1}{N}\mathbf{K}_1 \circ \ldots \circ \mathbf{K}_C,$$

since $\operatorname{tr}(\mathbf{K}_1 \circ \ldots \circ \mathbf{K}_C) = N$. Thus, element (i,j) is given by

$$\left(\frac{\mathbf{A}_1 \circ \ldots \circ \mathbf{A}_C}{\operatorname{tr}(\mathbf{A}_1 \circ \ldots \circ \mathbf{A}_C)}\right)_{ij} = \frac{1}{N}\prod_{c=1}^{C}(\mathbf{K}_c)_{ij} \quad (A4)$$
$$= \frac{1}{N}e^{-\sum_{c=1}^{C}\frac{1}{\sigma_c^2}\|\mathbf{x}_i^{(c)} - \mathbf{x}_j^{(c)}\|^2}.$$

If we let $\sigma = \sigma_1 = \sigma_2 = \ldots = \sigma_C$, this expression is reduced to

$$\frac{1}{N}e^{-\frac{1}{\sigma^2}\sum_{c=1}^{C}\|\mathbf{x}_i^{(c)} - \mathbf{x}_j^{(c)}\|^2} = \frac{1}{N}e^{-\frac{1}{\sigma^2}\|\mathbf{x}_i - \mathbf{x}_j\|^2} \quad (A5)$$
$$= \frac{1}{N}\kappa_{\text{ten}}(\mathbb{X}_i, \mathbb{X}_j).$$

Accordingly, $S_\alpha(\mathbf{A}_{\text{ten}}) = S_\alpha(\mathbf{A}_1, \ldots, \mathbf{A}_C)$, implying that the tensor method is equivalent to the multivariate matrix-based joint entropy when the width parameter is equal within a given layer, assuming an RBF kernel is used. However, the tensor-based approach eliminates the effect of numerical instabilities one encounters in layers with many filters, thereby enabling the training of complex neural networks.

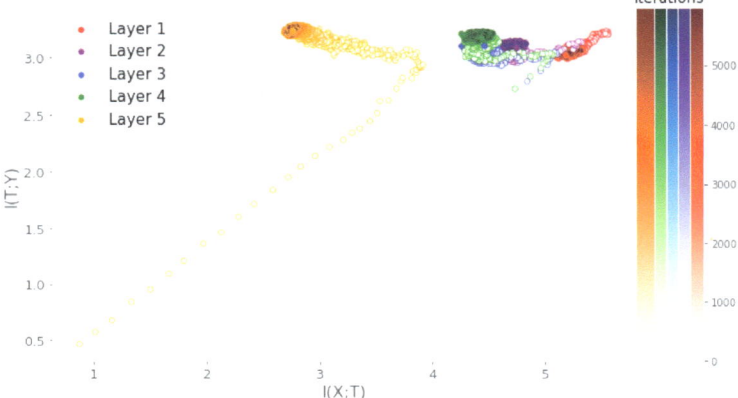

Figure A2. IP of an MLP consisting of four fully connected layers with 1024, 20, 20, and 20 neurons and a tanh activation function in each hidden layer. MI was measured using the training data of the MNIST dataset and averaged over 5 runs.

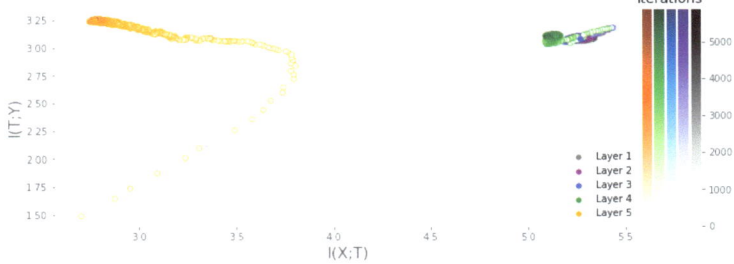

Figure A3. IP of a CNN consisting of three convolutional layers with 4, 8 and 12 filters and one fully connected layer with 256 neurons and a tanh activation function in each hidden layer. MI was measured using the training data of the MNIST dataset and averaged over 5 runs.

Appendix C. Structure Preserving Tensor Kernels and Numerical Instability of Multivariate Approach

As explained in Appendix A, the multivariate approach of [20] Equation (A1) struggles when the number of channels in an image tensor becomes large as a result of the Hadamard products in Equation (A1). To illustrate this instability, we have conducted a simple example. A subset of 50 samples is extracted from the MNIST dataset. Then, each image is duplicated (plus some noise) C times along the channel dimension of the same image, i.e., going from a grayscale image of size $(1, 1, 28, 28)$ to a new image of size $(1, C, 28, 28)$. Since the same image is added along the channel dimension, the kernel matrix should not change dramatically. Figure A1 displays the results of the experiment just described. The first row of Figure A1 shows the kernel matrices based on the multivariate approach proposed by [20]. When the tensor data only have one channel (first column), the kernel obtained is identical to the results obtained using the tensor kernel described in this paper. However, as the number of channels increases, the off-diagonal quickly vanishes and the kernel matrix tends toward a diagonal matrix. This is a result of vanishing Hadamard products, as described in Appendix A. Theoretically, the multivariate approach should yield the same kernel as with the tensor kernel approach, as explained in Section 3.3, but the off-diagonal elements decrease so quickly that they fall outside numerical precision. The second row of Figure A1 depicts the kernel matrices obtained using the tensor kernel approach described in Section 3.3. The kernel matrices in this row are almost unchanged as the number of channels increases, which is to be expected. Since the same image is added along the channel dimension, the similarity between the samples should not change drastically, which is what this row demonstrates. The third row of Figure A1 displays the kernel matrices obtained using so-called matricization-based tensor kernels [32], which are tensor kernels that preserve structure between the channels of the tensor. In this case, this approach produces similar results to the tensor kernel used in this paper, which is to be expected. Since the same image is added along the channel dimension, there is little information to extract between the channels. We hypothesize that for small images with centered objects, such as with MNIST and CIFAR10, the structured tensor kernel does not capture much more information than the tensor kernel described in Section 3.3. However, for more complex tensor data, exploring the potential of such structure-preserving tensor kernels is an interesting avenue for future studies.

Appendix D. Detailed Description of Networks from Section 4

We provide a detailed description of the architectures utilized in Section 4 of the main paper. Weights were initialized according to [42] when the ReLU activation function was applied and initialized according to [43] for the experiments conducted using the tanh activation function. Biases were initialized as zeros for all networks. A learning rate of 0.09 was used for the gradient descent algorithm. All networks were implemented using the deep learning framework Pytorch [44].

Appendix D.1. Multilayer Perceptron Used in Section 4

The MLP architecture used in our experiments is inspired by the architecture utilized in previous studies on the IP of DNN [4,5] but with batch normalization [45] included after the activation function of each hidden layer and an extra hidden layer. Specifically, the MLP in Section 5 includes (from input to output) the following components:

1. Fully connected layer with 784 inputs and 1024 outputs.
2. Activation function.
3. Batch normalization layer.
4. Fully connected layer with 1024 inputs and 20 outputs.
5. Activation function.
6. Batch normalization layer.
7. Fully connected layer with 20 inputs and 20 outputs.
8. Activation function.
9. Batch normalization layer.
10. Fully connected layer with 20 inputs and 20 outputs.
11. Activation function.
12. Batch normalization layer.
13. Fully connected layer with 784 inputs and 10 outputs.
14. Softmax activation function.

Appendix D.2. Convolutional Neural Network Used in Section 4

The CNN architecture in our experiments is a similar architecture to the one used by [4]. Specifically, the CNN in Section 5 includes (from input to output) the following components:

1. Convolutional layer with 1 input channel and 4 filters, filter size 3×3, stride of 1 and no padding.
2. Activation function.
3. Batch normalization layer.

4. Convolutional layer with 4 input channels and 8 filters, filter size 3 × 3, stride of 1 and no padding.
5. Activation function.
6. Batch normalization layer.
7. Max pooling layer with filter size 2 × 2, stride of 2 and no padding.
8. Convolutional layer with 8 input channels and 16 filters, filter size 3 × 3, stride of 1 and no padding.
9. Activation function.
10. Batch normalization layer.
11. Max pooling layer with filter size 2 × 2, stride of 2 and no padding.
12. Fully connected layer with 400 inputs and 256 outputs.
13. Activation function.
14. Batch normalization layer.
15. Fully connected layer with 256 inputs and 10 outputs.
16. Softmax activation function.

Appendix E. IP of MLP with Tanh Activation Function from Section 4

Figure A2 displays the IP of the MLP described above with a tanh activation function applied in each hidden layer. Similarly to the ReLU experiment in the main paper, a fitting phase is observed, where both $I(T;X)$ and $I(Y;T)$ increase rapidly, which is followed by a compression phase where $I(T;X)$ decreases and $I(Y;T)$ remains unchanged. In addition, note that similar to the ReLU experiment, $I(Y;T)$ stabilizes close to the theoretical maximum value of $\log_2(10)$.

Appendix F. IP of CNN with Tanh Activation Function from Section 4

Figure A3 displays the IP of the CNN described above with a tanh activation function applied in each hidden layer. Just as for the CNN experiment with the ReLU activation function in the main paper, no fitting phase is observed for the majority of the layers, which might indicate that the convolutional layers can extract the essential information after only a few iterations.

Appendix G. Data Processing Inequality with EDGE MI Estimator

Figure A4 displays the DPI of a simple MLP using the EDGE estimator as described by [4]. Results indicate that the EDGE estimator upholds the DPI. This agrees with our results with regard to the information flow in neural networks.

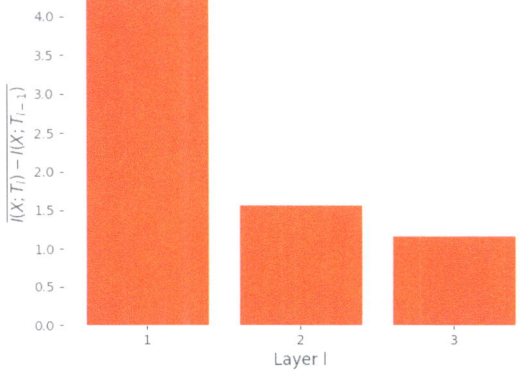

Figure A4. Mean difference in MI of subsequent layers ℓ and $\ell + 1$. Positive numbers indicate compliance with the DPI. MI was measured on the MNIST training using the EDGE MI estimator on a simple MLP [4].

Appendix H. Connection with Epoch-Wise Double Descent

One of the fundamental questions of deep learning is how heavily overparameterized models generalize well to unseen data. Recent studies have empirically demonstrated that having many more parameters than training points can be beneficial for generalization, which have been analyzed from the perspective of the double descent phenomenon [38,39]. The double descent phenomenon was proposed to qualitatively describe the behavior of complex models when the number of parameters is much larger than the number of samples, which is the heavily overparametrized regime that DNNs often operate in. Moreover, ref. [39] showed that overparametrized models can also exhibit epoch-wise double descent. Epoch-wise double descent refers to a phenomenon where the test error initially decreases and then increases before finally decreasing again and stabilizing. Such a behavior bears resemblance to the information flow discussed in this paper, where the information initially increases before decreasing.

To investigate the potential connection between our information theoretic analysis of DNNs and the epoch-wise double descent phenomenon, we train a heavily overparametrized neural network on a subset of the MNIST dataset (10,000 samples) inspired by [38]. The overparametrized network consists of one hidden layer and the output layer, where the hidden layer contains 50,000 neurons with a ReLU activation function. The training and analysis of this network is carried out in a similar manner as all the other reported experiments. Figure A5 displays training and test loss together with the MI between the input and each layer of the network. First, notice that the epoch-wise double descent phenomenon is clearly visible, as the test loss initially decreases, which is followed by an increase, and toward the end, there is another period of decrease. Simultaneously, the start of compression in $MI(X, \hat{Y})$ seems to coincide with the increase of the test loss, and it ends when the test loss stabilizes after going down again. These results suggests that there might be a link with the compression phase of DNNs and the epoch-wise double descent phenomenon, and that information theory can be used to gain new insights into the generalization capabilities of DNNs.

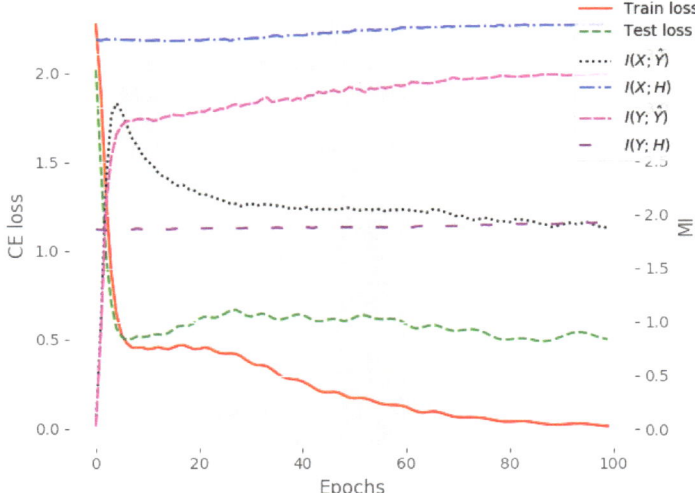

Figure A5. Training and test loss of neural network with one hidden layer with 50,000 neurons on a subset of the MNIST dataset. The figure also shows the MI between the input/labels and the hidden/output layer. The epoch-wise double descent phenomenon is visible in the test loss, and it seems to coincide with the start of the compression of MI between the input and output layer. Notice the different labels on the left and right y-axis. Curves represent the average over 3 training runs.

References

1. Shwartz-Ziv, R.; Tishby, N. Opening the Black Box of Deep Neural Networks via Information. *arXiv* **2017**, arXiv:1703.00810. [CrossRef]
2. Geiger, B.C. On Information Plane Analyses of Neural Network Classifiers—A Review. *IEEE Trans. Neural Netw. Learn. Syst.* **2021**, *33*, 7039–7051. [CrossRef]
3. Cheng, H.; Lian, D.; Gao, S.; Geng, Y. Evaluating Capability of Deep Neural Networks for Image Classification via Information Plane. In Proceedings of the European Conference on Computer Vision, Munich, Germany, 8–14 September 2018; pp. 168–182.
4. Noshad, M.; Zeng, Y.; Hero, A.O. Scalable Mutual Information Estimation Using Dependence Graphs. In Proceedings of the IEEE International Conference on Acoustics, Speech and Signal Processing, Brighton, UK, 12–17 May 2019; pp. 2962–2966.
5. Saxe, A.M.; Bansal, Y.; Dapello, J.; Advani, M.; Kolchinsky, A.; Tracey, B.D.; Cox, D.D. On the information bottleneck theory of deep learning. *J. Stat. Mech. Theory Exp.* **2019**, *2019*, 124020. [CrossRef]
6. Yu, S.; Wickstrøm, K.; Jenssen, R.; Príncipe, J.C. Understanding Convolutional Neural Network Training with Information Theory. *IEEE Trans. Neural Netw. Learn. Syst.* **2020**, *32*, 435–442. [CrossRef]
7. Yu, S.; Principe, J.C. Understanding autoencoders with information theoretic concepts. *Neural Netw.* **2019**, *117*, 104–123. [CrossRef] [PubMed]
8. Lorenzen, S.S.; Igel, C.; Nielsen, M. Information Bottleneck: Exact Analysis of (Quantized) Neural Networks. In Proceedings of the International Conference on Learning Representations, Virtual, 25–29 April 2022.
9. Goldfeld, Z.; Van Den Berg, E.; Greenewald, K.; Melnyk, I.; Nguyen, K.; Kingsbury, B.; Polyanskiy, Y. Estimating Information Flow in Deep Neural Networks. In Proceedings of the International Conference on Machine Learning, Long Beach, CA, USA, 9–15 June 2019; pp. 2299–2308.
10. Chelombiev, I.; Houghton, C.; O'Donnell, C. Adaptive Estimators Show Information Compression in Deep Neural Networks. *arXiv* **2019**, arXiv:1902.09037. [CrossRef]
11. Zhouyin, Z.; Liu, D. Understanding Neural Networks with Logarithm Determinant Entropy Estimator. *arXiv* **2021**, arXiv:2105.03705. [CrossRef]
12. Sanchez Giraldo, L.G.; Rao, M.; Principe, J.C. Measures of Entropy From Data Using Infinitely Divisible Kernels. *IEEE Trans. Inf. Theory* **2015**, *61*, 535–548. [CrossRef]
13. Tishby, N.; Zaslavsky, N. Deep learning and the information bottleneck principle. In Proceedings of the 2015 IEEE Information Theory Workshop (ITW), Jerusalem, Israel, 26 April–1 May 2015.
14. Kolchinsky, A.; Tracey, B.D.; Kuyk, S.V. Caveats for information bottleneck in deterministic scenarios. *arXiv* **2019**, arXiv:1808.07593. [CrossRef]
15. Amjad, R.A.; Geiger, B.C. Learning Representations for Neural Network-Based Classification Using the Information Bottleneck Principle. *IEEE Trans. Pattern Anal. Mach. Intell.* **2019**, *42*, 2225–2239. [CrossRef]
16. Kornblith, S.; Norouzi, M.; Lee, H.; Hinton, G. Similarity of Neural Network Representations Revisited. In Proceedings of the International Conference on Machine Learning, Long Beach, CA, USA, 10–15 June 2019; pp. 3519–3529.
17. Jónsson, H.; Cherubini, G.; Eleftheriou, E. Convergence Behavior of DNNs with Mutual-Information-Based Regularization. *Entropy* **2020**, *22*, 727. [CrossRef] [PubMed]
18. Belghazi, M.I.; Baratin, A.; Rajeshwar, S.; Ozair, S.; Bengio, Y.; Courville, A.; Hjelm, D. Mutual Information Neural Estimation. In Proceedings of the 35th International Conference on Machine Learning, Stockholm, Sweden, 10–15 July 2018; Dy, J., Krause, A., Eds.; Volume 80, pp. 531–540.
19. Geiger, B.C.; Kubin, G. Information Bottleneck: Theory and Applications in Deep Learning. *Entropy* **2020**, *22*, 1408. [CrossRef] [PubMed]
20. Yu, S.; Sanchez Giraldo, L.G.; Jenssen, R.; Principe, J.C. Multivariate Extension of Matrix-based Renyi's α-order Entropy Functional. *IEEE Trans. Pattern Anal. Mach. Intell.* **2019**, *42*, 2960–2966. [CrossRef]
21. Landsverk, M.C.; Riemer-Sørensen, S. Mutual information estimation for graph convolutional neural networks. In Proceedings of the 3rd Northern Lights Deep Learning Workshop, Tromso, Norway, 10–11 January 2022; Volume 3.
22. Bhatia, R. Infinitely Divisible Matrices. *Am. Math. Mon.* **2006**, *113*, 221–235. [CrossRef]
23. Renyi, A. On Measures of Entropy and Information. In *Proceedings of the Fourth Berkeley Symposium on Mathematical Statistics and Probability, Volume 1: Contributions to the Theory of Statistics*; University of California Press: Berkeley, CA, USA, 1961; pp. 547–561.
24. Nielsen, M.A.; Chuang, I.L. *Quantum Computation and Quantum Information*, 10th ed.; Cambridge University Press: Cambridge, UK, 2011.
25. Mosonyi, M.; Hiai, F. On the Quantum Rényi Relative Entropies and Related Capacity Formulas. *IEEE Trans. Inf. Theory* **2011**, *57*, 2474–2487. [CrossRef]
26. Kwak, N.; Choi, C.H. Input feature selection by mutual information based on Parzen window. *IEEE Trans. Pattern Anal. Mach. Intell.* **2002**, *24*, 1667–1671. [CrossRef]
27. Gretton, A.; Borgwardt, K.M.; Rasch, M.J.; Schölkopf, B.; Smola, A. A Kernel Two-sample Test. *J. Mach. Learn. Res.* **2012**, *13*, 723–773.
28. Muandet, K.; Fukumizu, K.; Sriperumbudur, B.; Schölkopf, B. Kernel Mean Embedding of Distributions: A Review and Beyond. In *Foundations and Trends® in Machine Learning*; Now Foundations and Trends: Boston, FL, USA, 2017; pp. 1–141.

29. Fukumizu, K.; Gretton, A.; Sun, X.; Schölkopf, B. Kernel Measures of Conditional Dependence. In Proceedings of the Advances in Neural Information Processing Systems, Vancouver, BC, Canada, 3–6 December 2008; pp. 489–496.
30. Smola, A.; Gretton, A.; Song, L.; Schölkopf, B. A Hilbert Space Embedding for Distributions. In Proceedings of the Algorithmic Learning Theory, Sendai, Japan, 1–4 October 2007; Hutter, M., Servedio, R.A., Takimoto, E., Eds.; pp. 13–31.
31. Evans, D. A Computationally Efficient Estimator for Mutual Information. *Proc. Math. Phys. Eng. Sci.* **2008**, *464*, 1203–1215. [CrossRef]
32. Signoretto, M.; De Lathauwer, L.; Suykens, J.A. A kernel-based framework to tensorial data analysis. *Neural Netw.* **2011**, *34*, 861–874. [CrossRef]
33. Shi, J.; Malik, J. Normalized Cuts and Image Segmentation. *IEEE Trans. Pattern Anal. Mach. Intell.* **2000**, *22*, 888–905.
34. Shi, T.; Belkin, M.; Yu, B. Data spectroscopy: Eigenspaces of convolution operators and clustering. *Ann. Stat.* **2009**, *37*, 3960–3984. [CrossRef]
35. Silverman, B.W. *Density Estimation for Statistics and Data Analysis*; CRC Press: Boca Raton, FL, USA, 1986; Volume 26.
36. Cristianini, N.; Shawe-Taylor, J.; Elisseeff, A.; Kandola, J.S. On kernel-target alignment. In Proceedings of the Advances in Neural Information Processing Systems, Vancouver, BC, Canada, 3–6 December 2002; pp. 367–373.
37. He, K.; Zhang, X.; Ren, S.; Sun, J. Deep Residual Learning for Image Recognition. In Proceedings of the IEEE Conference on Computer Vision and Pattern Recognition, Las Vegas, NV, USA, 27–30 June 2016; pp. 770–778.
38. Belkin, M.; Hsu, D.; Ma, S.; Mandal, S. Reconciling modern machine-learning practice and the classical bias–variance trade-off. *Proc. Natl. Acad. Sci. USA* **2019**, *116*, 15849–15854. [CrossRef] [PubMed]
39. Nakkiran, P.; Kaplun, G.; Bansal, Y.; Yang, T.; Barak, B.; Sutskever, I. Deep Double Descent: Where Bigger Models and More Data Hurt. *arXiv* **2020**, arXiv:1912.02292. [CrossRef]
40. Cover, T.M.; Thomas, J.A. *Elements of Information Theory*; Wiley Series in Telecommunications and Signal Processing; Wiley-Interscience: New York, NY, USA, 2006.
41. Yu, X.; Yu, S.; Príncipe, J.C. Deep Deterministic Information Bottleneck with Matrix-Based Entropy Functional. In Proceedings of the IEEE International Conference on Acoustics, Speech and Signal Processing, Toronto, ON, Canada, 6–11 June 2021; pp. 3160–3164.
42. He, K.; Zhang, X.; Ren, S.; Sun, J. Delving Deep into Rectifiers: Surpassing Human-Level Performance on ImageNet Classification. In Proceedings of the 2015 IEEE International Conference on Computer Vision (ICCV), Santiago, Chile, 7–13 December 2015; pp. 1026–1034.
43. Glorot, X.; Bengio, Y. Understanding the difficulty of training deep feedforward neural networks. In Proceedings of the International Conference on Artificial Intelligence and Statistics, Sardinia, Italy, 13–15 May 2010; pp. 249–256.
44. Paszke, A.; Gross, S.; Chintala, S.; Chanan, G.; Yang, E.; DeVito, Z.; Lin, Z.; Desmaison, A.; Antiga, L.; Lerer, A. Automatic Differentiation in PyTorch. 2017. Available online: https://pytorch.org (accessed on 1 January 2023).
45. Ioffe, S.; Szegedy, C. Batch Normalization: Accelerating Deep Network Training by Reducing Internal Covariate Shift. In Proceedings of the International Conference on Machine Learning, Lille, France, 6–11 July 2015; pp. 448–456.

Disclaimer/Publisher's Note: The statements, opinions and data contained in all publications are solely those of the individual author(s) and contributor(s) and not of MDPI and/or the editor(s). MDPI and/or the editor(s) disclaim responsibility for any injury to people or property resulting from any ideas, methods, instructions or products referred to in the content.

Ensemble Transductive Propagation Network for Semi-Supervised Few-Shot Learning

Xueling Pan [1,2], Guohe Li [1,2,*] and Yifeng Zheng [3,4]

1. Beijing Key Lab of Petroleum Data Mining, Department of Geophysics, China University of Petroleum, Beijing 102249, China; 2020310415@student.cup.edu.cn
2. College of Information Science and Engineering, China University of Petroleum, Beijing 102249, China
3. School of Computer Science, Minnan Normal University, Zhangzhou 363000, China; zhengyifengja@gmail.com
4. Key Laboratory of Data Science and Intelligence Application, Fujian Province University, Zhangzhou 363000, China
* Correspondence: lgh202310@163.com

Abstract: Few-shot learning aims to solve the difficulty in obtaining training samples, leading to high variance, high bias, and over-fitting. Recently, graph-based transductive few-shot learning approaches supplement the deficiency of label information via unlabeled data to make a joint prediction, which has become a new research hotspot. Therefore, in this paper, we propose a novel ensemble semi-supervised few-shot learning strategy via transductive network and Dempster–Shafer (D-S) evidence fusion, named ensemble transductive propagation networks (ETPN). First, we present homogeneity and heterogeneity ensemble transductive propagation networks to better use the unlabeled data, which introduce a preset weight coefficient and provide the process of iterative inferences during transductive propagation learning. Then, we combine the information entropy to improve the D-S evidence fusion method, which improves the stability of multi-model results fusion from the pre-processing of the evidence source. Third, we combine the L2 norm to improve an ensemble pruning approach to select individual learners with higher accuracy to participate in the integration of the few-shot model results. Moreover, interference sets are introduced to semi-supervised training to improve the anti-disturbance ability of the mode. Eventually, experiments indicate that the proposed approaches outperform the state-of-the-art few-shot model. The best accuracy of ETPN increases by 0.3% and 0.28% in the 5-way 5-shot, and by 3.43% and 7.6% in the 5-way 1-shot on miniImagNet and tieredImageNet, respectively.

Keywords: few-shot learning; meta learning; graph semi-supervision; label propagation; Gaussian kernel function; D-S evidence theory

1. Introduction

Deep learning is widely used in many practical applications, such as speech recognition [1], computer vision [2], and semantic segmentation [3]. It is data-driven and relies on a large amount of labeled data to train a model. However, in some scenarios, labeled data are costly to obtain. Therefore, how to utilize the limited labeled data to construct a reliable model is very important. Nowadays, inspired by human learning and utilizing prior knowledge to learn new concepts via only a handful of examples, few-shot learning (FSL) has attracted much more attention.

Few-shot learning has been divided into three categories, including augmentation, metric learning, and meta-learning. FSL usually adopts an episodic training mode. Each episodic training includes a support and a query set. The support set is constructed by randomly selecting K categories and N samples in each selected category from training data, namely the K-way N-shot. The query set is also randomly sampled from the K categories, but it has no intersection with the support set.

For augmentation approaches, they aim to increase the number of training samples or features to enhance data diversity. However, some basic augmentation operations need to be improved in the process of model training, such as rotating, flipping, cropping, translating, and adding noise into images [4,5]. With the development of deep learning, more sophisticated algorithms customized for FSL were proposed. Dual TriNet mapped the multi-level image feature into a semantic space to enhance the semantic vectors using the semantic Gaussian or neighborhood approaches [6]. ABS-Net established a repository of attribute features by conducting attribute learning on the auxiliary dataset to synthesize pseudo feature representations automatically [7].

Metric learning is designed to learn a pairwise similarity metric by exploiting the similarity information between samples. It means a similar sample pair has a high similarity score and vice versa. Matching Nets performed full context embeddings by adding external memories to extract features. It measures the similarity between samples via the cosine distance [8]. Proto Net constructed a metric space by computing distances between the prototype representations and test examples [9]. AM3 incorporated extra semantic representations into Proto Net [10]. TSCE utilized the mutual information maximization and ranking-based embedding alignment mechanism to implement knowledge transfer across domains, which maintains the consistency between the semantic and shared spaces, respectively [11]. Moreover, TSVR made the source and target domains have the same label space to quantify domain discrepancy by predicting the similarity/dissimilarity labels for semantic-visual fusions [12]. K-tuplet Nets changed the NCA loss of Proto Net into a K-tuplet metric loss [13]. The drawback of the above algorithms is that they cannot learn enough transferable knowledge in a small number of samples to enhance the model's performance.

Meta-learning approaches aim to utilize the transferring experience of the meta-learner to optimize a base learner. It is divided into three categories: Learn-to-Measure [14–16], Learn-to-Finetune [17,18], and Learn-to-Parameterize [19–21]. MAML learned a suitable initialization parameter via a multi-task training strategy to guarantee its generalization [22]. TAML utilized an entropy-maximization reduction to address the over-fitting problem [23]. DAE employed a graph neural network based on a denoising auto-encoder to generate model parameters [19]. However, the above solutions should further consider the related information between the support set and the query set. Even more importantly, learning a base learner for few-shot tasks is easy to overfit, which results in high-variance or low-confidence predictions by lacking training data [24].

Nowadays, some researchers focus on measuring the relations between the support and the query instances via transductive graph theory. The transductive graph-based approaches [25–27] can effectively obtain the labels of the query set based on a few labeled samples. The main idea is that, regarding the samples of the support set and the query set as graph nodes, the nearest neighbor relationship between the support set and the query set is utilized for joint prediction to supplement the lack of label information. TPN employed the Gaussian kernel function to calculate the similarity as the weight to build a k-nearest neighbor graph (KNN-Graph), which uses the label propagation algorithm to transductively propagate labels between the support and query examples [25]. The drawback is that it may divide all graph vertices into a vast community or trap them in a local maximum to affect the stability and robustness of a model.

To address the above problems, we propose an Ensemble Transductive Propagation Network (ETPN). Firstly, two types of ensemble strategies are proposed, based on homogeneous and heterogeneous algorithms. These are referred to as Ho-ETPN (Homogeneous Ensemble Transductive Propagation Network) and He-ETPN (Heterogeneous Ensemble Transductive Propagation Network), respectively. Transductive inference, based on a graph, is used to extract valuable information shared between support-query pairs for label prediction. This approach circumvents the intermediate problem of defining a prediction function on an entire space in inductive learning. Secondly, a novel fusion strategy is proposed, based on an improved D-S evidence theory, to enhance the robustness of our proposal. The improved D-S evidence fusion approach first uses the Bhattacharyya distance to construct a conflict matrix between the mass function, and then uses this conflict matrix to obtain the support matrix. It then combines information entropy to recalculate the mass weight, realizing the pre-processing of the evidence source. This enhances the robustness and stability of few-shot classification. Thirdly, we propose an improved ensemble pruning approach to select individual learners with higher accuracy to participate in the integration of the few-shot model results. It employs the L2 norm to make the model more stable to small changes in the input and improve the model's robustness.

In summary, the key contributions of our approaches are summarized as follows:

1. *Ensemble framework*: Based on the individual graph learner framework, we propose two ensemble strategies including the homogeneous and heterogeneous models, named Ho-ETPN and He-ETPN, respectively. Moreover, during transductive propagation learning, we add the preset weight coefficient and give the process of iterative inferences.
2. *Ensemble pruning*: Proposing an improved ensemble pruning method to conduct the selective results fusion by screening the individual learner with higher accuracy.
3. *Combination strategy*: An improved D-S evidence aggregation method is proposed for comprehensive evaluation. To the best of our knowledge, it is the first work that explicitly considers the D-S evidence theory in few-shot learning.
4. *Effectiveness*: Extension experiences about supervised and semi-supervised conducted on miniImageNet and tieredImageNet datasets show that our solution yields competitive results on a few-shot classification. More challenging is that distracted classes are introduced during the process of the semi-supervised experiment.

2. Related Work

(1) Transductive Graph Few-shot Learning

Recently, few-shot learning has become one of the hot spots. Transductive inference employs the valuable information between support and query sets to achieve predictions [25]. In a data-scarce scenario, it has been proven to improve the performance of few-shot learning over inductive solutions [28–30]. TPRN treated the sample relation of each support–query pair as a graph node, then resorted to the known relations between support samples to estimate the relational adjacency among the different support–query pairs [31]. DSN proposed an extension of existing dynamic classifiers by using subspaces and introduced a discriminative formulation to encourage maximum discrimination between subspaces during training, which avoids over-performing and boosts robustness against perturbations [32]. Huang et al. proposed PTN to revise the Poisson model tailored for few-shot problems by incorporating the query feature calibration and the Poisson MBO (Merriman–Bence–Osher) model to tackle the cross-class bias problems due to the data distribution drift between the support and query data [26]. EGNN exploited the edge labels rather than the node labels on the graph to exploit both intra-cluster similarity and inter-cluster dissimilarity to evolute an explicit clustering [33]. Unlike the above methods, in this paper, we adopt the transductive graph approach to construct the ETPN model. It leverages the related prior knowledge between support and query sets during the test phase and a novel fusion strategy to address the issue of high variance and over-fitting.

(2) Semi-supervised Few-shot Learning

Moreover, it is difficult to annotate samples in many fields, such as medicine, military, finance, etc. Thus, semi-supervised few-shot learning (SSFSL) approaches are proposed to leverage the extra unlabeled data to enhance the performance of few-shot learning. LTTL proposed a self-training model, which utilizes cherry-picking to search for valuable samples from pseudo-labeled data via a soft-weighting network [34]. PRWN proposed prototypical random walk networks to promote prototypical magnetization of the learning representation [35]. BR-ProtoNet exploited unlabeled data and constructed complementary constraints to learn a generalizable metric [36]. In this paper, we adopt transductive inference to utilize unlabeled data and distractor classes irrelevant to the classification task to boost robustness against perturbations.

(3) Ensemble Few-Shot Learning

Ensemble learning is widely used in classifications to enhance the generalization ability and robustness of models. Therefore, many researchers have applied the ensemble framework to few-shot learning. The main idea is to adopt a combination approach to reduce the over-fitting problem and enhance the stability of the model. DIVERSITY investigated an ensemble approach for training multiple convolutional neural networks (CNNs). Each network predicts class probabilities, which are then integrated by a mean centroid classifier constructed for each network. Moreover, it introduced penalty terms allowing the networks to cooperate during training to guarantee the diversity of predictions [37]. EBDM divided the feature extraction network into shared and exclusive components. The shared component aims to share and reduce parameters in the lower layers, while the exclusive component is designed to be unique to each learner in the higher layers [38]. HGNN proposed a novel hybrid GNN of a prototype and instance to address overlapping classes and outlying samples, respectively [39]. E^3BM introduced a Bayes model for each epoch, which leverages innovative hyperprior learners to learn task-specific hyperparameters and enhances model robustness [40]. However, the existing integration strategies mainly adopt a max-voting strategy without considering information uncertainty. Different from the above methods, we propose an improved D-S method to solve the above problem by preprocessing the data source; moreover, we improved the ensemble pruning method to perform a selective ensemble with better accuracy.

The contribution of our algorithm is summarized in Table 1, including transduction inference (trans_inference), semi-supervised few-shot learning (SSFSL), ensemble, ensemble pruning, and information uncertainty (infor_uncertainty).

Table 1. The key contributions. Where "w/D" means with distractors.

Model	trans_inference	SSFSL	Ensemble	Ensemble Pruning	infor_uncertainty
TPRN [31]	✓	✗	✗	✗	✗
DSN [32]	✓	✓ (w/D)	✗	✗	✗
PTN [26]	✓	✓ (w/D)	✗	✗	✗
EGNN [33]	✓	✓	✗	✗	✗
LTTL [34]	✗	✓	✗	✗	✗
PRWN [35]	✗	✓ (w/D)	✗	✗	✗
BR − ProtoNet [36]	✗	✓ (w/D)	✗	✗	✗
DIVERSITY [37]	✗	✗	✓	✗	✗
EBDM [38]	✗	✗	✓	✗	✗
HGNN [39]	✓	✗	✓	✗	✗
E^3BM [40]	✗	✗	✓	✗	✗
IG − semiTPN [41]	✓	✓ (w/D)	✗	✗	✗
He − ETPN (our)	✓	✓ (w/D)	✓	✓	✓
Ho − ETPN (our)	✓	✓ (w/D)	✓	✓	✓

3. Problem Definition

Given a label set $C = \{c_j | j = 1, 2, \ldots, N\}$, c_j represents the label (i.e., a discrete value). $S = \{s_i | i = 1, 2, \ldots, n\}$ denotes a sample set, $s_i = (x_i, y_i)$ represents a sample, x_i is the attribute values set, $\|x_i\|$ denotes number of dimensions, namely, $x_i = (x_i^1, x_i^2, \ldots, x^{\|x_i\|})$. If $y_i \in C$, s_i represents labeled samples, otherwise $s_i = (x_i, \_)$ represents unlabeled samples. Sample sets are divided into supervised represented S_{sup} and unsupervised sample sets represented by S_{uns}, thus, $S = S_{sup} \cup S_{uns}$, where $S_{sup} = \{(x_i, y_i) | (x_i, y_i) \in S, y_i \in C\}$, $S_{uns} = \{(x_i, \_) | (x_i, \_) \in S\}$.

For S_{sup}, let $X \longrightarrow C$ denote the process of predicting the labels by the classifier F for training samples, where $X = \{x_i | (x_i, y_i) \in S_{sup}\}$, namely $\forall (x_i, y_i) \in S_{sup}, \widetilde{y}_i = F(x_i)$. The accuracy rate of a classifier F is defined as $Acc(S_{sup}, F) = \frac{|\{(x_i,y_i)|(x_i,y_i) \in S_{sup}, \widetilde{y_i}=F(x_i), \widetilde{y_i}=y_i\}|}{|S_{sup}|}$. Supervised machine learning is the process of obtaining a classifier F from S_{sup}.

For F and S_{uns}, obtaining $S_{uns \to sup}$ from S_{uns} is the process of adding annotations, which can be defined as $S_{uns \to sup} = \{(x_i, \widetilde{y_i}) | (x_i, \_) \in S_{uns}, \widetilde{y_i} = F(x_i)\}$. For $S = S_{sup} \cup S_{uns}$ and $X \longrightarrow C$, where $X = \{x_i | (x_i, y_i) \in S_{sup} \text{ or} (x_i, \widetilde{y_i}) \in S_{uns \to sup}\}$, semi-supervised machine learning is the process of obtaining F from S.

For $S = S_T \cup S_V$, where S_T is the train set, S_V is validation set. F is learned from S_T. The validation is the process of calculating $Acc(S_V, F)$.

Few-shot learning constructing models generally adopt episodic training mode. According to the above notations, the episodic training (K-way, N-shot) is defined as follows: let the label set of the support set denote $C_K \subseteq C$, $|C_K| = K$, $\forall C_K, \exists y \in C_K$, $S^N \subseteq S$, $|S^N| = N$, $s \in S^N$, $s = (x,y)$; the support set is defined as $T^{K \cdot N} = \{S_i^N | i = 1, 2, \ldots, K\}$, $\exists y \in C_K$ and the query set is defined as $Q^M \subseteq S$, $|Q^M| = M$, $q \in Q^M$, $\forall S_i^N \in T^{K \cdot N}$, $q \notin S_i^N$.

For $S_{uns \to sup} = \{(x_i, \widetilde{y_i}) | (x_i, \_) \in S_{uns}, \widetilde{y_i} = F(x_i)\}$, the interference sets consist of the distractor classes irrelevant to the target tasks [42,43]. It is added in the support and query sets to boost model robustness.

4. Methodology

In this paper, we propose the ensemble transductive propagation network (ETPN). The whole framework of the ensemble model is shown in Figure 1. For ETPN, we propose Ho-ETPN and He-ETPN models according to different ensemble approaches. Additionally, we incorporate a preset weight coefficient and compute iterative inferences during transductive propagation learning. Moreover, an improved D-S evidence fusion strategy is proposed for comprehensive evaluation. Meanwhile, we improve the ensemble pruning method to screen individual learners of higher accuracy to conduct fusing.

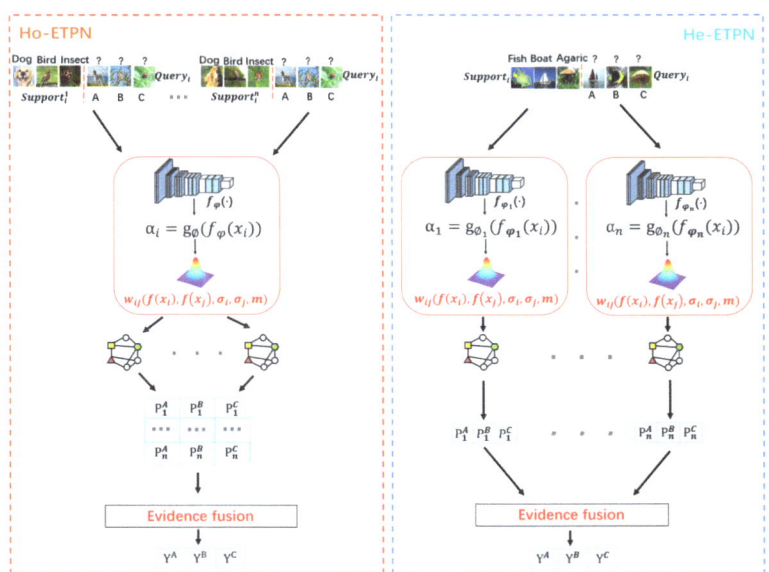

Figure 1. The overall framework diagram of the model.

There are several important parts in our ETPN model (as shown in Figure 2), including the framework of Ho-ETPN and He-ETPN, constructing KNN-Graphs using the improved Gaussian kernel [41], transductive propagation learning, and evidence fusion strategy. Next, we introduce the single model framework of IG-semiTPN simply, then introduce other parts of our ensemble model in detail.

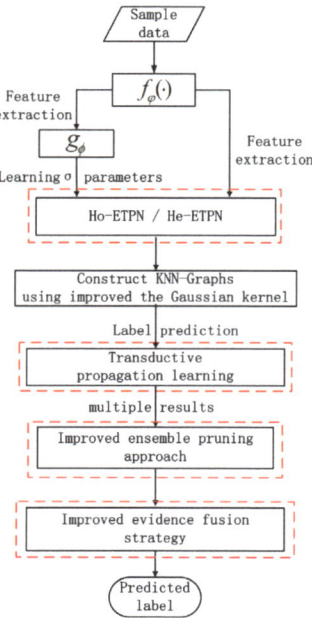

Figure 2. The overall flow chart of the ensemble model.

4.1. IG-semiTPN Model

We propose our ensemble semi-supervised graph network based on the individual learner framework of IG-semiTPN [41] to utilize the information shared between support and query datasets. The framework of IG-semiTPN is shown in Figure 3.

Firstly, it employs $f_\varphi(\cdot)$ to extract features of the input x_i and x_j (φ indicates a parameter of the network). Then, the graph construction module g_ϕ (as shown in Figure 4) is utilized to learn σ_i for every instance. Next, an improved Gaussian kernel $w_{ij}(f_\varphi(x_i), f_\varphi(x_j), \sigma_i, \sigma_j)$ is proposed to calculate the edge weight for constructing the k-nearest neighbor graph. Finally, the label propagation method is adopted to achieve transductive propagation learning.

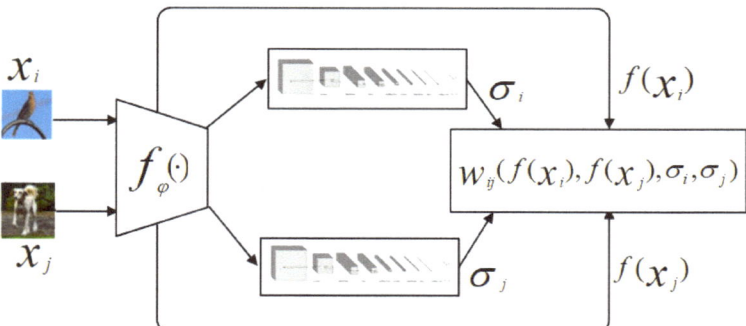

Figure 3. The framework of the IG-semiTPN model.

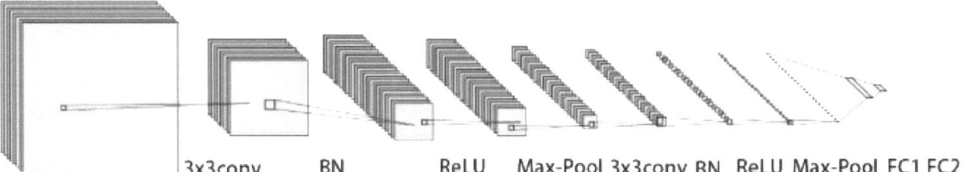

Figure 4. g_ϕ construction of model.

4.2. ETPN Model

Ensemble learning aims to enhance the generalization ability and stability of individual learners. The homogeneous framework employs a single base learning algorithm, i.e., learners of the same type but with multiple different sample inputs, leading to homogeneous ensembles (shown in Figure 5). The heterogeneous model utilizes multiple learning algorithms, i.e., learners of different types, leading to heterogeneous ensembles (shown in Figure 6).

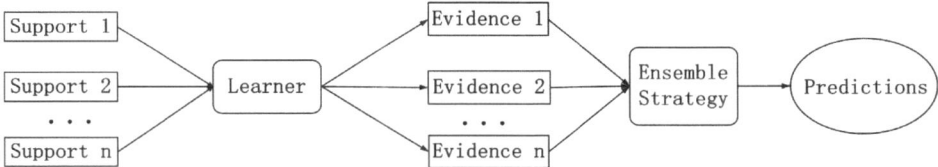

Figure 5. The process of homogeneous ensembles.

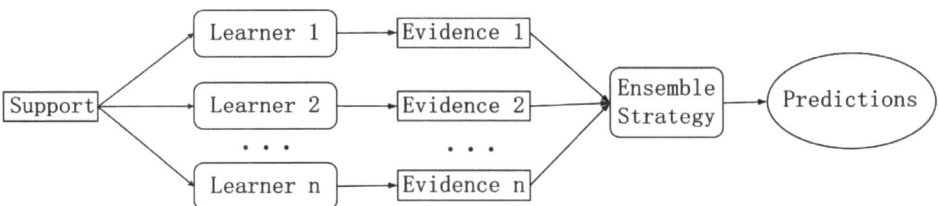

Figure 6. The process of heterogeneous ensembles.

4.2.1. The Ho-ETPN Model

In this section, we propose a homogeneous ensemble few-shot learning model (Ho-ETPN, shown in Figure 7). The Ho-ETPN model generates multiple results (evidence) by randomly selecting different support sets (i.e., $support_i^n$, being the same categories but different samples) in every episodic training. In contrast, the query set is selected only once in each episodic training. It generates multiple results by the same individual learner introduced in the last sector then integrates them via the the evidence fusion strategy proposed in this paper to accomplish predictions.

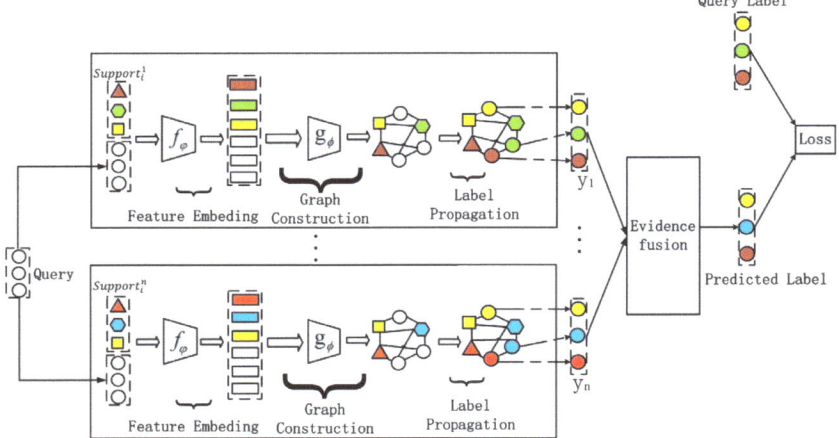

Figure 7. The framework of the Ho-ETPN model.

4.2.2. The He-ETPN Model

In this section, we propose a heterogeneous ensemble few-shot learning model (He-ETPN). The He-ETPN model generates multiple results (evidence) via multiple learners in every episodic training, and then integrates them via the evidence fusion strategy proposed in this paper to accomplish predictions. The model framework of base learners has been introduced in the last section. The He-ETPN model (shown in Figure 8) generates multiple results by constructing diverse KNN-graphs using different models that are the different initializations of $f_\varphi(\cdot)$ and g_ϕ, with different value settings of γ and m in an improved Gaussian kernel.

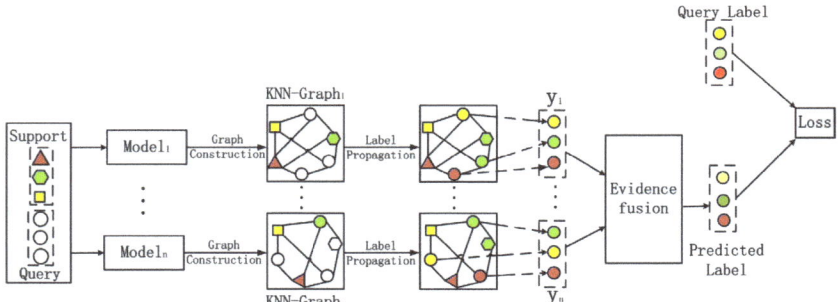

Figure 8. The framework of the He-ETPN model.

4.2.3. Construct KNN-Graphs

For dataset $S = S_{sup} \cup S_{uns}$, during the construction of KNN-graphs, let $s \in S$ represent the graph vertex to build the undirected graphs of labeled and unlabeled samples. We use the edge weights to measure the similarity between samples, the greater the weight of the edge, the greater the similarity between the two samples. Due to the improved Gaussian kernel [41] the nuclear truncation effect is alleviated by adding displacement parameters and corrections and learning a σ parameter suitable for each sample in the process of constructing the graph. Therefore, we utilize the improved Gaussian kernel to calculate the edge weight to construct more accurate KNN graphs for the transductive propagation ensemble network. The improved Gaussian kernel is defined as follows:

$$w_{ij} = exp(\frac{1}{md(\frac{f_\varphi(x_i)}{\sigma_i}, \frac{f_\varphi(x_j)}{\sigma_j}, m) + \gamma^2} + \lambda), i, j = 1, \ldots, n, \quad (1)$$

where $f_\varphi(\cdot)$ refers to the feature map, φ indicates a parameter of the network , σ is the variable bandwidth (length scale parameter) of the kernel function learned by g_ϕ, γ is the displacement parameters, λ is the fine-tuning variable. $d(\cdot)$ is the Euclidean distance.

4.3. Transductive Propagation Learning

Transductive propagation learning aims to predict unlabeled data from locally labeled training samples. It takes the support and query set as graph nodes, then makes joint predictions using the nearest neighbor relationship between the support and query sets (as shown in Figure 9), which can supplement the deficiency of label information through unlabeled data. Due to its low complexity and good classification effect, the label propagation algorithm is adopted to perform the transfer of label information between graph nodes. The process of predictions for the query set Q^M using label propagation is defined as follows:

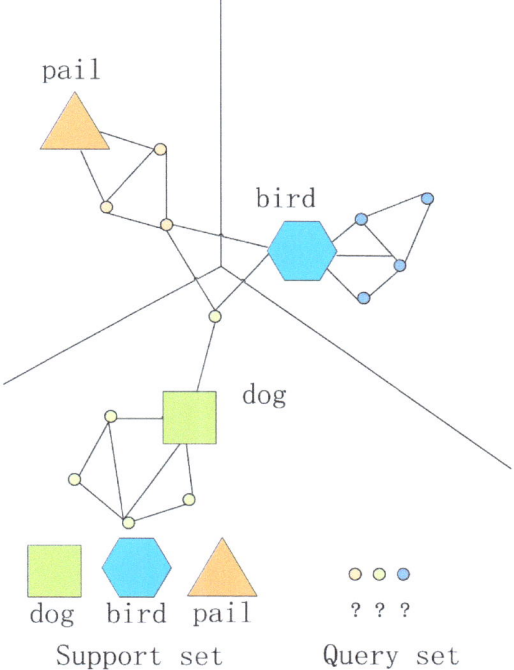

Figure 9. Transductive propagation algorithm based on K-nearest neighbor graph.

(1) Suppose $F = [Y_l, Y_u]$ is an annotation matrix with $(K \cdot N + M) \times K - dimension$. Y_l denotes the support set sample label matrix, and Y_u denotes the query set sample matrix Let Y is the initial annotation matrix $Y \in F$, Y_{ic} represents the membership degree to the

$c - th$ column category of $i - th$ node Y_i. If $Y_{ic} = 1$, which is mean the node Y_i belonging to the category c, else $Y_{ic} = 0$, that is,

$$Y_{ic} = \begin{cases} 1, & Y_i = c \\ 0, & otherwise \end{cases} \qquad (2)$$

(2) Given the initial label matrix Y_l, the query set labels are iteratively predicted according to the KNN-graphs. Let $\alpha \in (0,1)$ denote the pre-set weight coefficient to control the amount of propagated information. The transductive propagation learning iteratively inferences as follows:

$$\lim_{x \to \infty} T^t = \begin{pmatrix} I & 0 \\ \alpha \cdot T_{ul} & \alpha \cdot T_{uu} \end{pmatrix} \times \begin{pmatrix} I & 0 \\ \alpha \cdot T_{ul} & \alpha \cdot T_{uu} \end{pmatrix} \times \begin{pmatrix} I & 0 \\ \alpha \cdot T_{ul} & \alpha \cdot T_{uu} \end{pmatrix} \times \ldots$$

$$= \begin{pmatrix} I \cdot I + 0 + 0 + \ldots & 0 + 0 + 0 + \ldots \\ (\alpha \cdot T_{ul}) + (\alpha \cdot T_{ul}) \cdot (\alpha \cdot T_{uu}) + (\alpha \cdot T_{ul}) \cdot (\alpha \cdot T_{uu})^2 + \ldots & (\alpha \cdot T_{uu}) \cdot (\alpha \cdot T_{uu}) \cdot (\alpha \cdot T_{uu}) \ldots \end{pmatrix}$$

$$= \begin{pmatrix} I \cdot I + 0 + 0 + \ldots & 0 + 0 + 0 + \ldots \\ (I + (\alpha \cdot T_{uu}) + (\alpha \cdot T_{uu})^2 + \ldots) \cdot (\alpha \cdot T_{ul}) & (\alpha \cdot T_{uu}) \cdot (\alpha \cdot T_{uu}) \cdot (\alpha \cdot T_{uu}) \ldots \end{pmatrix} \qquad (3)$$

$$= \begin{pmatrix} I & 0 \\ (\sum_{t=0}^{\infty} (\alpha \cdot T_{uu})^t) \cdot (\alpha \cdot T_{ul}) & (\alpha \cdot T_{uu})^{\infty} \end{pmatrix}$$

$$= \begin{pmatrix} I & 0 \\ (I - \alpha T_{uu})^{-1} \cdot (\alpha \cdot T_{ul}) & 0 \end{pmatrix}$$

$$F_{t+1} = \lim_{x \to \infty} F_t = \lim_{t \to \infty} T^t \begin{pmatrix} (1-\alpha)Y_l \\ 0 \end{pmatrix} = \begin{pmatrix} I & 0 \\ (I - \alpha T_{uu})^{-1} \cdot (\alpha \cdot T_{ul}) & 0 \end{pmatrix} \begin{pmatrix} (1-\alpha)Y_l \\ 0 \end{pmatrix}, \qquad (4)$$

where $T = D^{-1/2} W D^{-1/2}$, T represents the normalized Laplace matrix. T_{ll} denotes the identity matrix; T_{lu} denotes the zero matrix; $T_{ul} \subset T$; $T_{uu} \subset T$. $W = [w_{ij}]$, $W \in R^{(K \cdot N + M) \times (K \cdot N + M)}$ for all instances in $S = S_{sup} \cup S_{uns}$.

We keep the $k - max$ values in each row of W calculating by Equation (1) to construct KNN-graphs. Then, the normalized graph Laplacian is applied [44] on W; D is the diagonal matrix, $D = diag([d_{ii} = \sum_{j=1}^{K \cdot N + M} w_{ij}])$. While α is bigger, the results tend to favor label propagation items T_{uu} and T_{ul}, else, results prefer the original annotated items Y_l. The final prediction results F^* ($F^* = [f_{i\eta}]$) are obtained through multiple iterations, as is shown in Equation (5).

$$F^* = \lim_{x \to \infty} F_t = (I - \alpha T_{uu})^{-1} (\alpha \cdot T_{ul}) \cdot (1 - \alpha) Y_l. \qquad (5)$$

4.4. Ensemble Pruning

The error-ambiguity decomposition [45] can show that the success of ensemble learning depends on a good trade off between the individual performance and diversity, which is defined as follows:

$$err(H) = \overline{err}(h) - \sqrt{ambi}(h), \qquad (6)$$

where $\overline{err}(h) = \sum_{i=1}^{N} \omega_i \cdot err(h_i)$ denotes the average error of the individual learners, and $\overline{err}(h) = \sum_{i=1}^{N} \omega_i \cdot ambi(h_i)$ denotes the weighted average of ambiguities. h denotes the individual learner.

The $\overline{err}(h)$ depends on the generalization ability of individual learners; the $\overline{ambi}(h)$ depends on the ensemble diversity. Since the $\overline{ambi}(h)$ is always positive, obviously, the error of the ensemble will never be larger than the average error of the individual learners. More importantly, Equation (6) shows that the more accurate and the more diverse the individual learners, the better the ensemble. Based on this, we propose an improved ensemble pruning approach to select more accurate learners to participate in the integration.

Ensemble pruning is to associate an individual learner with a weight that could characterize the goodness of including the individual learner in the final ensemble. RSE is a regularized selective ensemble algorithm; it adopted the L1 norm for feature selection to obtain sparse weights [46]. However, the sample space of few-shot learning is more sparse. To enhance data utilization and ensure that samples far away from decision boundaries still contribute to model training, we employ the L2 norm to obtain weights as small as possible but not zero. In addition, this makes the model more stable to small changes of the input and improves the robustness of the model. Moreover, to be suitable for few-shot learning, we redefine the improved ensemble pruning algorithm.

Given n individual learners for He-ETPN or Ho-ETPN, let $\omega = [\omega_1, \ldots, \omega_n]$ denote the n-dimensional weight vector of n individual learners, where small elements in the weight vector suggest that the corresponding individual learner from He-ETPN or Ho-ETPN should be excluded during the process of fusion.

$$\Theta(\omega) = \lambda \Lambda(\omega) + \Omega(\omega), \quad (7)$$

where $\Lambda(\omega)$ is the empirical loss, $\Omega(\omega)$ is the graph Laplacian regularization term to measure the misclassification, and λ is a regularization parameter which trades off the minimization of $\Lambda(\omega)$ and $\Omega(\omega)$.

By introducing slack variables η and minimizing the regularized risk function to determine the weight vector, Equation (7) is redefined as follows:

$$\begin{aligned} &\min_{\omega} \omega P^\top T P \omega^\top + \lambda(\eta_1^2 + \ldots + \eta_m^2) \\ &s.t. \ y_i p_i \omega^\top + \eta_i^2 \geq 1, (\forall i = 1, \ldots, m) \\ &\omega_1 + \ldots + \omega_m = 1, \omega \geq 0, \end{aligned} \quad (8)$$

where P denotes the prediction matrix of all individual learners on all support set instances, $p_i = (\max(F_1^*), \ldots, \max(F_n^*))$ denotes the predictions of the individual learner on x_i, and T represents the normalized Laplace matrix. y_i denotes the sample label of x_i. $\eta = (\eta_1, \ldots, \eta_m)^\top$ denotes the slack variables.

$$\omega_i = \begin{cases} 1, & top - n \\ 0, & otherwise \end{cases} \quad (9)$$

$$F_i^* = \omega_i \cdot F_i^*, i = 1, \ldots, n, \quad (10)$$

where $top - n$ is to select the top n best individual learners for the pruned ensemble. F_i^* denotes a piece of evidence, if the $\omega_i = 0$ denotes that the F_i^* does not participate in the fusion of the results.

The complexity of the pruning approach is $O(n^3)$. Equation (8) is a standard QP problem that can be efficiently solved by existing optimization packages. It is more suitable for small-scale datasets, especially few-shot learning.

4.5. Evidence Fusion Strategy

In this paper, we propose an improved D-S evidence fusion method to assemble the multiple pieces of evidence generated by the ensemble solutions of the Ho-ETPN and He-ETPN. Compared with the averaging and voting methods, the improved D-S evidence fusion method can enhance the stability of ensemble results and alleviate the problem of the "Zadeh paradox" to a certain extent. The D-S evidence theory was first proposed by Dempster [47,48]. Combining multiple information sources is an effective method of uncertainty reasoning. The research indicates that the synthetic consequence of conventional combination rules of Dempster is frequently contrary to the reality in the practical applications [49,50]. Two major approaches are proposed to improve the accuracy of synthetic results—one is to amend the composition rules; the second is to change the original evidence resources. In this paper, we focus on the latter. Next, we concretely introduce the process of the improved D-S evidence fusion method.

(1) Conflict Matrix

The Bhattacharyya distance [51] is utilized to construct the conflict matrix between evidence. According to the intension of Bhattacharyya distance, the formula is redefined as follows:

Definition 1 (Bhattacharyya Distance). *For probability distributions F_i^* and F_j^* over the same domain, the Bhattacharyya distance is defined as:*

$$Dis_{BC}(F_i^*, F_j^*) = \sum_{\eta=1}^{K} \sqrt{F_i^*(f_{i\eta}) F_j^*(f_{j\eta}))} \qquad (11)$$

$$fc_{ij} = -ln(Dis_{BC}(F_i^*, F_j^*)), \qquad (12)$$

where $Dis_{BC}(F_i^*, F_j^*)$ is the Bhattacharyya coefficient for discrete probability distributions. Let $n = K \cdot N + M$ denote the number of pieces of evidence. Each piece of normalized evidence is denoted by $F_i^* = (f_{i1}, f_{i2}, \ldots, f_{iK})$. F_i^* and $F_j^*(1 \leq i, j \leq n)$ represent two pieces of evidence. The K denotes the number of classes in each support set, $k_i \in K$. Then, the normalization conflict matrix is defined as:

$$Matrix_{conflict} = \begin{bmatrix} 0 & fc_{12} & \cdots & fc_{1j} & \cdots & fc_{1n} \\ fc_{21} & 0 & \cdots & fc_{2j} & \cdots & fc_{2n} \\ \vdots & \vdots & \vdots & \vdots & \vdots & \vdots \\ fc_{j1} & fc_{j2} & \cdots & 0 & \cdots & fc_{jn} \\ \vdots & \vdots & \vdots & \vdots & \vdots & \vdots \\ fc_{n1} & fc_{n2} & \cdots & fc_{nj} & \cdots & 0 \end{bmatrix}. \qquad (13)$$

(2) Support Degree

Evidence support degree indicates the support degree of evidence that is supported by other evidence. The higher the similarity with other evidence, the higher the support degree it is, and vice versa. According to $Matrix_{conflit}$ the following formula is utilized to calculate the similarity degree between F_i^* and F_j^*.

$$sd_{ij} = 1 - fc_{ij}, \quad i, j = 1, 2, \ldots, n. \qquad (14)$$

As a result, we can obtain the following similarity matrix of all evidence:

$$Matrix_{similarity} = \begin{bmatrix} 1 & sd_{12} & \cdots & sd_{1j} & \cdots & sd_{1n} \\ sd_{21} & 1 & \cdots & sd_{2j} & \cdots & sd_{2n} \\ \vdots & \vdots & \vdots & \vdots & \vdots & \vdots \\ sd_{j1} & sd_{j2} & \cdots & 1 & \cdots & sd_{jn} \\ \vdots & \vdots & \vdots & \vdots & \vdots & \vdots \\ sd_{n1} & sd_{n2} & \cdots & sd_{nj} & \cdots & 1 \end{bmatrix}. \tag{15}$$

And then, the support degree of each evident is calculated as:

$$Sup(F_i^*) = \sum_{j=1, j \neq i}^{n} sd_{ij}. \tag{16}$$

(3) Evident Weight

Credibility degree indicates the credibility of an evidence. It can be calculated by following formula.

$$CR(F_i^*) = \frac{Sup(F_i^*)}{\sum_{j=1}^{n} Sup(F_j^*)}. \tag{17}$$

Information entropy can be utilized to measure the informative quantity of evidence in the information fusion process. Integrated with D-S evidence theory, given a piece of evidence $F_i^* = (f_{i1}, f_{i2}, \ldots, f_{iK})$, and $\sum_{\eta=1}^{K} f_{i\eta} = 1$. The information quantity of the ith piece of evidence is defined as:

$$Info_e(F_i^*) = -\sum_{\eta=1}^{K} f_{i\eta} \log f_{i\eta}. \tag{18}$$

For information entropy, the larger the uncertainty, the smaller its weight. On the other hand, the smaller the information entropy, the larger its weight. The method mentioned above can be used to reduce the weight ratio of the evidence with higher indeterminacy in the fusion process. Therefore, the weight of each evidence is defined as:

$$weight(F_i^*) = \frac{CR(F_i^*)}{Normalization(Info_e(F_i^*))}, \; 1 \leq i \leq n \tag{19}$$

$$F_i^* = weight(F_i^*) \times F_i^*. \tag{20}$$

(4) Evidence Combination Rule

Suppose that the feature subsets generated in the previous chapter are independent. The D-S evidence theory improved in this paper allows the fusion of information coming from different feature subsets. Therefore, the evidence combination rule is utilized to combine different weighted feature subsets in a manner that is both accurate and robustness. For $F_i^* (i = 1, 2, \ldots, n), \forall k \in K$, the combination rule is redefined as:

$$F_{fusion}^* = (F_1^* \uplus F_2^* \uplus \cdots \uplus F_n^*)(k) = \frac{1}{Q} \prod_{i=1}^{n} F_i^*(k), \tag{21}$$

where Q means the conflict between different pieces of evidence, is given by:

$$Q = \sum_{i=1}^{K} \prod_{j=1}^{n} F_j^*(k_i). \tag{22}$$

4.6. Loss Generation

In this paper, we adopt cross-entropy loss to calculate the similarity between predictive values and true values.

(1) We adopt the softmax function to transform the F^*_{fusion} of the ETPN model to probability, which is defined as follows:

$$P(\widetilde{y}_i = j|x_i) = \frac{exp(f_{i\eta})}{\sum_{j=1}^{N} exp(f_{i\eta})}, \quad (23)$$

where $\widetilde{y}_i$ is the final prediction value of $i - th$ samples in query. $f_{i\eta}$ is the component of the prediction values in label propagation.

(2) We calculate the loss by the cross entropy loss:

$$J(\varphi, \phi) = \sum_{i=1}^{T} \sum_{j=1}^{N} -\mathbb{I}(y_i = j) log(P(\widetilde{y}_i = j|x_i)), \quad (24)$$

where y_i is the true value of the instance. $\mathbb{I}(b)$ is the indicator function. If b is right, and $\mathbb{I}(b) = 1$, else $\mathbb{I}(b) = 0$.

5. Experiments

In this section, to validate the performance of models, we contrast our proposal against state-of-the-art techniques on miniImageNet and tieredImageNet datasets. In addition, we set a supervised experiment including the ensemble model Ho-ETPN and He-ETPN, and a semi-supervised experiment including the setting of distractor classes. These approaches are particularly divided into optimization-based (MAML [22]), ensemble-based (EBDM-Euc [38], HGNN [39], E³BM+MAML [40]), graph-based (TPN [25], EPNet [27], TPRN [31], DSN [32], EGNN [33], PRWN [35], GNN [52], BGNN* [53], DPGN* [54]), and metric-based (MatchingNet [8], Proto Net [9], TADAM [13], BR-ProtoNet [36], SSFormers [55], CGRN [56], HMRN [57]) approaches. Moreover, we conduct 5-way 1-shot and 5-shot experiments, which are standard few-shot learning settings.

5.1. Datasets

miniImageNet [8]. A subset of the ImageNet datasets [58] consists of 60,000 images. Each image is of size 84 × 84, and classes with 600 samples per class are divided into 64, 16, and 20 for meta-training, meta-validation, and meta-testing, respectively. We use the miniImageNet for semi-supervised classification with 40% of labeled data.

tieredImageNet [41]. A more challenging subset derived from ImageNet datasets, its class subsets are chosen from supersets of the wordnet hierarchy. The top hierarchy has 34 super-classes, which are split into 20 different categories (351 classes) for training, six different categories (97 classes) for validation, and eight different categories (160 classes) for testing. We follow the implementation of 4-convolutional layer ($Conv - 4$) backbones and the image size of 84 × 84 as on miniImageNet. Moreover, the tieredImageNet is used for semi-supervised classification with 10% of labeled data.

5.2. Implementation Details

Following the Matching Networks [8], we also adopt the episodic training procedure. Moreover, we used a common feature extractor, which is a $Conv - 4$ as implemented in [8] during the entire comparision experiments for standard few-shot classification. It makes up four convolutional blocks where each block begins with a 2D convolutional layer with a 3 × 3 kernel and a filter size of 64. Each convolutional layer is followed by a batch-normalization layer [43], a ReLU nonlinearity, and a 2 × 2 max-pooling layer. Moreover, g_ϕ utilized to learn σ_i for every instances, consists of two convolutional blocks (64 and 1 filters) and two fully-connected layers (8 and 1 neurons) similar to TPN [25]. The convolutional blocks are made up of four convolutional blocks and each block begins with a 2D convolutional layer with a 3 × 3 kernel and filter size of 64. Each convolutional layer is followed by a batch-normalization layer [43], a ReLU nonlinearity and a 2 × 2 max-pooling layer. In the experiments, we follow a general practice to evaluate the model with N-way K-shot and 15 query images; the value of λ is set to 0.75. And we use Adam optimizer [59] with an initial learning rate of 0.001, we use the validation set to select the training episodes with the best accuracy, and run the training process until the validation loss reaches a plateau.

In addition, we utilize the improved Gaussian kernel proposed in the single model framework IG-semiTPN to construct the KNN graphs. IG-semiTPN experiments showed the superior effects of the improved Gaussian kernel function. It also indicated that the optimal models have relations with the value of γ [60,61]. Therefore, ETPN utilizes the parameter settings of the improved Gaussian kernel of the IG-semiTPN to perform supervised and semi-supervised experiments. Specifically, Ho-ETPN adopts the Minkowski distance with γ being 3 and m being 3 or the Minkowski distance with m being 2 and λ is 0.75. In addition, there are three learners in our He-ETPN ensemble models; learner 1 adopts a Minkowski distance with γ being 3 and m being 3; learner 2 adopts a Minkowski distance with γ being 0.2 and m being 2; learner 3 adopts a Minkowski distance with m being 2, and λ is 0.75.

5.3. Supervised Experiment

ETPN Experiment

In our experiments, we compare ensemble model ETPN with other classic and advanced algorithms in four categories, including graph-based (TPN [25], EPNet [27], TPRN [31], DSN [32], EGNN [33], PRWN [35], GNN [52], BGNN* [53], DPGN* [54]), metric-based (MatchingNet [8], Proto Net [9], TADAM [13], BR-ProtoNet [36], SSFormers [55], CGRN [56], HMRN [57]), optimization-based (MAML [22]) and ensemble-based (EBDM-Euc [38], HGNN [39], E^3BM+MAML [40]) approaches. The performance of the proposed ETPN and state-of-the-art models in the 5-way 5-shot/1-shot accuracy on the miniImageNet and tieredImageNet datasets are summarized in Tables 2 and 3, and "*" in the table indicates results re-implemented in HGNN [39] for a fair comparison. Our proposed ETPN outperforms few-shot models by large margins, indicating that the proposed ensemble model effectively assists few-shot recognition. Specifically, we can obtain the following observations:

(1) **Comparison with the latest model.** Ho-ETPN is 8.32% higher than SSFormers in 5-shot on miniImageNet and 5.58% higher than HMRN in 5-shot on tieredImageNet; Ho-ETPN is 7.86% higher than SSFormers in 1-shot on miniImageNet and 9.59% higher than HMRN in 1-shot on tieredImageNet. It confirms that our model has a good ability for classification discrimination, which benefits from our ensemble model and D-S evidence fusion strategy based on improved ensemble pruning.

(2) **Comparison with the state-of-the-art.** Under the 5-way-5-shot setting, the ETPN classification accuracies are 78.87% vs. 78.57% for the transductive learning model TPRN, 80.28% vs. 80.0% ensemble model BR-ProtoNet on miniImageNet and tieredImageNet, respectively. It is 0.3% higher than the transductive learning model TPRN in 5-shot on miniImageNet and 0.28% higher than the ensemble model BR-ProtoNet in 5-shot on tieredImageNet. Under the 5-way-1-shot setting, the ETPN classification accuracies are 63.06% vs. 57.84% for the transductive learning model TPRN, 67.57% vs. 62.7% for the ensemble model BR-ProtoNet on miniImageNet and tieredImageNet, respectively. It is 5.22% higher than the transductive model TPRN in 1-shot on miniImageNet and 4.87% higher than the ensemble model BR-ProtoNet in 1-shot on tieredImageNet. ETPN outperforms state-of-the-art few-shot models by large margins, especially under the 5-way-1-shot setting. This indicates that our ensemble model and improved evidence fusion strategy are effective, particularly for scenarios with a small sample size, which can increase the performance by enhancing the stability of the model.

Table 2. Few-shot classification accuracies on the miniImageNet dataset are cited.

Methods	m	γ	λ	5way5shot	5way1shot
MatchingNet [8]				55.31%	43.56%
Proto Net [9]				68.20%	49.42%
TADAM [13]				76.7%	58.5%
BR-ProtoNet [36]				74.5%	58.4%
Relation Network [62]				65.32%	50.44%
MAML [22]				63.11%	48.70%
PRWN [35]				67.82%	50.89%
TPN [25]				67.79%	53.42%
EPNet [27]				72.95%	59.32%
TPRN [31]				78.57%	57.84%
DSN [32]				68.99 %	51.78%
EGNN [33]				66.85%	59.63%
GNN [52]				66.41%	50.33%
BGNN* [53]				67.35	52.35%
DPGN* [54]				65.34	53.22%
EBDM-Euc (2heads) [38]				68.30%	49.96%
EBDM-Euc (3heads) [38]				69.14%	50.49%
EBDM-Euc (5heads) [38]				69.64%	52.53%
EBDM-DD (2heads) [38]				67.99%	51.42%
EBDM-DD (3heads) [38]				68.74%	52.56%
EBDM-DD (5heads) [38]				70.17%	53.08%
HGNN [39]				72.48%	55.63%
E^3BM + MAML [40]				65.1%	53.2%
SSFormers [55]				70.55%	55.2%
CGRN [56]				64.13%	50.85%
He-ETPN (our)			0.75	72.94%	59.87%
Ho-ETPN (our)	3	3	0.75	77.13%	**63.06**%
Ho-ETPN (our)	2		0.75	**78.87%**	62.33%

Table 3. Few-shot classification accuracies on the tieredImageNet dataset are cited.

Methods	m	γ	λ	5way5shot	5way1shot
Proto Net [9]				72.69%	53.31%
MAML [22]				70.30%	51.67%
PRWN [35]				70.52%	54.87%
BR-ProtoNet [36]				80.0%	62.7%
Relation Network [62]				71.32%	54.48%
TPN [25]				71.2%	56.17%
EGNN [33]				70.96%	
TPRN [31]				79.66%	59.26%
HGNN [39]				72.82%	56.05%
BGNN* [53]				65.27%	49.41%
DPGN* [54]				69.86%	53.99%
EPNet [27]				73.91%	59.97%
EBDM-Euc (3 heads) [38]				72.24%	51.22%
EBDM-Euc (1-st head) [38]				71.07%	50.04%
EBDM-Euc (2-nd head) [38]				71.28%	50.29%
EBDM-Euc (3-rd head) [38]				70.84%	50.52%
E^3BM + MAML [40]				70.2%	52.1%
SSFormers [55]				73.72%	55.54%
CGRN [56]				71.34%	55.07%
HMRN [57]				74.70%	57.98%
He-ETPN (our)			0.75	74.08%	62.75%
Ho-ETPN (our)	3	3	0.75	**80.28%**	66.24%
Ho-ETPN (our)	2		0.75	80.18%	**67.57%**

(3) **Compare with individual learner IG-semiTPN.** In this section, we compare our ensemble model ETPN with our single supervised model IG-semiTPN [41]; this is to show that the homogeneous strategy, heterogeneous strategy, and improved D-S evidence fusion strategy based on improved ensemble pruning facilitate the model performance. For the fairness of the experiment, we ensure other settings are the same, only changing the ensemble strategy and the parameter settings in the improved Gaussian kernel to perform the ablation experiment. The comparison results are shown in Figures 10 and 11. Under the 5-way 5-shot setting, the classification accuracies of Ho-ETPN and IG-semiTPN are 78.87% vs. 69.31% on miniImageNet, and 80.28% vs. 73.21% on tieredImageNet, respectively. Ho-ETPN is 9.56% and 7.07% higher than IG-semiTPN in 5-shot on miniImageNet and tieredImageNet, respectively. Under the 5-way 1-shot setting, the classification accuracies of Ho-ETPN and IG-semiTPN are 63.06% vs. 54.03% on miniImageNet, and 67.57% vs. 57.35% on tieredImageNet, respectively. Ho-ETPN is 9.03% and 10.22% higher than IG-semiTPN in 1-shot on miniImageNet and tieredImageNet, respectively. In addition, under the 5-way 5-shot setting, the classification accuracies of He-ETPN and IG-semiTPN are 72.94% vs. 69.31% on miniImageNet, and 74.08% vs. 73.21% on tieredImageNet, respectively. He-ETPN is 3.63% and 0.87% higher than IG-semiTPN in 5-shot on miniImageNet and tieredImageNet, respectively. Under the 5-way 1-shot setting, the classification accuracies of He-ETPN and IG-semiTPN are 59.87% vs. 54.03% on miniImageNet, and 62.75% vs. 57.35% on tieredImageNet, respectively. He-ETPN is 5.84% and 5.4% higher than IG-semiTPN in 1-shot on miniImageNet and tieredImageNet, respectively. The results indicate the effectiveness of the proposed ensemble solutions, which achieve a state-of-the-art performance compared to the single model IG-semiTPN, especially in 1-shot. Moreover, the Ho-ETPN is superior to the He-ETPN, which is related to the problem of multiple learner selection. In our paper, we only select different parameter settings of f_φ, g_ϕ and an improved Gaussian kernel.

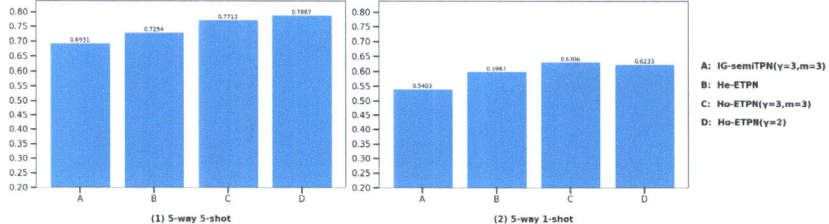

Figure 10. Comparison of the IG-semiTPN and ETPN (He-ETPN and Ho-ETPN) on miniImageNet.

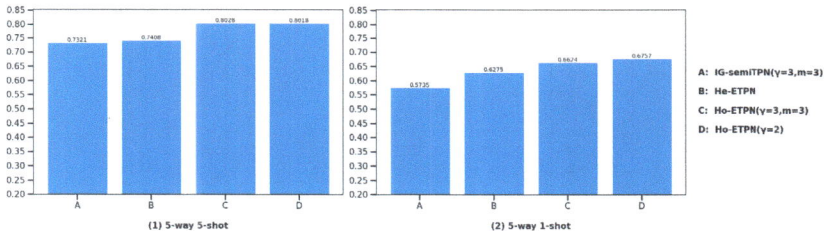

Figure 11. Comparison of the IG-semiTPN and ETPN (He-ETPN and Ho-ETPN) on tieredImageNet.

5.4. Semi-Supervised Experiment

Since labeled data are scarce and their collection is expensive, in this section, we leverage the extra unlabeled data to improve the performance of few-shot classifiers. Our model was trained on miniImageNet and tieredImageNet with 40% and 10% of labeled data, respectively. What is more, another key challenge is that the distractor classes, being an unlabeled set that is irrelevant to the classification task, are introduced to boost robustness against perturbations. We follow the settings in papers [41,63]. Our models outperforms inference (TADAM-semi [13], BR-ProtoNet [36] and PN+Semi [41]) and transduction (TPN-semi [25], Semi-EPNet [27], Semi DSN [32], Semi-EGNN [33]and PRWN-semi [35]) semi-supervised few-shot models by large margins.

(1) **Comparison with the state-of-the-art.** In order to ensure the effectiveness of the semi-supervised experiment, every category in the datasets was divided into labeled datasets and unlabeled datasets without intersection [39]. In this paper, we utilize the label propagation algorithm to perform the annotation for unlabeled data, which is different from traditional inductive reasoning semi-supervised approaches. As is shown in Tables 4 and 5 , it can be observed that the classification results of all semi-supervised few-shot models are degraded due to the distractor classes. However, even with the distractor class represented as w/D in the table, the ensemble semi-supervised model semi-HoTPN achieves the highest performance among the compared methods, especially in the scenario of 1-shot, which indicates the robustness of the proposed semi-HoTPN in dealing with distracted unlabeled data. In addition, this indicates that the proposed D-S evidence fusion strategy based on improved ensemble pruning, transductive propagation learning and homogeneous ensemble semi-supervised model semi-HoTPN effectively assists few-shot recognition.

Table 4. Semi-supervised comparison on the miniImageNet dataset.

Models	m	γ	λ	5way5shot	5way1shot	5way5shot (w/D)	5way1shot (w/D)
PN + Semi [41]				63.77%	49.98%	62.62%	47.42%
Soft k-Means [41]				64.59%	50.09%	63.55%	48.70%
Soft k-Means + Cluster [41]				63.08%	49.03%	61.27%	48.86%
Masked Soft k-Means [41]				64.39%	50.41%	62.96%	49.04%
TADAM-semi [13]						68.92%	54.81%
BR-ProtoNet [36]				73.1%	57.4%	72.4%	55.9%
Semi-EPNet [27]				67.08%			
Semi DSN [32]						67.12%	51.01%
Semi-EGNN [33]				64.32%			
PRWN-semi [35]				69.65%	56.65%	67.45%	53.61%
TPN-semi [25]				64.95%	50.43%	64.95%	50.43%
semi-HoETPN (our)	3	3	0.75	**73.87%**	60.57%	72.64%	**59.34%**
semi-HoETPN (our)	2		0.75	73.74%	**61.31%**	**73.24%**	59.28%

Table 5. Semi-supervised comparison on the tieredImageNet dataset.

Models	m	γ	λ	5way5shot	5way1shot	5way5shot (w/D)	5way1shot (w/D)
PN + Semi [41]				69.37%	50.74%	67.46%	48.67%
Soft k-Means [41]				70.25%	51.52%	68.32%	49.88%
Soft k-Means + Cluster [41]				69.42%	51.85%	67.56%	51.36%
Masked Soft k-Means [41]				69.88%	52.39%	69.08%	51.38%
BR-ProtoNet [36]				79.1%	61.8%	77.4%	60.1%
TPN-semi [25]				71.01%	55.74%	69.93%	53.45%
Semi DSN [32]						70.15%	53.89%
PRWN+Semi [35]				71.06%	59.17%	69.58%	56.59%
semi-HoETPN (our)	3	3	0.75	77.87%	63.87%	77.17%	63.16%
semi-HoETPN (our)	2		0.75	**78.94%**	**65.21%**	**78.45%**	**64.80%**

(2) **Compare with individual learner IG-semiTPN.** In this section, we show that the semi-supervised homogeneous ensemble model and improved D-S evidence fusion strategy based on improved ensemble pruning facilitate the model performance. For the fairness of the experiment, we compare semi-HoETPN with IG-semiTPN and other settings are the same. The comparison results are shown in Figures 12 and 13. We compare ensemble semi-supervised model semi-HoETPN with single semi-supervised model IG-semiTPN; under the 5-way-5-shot setting, the classification accuracies of semi-HoTPN and IG-semiTPN are

73.87% vs. 67.24% on miniImageNet, and 78.94% vs. 72.32% on tieredImageNet, respectively. Under the 5-way-1-shot setting, the classification accuracies of semi-HoTPN and IG-semiTPN are 61.31% and 53.48% on miniImageNet, and 65.21% and 57.28% on tieredImageNet, respectively. With the distractor class experiments, under the 5-way-5-shot setting, the classification accuracies of semi-HoTPN and IG-semiTPN are 73.24% vs. 66.8% on miniImageNet, and 78.45% vs. 70.08% on tieredImageNet, respectively; under the 5-way-1-shot setting, the classification accuracies of semi-HoTPN and IG-semiTPN are 59.34% vs. 53.13% on miniImageNet, and 64.80% vs. 56.09% on tieredImageNet, respectively. The results demonstrate the superior capacity of the proposed ensemble strategy in using the extra unlabeled information for boosting few-shot methods. Moreover, the addition of the distractor class enhances the robustness of the model.

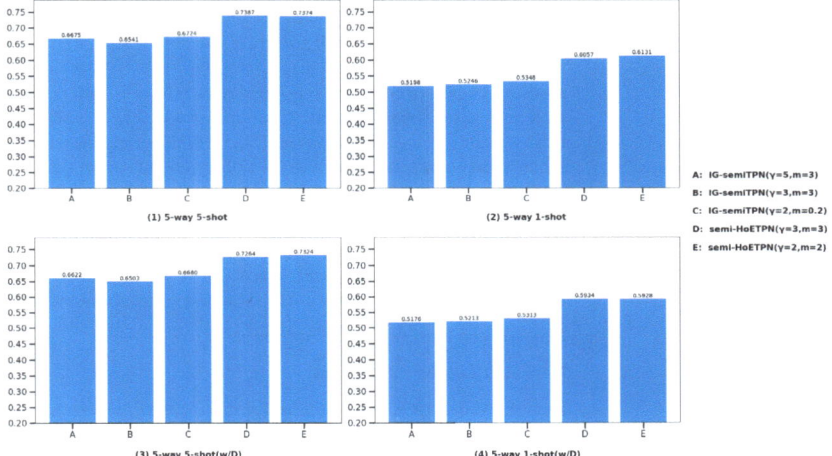

Figure 12. Comparison of the IG-semiTPN and semi-HoETPN on miniImageNet.

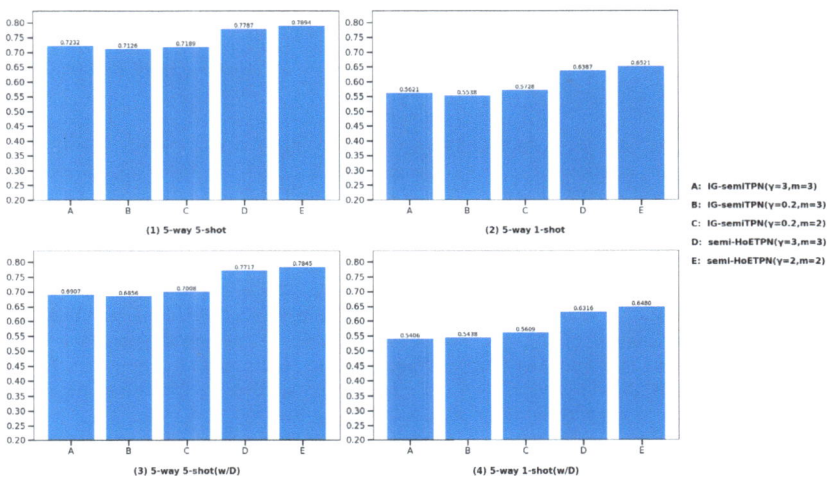

Figure 13. Comparison of the IG-semiTPN and semi-HoETPN on tieredImageNet.

6. Conclusions and Future Work

Few-shot learning aims to construct a classification model using limited samples. In this paper, we propose a novel ensemble semi-supervised few-shot learning with a transductive propagation network and evidence fusion. During the process of transductive propagation learning, we introduce the preset weight coefficient and calculate the process of iterative inferences to present homogeneous and heterogeneous models to improve the stability of the model. Then, we propose the improved D-S evidence ensemble strategy to enhance the stability of the final results. It combines the information entropy to realize the pre-processing of the evidence source. Then, an improved ensemble pruning method adopting the L2 norm is proposed to maintain a better performance of individual learners to enhance the accuracy of model fusion. Furthermore, an interference set is introduced to improve the robustness of the semi-supervised model. Experiments on miniImagnet and tieredImageNet indicate that the proposed approaches outperform the state-of-the-art few-shot model. However, our proposal directly utilizes a label propagation approach to transfer information between nodes in the graph-constructing phase. Therefore, in our future work, we will consider adopting the reality-semantic and cross-modal information to improve the accuracy of the transduction inference graph in few-shot learning.

Author Contributions: Writing—original draft preparation, Conceptualization, Methodology, Software,validation, investigation, X.P.; writing—review and editing, supervision, funding acquisition, G.L.; writing—review and editing, Conceptualization, Formal analysis, funding acquisition, Y.Z. All authors have read and agreed to the published version of the manuscript.

Funding: This work is partly supported by the Nature Science Foundation of China under Grant (Nos. 60473125), Science Foundation of China University of Petroleum-Beijing At Karamay under Grant (Nos. RCYJ2016B-03-001), Kalamay Science & Technology Research Project (Nos. 2020CGZH0009), Natural Science Foundation of Fujian Province, China under Grant (Nos. 2021J011004 and 2021J011002), the Ministry of Education Industry-University-Research Innovation Program (Grant No. 2021LDA09003).

Institutional Review Board Statement: Not applicable.

Informed Consent Statement: Not applicable.

Data Availability Statement: The miniImageNet dataset and tieredImageNet dataset can be found at: https://github.com/renmengye/few-shot-ssl-public (accessed on 29 January 2023).

Acknowledgments: We are greatly indebted to colleagues at Data and Knowledge Engineering Center, School of Information Technology and Electrical Engineering, the University of Queensland, Australia. We thank Xiaofang Zhou, Xue Li, Shuo Shang and Kai Zheng for their special suggestions and many interesting discussions.

Conflicts of Interest: The authors declare no conflicts of interest.

References

1. Aouani, H.; Ayed, Y.B. Speech Emotion Recognition with deep learning. *Procedia Comput. Sci.* **2020**, *176*, 251–260. [CrossRef]
2. LeCun, Y.; Yoshua, B.; Hinton, G. Deep learning. *Nature* **2015**, *521*, 436–444. [CrossRef] [PubMed]
3. Wang, C.; Wang, C.; Li, W.; Wang, H. A brief survey on RGB-D semantic segmentation using deep learning. *Displays* **2021**, *70*, 102080. [CrossRef]
4. Chatfield, K.; Simonyan, K.; Vedaldi, A.; Zisserman, A. Return of the devil in the details: Delving deep into convolutional nets. In Proceedings of the British Machine Vision Conference 2014, Nottingham, UK, 1–5 September 2014.
5. Zeiler, M.D.; Fergus, R. Visualizing and understanding convolutional networks. In Proceedings of the 13th European Conference, Zurich, Switzerland, 6–12 September 2014; Springer: Cham, Switzerland, 2014; pp. 818–833.
6. Chen, Z.; Fu, Y.; Zhang, Y.; Jiang, Y.G.; Xue, X.; Sigal, L. Semantic feature augmentation in few-shot learning. In Proceedings of the 5th European Conference on Computer Vision, Munich, Germany, 8–14 September 2018.
7. Lu, J.; Li, J.; Yan, Z.; Mei, F.; Zhang, C. Attribute-based synthetic network (abs-net): Learning more from pseudo feature representations. *Pattern Recognit.* **2018**, *80*, 129–142. [CrossRef]
8. Vinyals, O.; Blundell, C.; Lillicrap, T.; Wierstra, D. Matching networks for one shot learning. *Adv. Neural Inf. Process. Syst.* **2016**, *29*, 3630–3638.
9. Snell, J.; Swersky, K.; Zemel, R. Prototypical networks for fewshot learning. *Adv. Neural Inf. Process. Syst.* **2017**, *30*, 4077–4087.
10. Xing, C.; Rostamzadeh, N.; Oreshkin, B.; Pinheiro, P.O. Adaptive cross-modal few-shot learning. *Adv. Neural Inf. Process. Syst.* **2019**, *32*, 4848–4858.
11. Lv, F.; Zhang, J.; Yang, G.; Feng, L.; Yu, Y.; Duan, L. Learning cross-domain semantic-visual relationships for transductive zero-shot learning. *Pattern Recognit.* **2023**, *141*, 109591. [CrossRef]

12. Zhang, J.; Yang, G.; Hu, P.; Lin, G.; Lv, F. Semantic Consistent Embedding for Domain Adaptive Zero-Shot Learning, *IEEE Trans. Image Process.* **2023**, *32*, 4024–4035. [CrossRef]
13. Oreshkin, B.; López, P.R.; Lacoste, A. Tadam: Task dependent adaptive metric for improved few-shot learning. *Adv. Neural Inf. Process. Syst.* **2018**, *31*, 721–731.
14. Tang, K.D.; Tappen, M.F.; Sukthankar, R.; Lampert, C.H. Optimizing one-shot recognition with micro-set learning. In Proceedings of the 2010 IEEE Computer Society Conference on Computer Vision and Pattern Recognition, San Francisco, CA, USA, 13–18 June 2018; pp. 3027–3034.
15. Zheng, Y.; Wang, R.; Yang, J.; Xue, L.; Hu, M. Principal characteristic networks for few-shot learning. *J. Vis. Commun. Image Represent.* **2019**, *59*, 563–573. [CrossRef]
16. Wang, D.; Zhang, M.; Xu, Y.; Lu, W.; Yang, J.; Zhang, T. Metric-based meta-learning model for few-shot fault diagnosis under multiple limited data conditions, *Mech. Syst. Signal Process.* **2021**, *155*, 107510. [CrossRef]
17. Rusu, A.A.; Rao, D.; Sygnowski, J.; Vinyals, O.; Pascanu, R.; Osindero, S.; Hadsell, R. Meta-learning with latent embedding optimization. In Proceedings of the 7th International Conference on Learning Representations, New Orleans, LA, USA, 6–9 May 2019.
18. Jiang, X.; Havaei, M.; Varno, F.; Chartr, G.; Chapados, N.; Matwin, S. Learning to learn with conditional class dependencies. In Proceedings of the 7th International Conference on Learning Representations, New Orleans, LA, USA, 6–9 May 2019.
19. Gidaris, S.; Komodakis, N. Generating classification weights with gnn denoising autoencoders for few-shot learning. In Proceedings of the IEEE/CVF Conference on Computer Vision and Pattern Recognition (CVPR), Long Beach, CA, USA, 16–20 June 2019; pp. 21–30.
20. Gordon, J.; Bronskill, J.; Bauer, M.; Nowozin, S.; Turner, R.E. Meta-learning probabilistic inference for prediction. In Proceedings of the 7th International Conference on Learning Representations, New Orleans, LA, USA, 6–9 May 2019.
21. Bertinetto, L.; Henriques, J.F.; Torr, P.H.; Vedaldi, A. Meta learning with differentiable closed-form solvers. In Proceedings of the 7th International Conference on Learning Representations, New Orleans, LA, USA, 6–9 May 2019.
22. Finn, C.; Abbeel, P.; Levine, S. Model-agnostic meta-learning for fast adaptation of deep networks. In Proceedings of the International Conference on Machine Learning, Sydney, Australia, 6–11 August 2017; pp. 1126–1135.
23. Jamal, M.A.; Qi, G.J. Task agnostic meta-learning for few shot learning. In Proceedings of the IEEE/CVF Conference on Computer Vision and Pattern Recognition (CVPR), Long, Beach, CA, USA, 16–20 June 2019; pp. 11719–11727.
24. Antoniou, A.; Edwards, H.; Storkey, A. How to train your maml. In Proceedings of the 7th International Conference on Learning Representations, New Orleans, LA, USA, 6–9 May 2019.
25. Liu, Y.; Lee, J.; Park, M.; Kim, S.; Yang, E.; Hwang, S.J.; Yang, Y. Learning to propagate labels: Transductive propagation network for few-shot learning. In Proceedings of the 7th International Conference on Learning Representations, New Orleans, LA, USA, 6–9 May 2019.
26. Huang, H.; Zhang, J.; Zhang, J.; Wu, Q.; Xu, C. PTN: A Poisson Transfer Network for Semi-supervised Few-shot Learning. In Proceedings of the AAAI Conference on Artificial Intelligence, Virtual, 2–9 February 2021; pp. 1602–1609.
27. Rodríguez, P.; Laradji, I.H.; Drouin, A.; Lacoste, A. Embedding Propagation: Smoother Manifold for Few-Shot Classification. In Proceedings of the 16th European Conference, Glasgow, UK, 23–28 August 2020; pp. 121–138.
28. Iscen, A.; Tolias, G.; Avrithis, Y.; Chum, O. Label propagation for deep semisupervised learning. In Proceedings of the IEEE/CVF Conference on Computer Vision and Pattern Recognition (CVPR), Long Beach, CA, USA, 16–20 June 2019; pp. 5070–5079.
29. Liu, B.; Wu, Z.; Hu, H.; Lin, S. Deep Metric Transfer for Label Propagation with Limited Annotated Data. In Proceedings of the IEEE/CVF International Conference on Computer Vision (ICCV), Seoul, Republic of Korea, 27October–2 November 2019; pp. 1317–1326.
30. Zhang, R.; Yang, S.; Zhang, Q.; Xu, L.; He, Y.; Zhang, F. Graph-based few-shot learning with transformed feature propagation and optimal class allocation. *Neurocomputing* **2022**, *470*, 247–256. [CrossRef]
31. Ma, Y.; Bai, S.; An S.; Liu, W.; Liu, A.; Zhen, X.; Liu, X. Transductive Relation-Propagation Network for Few-shot Learning. In Proceedings of the Twenty-Ninth International Joint Conference on Artificial Intelligence (IJCAI-20), Yokohama, Japan, 7–15 January 2021; pp. 804–810.
32. Simon, C.; Koniusz, P.; Nock, R.; Harandi, M. Adaptive Subspaces for Few-Shot Learning. In Proceedings of the IEEE/CVF Conference on Computer Vision and Pattern Recognition (CVPR) Seattle, WA, USA, 13–19 June 2020; pp. 4135–4144.
33. Kim, J.; Kim, T.; Kim, S.; Yoo, C.D. Edge-Labeling Graph Neural Network for Few-Shot Learning. In Proceedings of the IEEE/CVF Conference on Computer Vision and Pattern Recognition (CVPR), Long Beach, CA, USA, 16–20 June 2019; pp. 11–20.
34. Li, X.; Huang, J.; Liu, Y.; Zhou, Q.; Zheng, S.; Schiele, B.; Sun, Q. Learning to teach and learn for semi-supervised few-shot image classification. *Comput. Vis. Image Underst.* **2021**, *212*, 103270. [CrossRef]
35. Ayyad, A.; Li, Y.; Muaz, R.; Albarqouni, S.; Elhoseiny, M. *Semi-Supervised Few-Shot Learning with Prototypical Random Walks; arXiv* **2019**, arXiv:1903.02164 .
36. Huang, S.; Zeng, X.; Wu, S.; Yu, Z.; Azzam, M.; Wong, H.S. Behavior regularized prototypical networks for semi-supervised few-shot image classification. *Pattern Recognit.* **2021**, *112*, 107765. [CrossRef]
37. Dvornik, N.; Mairal, J.; Schmid, C. Diversity With Cooperation: Ensemble Methods for Few-Shot Classification. In Proceedings of the IEEE/CVF International Conference on Computer Vision (ICCV), Seoul, Republic of Korea, 27 October–2 November 2019; pp. 3722–3730.

38. Zhou, M.; Li, Y.; Lu, H. Ensemble-Based Deep Metric Learning for Few-Shot Learning. In Proceedings of the 29th International Conference on Artificial Neural Networks, Bratislava, Slovakia, 15–18 September 2020; pp. 406–418.
39. Yu, T.; He, S.; Song, Y.Z.; Xiang, T. Hybrid Graph Neural Networks for Few-Shot Learning. In Proceedings of the AAAI—Thirty-Eighth Conference on Artificial Intelligence, Vancouver, BC, USA, 20–27 February 2022; pp. 3179–3187.
40. Liu, Y.; Schiele, B.; Sun, Q. An Ensemble of Epoch-Wise Empirical Bayes for Few-Shot Learning. In Proceedings of the 16th European Conference, Glasgow, UK, 23–28 August 2020; Volume 16, pp. 404–421.
41. Pan, X.; Li, G.; Yu, Q.; Guo, K.; Li, Z. Novel Graph Semi-Supervised Transduction Approach with lmproved Gauss Kernel for Few-Shot Learning. *Comput. Eng. Appl.* **2023**, *59*, 328–333.
42. Ren, M.; Triantafillou, E.; Ravi, S.; Snell, J.; Swersky, K.; Tenenbaum, J.B.; Larochelle, H.; Zemel, R.S. Meta-learning for semi-supervised few-shot classification. In Proceedings of the 6th International Conference on Learning Representations, Vancouver, BC, Canada, 30 April–3 May 2018.
43. Yu, Z.; Chen, L.; Cheng, Z.; Luo, J. TransMatch: A Transfer-Learning Scheme for Semi-Supervised Few-Shot Learning. In Proceedings of the 2020 IEEE/CVF Conference on Computer Vision and Pattern Recognition (CVPR), Seattle, WA, USA, 13–19 June 2020; pp. 12856–12864.
44. Greenleaf, G.; Mowbray, A.; King, G.; Cant, S.; Chung, P. More than wyshful Thinking: AustLII's Legal Inferencing via the World Wide Web. In Proceedings of the ICAIL97: International Conference on Artificial Intelligence and Law, Melbourne, Australia, 30 June–3 July 1997; pp. 47–55.
45. Krogh, A.; Vedelsby, J. Neural Network Ensembles, Cross Validation, and Active Learning. In Proceedings of the International Conference on Neural Information Processing Systems, Denver, CO, USA, 27 November–2 December 1995.
46. Li, N.; Zhou, Z.H. *Selective Ensemble under Regularization Framework*; Springer: Berlin/Heidelberg, Germany, 2009.
47. Dempster, A.P. Upper and lower probabilities induced by a multivalued mapping. *Ann. Math. Statist.* **1967**, *38*, 325–339. [CrossRef]
48. Shafer, G. *A Mathematical Theory of Evidence*; Princeton University Press: Princeton, NJ, USA, 1976.
49. Xiao, J.; Tong, M.; Zhu, C.; Fan, Q. Improved combination rule of evidence based on pignistic probability distance. *J. Shanghai Jiaotong Univ.* **2012**, *46*, 636–641+645.
50. Deng, Y.; Shi, W.; Zhu, Z. Efficient combination approach of conflict evidence, in Chinese. *J. Infr. Millim. Waves* **2004**, *23*, 27–32.
51. Choi, E.; Lee, C. Feature extraction based on the Bhattacharyya distance. *Pattern Recognit.* **2003**, *36*, 1703–1709. [CrossRef]
52. Satorras, V.G.; Estrach, J.B. Few-Shot Learning with Graph Neural Networks. In Proceedings of the 6th International Conference on Learning Representations, Vancouver, BC, Canada, 30 April–3 May 2018.
53. Luo, ; Y.; Huang, Z.; Zhang, Z.; Wang, Z.; Baktashmotlagh, M.; Yang, Y. Learning from the Past: Continual Meta-Learning via Bayesian Graph Modeling. In Proceedings of the AAAI—Thirty-Fourth AAAI Conference on Artificial Intelligence, New York, NY, USA, 7–12 February 2020.
54. Yang, L.; Liangliang, L.; Zilun, Z.; Xinyu, Z.; Erjin, Z.; Yu, L. DPGN: Distribution Propagation Graph Network for Few-Shot Learning. In Proceedings of the 2020 IEEE/CVF Conference on Computer Vision and Pattern Recognition (CVPR), Seattle, WA, USA, 13–19 June 2020; pp. 13387–13396.
55. Chen, H.; Li, H.; Li, Y.; Chen, C. Sparse spatial transformers for few-shot learning. *Sci. China Inf. Sci.* **2023**, *66*, 210102. [CrossRef]
56. Jia, X.; Su, Y.; Zhao, H. Few-shot learning via relation network based on coarse-grained granulation. *Appl. Intell.* **2023**, *53*, 996–1008. [CrossRef]
57. Su, Y.; Zhao, H.; Lin, Y. Few-shot learning based on hierarchical classification via multi-granularity relation networks. *Int. J. Approx. Reason.* **2022**, *142*, 417–429. [CrossRef]
58. Russakovsky, O.; Deng, J.; Su, H.; Krause, J.; Satheesh, S.; Ma, S.; Huang, Z.; Karpathy, A.; Khosla, A.; Bernstein, M.; et al. Imagenet large scale visual recognition challenge. *Int. J. Comput. Vis.* **2015**, *115*, 211–252. [CrossRef]
59. Kingma, D.P.; Jimmy, B. Adam: A Method for Stochastic Optimization. In Proceedings of the 3rd International Conference on Learning Representations, San Diego, CA, USA, 7–9 May 2015.
60. Chang, C.C.; Li, C.J. LIBSVM: A library for support vector machines. *ACM Trans. Intell. Syst. Technol.* **2011**, *2*, 1–39. [CrossRef]
61. Hsu, C.; Chang, C.; Lin, C. A practical guide to support vector classification, *BJU Int.* **2008**, *101*, 1396–1400.
62. Sung, F.; Yang, Y.; Zhang, L.; Xiang, T.; Torr, P.H.; Hospedales, T.M. Learning to compare: Relation network for few-shot learning. In Proceedings of the IEEE Conference on Computer Vision and Pattern Recognition (CVPR), Salt Lake City, UT, USA, 18–22 June 2018.
63. Qiao, S.; Liu, C.; Shen, W.; Yuille, A.L. Few-Shot Image Recognition by Predicting Parameters from Activations. In Proceedings of the IEEE Conference on Computer Vision and Pattern Recognition (CVPR), Salt Lake City, UT, USA, 18–22 June 2018; pp. 7229–7238.

Disclaimer/Publisher's Note: The statements, opinions and data contained in all publications are solely those of the individual author(s) and contributor(s) and not of MDPI and/or the editor(s). MDPI and/or the editor(s) disclaim responsibility for any injury to people or property resulting from any ideas, methods, instructions or products referred to in the content.

Article

Continual Reinforcement Learning for Quadruped Robot Locomotion

Sibo Gai [1,2], Shangke Lyu [2], Hongyin Zhang [2] and Donglin Wang [2,*]

1 School of Computer Science, Fudan University, Shanghai 200433, China; 17114010010@fudan.edu.cn or gaisibo@westlake.edu.cn
2 School of Engineer, Westlake Univercity, Hangzhou 310030, China; lyushangke@westlake.edu.cn (S.L.); zhanghongyin@westlake.edu.cn (H.Z.)
* Correspondence: wangdonglin@westlake.edu.cn

Abstract: The ability to learn continuously is crucial for a robot to achieve a high level of intelligence and autonomy. In this paper, we consider continual reinforcement learning (RL) for quadruped robots, which includes the ability to continuously learn sub-sequential tasks (plasticity) and maintain performance on previous tasks (stability). The policy obtained by the proposed method enables robots to learn multiple tasks sequentially, while overcoming both catastrophic forgetting and loss of plasticity. At the same time, it achieves the above goals with as little modification to the original RL learning process as possible. The proposed method uses the Piggyback algorithm to select protected parameters for each task, and reinitializes the unused parameters to increase plasticity. Meanwhile, we encourage the policy network exploring by encouraging the entropy of the soft network of the policy network. Our experiments show that traditional continual learning algorithms cannot perform well on robot locomotion problems, and our algorithm is more stable and less disruptive to the RL training progress. Several robot locomotion experiments validate the effectiveness of our method.

Keywords: continual learning; quadruped robot locomotion; reinforcement learning; plasticity; entropy

Citation: Gai, S.; Lyu, S.; Zhang, H.; Wang, D. Continual Reinforcement Learning for Quadruped Robot Locomotion. *Entropy* **2024**, *26*, 93. https://doi.org/10.3390/e26010093

Academic Editor: Adam Lipowski

Received: 1 December 2023
Revised: 12 January 2024
Accepted: 15 January 2024
Published: 22 January 2024

Copyright: © 2024 by the authors. Licensee MDPI, Basel, Switzerland. This article is an open access article distributed under the terms and conditions of the Creative Commons Attribution (CC BY) license (https://creativecommons.org/licenses/by/4.0/).

1. Introduction

In recent years, deep reinforcement learning (RL) has shown remarkable success in various decision-making tasks [1–4], especially in the field of robot manipulation. The success of these tasks can be attributed to a nearly stable manipulation environment (for inference), a high-quality simulation platform, and also multi-task behavioral data at this stage. Naturally, prior works thus conduct a multi-task RL formulation [5,6], exploiting the potential behavioral correlations between tasks to further boost the performance. However, the same level of success progress has not been achieved in the context of complex locomotion tasks for quadruped robots. The primary reasons behind this challenge are the lack of a stable inference environment (diverse quadruped locomotion terrains), an accurate simulator, and a publicly verifiable dataset for quadruped robots to date. Further, this makes it difficult to model the quadruped locomotion as a traditional multi-task objective. Therefore, a question naturally arises: is there any other way, besides the multi-task paradigm, for training reliable quadruped robots?

We note that even without the presence of an accurate simulator, as well as the pre-collected multi-task offline data, it is feasible to learn a base quadruped policy in a single, static environment. Therefore, we can use base policy (or other behavior policies) to collect new offline data by visiting new tasks (e.g., terrains and commands) and then further boost the policy. In this way, we can continuously learn in multiple environments, and each new policy is trained to be adaptable to the corresponding environment. As depicted above, we thus propose a continual learning approach for quadruped locomotion tasks, shifting the demanding training requirements of a multi-task formulation (see Figure 1).

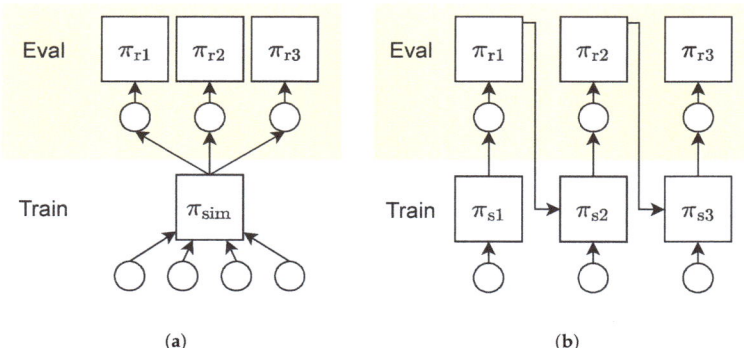

Figure 1. (**a**) Multi-task RL formulation: the agent learns from a set of pre-defined environments. (**b**) Continual RL formulation: the agent learns from sequential environments.

The decision to model quadruped robot locomotion as a continual learning problem is driven by several key factors. Firstly, continual learning offers the advantage of adaptability and flexibility, enabling the quadruped robot to continually learn and improve its locomotion skills with new experiences. This is particularly crucial in dynamic and real-world scenarios where the quadruped environment and task requirements may change over time. Also, robot locomotion for complex tasks in large spaces is, itself, a combination of numerous tasks. New tasks will naturally emerge as the exploration capabilities of the quadruped robot improve. Secondly, continual learning allows for the accumulation of knowledge, enabling the quadruped robot to build upon its previous experiences and avoid catastrophic forgetting. This is especially important for long-term deployment and robust quadruped locomotion performance.

However, modeling quadruped robot locomotion as a continual learning problem poses several challenges that need to be addressed.

Firstly, the issue of catastrophic forgetting arises, where the robot may lose previously acquired locomotion skills when learning new tasks. Secondly, the loss of plasticity problem becomes obvious, the plasticity of the RL network will be soon saturated after learning several tasks. Additionally, the trade-off between the exploitation of existing knowledge and the exploration of new locomotion strategies needs to be carefully managed to ensure continual improvement.

To overcome these challenges, our approach incorporates a dynamic-architecture strategy. Dynamic-architecture-based algorithms allow the robot to select and learn the most critical parameters for each task, and save and lock the learned parameters for each task. On the one hand, saving and locking these parameters ensures that the robot does not forget learned skills. On the other hand, the robot can also select and leverage parameters learned in the past, allowing the robot to build on previous experience. We also indicate that re-initialization the parameters and appending the entropy of the output of the policy network can help the robot maintain its plasticity.

The main contributions of this paper are as follows:

- We introduce the concept of continual reinforcement learning for quadruped robot locomotion, addressing the limitations imposed by the lacking requirements of multi-task formulation.
- We propose a dynamic-architecture-based framework that enables continual learning, relieves the catastrophic forgetting in quadruped robot and improves complex locomotion capabilities. Then, we introduce the re-initialization and the entropy to help the robot maintain its plasticity.
- We present experimental results demonstrating the effectiveness of our approach in achieving robust and adaptive locomotion performance in dynamic environments.

In the following sections, we will discuss the challenges associated with modeling quadruped robot locomotion as a continual learning problem and present our approach to address these challenges. We will then present experimental results and discuss the implications of our findings.

2. Materials and Methods

2.1. Preliminary

In this work, we model the interaction between the quadruped robot and the environment as a partially observable Markov decision process (POMDP), denoted by the tuple $\mathcal{M} = \{\mathcal{S}, \Omega, \mathcal{A}, \mathcal{T}, \mathcal{O}, r, \gamma, p_0, \rho_0\}$, where $\mathcal{S}$ is the full state space, Ω is the observation space, $\mathcal{A}$ is the action space, $\mathcal{T} : \mathcal{S} \times \mathcal{A} \times \mathcal{S} \to \mathbb{R}$ is the transition dynamics function, $\mathcal{O} : \mathcal{S} \times \mathcal{A} \to \Omega$ is the observation probability, $r : \mathcal{S} \times \mathcal{A} \to \mathbb{R}$ is the reward function, γ is the discount factor, p_0 is the distribution of initial states, and ρ_0 is the distribution of initial observation.

The goal in a reinforcement learning (RL) decision-making task is to learn a policy $\pi_\theta(\mathbf{a}|\mathbf{o})$ that maximizes the expected sum of discounted rewards $\mathbb{E}_{\pi_\theta(\tau)}\left[\sum_{t=0}^{T-1} \gamma^t r(\mathbf{s}_t, \mathbf{a}_t)\right]$, where $\tau := \{\mathbf{s}_0, \mathbf{o}_0, \mathbf{a}_0, \cdots, \mathbf{s}_{K-1}, \mathbf{o}_{K_1}, \mathbf{a}_{K-1}\}$ denotes the trajectory and the generated trajectory distribution $\pi_\theta(\tau) = \mathcal{A}_0 \prod_{t=1}^{K-1} \pi_\theta(\mathbf{a}_t|\mathbf{o}_t)\mathcal{O}(\mathbf{o}_t|\mathbf{s}_t, \mathbf{a}_{t-1})\mathcal{T}(\mathbf{s}_t|\mathbf{s}_{t-1}, \mathbf{a}_{t-1})$, where K is the upper limit of the number of running steps and $\mathcal{A}_0 = p_0(\mathbf{s}_0)\mathcal{O}(\mathbf{s}_0)\pi_\theta(\mathbf{a}_0|\mathbf{o}_0)$.

We would like to emphasize that our method can also be used in the Markov decision process (MDP) environment. We model the environment into a POMDP because the robot locomotion task usually model the environment into a POMDP. The propose of our continual RL method is to not affect the origin method much and keep the plug-and-play capability.

2.2. Continual Quadruped Robot Locomotion

Compared to other robot control tasks, quadruped robots have greater flexibility in exploring a complex real world. In the exploration process, quadruped robots will naturally encounter more environments and tasks. However, compared to the complex real world, the environments and tasks that a robot can explore in a given time are limited. Also, due to limited onboard resources, robots cannot store all the experiences they have explored. Therefore, we define the learning process of quadruped robot locomotion as a continual learning process, where the current task refers to the locomotion task within the region that a robot can freely explore when the environment, task, and physical structure of the robot remain unchanged. As soon as the environment, task, or robot dynamics change, or the physical structure that the robot can freely explore changes, the robot is faced with a new task.

We define a robot locomotion RL task as a continual RL process in which the robot has to learn a sequence of tasks $\{T_n\}, n \in \{1, \cdots, N\}$, where N is the length of the sequence. Considering that tasks faced by robots can be repetitive, we consider each task to be sampled from a task set $\mathcal{T} = \{T_1, \cdots, T_{\tilde{N}}\}$, where $\tilde{N}$ is the set of all tasks, $\tilde{N} < N$. In the remainder of this paper, we will use T_n to denote the task the robot is learning, $\mathcal{T}'$ to denote the set of all learned tasks, and $T'_n \in \mathcal{T}'$ to denote a previous task. For convenience, we will omit the subscript of the task index $*_n$ if we do not specify a particular task.

In the next section, we introduce the Piggyback network [7] to relieve the catastrophic forgetting problem for the Q network, the policy network, and the CENet (all three networks adopt the same anti-forgetting method).

2.3. Catastrophic Forgetting and Piggyback

Our architecture of each network is shown in Figure 2, which is based on the Piggyback algorithm.

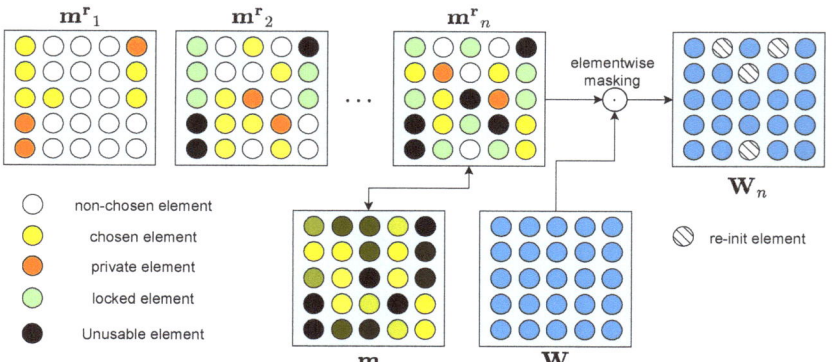

Figure 2. For each task, we only select the most important subset of parameters to compose a sub-network for training and utilization. Among them, only the parameters never selected by other tasks before (chosen elements) will be updated in order not to affect learned task performance, while parameters previously selected by other tasks are used without updating (locked elements). After learning each task, some parameters will be selected (private elements) for later fine-tuning on this task. Private parameters of previous tasks (unusable elements) avoid being chosen by subsequent tasks for both training and utilization thus preventing influencing the performance of other tasks. After all, those parameters that never chosen by any task will be re-initialization after training a task.

First, when learning the first task T_1, for the policy network π, the critic network Q, and the CENet, the algorithm proposes to select and fine-tune a part of the parameters $\mathbf{W}_1$ to consist a sub-network from the intact parameter $\mathbf{W}$. For simplicity, we will use $\mathbf{W} = [w]_{ij}$ and $\mathbf{W}_1 = [w_1]_{ij}$ if the network is not specified. In the following, we will refer to the three as the base network and the dense network, respectively. To do this, our approach learns both the parameters of the base network $\mathbf{W}$ and the parameters of the binary mask $\mathbf{m}_1$, and masks the base network with the binary mask $\mathbf{W}_1 = \mathbf{W} \cdot \mathbf{m}_1$, where '·' means the element-wise multiplication. Since the binary mask cannot be learned with backward propagation, Piggyback introduces a soft network $\mathbf{m^r}_1 = [m^r]_{1,ij}$. Each time, the algorithm selects a binary mask from the soft network by a threshold and copies the gradient of the binary mask to the soft network, as shown below:

$$m_{1,ij} = \begin{cases} 1, \text{if } ij \in \text{topk } \mathbf{m^r} \\ 0, \text{otherwise} \end{cases}, \delta m^r_{1,ij} = \delta m_{1,ij}. \tag{1}$$

Then, for the following continual learning tasks, suppose we have learned task $n-1$; next, we will learn task n. In the experiment, to control the capacity of the network, we choose the threshold k by a ratio of the size of the network, i.e., $k = c\|\mathbf{W}\|, c \in [0, 1]$.

However, the traditional Piggyback algorithm performs poorly when controlling quadruped robots. Despite high payoffs during training, test performance is poor. Even when the size of the base network is increased by a factor of $\frac{1}{c}$, the performance of the piggyback network still fails to match that of regular dense networks. We believe that one reason for this is the choice of metrics. Freely chosen parameters have validity problems. That is, if none of a neuron's output parameters are selected, its input parameters cannot be learned. Similarly, if too many of a neuron's output parameters are selected, the importance of its input parameters will also increase. Therefore, we use an element-based ratio to select parameters, i.e., we ensure the same ratio of activated parameters for each neuron. This allows our network to achieve performance commensurate with its capacity. When the size of the basic network is increased, each parameter of the network can still operate normally, thus improving the learning ability of our network. So, the element-based ratio mask should be optimized:

$$m_{1,ij} = \begin{cases} 1, \text{if } ij \in \text{topk } \mathbf{m}_i^{\mathbf{r}} \\ 0, \text{otherwise} \end{cases}, \delta m_{1,ij}^r = \delta m_{1,ij}. \qquad (2)$$

Selecting and learning a new part of **W** from scratch will be a naive way to learn subsequent tasks like Piggybacking. However, unlike the traditional continual learning hypothesis, tasks in quadruped robot control are much more general. Instead of learning completely new parameters, we perform further training on the originally learned network. Thus, we add some vacant parameters to the original parameters of task $n-1$ as the network of the new task n.

Following the idea of soft network from the WSN method [8], we further allow the binary masks **m** for different tasks to overlap, but only one parameter that is never selected by any task (vacant parameters) will be updated and one parameter that is selected by the previous task will not be updated, called the occupied parameters:

$$\delta m_{n,ij}^r = \begin{cases} \delta m_{n,ij}, \text{if } m'_{n,ij} = 0 \\ 0, \text{otherwise} \end{cases}, \qquad (3)$$

where $m'_{n,ij} = \prod_{n' \in \{1,\cdots,n-1\}} m_{n',ij} = 0$ is a parameter is vacant (=0) or occupied (=1). **W**, **m** and $\mathbf{m^r}$ are learned together. However, in the vanilla WSN method [8], the soft network is updated by a Straight-through Estimator [9], which needs to update the soft network while ignoring the mask. However, exploration and learning without the mask will be dangerous and inefficient for the robot. Therefore, unlike WSN, optimizing the soft network by Piggyback will suffer from low plasticity because the soft network cannot distinguish between free and occupied parameters. Once the selected parameters consist mainly of occupied parameters, the algorithm will stop learning. Therefore, for each new task n, we force at least λ vacant parameters to be introduced along with $1-\lambda$ occupied parameters to learn the new task n. Both vacant and filled parameters are selected by the soft network, i.e.,

$$m_{n,ij} = \begin{cases} 1, \text{if } m_{n,ij}^r \geq r_{\text{vacant}} \text{ and } m^* \\ 1, \text{if } m_{n,ij}^r \geq r_{\text{occupied}} \text{ and } m^* \\ 0, \text{otherwise} \end{cases}, \delta m_{1,ij}^r = \delta m_{1,ij}. \qquad (4)$$

In this way, we can control the network parameters consumed by each task, avoiding the failure of some tasks during the learning process. In our experience, we choose the λ by proportion, which allows us to better control the learning capacity of the network.

After learning a task, only the binary mask will be saved.

2.4. Loss of Plasticity and Re-Initialization

Simply applying dynamic structure algorithms directly to the robot RL performs poorly, as shown in our experiments. The additional attached loss function and the loss of plasticity problem introduced by the dynamic structure make it difficult to learn tasks other than the initial task. We believe that this problem could possibly be solved by carefully tuning the hyperparameters and designing the network architecture and learning processes. However, such an approach would require re-tuning the hyperparameters from scratch each time we face a new task. It is well-known that tuning hyperparameters for quadruped robot control problems is an extremely complex and tedious process [10]. This would cause our method to lose its plug-and-play capability.

In order to compensate for the loss of plasticity, we propose to reinitialize the base and soft networks after learning each task. Besides leaving the occupied parameters of the base network unchanged, other parameters are reset to random initialization states (our experiments show that re-initializing the soft network for vacant parameters or the entire soft network leads to similar results). Note that for vacant parameters, although they are not selected in the end, they may still have been updated during optimization. Meanwhile, random initialization of the soft network also avoids problems where soft network values become too large or too small during the previous task, preventing learning in the new task. Also, since we are optimizing the soft network using the Piggyback algorithm and using the gradient of **m** instead of **m**^{r}, the size of **m**^{r} does not affect the gradient scale. Thus, the convergence speed of the soft mesh is influenced by the scale of **m**^{r}.

Another factor affecting plasticity is the exploration ability of the robot, which is correlated with the entropy of robot actions. Robots that output actions with higher entropy can retain higher levels of exploration in following environments. With the learned skills and knowledge, the robot will tend to choose the actions that is stable and secure in order to avoid degradation in performance. However, the stable skills that learned by past tasks cannot obtain the optimal performance in the new task without exploration with more flexible and random actions, so that to keep the entropy when selecting the occupied parameters is important. Therefore, we have introduced a reward function in our robot learning to encourage the robot to maintain the soft network with high entropy. Therefore, avoiding adding the entropy into the loss function of the base network, we take it as a term of the loss function of the soft network; that is:

$$m^r_{n,ij} = \text{Normal}\left(m^{r,\text{base}}_{n,ij}, \sigma^2\right), \delta m^r_{n,ij} = \begin{cases} \delta m_{n,ij} + \delta \mathcal{H}, \text{if } m'_{n,ij} = 0 \\ 0, \text{otherwise} \end{cases}, \quad (5)$$

where $\mathcal{H} = \frac{1}{2}\ln(2\pi e\sigma^2)$ is the entropy, $m^{r,\text{base}}_{n,ij}$ is the mean of the distribution of the soft network, and σ is the variance of the output of the soft network. After learning several steps (100 in our experiment), we reduce the entropy on the soft network and let the base network enhance the final rewards.

Forward transferability and maintaining plasticity are a trade-off in continual learning. Our algorithm reconciles this dilemma well by reinitializing vacant parameters while still allowing access to occupied parameters.

2.5. Sim to Real in Continual Learning

Another aspect of the real-world robot control problem is the sim-to-real shift. Although they have learned in simulation environments, quadruped robots still need to be fine-tuned in real environments in order to be deployed there. However, due to conditional constraints, it is ideal but often infeasible to immediately fine-tune in the real environment after learning a task in simulation. Thus, fine-tuning a task in the real environment can still lead to catastrophic forgetting of other tasks. Therefore, we propose a method to isolate some parameters as private parameters for each task, which are not accessible by other tasks, to prevent the network from forgetting even after fine-tuning. Only these parameters are optimized during the real fine-tuning. In addition, our method allows for multiple learning of the same task to adapt to small variations in the environment or task. Due to the complexity of control tasks, robots often find it difficult to fully explore the state space once. Repeated learning of the same task is important in reinforcement learning [11]. In practice, we directly use the soft network to select parameters. The soft mesh cannot accurately reflect the importance of the parameters, but has a lower computational cost.

2.6. Compare to the Past Works

Our work is mainly based on the two algorithms, Piggyback [7] and Winning Soft-network [8]. We would like to emphasize the difference between our method and these two methods here. Comparing with Piggyback, our method can leverage experience from past tasks. This not only improves learning capability for subsequent tasks, but also saves space usage for the subsequent tasks. Also, to address the issue of loss of plasticity in Piggyback, we employed re-initialization and maintaining the entropy of soft-network to increase the plasticity, ensuring that our algorithm can extensively explore all parameters. Then, comparing with the WSN, our method uses the Piggyback soft-network updating, which not only can be easily used in RL setting, but also saves the computation time. Finally, we introduce a simple way to efficiently choose and keep some private parameters for sim-to-real transfer.

3. Results

3.1. Compared Methods

To evaluate the performance of our method, we compare it with six widely used continual learning methods:

- Experience Replay (ER) [12]: a basic rehearsal-based continual method that adds a behavior cloning term to the loss function of the policy network.
- Averaged gradient episodic memory (AGEM) [13]: a method based on gradient episodic memory that uses only a batch of gradients to limit the policy update.
- Elastic weight consolidation (EWC) [14]: constraining changes to critical parameters by the Fisher information matrix.
- Riemannian Walk (R-Walk) [15]: a method adds a parameter importance score on the Riemannian manifold based on EWC.
- Synaptic Intelligence (SI) [16]: a method that constrain the changes after each optimization step.
- Packnet [17]: a method to sequentially "pack" multiple tasks into a single network by performing iterative pruning and network re-training.

We evaluate these methods using the same network architecture as our method, but a multi-head network. For the two rehearsal-based methods compared (ER and AGEM), we used a replay buffer with a capacity of a trajectory of the data collected for each task, which is a large proportion for general applications [18]. For each task, we select 20% of the parameters and keep 2% of the parameters for online tuning.

3.2. Implementation Details

Each task in the sequence is a robot locomotion task, which we model as an RL task. According to [19], we define a Q-function $Q(\mathbf{s}_t, \mathbf{a}_t)$, a policy $\pi(\mathbf{a}_t|\mathbf{o}_t, \mathbf{z}_t, \mathbf{v}_t)$ and a context-aided estimator network (CENet) $C(\tilde{\mathbf{o}}_t, \mathbf{v}_t|\mathbf{o}_t^H)$. Q-learning methods train a Q-function by iteratively applying the Bellman operator $\mathcal{B}^*Q(\mathbf{s}_t, \mathbf{a}_t) = r(\mathbf{s}_t, \mathbf{a}_t) + \gamma \mathbb{E}_{\mathbf{s}_{t+1} \sim P(\mathbf{s}_t|\mathbf{s}_t, \mathbf{s}_t)}(\max_{\mathbf{a}_{t+1}} Q(\mathbf{s}_{t+1}, \mathbf{a}_{t+1}))$. By introducing the privileged observation $\mathbf{s}_t$ only into the Q-network, the agent (policy) also can makes decisions without privileged observation when evaluating in the real world. The implementation also follows the definition of the privileged observation s_t in [19]. The CENet from [19] is used to jointly learn to estimate and infer a latent representation of the environment. The architecture of the CENet consists of a single encoder and a multi-head decoder to encode $\mathbf{o}_t^H$ into $\mathbf{v}_t$ and $\tilde{\mathbf{o}}_t$.

Our basic actor-critical RL method is from [19]. For details on the specific state space $\mathcal{S}$, action space $\mathcal{A}$, and reward function r, we follow [19]. We also list the elements of the reward function in Table 1, where $\cdot_{target}$ indicates the desired values. x, y, and z are defined on the body frame of the robot, with x and z pointing forward and upward, respectively. g, v_z, ω, h, p, and v_f are the gravity vector projected onto the robot's body frame, linear velocities in the z-plane, yaw rate, body height above ground, foot height, and foot lateral velocity, respectively.

We mainly follow the setting of the RL network in [19]. Both the actor and the critic are multi-layer perceptron (MLP) with three hidden layers of 512, 256, and 128 neurons, respectively, each with ReLU non-linearity. The CENet is also a multi-layer perceptron with two hidden layers of 256 neurons for the encoder and decoder. We also use Adam [20] with a learning rate of 0.001 to update both the basic network and the soft network of actor, critic, and CENet. According to [21], we increase the epsilon of Adam to 1×10^{-5}. We update each task by 500 epochs. Unlike the vanilla Piggyback algorithm, we initialize the soft network with a random Gaussian noise, which works better than a fixed value for all tasks except the first.

Table 1. Reward structure.

Term	Equation	Weight
linear velocity tracking	$\exp\{-|v_{xy} - v_{xy}^{cmd}|^2/0.25\}$	1.0
angular velocity tracking	$\exp\{-|\omega_z - \omega_z^{cmd}|^2/0.25\}$	0.5
z velocity	v_z^2	-2.0
roll-pitch velocity	$|\omega_{xy}|^2$	-0.05
orientation	$|g|^2$	-5.0
joint limit violation	$\sum_{j=1}^{12} \phi(q_{bj}, q_{bj,lower}, q_{bj,upper})$	-10.0
joint torques	$|\tau|^2$	-2×10^{-4}
joint accelerations	$|\ddot{q}_b|^2$	-2.5×10^{-7}
body height	$(h - h_{target})^2$	-30.0
feet clearance	$(p - p_{target})^2 * v_f$	1.0
thigh/calf collision	$\mathbb{1}_{collision}$	-1.0
action smoothing	$|a_{t-1} - a_t|^2$	-0.01

For each task, we keep 20% private parameters and keep 2% parameters for sim-to-real learning. In the 20% private parameters, we choose 25% vacant parameters and 75% occupied parameters so that the λ is 25%. For each task, we train it 500 epochs and turn to the next task.

3.3. Experimental Environments

We will discuss the three sets of tasks we are evaluating (see Figure 3).

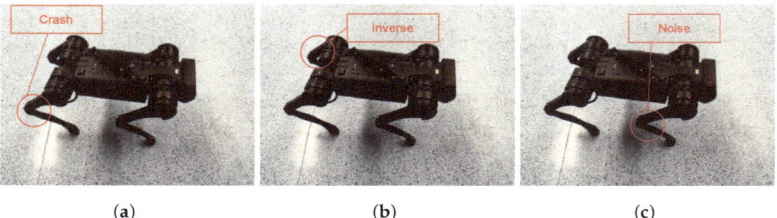

Figure 3. (**a**) In the Leg Crash task, we set the output of each leg into zero, respectively. (**b**) In the Leg Inversion task, we inverse the output of each leg, respectively. (**c**) In the Leg Noise task, we add a random noise into the output of each leg, respectively.

- Leg Crash: we set the output of different legs of the robot to zero for each task to simulate the situation where the leg crashes and cannot move.
- Leg Inversion: for each task, we invert the outputs of the neural network for one leg of the robot.
- Leg Noise: we add random Gaussian noise to the output of the robot. From the first task to the fourth task, we add the noise to the left front leg, the right front leg, the left rear leg, and the right rear leg.

In order to make our experiments as long as possible and increase the number of tasks, we randomly mix the three cases to obtain the final experimental tasks.

4. Discussion

4.1. Episode Reward

We report part of the result in Figure 4. From the figure, we can see that a traditional continual learning architecture cannot solve the complex problem of the locomotion of a quadruped robot. Among them, regularization-based algorithms (EWC, SI, and R-Walk) have difficulty maintaining acquired performance. After several tasks, the performance of learned tasks decreases notably. In comparison, rehearsal-based algorithms (ER and AGEM) perform better, but robot performance still declines after multiple tasks. This may be because robot locomotion poses higher requirements on network parameter stability. Even small changes in network parameters can lead to a damaged locomotion ability. The pruning-based dynamic-architecture-method (Packnet) performs the worst because the additional L1 loss will affect the learning of the robot.

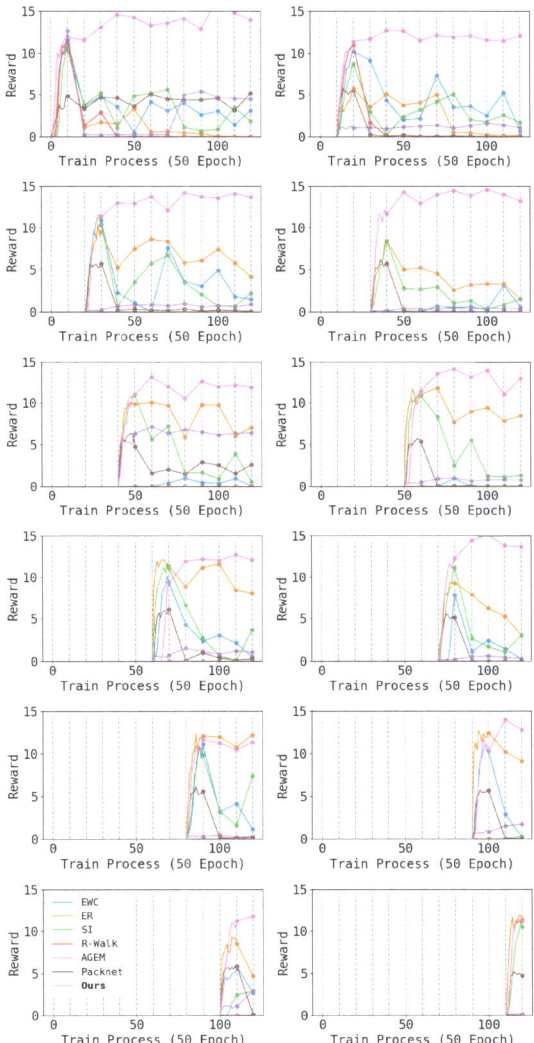

Figure 4. Each figure shows the performance of one task during the entire learning phase: the first row is for tasks 1–2, the second row is for tasks 3–4, and so on. Throughout the learning process, we train each task 500 epochs and switch to the next task. The first 500 epochs of each task show the reward during training, while subsequent data are results of testing the performance on that task each 500 epochs. Higher results are better. We can see that our algorithm maintains the performance achieved during training on all tasks, while all baselines exhibit decreased performance during later testing.

Finally, we report the performance of the Piggyback methods with different hyperparameters and random seeds in Figure 5. It can be seen that Piggyback perform well in first few tasks, but the learning ability will reduce after learning several tasks. This is because the Piggyback method cannot leverage the occupied parameters as well as ours.

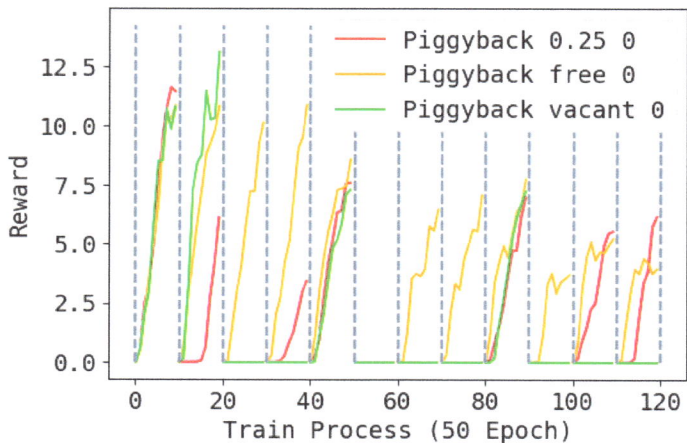

Figure 5. Training rewards of the Piggyback method during the whole training process. A value of 0.25 means each task uses 25% vacant parameters and 75% occupied parameters; free means select using vacant parameters and the occupied parameters freely like WSN; vacant means only use the vacant parameters for new tasks. The task changes every 500 epochs. Higher is better.

In comparison, our method not only has significant advantages in mitigating catastrophic forgetting, but also maintains better plasticity as the number of learned tasks increases than baselines. Although each task requires a long exploration and training process, our method can still maintain the original locomotion ability. Even though we use only 20% of the parameters for a task, the learning ability is sufficient to learn such complex RL tasks as controlling quadruped robots without enlarging the neural network. Furthermore, even though our method has slightly lower performance for the first task in some cases compared to the incomplete version, the higher plasticity will be reflected in the performance of subsequent tasks. The learning capabilities of AGEM and R-Walk significantly decrease after learning several tasks, showing an inability to learn new tasks to adequate levels during training. In contrast, EWC, ER, and SI ensure higher learning ability on new tasks, and Piggyback suffers almost no loss of plasticity problem.

4.2. Commands Tracking

The other two important arguments for robot locomotion are the line velocity and the angle velocity. These two arguments are commonly used to measure the correct locomotion of the quadruped robots [19]. We compare the difference between the output velocity and input command with three random commands. Each command is the expected line speed sampled from $[-1.0, 1.0]$ m/s and the angle speed sampled from $\left[-\frac{\pi}{2}, \frac{\pi}{2}\right]$ rad/s. We give the tracking performance of the line velocity in Figure 6 and the angle velocity in Figure 7.

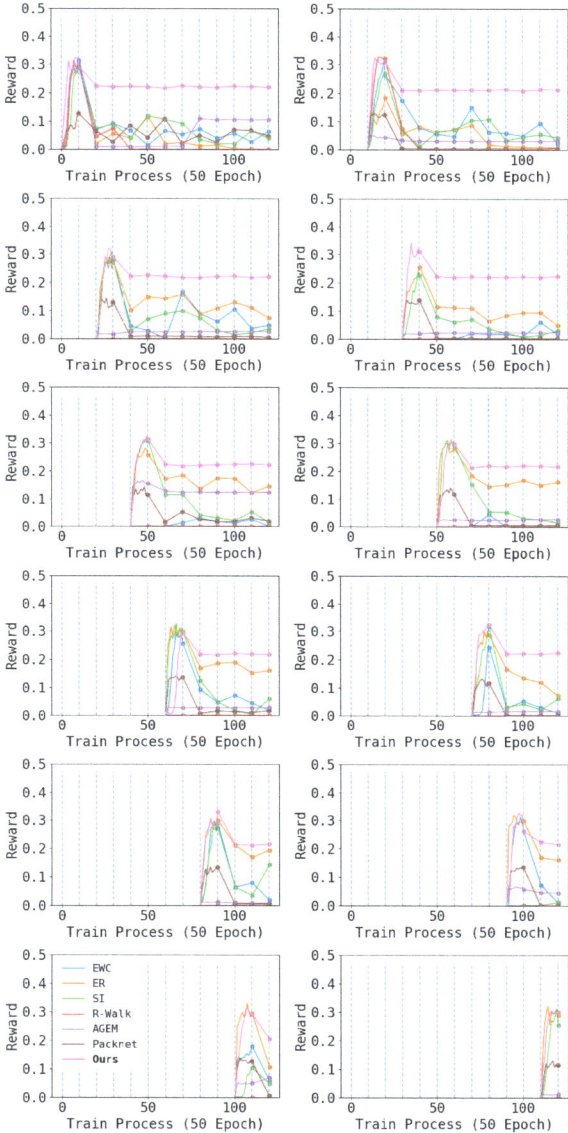

Figure 6. Each figure shows the performance of tracking the line velocity of one task during the entire learning phase: the first row is for tasks 1–2, the second row is for tasks 3–4, and so on. Throughout the learning process, we switch the robot to another task every 500 epochs. The first 500 epochs of each task show the performance of tracking the line velocity during training, while subsequent data are the results of testing the performance on that task for each 500 epochs. Higher results are better. We can see that the performance of our method only drops just after training (because of the shift between training and testing), and can keep a steady performance in the remaining learning process.

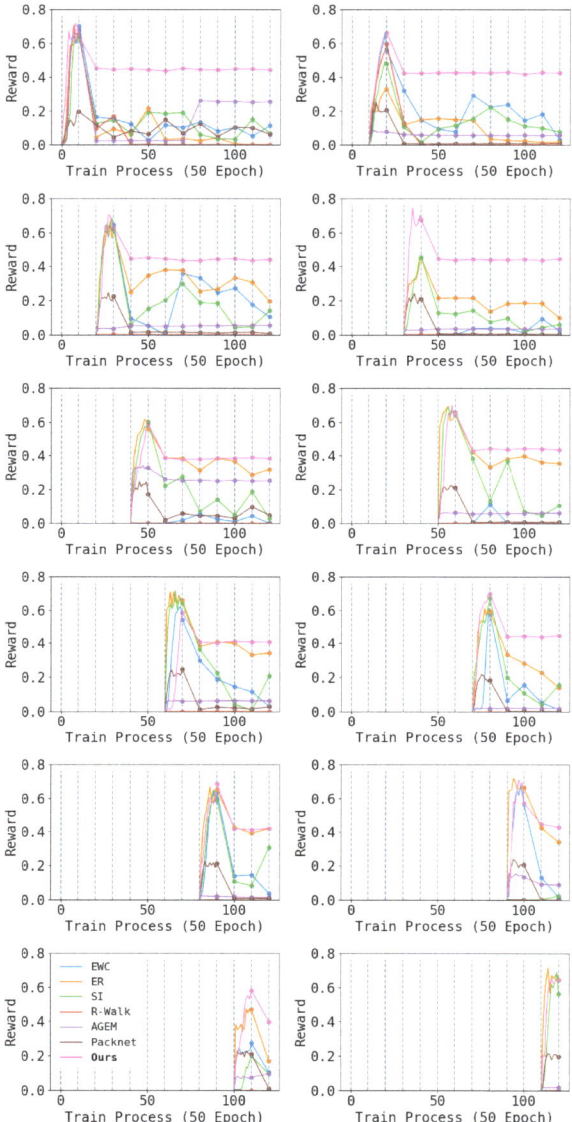

Figure 7. Each figure shows the performance of tracking the angle velocity of one task during the entire learning phase: the first row is for tasks 1–2, the second row is for tasks 3–4, and so on. Throughout the learning process, we switch the robot to another task every 500 epochs. The first 500 epochs of each task show the performance of tracking the line velocity during training, while subsequent data are the results of testing the performance on that task for each 500 epochs. Higher results are better. We can see that the performance of our method only drops just after training (because of the shift between training and testing), and can keep a steady performance in the remaining learning process.

We can see that after learning the follow-up task, the ability to follow the moving commands decreases. In particular, the robot tends to reduce speed to ensure safety.

4.3. Effect of Re-Initialization and Entropy

In Figures 8–10, we show the reward during training on each task under three different re-initialization schemes. We can see that re-initialization enhances the plasticity for the following tasks. For most tasks, whether the base network is reinitialized also does not have an obvious impact, but for some tasks, not re-initializing parameters can lead to slower training. Also, optimizing the entropy for soft network also hastens the learning process of the following tasks.

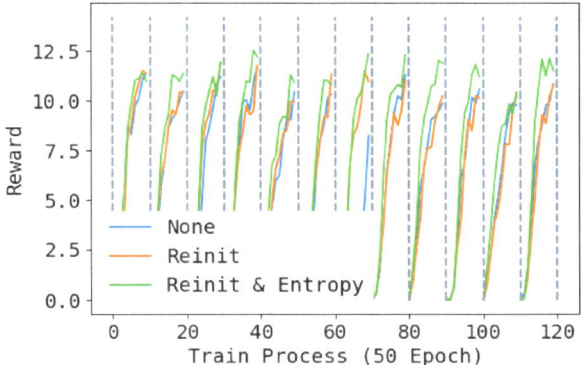

Figure 8. Training rewards during the whole training process. None means not to reinitialize; Reinit means to reinitialize unused parameters of the base network and the soft network; Reinit & Entropy means to reinitialize the unused parameters of the base networks and the soft network, and raise the entropy of the action when learning the soft network. The task changes every 500 epochs. Higher is better.

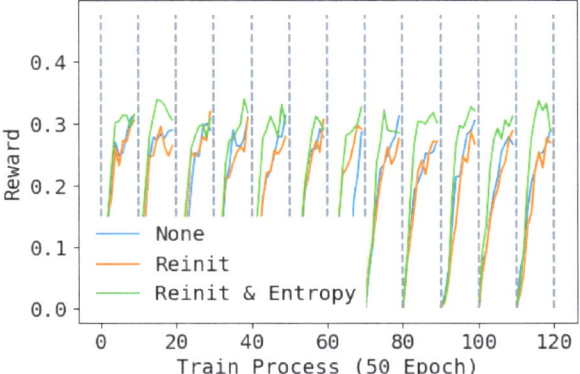

Figure 9. Training performance of tracking line velocity during the whole training process. None means not to reinitialize; Reinit means to reinitialize unused parameters of the base network and the soft network; Reinit & Entropy means to reinitialize the unused parameters of the base networks and the soft network, and raise the entropy of the action when learning the soft network. The task changes every 500 epochs. Higher is better.

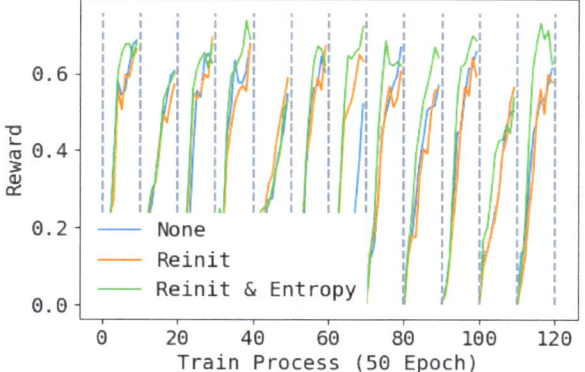

Figure 10. Training performance of tracking angle velocity during the whole training process. None means not to reinitialize; Reinit means to reinitialize unused parameters of the base network and the soft network; Reinit & Entropy means to reinitialize the unused parameters of the base networks and the soft network, and raise the entropy of the action when learning the soft network. The task changes every 500 epochs. Higher is better.

4.4. Forward Transfer

An important capability of our architecture is forward transfer. We evaluate the forward transfer ability by a newly designed environment consisting of all the interference of tasks. We mix a new task by two learned task, i.e., a robot have both a inverse right back leg and a noise right forward leg. Then, we learn this new task with a soft network that the chosen parameters by the task "inverse right back leg" and the task "noise right forward leg" has a higher initialization than other occupied parameters. We called this way "related task". As a contrast, we propose two other learning ways: "random select", which initialize the soft network by other two random tasks, and "learn from scratch", which does not change the initialize way. The result is shown in Figure 11. This result reflects the forward transferability of our methods. We can see that the "related task" learns faster than "learn from scratch" because it has a better foundation. Then, "random task" learn the slowest and cannot match the performance because the extraneous parameters interfere with the learning process.

Figure 11. The learning process of the mixed environment. We can see that learning a new task that combination of two learned tasks from a combination of the soft network can speed up the training process.

5. Conclusions

In this paper, we propose an algorithm that performs continual learning on a quadruped robot control using a dynamic architecture approach. We point out that complex quadruped control environments make traditional continual learning algorithms difficult to adapt, while dynamic-architecture-based continual learning algorithms can achieve greater advantages with their excellent stability. We also propose to maintain the plasticity of the policies by resetting the parameters to avoid plasticity loss, which has a significant impact on the final performance. Finally, our experiments validate that our algorithm can enable positive transfer for skill composition, demonstrating the unique advantages of continual learning algorithms.

Author Contributions: Conceptualization, S.G. and S.L.; methodology, S.G.; software, S.G. and H.Z.; validation, H.Z. and S.L.; formal analysis, S.G.; investigation, D.W.; resources, D.W.; data curation, H.Z.; writing—original draft preparation, S.G.; writing—review and editing, S.G. and S.L.; visualization, S.G.; supervision, D.W.; project administration, D.W.; funding acquisition, D.W. All authors have read and agreed to the published version of the manuscript.

Funding: This work was supported by the National Science and Technology Innovation 2030-Major Project (Grant No. 2022ZD0208800), and NSFC General Program (Grant No. 62176215).

Data Availability Statement: No new data were created or analyzed in this study. Data sharing is not applicable to this article.

Conflicts of Interest: The authors declare no conflicts of interest.

References

1. Zitkovich, B.; Yu, T.; Xu, S.; Xu, P.; Xiao, T.; Xia, F.; Wu, J.; Wohlhart, P.; Welker, S.; Wahid, A.; et al. Rt-2: Vision-language-action models transfer web knowledge to robotic control. In Proceedings of the 7th Annual Conference on Robot Learning, Atlanta, GA, USA, 6–9 November 2023.
2. Brohan, A.; Brown, N.; Carbajal, J.; Chebotar, Y.; Dabis, J.; Finn, C.; Gopalakrishnan, K.; Hausman, K.; Herzog, A.; Hsu, J.; et al. Rt-1: Robotics transformer for real-world control at scale. *arXiv* **2022**, arXiv:2212.06817.
3. Kang, Y.; Shi, D.; Liu, J.; He, L.; Wang, D. Beyond reward: Offline preference-guided policy optimization. *arXiv* **2023**, arXiv:2305.16217.
4. Liu, J.; Zhang, H.; Zhuang, Z.; Kang, Y.; Wang, D.; Wang, B. Design from Policies: Conservative Test-Time Adaptation for Offline Policy Optimization. *arXiv* **2023**, arXiv:2306.14479.
5. Reed, S.; Zolna, K.; Parisotto, E.; Colmenarejo, S.G.; Novikov, A.; Barth-Maron, G.; Gimenez, M.; Sulsky, Y.; Kay, J.; Springenberg, J.T.; et al. A generalist agent. *arXiv* **2022**, arXiv:2205.06175.
6. Yang, R.; Xu, H.; Wu, Y.; Wang, X. Multi-task reinforcement learning with soft modularization. *Adv. Neural Inf. Process. Syst.* **2020**, *33*, 4767–4777.
7. Mallya, A.; Davis, D.; Lazebnik, S. Piggyback: Adapting a Single Network to Multiple Tasks by Learning to Mask Weights. In *Computer Vision—ECCV 2018, Proceedings of the 15th European Conference, Munich, Germany, 8–14 September 2018*; Proceedings, Part IV; Lecture Notes in Computer Science; Ferrari, V., Hebert, M., Sminchisescu, C., Weiss, Y., Eds.; Springer: Cham, Switzerland, 2018; Volume 11208, pp. 72–88. [CrossRef]
8. Kang, H.; Yoon, J.; Madjid, S.R.; Hwang, S.J.; Yoo, C.D. Forget-free Continual Learning with Soft-Winning SubNetworks. *arXiv* **2023**, arXiv:2303.14962.
9. Ramanujan, V.; Wortsman, M.; Kembhavi, A.; Farhadi, A.; Rastegari, M. What's hidden in a randomly weighted neural network? In Proceedings of the IEEE/CVF Conference on Computer Vision and Pattern Recognition, Seattle, WA, USA, 13–19 June 2020; pp. 11893–11902.
10. Zhang, H.; Yang, S.; Wang, D. A Real-World Quadrupedal Locomotion Benchmark for Offline Reinforcement Learning. *arXiv* **2023**, arXiv:2309.16718.
11. Van de Ven, G.M.; Tolias, A.S. Three scenarios for continual learning. *arXiv* **2019**, arXiv:1904.07734.
12. Rolnick, D.; Ahuja, A.; Schwarz, J.; Lillicrap, T.P.; Wayne, G. Experience Replay for Continual Learning. In Proceedings of the Advances in Neural Information Processing Systems 32: Annual Conference on Neural Information Processing Systems 2019, NeurIPS 2019, Vancouver, BC, Canada, 8–14 December 2019; pp. 348–358.
13. Chaudhry, A.; Ranzato, M.; Rohrbach, M.; Elhoseiny, M. Efficient Lifelong Learning with A-GEM. In Proceedings of the ICLR, New Orleans, LA, USA, 6–9 May 2019.
14. Kirkpatrick, J.; Pascanu, R.; Rabinowitz, N.; Veness, J.; Desjardins, G.; Rusu, A.A.; Milan, K.; Quan, J.; Ramalho, T.; Grabska-Barwinska, A.; et al. Overcoming catastrophic forgetting in neural networks. *Proc. Natl. Acad. Sci. USA* **2017**, *114*, 3521–3526. [CrossRef] [PubMed]

15. Chaudhry, A.; Dokania, P.K.; Ajanthan, T.; Torr, P.H. Riemannian Walk for Incremental Learning: Understanding Forgetting and Intransigence. In Proceedings of the European Conference on Computer Vision, Munich, Germany, 8–14 September 2018; pp. 556–572.
16. Zenke, F.; Poole, B.; Ganguli, S. Continual Learning Through Synaptic Intelligence. In Proceedings of the International Conference on Machine Learning. PMLR, Sydney, Australia, 6–11 August 2017; pp. 3987–3995.
17. Mallya, A.; Lazebnik, S. Packnet: Adding multiple tasks to a single network by iterative pruning. In Proceedings of the IEEE conference on Computer Vision and Pattern Recognition, Salt Lake City, UT, USA, 18–23 June 2018; pp. 7765–7773.
18. Gai, S.; Wang, D.; He, L. Offline Experience Replay for Continual Offline Reinforcement Learning. In Proceedings of the 26th European Conference on Artificial Intelligence, Kraków, Poland, Wed, 18 October 2023; pp. 772–779.
19. Nahrendra, I.M.A.; Yu, B.; Myung, H. DreamWaQ: Learning Robust Quadrupedal Locomotion with Implicit Terrain Imagination via Deep Reinforcement Learning. In Proceedings of the IEEE International Conference on Robotics and Automation, ICRA 2023, London, UK, 29 May–2 June 2023; IEEE: Piscataway, NJ, USA, 2023; pp. 5078–5084. [CrossRef]
20. Kingma, D.P.; Ba, J. Adam: A Method for Stochastic Optimization. In Proceedings of the 3rd International Conference on Learning Representations, ICLR 2015, San Diego, CA, USA, 7–9 May 2015.
21. Lyle, C.; Zheng, Z.; Nikishin, E.; Pires, B.Á.; Pascanu, R.; Dabney, W. Understanding Plasticity in Neural Networks. In Proceedings of the International Conference on Machine Learning, ICML 2023, Honolulu, HI, USA, 23–29 July 2023; Volume 202, pp. 23190–23211.

Disclaimer/Publisher's Note: The statements, opinions and data contained in all publications are solely those of the individual author(s) and contributor(s) and not of MDPI and/or the editor(s). MDPI and/or the editor(s) disclaim responsibility for any injury to people or property resulting from any ideas, methods, instructions or products referred to in the content.

Article

A Deep Neural Network Regularization Measure: The Class-Based Decorrelation Method

Chenguang Zhang [1,*], Tian Liu [2] and Xuejiao Du [1]

[1] School of Mathematics and Statistics, Hainan University, Haikou 570100, China; xuejiao_du@hainanu.edu.cn
[2] School of Information and Communication Engineering, Hainan University, Haikou 570100, China; liutian@hainanu.edu.cn
* Correspondence: chenguang_zhang@hainanu.edu.cn

Abstract: In response to the challenge of overfitting, which may lead to a decline in network generalization performance, this paper proposes a new regularization technique, called the class-based decorrelation method (CDM). Specifically, this method views the neurons in a specific hidden layer as base learners, and aims to boost network generalization as well as model accuracy by minimizing the correlation among individual base learners while simultaneously maximizing their class-conditional correlation. Intuitively, CDM not only promotes diversity among the hidden neurons, but also enhances their cohesiveness among them when processing samples from the same class. Comparative experiments conducted on various datasets using deep models demonstrate that CDM effectively reduces overfitting and improves classification performance.

Keywords: deep neural network; generalization ability; regularization method

Citation: Zhang, C.; Liu, T.; Du, X. A Deep Neural Network Regularization Measure: The Class-Based Decorrelation Method. *Entropy* **2024**, *26*, 7. https://doi.org/10.3390/e26010007

Academic Editors: Badong Chen, Luis Gonzalo Sánchez Giraldo, Shuangming Yang and Shujian Yu

Received: 7 November 2023
Revised: 10 December 2023
Accepted: 13 December 2023
Published: 20 December 2023

Copyright: © 2023 by the authors. Licensee MDPI, Basel, Switzerland. This article is an open access article distributed under the terms and conditions of the Creative Commons Attribution (CC BY) license (https://creativecommons.org/licenses/by/4.0/).

1. Introduction

Deep neural networks (DNNs) have demonstrated the highest accuracy in many artificial intelligence (AI) tasks, including computer vision, speech recognition, and robotics, due to their deep learning architecture and parallel learning mechanism, which guarantees its powerful expressive capacity to learn complex things [1]. However, overparameterization may also bring the risk of overfitting. How to maintain or even improve the learning advantages brought by deep architecture while avoiding overfitting is a continuous research topic in the field of deep learning.

In recent years, some studies have shown that DNNs may have a self-regularization effect [2], and the classical generalization theory [3,4] may not be applicable to deep learning. They suggested that the mechanism and effect of the regularization methods such as L_2 regularization [5,6], Weight Decay [7], Dropout [8], etc., which enhance the generalization ability by limiting the model complexity, need to be further explored and clarified.

On the other hand, certain studies also argue that traditional mean deviation theory remains effective, but requires a revision for the concept of model complexity, which should contain not only the parameter numbers but also the data, optimization methods, and model structure [9,10]. Some corresponding explicit regularization methods are explored and testified to have positive effect on reducing the generalization gap (performance gap between the test dataset and the train dataset) [11–13]. For example, Achille et al. [14] proposed that the mutual information between labels and model parameters can be used as a regularization term to predict sharp phase transitions between underfitting and overfitting of random labels.

Recently, in contrast to treating the whole deep learning network as a single black box, several studies begin to explore its parallel mechanism. By viewing the network output as a collection of fundamental mappings or combinations of individual learners [12,15,16], these studies analyze the influence of their correlations on the generalization capabilities of deep learning models, introducing novel concepts for devising regularization techniques to enhance generalization. This concept of correlation is referred to as the disentanglement measure in representation learning and the diversity measure in ensemble learning. Several well-established disentanglement measures [17,18] as well as diversity measures [19,20] have been introduced, and their validity has been verified theoretically and experimentally.

Inspired by ensemble learning and representation learning, this paper proposes a novel approach based on class labels for decorrelating neurons within a hidden layer of deep neural networks, called the class-based decorrelation method (CDM). This method takes into account both the unsupervised decorrelation between hidden neurons and the supervised requirement for collaboration of neurons in the same class. The unsupervised decorrelation term has been explored in a large amount of the literature. For example, Cogswell et al. [11] and Gu et al. [12] consider hidden layer neurons, or their groupings, as basic mappings to improve the generalization of deep networks by limiting the correlation between mappings. In the field of representation learning, methods such as variational autoencoders (VAE) [21] and β-VAE [22] have demonstrated the beneficial impact of disentanglement on downstream tasks, including improving interpretability, controllability, and robustness.

Furthermore, the research conducted by Zhou et al. [23] in the field of ensemble learning has shown that in addition to the aforementioned unsupervised term, a supervised term formalized as mutual information that reflects clustering characteristics is also helpful in improving prediction accuracy on future data. A similar conclusion was drawn by Zhang et al. [24], who decomposed the upper bound of the generalization error from information perspective. However, considering the complexity of estimating mutual information and that covariance is straightforward proxy for mutual information, CDM provides a regularization method with the above supervised and unsupervised terms estimated by covariance. Intuitively, CDM encourages the diversity among hidden neurons to diminish data redundancy while simultaneously strengthening neuron collaboration when dealing with samples from the same class, which helps to preserve useful information for classification, ensuring significantly higher classification accuracy and improved generalization performance.

We conducted comparative experiments on different depths of network structures. A large number of experiments have shown that compared to other regularization methods, CDM can effectively reduce overfitting and generalization errors while improving model accuracy. Due to the simplicity of CDM, it can be easily applied to any layer of a neural network. In addition, the experiment also verified that the class label-related terms in the supervised setting are a key factor in improving the generalization ability of DNNs.

2. Related Work

Understanding the generalization mechanism of deep learning and how it differs from classic methods is a crucial step to improve the generality of deep models. Recently, some studies have sought to provide more compact new generalization upper bounds by taking the special situations of the current training dataset, model frameworks, training methods, etc., into account. Here are some notable examples. Bartlett and Maiorov [25], Bartlett and Harvey [26], and Yang et al. [27] proposed upper bounds of DNNs based on the VC-dimension. Dziugaite and Roy [28] and Neyshabur et al. [29,30] used PAC-Bayesian analysis to derive bounds related to deep polynomials. Neyshabur et al. [31] proved the depth exponential dependence bound of ReLU networks by using Rademacher complexity, and Bartlett et al. [32] proposed a norm-based generalization bound of neural networks. Based on a ReLU kernel function, Arora et al. [33] proposed a generalization error bound for two-layer ReLU networks with fixed second-layer weights. Daniely and Granot [34] obtained improved bounds for constant-depth fully connected networks. They also introduce some empirical-based measures, such as the Fisher–Rao norm proposed by Liang et al. [35] and the study of generalization gaps with various dependencies, including distance from initialization, conducted by Jiang et al. [36].

The parallel mechanism of neural networks naturally lends itself to mutual inspiration from ensemble learning. Moreover, the divergence measure among individual learners in ensemble learning usually corresponds to the degree of disentanglement in representation learning. For example, the variational autoencoder (VAE) [21] applies a constraint on the learned representations of a neural network based on the Kullback–Leibler (KL) divergence between the variational posterior distribution and the true posterior distribution, thereby endowing the method with the potential for disentanglement capability. Furthermore, methods like β-VAE [22], DIP-VAE [37], and β-TCVAE [38] enhance the disentanglement ability and improve model generalization by incorporating implicit or explicit inductive biases into the original VAE loss function. Although the above method successfully implements the attribute "encouraged" by the corresponding loss, some researchers argue that identifying a well-disentangled model is virtually impossible without inductive biases in the absence of supervised settings.

Another important paradigm for improving the generalization performance of neural networks is regularization. Traditional regularization methods focus on constraining the complexity of the model, such as Weight Decay [7], Dropout [8] and DropConnect [39]. Although these methods have made improvements in terms of generalization, the random reduction in parameters may affect the expressive power of the model. In response, some research focuses on improving the generalization of neural networks while preserving their expressive power. For example, Bengio and Bergstra [40] proposed a pretraining algorithm for learning decorrelation features. Bao et al. [41] discussed decorrelation activation using incoherent training. Combining ensemble learning, Gu et al. [12] and Yao et al. [13] proposed corresponding decorrelation regularization methods by treating the network output as a combination of learners. Ayinde et al. [20] proposed an effective method for regularizing deep neural networks by leveraging the correlation between features. However, these regularization methods only emphasize the impact of unsupervised decoupling in hidden neurons, while neglecting the positive effect of supervised term that captures clustering characteristics on DNNs. Addressing this, Zhang et al. [24] obtained a regularization method containing both supervised and unsupervised items from the perspective of mutual information, and emphasized the importance of label-based inductive bias under the supervision setting to improve the network generalization ability. While this method is theoretically feasible, it may be less accessible due to the difficulty in estimating mutual information. Our work aims to overcome these limitations and proposes a simpler and more generalizable solution.

3. Class-Based Decorrelation Method

This section provides a detailed introduction to the class-based decorrelation method (CDM), which is a regularization method aimed at promoting the diversity of hidden neurons while enhancing collaboration among neurons when processing samples from the same class.

3.1. Theoretical Motivation

CDM is grounded in the newly introduced label-based diversity measure, which amalgamates the unsupervised diversity measure with supervised class-conditional diversity measure among hidden neurons, shedding light on the improvement of generality without compromising classification accuracy. Let $S = \{(X, Y) \mid (X, Y) \in \mathcal{X} \times \mathcal{Y}\}$ be the given dataset, and let $h_i(X)$ represent the activation of the sample in the i-th hidden neuron; the label-based diversity (LDiversity) among hidden neurons can be expressed as:

$$D_{LB}(S) = I(h_1(X); \ldots; h_m(X)) - I(h_1(X); \ldots; h_m(X) \mid Y), \tag{1}$$

where the initial mutual information term in the right-hand side serves the purpose of extracting independent features, aligning with the typical notion of an unsupervised diversity measure. Conversely, the second class-conditional term is intricately linked with labels, reflecting the underlying inductive bias inherent in the new representations of samples.

The work of Zhou et al. [23] shows that if only 0–1 loss is permitted, given $\hat{h} = (h_1, h_2, \ldots, h_m)$ as a set of base classifiers h_i for the labeled sample (X, Y), and $C(\cdot)$ as any given combination function that minimizes the probability $P(C(\hat{h}(X)) \neq Y)$, the probability is bounded as follows:

$$P(C(\hat{h}(X)) \neq Y) \leq \frac{H(Y) - \sum_{i=1}^{m} I(h_i(X); Y) + D_{LB}(S)}{2}, \qquad (2)$$

which indicates that there is an inverse relationship between the test error and LDiversity.

Zhang et al. [24] obtained a similar result. Further, their work is directly founded on the decomposition of the generalization error bound and reveals that reducing the value of LDiversity can enhance the generality.

Given the intricacies in estimating mutual information and the direct correlation between covariance and mutual information where mutual information is a monotone transformation of covariance, we opt to use covariance as a proxy in Equation (1), thereby deriving the following expression:

$$D'_{LB}(S) = \sum_{i,j} \mathbb{E}_S[(h_i(X) - \mathbb{E}_S[h_i(X)])(h_j(X) - \mathbb{E}_S[h_j(X)])] \\ - \sum_{i,j} \mathbb{E}_{S_Y}[(h_i(X) - \mathbb{E}_{S_Y}[h_i(X)])(h_j(X) - \mathbb{E}_{S_Y}[h_j(X)]) \mid Y]. \qquad (3)$$

Clearly, the covariance-based redefinition of LDiversity still retains the core idea of Equation (1), with the goal of encouraging diversity among hidden neurons while fostering stronger collaboration among neurons within the same class. Furthermore, covariance exhibits a straightforward and easily estimable characteristic, making CDM a more versatile and readily implementable approach.

3.2. CDM Application in the Fully Connected Layer

As illustrated in Figure 1, when applying CDM to a specific fully connected layer of a neural network, each hidden neuron within this layer is treated as a base learner. By exemplifying the calculation on a batch of samples, we demonstrate the specific process of applying CDM to any fully connected layer.

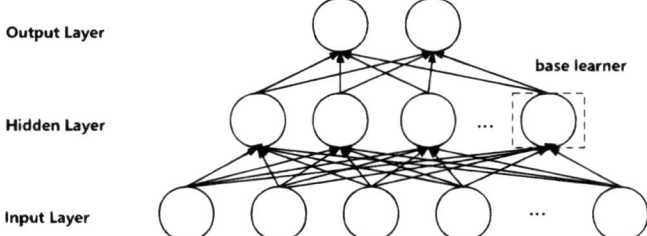

Figure 1. Architecture of a fully connected neural network based on CDM. Each neuron of the specified hidden layer is treated as a base learner.

Let n be the number of neurons in the target hidden layer. Consider a batch of N samples categorized into K classes, where each class contains n_k samples (with $k = 1, \ldots, K$) and $N = \sum_{k=1}^{K} n_k$. Let h_i^n represent the activation originating from the n-th sample in the input to the i-th hidden neuron in the target layer. To represent the correlation between the

i-th and j-th base learners across the entirety of the mixed distribution, we introduce the notation $LnCor_{ij}^{mix}$, which is formally expressed as follows:

$$LnCor_{ij}^{mix} = \frac{1}{N} \sum_{n=1}^{N} (h_i^n - \mu_i)\left(h_j^n - \mu_j\right), \quad (4)$$

$$\mu_i = \frac{1}{N} \sum_{n=1}^{N} h_i^n, \quad (5)$$

where μ_i denotes the activation mean of the i-th base learner across N samples. As covariance quantifies the correlation between variables, lower covariance usually implies reduced correlation. Consequently, we need to minimize this item, aiming to maintain a minimal level of correlation among the base learners, thus fostering greater diversity in sample representations.

The class-conditional correlation between the i-th and j-th base learners denoted as $LnCor_{ij}^{class}$ is expressed as follows:

$$LnCor_{ij}^{class} = \sum_{k=1}^{K} \frac{n_k}{N} LnCor_{(k,ij)}^{class}, \quad (6)$$

$$LnCor_{(k,ij)}^{class} = \frac{1}{n_k} \sum_{n=1}^{n_k} \left(h_{(k,i)}^n - \mu_i^k\right)\left(h_{(k,j)}^n - \mu_j^k\right), \quad (7)$$

$$\mu_i^k = \frac{1}{n_k} \sum_{n=1}^{n_k} h_{(k,i)}^n, (k = 1, \ldots, K), \quad (8)$$

where $LnCor_{(k,ij)}^{class}$ represents the covariance between the i-th and j-th base learners within the k-th class; $h_{(k,i)}^n$ represents the activation value from n-th sample in the k class to the i-th hidden neuron, and μ_i^k signifies the mean activation value of the i-th hidden neuron over the samples within this class. Formula (4) pertains to the class labels and describes local clustering features captured by hidden neurons. Enhancing the class-conditional term, especially by maximizing its value, is anticipated to promote cohesiveness of base learners when the input samples originate from the same class.

By utilizing $LnCor_{ij}^{mix}$ and $LnCor_{(k,ij)}^{class}$ as the entries in the i-th row and j-th column of matrices, we can construct the covariance matrix $LnCor^{mix}$ and the class-conditional covariance matrix $LnCor^{class}$, respectively. Let S_L^{mix} and S_L^{class} denote the final total correlation over the mixed distribution and total class-conditional correlation, respectively. From these, we derive the ultimate penalty regularization term, denoted as $LnCor_{Loss}$:

$$LnCor_{Loss} = ln(S_L^{mix}) - ln(S_L^{class}), \quad (9)$$

$$S_L^{mix} = \frac{1}{2}(\|LnCor^{mix}\|_F^2 - \|diag(LnCor^{mix})\|_2^2), \quad (10)$$

$$S_L^{class} = \frac{1}{2}(\|LnCor^{class}\|_F^2 - \|diag(LnCor^{class})\|_2^2), \quad (11)$$

where $\|\cdot\|_F$ is the Frobenius norm, the $diag(\cdot)$ operator returns the main diagonal elements of the matrix as vectors, and $ln(\cdot)$ represents logarithmic operation. It is worth noting that the diagonal elements of the two matrices have been excluded from their respective correlation measures since these elements indicate self-correlation. Minimizing the regularization term $LnCor_{Loss}$ is expected to encourage nonredundant representations of samples.

Finally, the total loss of the neural network applying CDM at the fully connected layer can be expressed as:

$$T_{Loss} = E_{Loss} + \lambda LnCor_{Loss}, \quad (12)$$

where E_{Loss} is the cross-entropy loss, and $\lambda \geq 0$ is the hyperparameter.

Specially, to illustrate the training process on the l-th layer, we assume that W^l represents the weight matrix from the $(l-1)$-th to the l-th layer, and H^l denotes the activations of the l-th layer. Now, let us examine the gradient of the total loss for a specific sample:

$$\frac{\partial T_{Loss}}{\partial W_i^l} = \frac{\partial T_{Loss}}{\partial h_i} \cdot \frac{\partial h_i}{\partial W_i^l}, \tag{13}$$

$$\frac{\partial LnCor_{Loss}}{\partial h_i} = \frac{1}{N} \sum_{i \neq j} LnCor_{i,j} \cdot (h_j - \mu_j) + \sum_k \frac{n_k}{N} \sum_{i \neq j} LnCor_{i,j} \cdot \left(h_j^k - \mu_j^k\right), \tag{14}$$

$$\frac{\partial h_i}{\partial W_i^l} = H^{l-1}, \tag{15}$$

where we have not shown the gradient of the cross-entropy part since it is common. From Equations (13)–(15), it has been demonstrated that the gradient can be conveniently computed through covariance-based backpropagation. Then, the obtained gradient is subsequently utilized for updating the weights.

3.3. CDM Application in Convolutional Layer

The application of CDM in convolutional layers differs from its use in fully connected layers in that each neuron is no longer treated as an individual base learner; instead, the convolutional feature map is considered as the base learner. Two primary reasons underlie this approach: (1) Decorrelating all the hidden neurons within a convolutional layer incurs a significant computational cost. (2) Distinct neurons may share the same convolutional feature map, rendering decorrelation efforts on these neurons essentially futile. In fact, it is the feature map that fundamentally reflects the mapping relationship from samples to their representations. In a similar vein, we illustrate how CDM can be applied to any convolutional layer and trained on a batch of samples with size N.

Given the convolutional layer to be processed, let M, $H \cdot W$ be the number of convolutional feature maps and the output spatial dimensions. We use $CoCor_{ij}^{mix}$ to represent the correlation between the i-th and j-th base learners over the mixed distribution, which is expressed as follows:

$$CoCor_{ij}^{mix} = \frac{1}{N} \sum_{n=1}^{N} (g_i^n - \overline{\mu}_i)\left(g_j^n - \overline{\mu}_j\right), \tag{16}$$

$$\overline{\mu}_i = \frac{1}{N} \sum_{n=1}^{N} g_i^n, \tag{17}$$

$$g_i^n = \frac{1}{HW} \sum_{h=1}^{H} \sum_{w=1}^{W} v_i^{(h,w)}, \tag{18}$$

where $v_i^{(h,w)}$ represents the value whose coordinate position is (h,w) in the output of the i-th convolutional feature map; g_i^n is regarded as the activation originated from the n-th sample in the input batch of the i-th base learner, and $\overline{\mu}_i$ represents the mean of the activations across the samples. Correspondingly, the conditional correlation between the i-th and j-th base learner, denoted as $CoCor_{ij}^{class}$, is defined as follows:

$$CoCor_{ij}^{class} = \sum_{k=1}^{K} \frac{n_k}{N} CoCor_{(k,ij)}^{class}, \tag{19}$$

$$CoCor_{(k,ij)}^{class} = \frac{1}{n_k} \sum_{n=1}^{n_k} \left(g_{(k,i)}^n - \overline{\mu}_i^k\right)\left(g_{(k,j)}^n - \overline{\mu}_j^k\right), \tag{20}$$

$$\overline{\mu}_i^k = \frac{1}{n_k} \sum_{n=1}^{n_k} h_{(k,i)}^n, (k = 1, \ldots, K), \tag{21}$$

$$g_{(k,i)}^n = \frac{1}{HW} \sum_{h=1}^{H} \sum_{w=1}^{W} v_{(k,i)}^{(h,w)}, \tag{22}$$

where $CoCor_{(k,ij)}^{class}$ represents the covariance between the i-th and j-th feature maps within the class k; $g_{(k,i)}^n$ denotes the activation value of the n-th sample in k-th class by the i-th hidden neuron, and $\overline{\mu}_i^k$ signifies the mean activation value across different samples. Similar to the fully connected layer, we construct the covariance matrix $CoCor^{mix}$ and the class conditional covariance matrix $CoCor^{class}$ by using $CoCor_{ij}$ and $CoCor_{(k,ij)}^{class}$ as entries. The regularization term $CoCor_{Loss}$ for the convolutional layer is then defined as follows:

$$CoCor_{Loss} = ln(S_C^{mix}) - ln(S_C^{class}), \tag{23}$$

$$S_C^{mix} = \frac{1}{2}(\|LnCor^{mix}\|_F^2 - \|diag(LnCor^{mix})\|_2^2), \tag{24}$$

$$S_C^{class} = \frac{1}{2}(\|LnCor^{class}\|_F^2 - \|diag(LnCor^{class})\|_2^2). \tag{25}$$

where S_C^{mix} and S_C^{class} are the total correlation over the entire mixed distribution and the total class-conditional correlation.

Adding $CoCor_{Loss}$ to the cross-entropy loss, we define the final loss for neural networks with convolutional layer as follows:

$$T_{Loss} = E_{Loss} + \gamma CoCor_{Loss}, \tag{26}$$

where $\gamma \geq 0$ is the hyperparameter.

4. Experimental Section

In this section, to validate the efficacy of CDM in deep neural networks, we performed experiments on diverse datasets using different neural networks of varying depths. The control group encompassed several methods: nonregularization (None); Dropout [8] with a random probability of 0.5; the decorrelation regularization method (DeCov) [11] with a hyperparameter set to 0.1; and the ensemble-based decorrelation method (EDM) [12] with a balance parameter of 0.1. Notably, since DeCov, EDM, and CDM all fall under decorrelation techniques, for fairness, they were applied to the same hidden layer. For Dropout, it is commonly utilized for fully connected layers.

Additionally, we also tested the effectiveness of CDM when applied to the state-of-the-art methods, including Inception [42] and MobileNet [43], focusing on the challenge of relatively limited training samples encountered commonly in real-world applications.

4.1. Datasets

The study presented in this paper makes use of two publicly available datasets: MNIST [44], CIFAR-10 [45] and mini-ImageNet [46]. A brief overview of these datasets is presented below.

- **MNIST:** The MNIST dataset is a collection of handwritten digit images, totaling 70,000 grayscale images across 10 different classes. Each image is 28 pixels in height and 28 pixels in width. The training set comprises 60,000 images, while the test set contains 10,000 images.
- **CIFAR-10:** The CIFAR-10 dataset comprises 10 classes, with each class containing 6000 color images sized at 32 × 32 pixels and composed of RGB three-channel data. The training set encompasses 50,000 images, while the test set includes 10,000 images.

- **Mini-ImageNet**: The mini-ImageNet dataset consists of 50,000 training images and 10,000 testing images, evenly distributed across 100 classes. The images have a size of 84 × 84 × 3.

Moreover, to effectively highlight the generalization capabilities of each method, we introduced noise to the test images. The noise adheres to a standard Gaussian distribution. For MNIST and CIFAR-10 as well as mini-ImageNet, we multiplied the noise by weights of 0.2 and 0.05, respectively, when adding it to the original pixel values. It is important to note that prior to introducing the noise, we standardized pixel values within the range $[-1, 1]$ (refer to Figure 2).

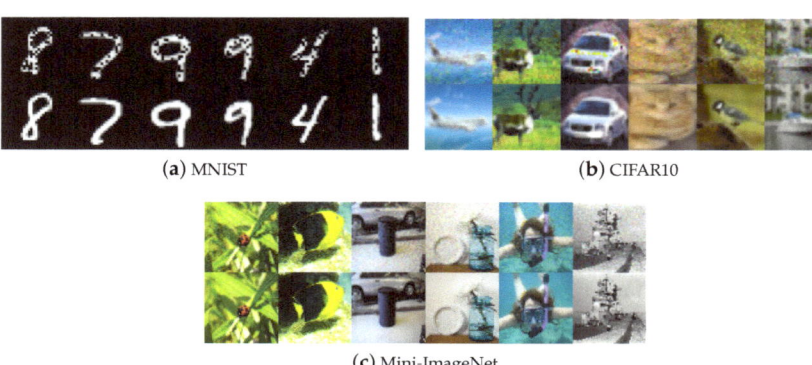

(a) MNIST (b) CIFAR10

(c) Mini-ImageNet

Figure 2. Some examples of introducing Gaussian noise to (**a**) MNIST, (**b**) CIFAR-10 and (**c**) Mini-ImageNet datasets to generate noisy images (**top row**) from original images (**bottom row**).

4.2. Network Frameworks

The study employs fully connected neural networks (FCNNs) and residual neural networks (ResNets) with two distinct depths. In this context, "depth" refers to the number of layers that undergo parameter updates during training, encompassing convolutional layers, fully connected layers, and so forth. Additionally, aiming at the challenge of relatively limited training samples, the learning architectures from approaches such as Inception and MobileNet are included for comparative analysis.

The architecture of FCNNs is composed of layers in the order of D(512)-D(256)-D*(100)-D(256)-D(128)-D(64), where D(N) signifies a dense layer with N neurons. The introduced regularizer is specifically applied to the D* layer. Furthermore, for residual neural networks, we make use of ResNet18 [47] and ResNet50 [48]. Specific details regarding the parameters can be found in Table 1. Besides ResNet18 and ResNet50, the learning methods of Inception and MobileNet are also utilized. All the models are pretrained on the ImageNet dataset [49]. Throughout the training phase, transfer learning and fine-tuning methodologies are employed, allowing for active adjustment of the model's layer parameters without freezing. This approach ensures continuous updates to the parameters to enhance the network's performance. Notably, the regularizer is implemented either on the topmost fully connected layer (excluding the output layer) or on the convolutional layer, as applicable. The entire experiment is carried out using PyTorch [50].

Table 1. Structure diagram of residual neural networks at different depths.

Layer	18-Layer (ResNet18)	50-Layer (ResNet50)
Conv 1	$7 \times 7, 64$, stride2	
	3×3, maxpool, stride2	
Conv 2	$\begin{bmatrix} 3 \times 3, 64 \\ 3 \times 3, 64 \end{bmatrix} \times 2$	$\begin{bmatrix} 1 \times 1, 64 \\ 3 \times 3, 64 \\ 1 \times 1, 256 \end{bmatrix} \times 3$
Conv3	$\begin{bmatrix} 3 \times 3, 128 \\ 3 \times 3, 128 \end{bmatrix} \times 2$	$\begin{bmatrix} 1 \times 1, 128 \\ 3 \times 3, 128 \\ 1 \times 1, 512 \end{bmatrix} \times 4$
Conv4	$\begin{bmatrix} 3 \times 3, 256 \\ 3 \times 3, 256 \end{bmatrix} \times 2$	$\begin{bmatrix} 1 \times 1, 256 \\ 3 \times 3, 256 \\ 1 \times 1, 1024 \end{bmatrix} \times 6$
Conv5	$\begin{bmatrix} 3 \times 3, 512 \\ 3 \times 3, 512 \end{bmatrix} \times 2$	$\begin{bmatrix} 1 \times 1, 512 \\ 3 \times 3, 512 \\ 1 \times 1, 2048 \end{bmatrix} \times 3$
Last	average pool/D(1000), D(10)/D(100), softmax	

The structure of residual neural network with different depths (18, 50) is given in the table. The number of neurons in the output layer is aligned with the quantity of categories present in the datasets.

4.3. Effect on the Covariance Gap

We initially conducted an investigation to determine whether the CDM can boost the diversity among hidden neurons while simultaneously strengthening neuron collaboration when the samples are from the same classes. We varied the weight λ of the regularization term in Equations (12) and (26) from 0 to 0.4 in increments of 0.1. The average results of experiments conducted on the MNIST and CIFAR-10 datasets are illustrated in Figure 3, where FCNNs and ResNet50 with the regularizer applied on their topmost convolutional layers were employed for the above datasets, respectively.

Significantly, the covariance gap, denoting the variance between the covariance and the class-conditional covariance, displays a decreasing pattern as the number of iterations rises when $\lambda > 0$. This trend indicates that CDM actively aids in decreasing regularizer values, aligning with its intended design. Notably, with $\lambda = 0$, the regularizer value remains static, consistently near zero but higher compared to other instances. Moreover, an increase in λ value correlates with a reduction in the regularizer over the same training period.

4.4. Hyperparameter

To assess the impact of hyperparameters on experimental outcomes, we conducted multiple experiments using exclusively FCNNs for the MNIST dataset and ResNet50 for the CIFAR-10 dataset. Specifically, for the CIFAR-10 dataset, the regularizer was implemented on the topmost convolutional layer of ResNet50. The test results on the original test set, which is devoid of artificial noise, are illustrated in Figure 4. Upon observing the trends portrayed in Figure 4, it becomes apparent that a gradual increment in the regularization term weight within a narrow range leads to improved classification accuracy and a slight reduction in generalization error. However, if the weight is larger, the classification performance may, conversely, begin to slightly decrease. Nonetheless, the experimental findings suggest that the influence of hyperparameters on performance remains relatively stable, providing a broad spectrum of choices. Given that CDM exhibits a relatively minor covariance gap and performs quite well at $\lambda = 0.3$, subsequent experiments will maintain a fixed λ at 0.3.

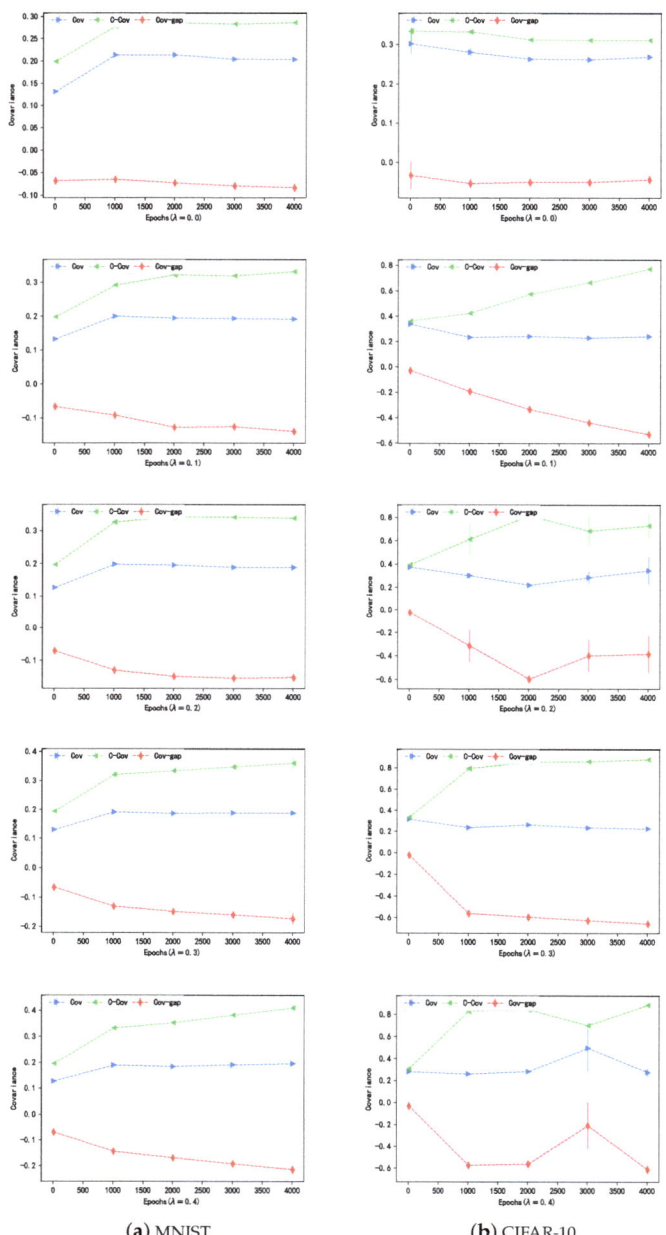

Figure 3. Given the values of λ in the range [0, 0.4], the changes in covariance (Cov), class-conditional covariance (C-Cov), and the covariance gap (Cov-gap) with increasing training iterations on (**a**) MNIST and (**b**) CIFAR-10 datasets.

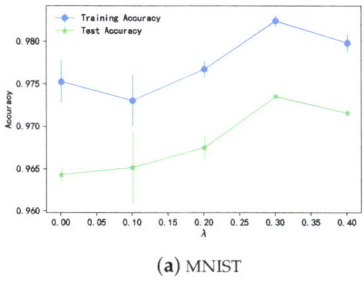
(a) MNIST

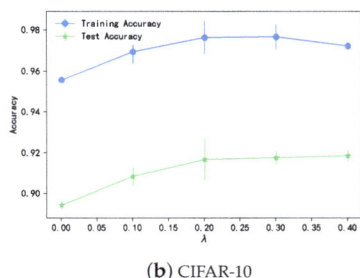
(b) CIFAR-10

Figure 4. The changes in classification accuracy by varying the value of λ on (**a**) MNIST and (**b**) CIFAR-10 datasets.

4.5. Experiment on Fully Connected Layer

The purpose of this experiment is to evaluate the effect of CDM in contrast to other regularization techniques when applied to the fully connected layer. Throughout all method experiments, the Adam algorithm was utilized for training, the initial learning rate was set at 0.001, and a consistent batch size of 128 was maintained. Comparative experiments were conducted on both the MNIST and CIFAR-10 datasets using images with added noise. The final results of the experiment were averaged with the accuracy of five experiments and are recorded in Table 2.

The experimental results, as presented in Table 2, demonstrate that CDM achieves significant test accuracy and the smallest train–test accuracy gap on both the MNIST and CIFAR-10 datasets. Specifically, in the case of MNIST, CDM yielded an impressive 1.8 improvement in test accuracy and simultaneously reduced the train–test accuracy gap by 0.8 when contrasted to suboptimal methods. Similarly, for CIFAR-10, CDM exhibits a remarkable 2.6 increase in test accuracy, accompanied by a substantial reduction of 1.9 in the train–test accuracy gap. It is noteworthy that CDM's impact on network generalization becomes progressively more pronounced as the dataset's complexity increases.

Furthermore, it is pertinent to mention that both DeCov and CDM share the same unsupervised disentanglement term. However, DeCov as well as EDM do not consistently enhance performance. For example, on the MNIST dataset, their test accuracy is marginally lower compared to methods with no regularization. This could be due to the dataset's simplicity, where mandating independence among hidden neurons disrupts their intrinsic relationships. Therefore, attributing the superior performance of CDM to the role of the supervised term is a reasonable and well-supported conclusion, indicating that this supervision term can help extract beneficial clustering information for classification.

Table 2. Compartive experiment of different datasets on the full connection layer.

Method	MNIST			CIFAR-10		
	Train	Test	Train–Test	Train	Test	Train–Test
None	97.52 ±0.14	92.10 ± 0.67	5.42	95.58 ± 0.33	71.33 ± 1.48	24.25
Dropout	97.58 ± 0.06	91.41 ± 0.58	6.17	96.99 ± 0.35	75.20 ± 0.40	21.78
DeCov	97.78 ± 0.10	91.35 ± 1.11	6.42	95.81 ± 0.16	74.35	21.42
EDM	98.18 ± 0.05	91.95 ± 0.07	6.23	96.26 ± 0.27	75.23 ± 1.01	21.03
CDM	98.24 ± 0.12	**93.99 ± 0.16**	**4.25**	96.95 ± 0.23	**77.83 ± 0.30**	**19.12**

The average accuracy of five repeated tests was used as the final result. Best scores are shown in bold.

4.6. Experiments on Convolutional Layer

We applied CDM, DeCov, and EDM to the final convolutional layer of the network, comparing CDM with other regularization methods in terms of network performance. The training setups, such as learning rate and batch size, remained consistent with those used for fully connected layers. We explored different depths of residual neural networks on the CIFAR-10 dataset with added artificial noise. The results, specifically the average classification accuracy derived from five experiments, are documented in Table 3.

As shown in Table 3, CDM consistently achieved the highest test accuracy and the smallest train–test accuracy gap in all comparative experiments, affirming its effective impact on enhancing network generalization, particularly for complex datasets. Moreover, it is worth noting that the overall performance of all regularization methods based on ResNet18 appears more similar compared to those using ResNet50, which could be attributed to the ResNet18 model's simplicity and reduced susceptibility to overfitting, leading to a relatively constrained impact of regularization. Moreover, at times, the performance of Decov and EDM falls even below that of the Dropout method, especially when confronted with more intricate network structures. Given that the regularization terms in Decov and EDM exclusively encompass unsupervised elements, the superior performance of CDM can be credited to its incorporation of a supervised term, thereby preventing the disruption of valuable classification information.

Table 3. Comparative experiment of different methods on CIFAR-10 dataset with regularizers applied on the topmost convolutional layer of ResNet18 and ResNet50.

Method	ResNet18			ResNet50		
	Train	Test	Train–Test	Train	Test	Train–Test
None	97.12 ± 0.04	76.94 ± 0.07	20.17	97.10 ± 0.04	78.7 ± 0.09	18.40
Dropout	97.22 ± 0.02	80.05 ± 0.19	17.16	97.62 ± 0.02	81.65 ± 0.08	15.96
DeCov	97.34 ± 0.09	80.19 ± 0.12	17.15	96.81 ± 0.06	79.98 ± 0.10	16.82
EDM	97.17 ± 0.07	79.99 ± 0.11	17.18	96.94 ± 0.05	80.12 ± 0.10	16.81
CDM	97.32 ± 0.04	**81.14 ± 0.09**	**16.17**	97.09 ± 0.06	**82.23 ± 0.08**	**14.85**

The average accuracy of five repeated tests was used as the final result. Best scores are shown in bold.

4.7. Experiments with a Comparatively Small Training Dataset

In practical applications, the relative scarcity of training samples is a commonly encountered issue, especially in the case of deep network structures, which can lead to problems related to overfitting. Specifically, the classification task on the mini-ImageNet dataset exemplifies such a challenge, as each class among the 100 classes comprises only 500 image samples for training. This characteristic renders learning methods applied to this dataset particularly susceptible to overfitting.

To further assess the effectiveness of CDM in addressing this challenge, we applied it to pretrained Inception and MobileNet models, both of which have demonstrated state-of-the-art (SOTA) results on the ImageNet dataset. A comprehensive comparative analysis of experimental results was conducted both before and after the addition of CDM on mini-ImageNet. Additionally, noise was introduced into the test images. As depicted in Table 4, it is evident that all methods exhibit a certain degree of overfitting. However, the methods incorporating CDM result in improved classification accuracy for all methods compared to the original approach, with increases of 1.7 and 4.72 points, respectively. Concurrently, the integration of CDM reduces generalization errors by 3.53 and 2.31 points, respectively. The comparison with the SOTA methods strongly demonstrates the effectiveness of CDM regularization.

Table 4. Applying CDM to the topmost layer of Inception and MobileNet methods: a performance comparison before and after CDM implementation.

Method	Inception			MobileNet		
	Train	Test	Train–Test	Train	Test	Train–Test
Before	93.02 ± 0.05	65.75 ± 0.08	27.27	90.60 ± 0.05	61.64 ± 0.06	28.96
After	91.19 ± 0.09	**67.45 ± 0.11**	**23.74**	93.01 ± 0.03	**66.36 ± 0.06**	**26.65**

The average accuracy of five repeated tests was used as the final result. Best scores are shown in bold.

5. Conclusions

Overfitting is one of the key factors that can affect the performance of DNNs. This paper proposes a new regularization technique called CDM to address the overfitting problem in DNNs. Experimental results demonstrate that CDM consistently enhances network generalization while maintaining or improving network expressiveness, thus preventing overfitting. Furthermore, CDM is easily applicable and can be added to any layer of existing networks.

While our method performs well, there are also some limitations. For example, the combination effect of CDM with other regularization methods is still worth investigating.

Author Contributions: T.L., validation, visualization, writing—original draft, writing—review and editing; C.Z., conceptualization, formal analysis, writing—review and editing; X.D., writing—review and editing. All authors have read and agreed to the published version of the manuscript.

Funding: This research was funded by the National Natural Science Foundation of China (Project Number 62166016) and the Hainan Provincial Natural Science Foundation of China (Project Number 119MS004).

Institutional Review Board Statement: Not applicable.

Informed Consent Statement: Not applicable.

Data Availability Statement: The paper itself contains all the information required to assess the conclusions. Additional data related to this paper may be requested from the corresponding author.

Conflicts of Interest: The authors declare no conflicts of interest.

References

1. LeCun, Y.; Bengio, Y.; Hinton, G. Deep learning. *Nature* **2015**, *521*, 436–444. [CrossRef] [PubMed]
2. Martin, C.H.; Mahoney, M.W. Implicit self-regularization in deep neural networks: Evidence from random matrix theory and implications for learning. *J. Mach. Learn. Res.* **2021**, *22*, 7479–7551.
3. Bartlett, P. The sample complexity of pattern classification with neural networks: The size of the weights is more important than the size of the network. *IEEE Trans. Inf. Theory* **1998**, *44*, 525–536. [CrossRef]
4. Bartlett, P.L.; Mendelson, S. Rademacher and Gaussian complexities: Risk bounds and structural results. *J. Mach. Learn. Res.* **2002**, *3*, 463–482.
5. Hoerl, A.E.; Kennard, R.W. Ridge Regression: Biased Estimation for Nonorthogonal Problems. *Technometrics* **1970**, *12*, 55–67. [CrossRef]
6. Willoughby, R.A. Solutions of Ill-Posed Problems (A. N. Tikhonov and V. Y. Arsenin). *SIAM Rev.* **1979**, *21*, 266–267. [CrossRef]
7. Krogh, A.; Hertz, J. A simple weight decay can improve generalization. *Adv. Neural Inf. Process. Syst.* **1991**, *4*.
8. Srivastava, N.; Hinton, G.; Krizhevsky, A.; Sutskever, I.; Salakhutdinov, R. Dropout: A simple way to prevent neural networks from overfitting. *J. Mach. Learn. Res.* **2014**, *15*, 1929–1958.
9. Neal, B.; Mittal, S.; Baratin, A.; Tantia, V.; Scicluna, M.; Lacoste-Julien, S.; Mitliagkas, I. A Modern Take on the Bias-Variance Tradeoff in Neural Networks. In Proceedings of the ICML 2019 Workshop on Identifying and Understanding Deep Learning Phenomena, Long Beach, CA, USA, 15 August 2019.
10. Belkin, M.; Hsu, D.; Ma, S.; Mandal, S. Reconciling modern machine-learning practice and the classical bias–variance trade-off. *Proc. Natl. Acad. Sci. USA* **2019**, *116*, 15849–15854. [CrossRef]
11. Cogswell, M.; Ahmed, F.; Girshick, R.; Zitnick, L.; Batra, D. Reducing overfitting in deep networks by decorrelating representations. *arXiv* **2015**, arXiv:1511.06068.
12. Gu, S.; Hou, Y.; Zhang, L.; Zhang, Y. Regularizing Deep Neural Networks with an Ensemble-based Decorrelation Method. In Proceedings of the Twenty-Seventh International Joint Conference on Artificial Intelligence (IJCAI-18), Stockholm, Sweden, 13–19 July 2018; pp. 2177–2183.
13. Yao, S.; Hou, Y.; Ge, L.; Hu, Z. Regularizing Deep Neural Networks by Ensemble-based Low-Level Sample-Variances Method. In Proceedings of the 28th ACM International Conference on Information and Knowledge Management, Beijing, China, 3–7 November 2019; pp. 1111–1120.
14. Achille, A.; Soatto, S. Emergence of invariance and disentanglement in deep representations. *J. Mach. Learn. Res.* **2018**, *19*, 1947–1980.
15. Liu, Y.; Yao, X. Ensemble learning via negative correlation. *Neural Netw.* **1999**, *12*, 1399–1404. [CrossRef] [PubMed]
16. Alhamdoosh, M.; Wang, D. Fast decorrelated neural network ensembles with random weights. *Inf. Sci.* **2014**, *264*, 104–117. [CrossRef]
17. Wang, X.; Chen, H.; Tang, S.; Wu, Z.; Zhu, W. Disentangled representation learning. *arXiv* **2022**, arXiv:2211.11695.

18. Carbonneau, M.A.; Zaidi, J.; Boilard, J.; Gagnon, G. Measuring disentanglement: A review of metrics. *arXiv* **2020**, arXiv:2012.09276.
19. Bian, Y.; Chen, H. When does diversity help generalization in classification ensembles? *IEEE Trans. Cybern.* **2021**, *52*, 9059–9075. [CrossRef]
20. Ayinde, B.O.; Inanc, T.; Zurada, J.M. Regularizing deep neural networks by enhancing diversity in feature extraction. *IEEE Trans. Neural Netw. Learn. Syst.* **2019**, *30*, 2650–2661. [CrossRef]
21. Kingma, D.P.; Welling, M. Auto-encoding variational bayes. *arXiv* **2013**, arXiv:1312.6114.
22. Higgins, I.; Matthey, L.; Pal, A.; Burgess, C.; Glorot, X.; Botvinick, M.; Mohamed, S.; Lerchner, A. beta-vae: Learning basic visual concepts with a constrained variational framework. In Proceedings of the International Conference on Learning Representations, San Juan, Puerto Rico, 2–4 May 2016.
23. Zhou, Z.H. *Ensemble Methods: Foundations and Algorithms*; CRC Press: Boca Raton, FL, USA, 2012.
24. Zhang, C.; Hou, Y.; Song, D.; Ge, L.; Yao, Y. Redundancy of Hidden Layers in Deep Learning: An Information Perspective. *arXiv* **2020**, arXiv:2009.09161.
25. Bartlett, P.; Maiorov, V.; Meir, R. Almost linear VC dimension bounds for piecewise polynomial networks. *Adv. Neural Inf. Process. Syst.* **1998**, *11*. [CrossRef]
26. Bartlett, P.L.; Harvey, N.; Liaw, C.; Mehrabian, A. Nearly-tight VC-dimension and pseudodimension bounds for piecewise linear neural networks. *J. Mach. Learn. Res.* **2019**, *20*, 2285–2301.
27. Yang, Y.; Yang, H.; Xiang, Y. Nearly Optimal VC-Dimension and Pseudo-Dimension Bounds for Deep Neural Network Derivatives. *arXiv* **2023**, arXiv:2305.08466.
28. Dziugaite, G.K.; Roy, D.M. Computing nonvacuous generalization bounds for deep (stochastic) neural networks with many more parameters than training data. *arXiv* **2017**, arXiv:1703.11008.
29. Neyshabur, B.; Bhojanapalli, S.; McAllester, D.; Srebro, N. Exploring generalization in deep learning. *Adv. Neural Inf. Process. Syst.* **2017**, *30*.
30. Neyshabur, B.; Bhojanapalli, S.; Srebro, N. A pac-bayesian approach to spectrally-normalized margin bounds for neural networks. *arXiv* **2017**, arXiv:1707.09564.
31. Neyshabur, B.; Tomioka, R.; Srebro, N. Norm-based capacity control in neural networks. In Proceedings of the Conference on Learning Theory, PMLR, Paris, France, 3–6 July 2015; pp. 1376–1401.
32. Bartlett, P.L.; Foster, D.J.; Telgarsky, M.J. Spectrally-normalized margin bounds for neural networks. *Adv. Neural Inf. Process. Syst.* **2017**, *30*.
33. Arora, S.; Du, S.S.; Hu, W.; Li, Z.; Salakhutdinov, R.R.; Wang, R. On exact computation with an infinitely wide neural net. *Adv. Neural Inf. Process. Syst.* **2019**, *32*.
34. Daniely, A.; Granot, E. Generalization bounds for neural networks via approximate description length. *Adv. Neural Inf. Process. Syst.* **2019**, *32*.
35. Liang, T.; Poggio, T.; Rakhlin, A.; Stokes, J. Fisher-rao metric, geometry, and complexity of neural networks. In Proceedings of the The 22nd International Conference on Artificial Intelligence and Statistics, PMLR, Okinawa, Japan, 16–18 April 2019; pp. 888–896.
36. Jiang, Y.; Neyshabur, B.; Mobahi, H.; Krishnan, D.; Bengio, S. Fantastic generalization measures and where to find them. *arXiv* **2019**, arXiv:1912.02178.
37. Kumar, A.; Sattigeri, P.; Balakrishnan, A. Variational inference of disentangled latent concepts from unlabeled observations. *arXiv* **2017**, arXiv:1711.00848.
38. Chen, R.T.; Li, X.; Grosse, R.B.; Duvenaud, D.K. Isolating sources of disentanglement in variational autoencoders. *Adv. Neural Inf. Process. Syst.* **2018**, *31*.
39. Wan, L.; Zeiler, M.; Zhang, S.; Le Cun, Y.; Fergus, R. Regularization of neural networks using dropconnect. In Proceedings of the International Conference on Machine Learning, PMLR, Atlanta, GA, USA, 17–19 June 2013; pp. 1058–1066.
40. Bengio, Y.; Bergstra, J. Slow, decorrelated features for pretraining complex cell-like networks. *Adv. Neural Inf. Process. Syst.* **2009**, *22*.
41. Bao, Y.; Jiang, H.; Dai, L.; Liu, C. Incoherent training of deep neural networks to de-correlate bottleneck features for speech recognition. In Proceedings of the 2013 IEEE International Conference on Acoustics, Speech and Signal Processing, Vancouver, BC, Canada, 26–31 May 2013; IEEE: Piscataway Township, NJ, USA; pp. 6980–6984.
42. Szegedy, C.; Vanhoucke, V.; Ioffe, S.; Shlens, J.; Wojna, Z. Rethinking the inception architecture for computer vision. In Proceedings of the IEEE Conference on Computer Vision and Pattern Recognition, Las Vegas, NV, USA, 27–30 June 2016; pp. 2818–2826.
43. Howard, A.G.; Zhu, M.; Chen, B.; Kalenichenko, D.; Wang, W.; Weyand, T.; Andreetto, M.; Adam, H. Mobilenets: Efficient convolutional neural networks for mobile vision applications. *arXiv* **2017**, arXiv:1704.04861.
44. Lecun, Y.; Bottou, L.; Bengio, Y.; Haffner, P. Gradient-based learning applied to document recognition. *Proc. IEEE* **1998**, *86*, 2278–2324. [CrossRef]
45. Krizhevsky, A.; Hinton, G. Learning multiple layers of features from tiny images. In *Handbook of Systemic Autoimmune Diseases*; Univeristy of Toronto: Toronto, ON, Canada, 2009; Volume 1 .
46. Ravi, S.; Larochelle, H. Optimization as a model for few-shot learning. In Proceedings of the International Conference on Learning Representations, San Juan, Puerto Rico, 2–4 May 2016.

47. Zhang, Y.; Wang, C.; Deng, W. Relative uncertainty learning for facial expression recognition. *Adv. Neural Inf. Process. Syst.* **2021**, *34*, 17616–17627.
48. Zhang, Y.; Wang, C.; Ling, X.; Deng, W. Learn From All: Erasing Attention Consistency for Noisy Label Facial Expression Recognition. *arXiv* **2022**, arXiv:cs.CV/2207.10299.
49. Krizhevsky, A.; Sutskever, I.; Hinton, G.E. ImageNet classification with deep convolutional neural networks. *Commun. ACM* **2017**, *60*, 84–90. [CrossRef]
50. Paszke, A.; Gross, S.; Massa, F.; Lerer, A.; Bradbury, J.; Chanan, G.; Killeen, T.; Lin, Z.; Gimelshein, N.; Antiga, L.; et al. Pytorch: An imperative style, high-performance deep learning library. *Adv. Neural Inf. Process. Syst.* **2019**, *32*.

Disclaimer/Publisher's Note: The statements, opinions and data contained in all publications are solely those of the individual author(s) and contributor(s) and not of MDPI and/or the editor(s). MDPI and/or the editor(s) disclaim responsibility for any injury to people or property resulting from any ideas, methods, instructions or products referred to in the content.

Article

Position-Wise Gated Res2Net-Based Convolutional Network with Selective Fusing for Sentiment Analysis

Jinfeng Zhou , Xiaoqin Zeng *, Yang Zou and Haoran Zhu

College of Computer and Information, Hohai University, Nanjing 210098, China; zhoujinfeng@hhu.edu.cn (J.Z.)
* Correspondence: xzeng@hhu.edu.cn

Abstract: Sentiment analysis (SA) is an important task in natural language processing in which convolutional neural networks (CNNs) have been successfully applied. However, most existing CNNs can only extract predefined, fixed-scale sentiment features and cannot synthesize flexible, multi-scale sentiment features. Moreover, these models' convolutional and pooling layers gradually lose local detailed information. In this study, a new CNN model based on residual network technology and attention mechanisms is proposed. This model exploits more abundant multi-scale sentiment features and addresses the loss of locally detailed information to enhance the accuracy of sentiment classification. It is primarily composed of a position-wise gated Res2Net (PG-Res2Net) module and a selective fusing module. The PG-Res2Net module can adaptively learn multi-scale sentiment features over a large range using multi-way convolution, residual-like connections, and position-wise gates. The selective fusing module is developed to fully reuse and selectively fuse these features for prediction. The proposed model was evaluated using five baseline datasets. The experimental results demonstrate that the proposed model surpassed the other models in performance. In the best case, the model outperforms the other models by up to 1.2%. Ablation studies and visualizations further revealed the model's ability to extract and fuse multi-scale sentiment features.

Keywords: sentiment analysis; deep neural networks; convolutional neural network; ResNet; Res2Net

Citation: Zhou, J.; Zeng, X.; Zou, Y.; Zhu, H. Position-Wise Gated Res2Net-Based Convolutional Network with Selective Fusing for Sentiment Analysis. *Entropy* **2023**, *25*, 740. https://doi.org/10.3390/e25050740

Academic Editors: Badong Chen, Luis Gonzalo Sánchez Giraldo, Shuangming Yang and Shujian Yu

Received: 25 February 2023
Revised: 23 April 2023
Accepted: 28 April 2023
Published: 30 April 2023

Copyright: © 2023 by the authors. Licensee MDPI, Basel, Switzerland. This article is an open access article distributed under the terms and conditions of the Creative Commons Attribution (CC BY) license (https:// creativecommons.org/licenses/by/ 4.0/).

1. Introduction

Sentiment analysis (SA) is one of the most fundamental tasks in the field of natural language processing (NLP). With the support of massive subjective-opinion data and the development of artificial neural networks (ANNs), various neural networks, including recurrent neural networks (RNNs), memory networks, and convolutional neural networks (CNNs), have been widely applied in this field. In particular, following the remarkable success of CNNs across numerous fields, including computer vision, speech recognition, and signal processing, they have also been successfully applied to NLP tasks [1–4].

One of the significant advantages of CNNs in SA is that they naturally learn coarse-to-fine multi-scale sentiment features using a stack of convolutional layers. Similarly, the text structure is hierarchical, and sentiment occurs in natural language in a multi-scale form. Most CNN-based models employ convolution filters with fixed window sizes to extract fixed-scale sentiment features [5–7]. However, the formation of a scale of sentiment features requires the flexible synthesis of various small-scale sentiment features. For example, the sentiment feature synthesis of "*nice to talk to without being patronizing*" (as shown in Figure 1a) preferably requires the sentiment features of "*nice*" (1-scale) and "*without being patronizing*" (3-scale). If the input feature scale is 1, the positive sentiment feature of "*nice*" and the negative sentiment feature of "*patronizing*" will be used as part of the input, which may introduce noise to the new sentiment feature. If the input feature scale is 3, the sentiment features of "*He's nice to*" and "*nice to talk*" will be used as part of the input, which may add a large amount of unnecessary information to "*nice*" and weaken the response of the new sentiment feature to "*nice*". Therefore, the interactions and fusion of multi-scale sentiment features are very important for learning large-scale sentiment features.

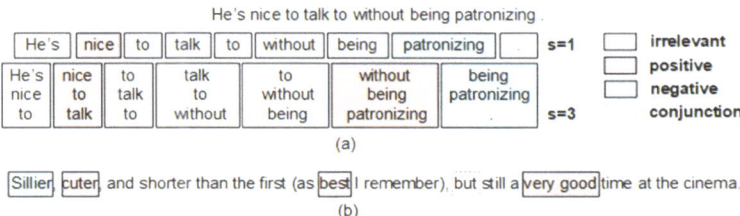

Figure 1. Impacts of multi-scale words and phrases on analyzing the sentiment of a text. (**a**) Limitations of the use of fixed scales to extract sentiment features. (**b**) Importance of jointly determining text sentiment by local sentiment words and phrases of different positions and scales.

Furthermore, the sentiment of a text is jointly determined by local sentiment words or phrases of different positions and scales; conjunctions also play an important role. Most traditional CNNs obtain a global text sentiment representation by stacking convolutional and pooling layers [8–10]. This requires the resolution of two problems: fully using different scales of sentiment features to generate the text sentiment representation and reducing the loss of local detailed information in the convolution and pooling processes. Taking the sentence—"*Sillier, cuter, and shorter than the first (as best I remember), but still a very good time at the cinema.*"—as an example (as shown in Figure 1b), it has a positive global sentiment polarity and contains conjunctions, words, and phrases of different sentiment polarities. The source of its text sentiment should preferably include these features of 1-scale and 2-scale that highlight the sentiment of "*sillier*", "*cuter*", "*best*", and "*very good*", as well as the features that emphasize the semantics of "*but*". For CNNs, if a text sentiment representation depends solely on the downstream layers, some information contained in small-scale sentiment features may be lost. Therefore, it is helpful for a task-friendly text sentiment representation to selectively reuse all scales of sentiment features.

Currently, there are two approaches to alleviate the above limitations: convolution filters with various window sizes in a layer and densely connected layers [6,11,12]. The first approach utilizes filters with different window sizes to extract multi-scale sentiment features. However, it is difficult to find the optimized combination of different window sizes. The interactions of sentiment features from different window sizes have also not been fully exploited, resulting in an insufficient ability to learn multi-scale sentiment features. A large-scale sentiment feature can be elegantly constructed through interactions between various small-scale features without relearning redundant features. The second approach can form a large-scale sentiment feature using various small-scale sentiment features and gracefully reuse all scales of sentiment features using dense connections [13,14]. However, this approach requires the stacking of multiple layers or blocks to obtain multi-scale sentiment features over a large range, resulting in a sharp increase in memory because of the dense connections. Recently, [15] proposed Res2Net in computer vision. Residual-like connections may provide interactions among various small-scale sentiment features to help synthesize large-scale sentiment features. However, these connections are implemented by direct addition, which cannot optimally select the appropriate sentiment features.

In this study, a new CNN-based model is proposed to adaptively learn more scales of sentiment features and fuse them selectively into a task-friendly text sentiment representation. Specifically, it comprises two important modules: a position-wise gated Res2Net (PG-Res2Net) module and a selective fusing module. First, each text is fed into the PG-Res2Net module to obtain different scales of sentiment features over a large range. Each block in the module uses multi-way convolution, residual-like connections, and position-wise gates to implicitly learn multi-scale sentiment features within a certain range. Multi-way convolution enables the module to stack a few residual blocks to obtain multi-scale sentiment features over a wide range. Residual-like connections also provide a bridge for the interactions between multi-scale sentiment features. Position-wise gates optimize the interactions. Furthermore, the selective fusing module integrates these sentiment features to generate a task-friendly text sentiment representation. Specifically, its dense-like connections reuse these features, and its selection operation selects the appropriate information from these features to generate a text sentiment representation. Finally, the text sentiment representation is fed into a classifier for prediction. These two modules enable the model to achieve competitive results on multiple SA datasets, particularly document-level datasets.

The major contributions of this work are as follows:

(1) This paper proposed a PG-Res2Net module to learn different scales of sentiment features over a large range. In contrast to convolution filters with fixed window sizes or dense connections for learning sentiment features, a single residual block in the module can learn multi-scale sentiment features within a certain range. Essentially, the module achieves the first selection of multi-scale features based on local statistics.

(2) Moreover, a selective fusing module is proposed to fully reuse and selectively fuse all scales of sentiment features. This is the second selection of multi-scale sentiment features based on global statistics. The module also effectively alleviates the loss of local detailed information caused by the convolution operation.

(3) The model is extensively evaluated on five datasets. The experimental results demonstrated the competitive performance of the model on these datasets. In the best case, the model outperforms the other models by up to 1.2%. In addition, visualizations and ablation studies demonstrated the effectiveness of the model.

The rest of this paper is organized as follows. Section 2 presents a brief survey of related work. A detailed description of the proposed model and the knowledge relevant to the model are presented in Section 3. Section 4 presents experimental results, ablation studies, and visual analysis. Finally, Section 5 is the conclusion that summarizes the work of this paper.

2. Related Work

SA is typically represented as a tuple (*target*, *sentiment*, *opinion holder*, and *time*). The element *target* is represented as a tuple (*category*, *entity*, and *aspect*), and the element *sentiment* is represented as a tuple (*type*, *intensity*, and *opinion terms*). Currently, most SA methods focus on these tuples or part of their elements. For example, structured sentiment analysis attempts to predict structured sentiment graphs by discovering all opinions and focusing on the whole entire tuple of SA [16]. As another example, emotion cause analysis is the detection of potential causes for certain emotional expressions in a text [17]. This is a study of the tuple *sentiment*. In addition, many interactive correlations between different elements can be shared by incorporating subtasks for handling combinations of different elements. As examples, Fei [18] and Yan et al. [19] proposed unified frameworks for aspect-based SA tasks. Our study focuses on the elements *intensity* and *opinion terms* within the tuple *sentiment* using sentiment modeling. This section presents some multi-scale sentiment modeling methods, including CNNs, residual networks (ResNets), and attention mechanisms relevant to this study.

2.1. CNNs and ResNets in SA Tasks

CNNs are suitable for extracting text sentiment because they naturally correspond to the multi-scale form of sentiment occurrence and the hierarchical structure of texts. Generally, a filter with a fixed window size learns fixed-scale sentiment features. Kim [11] first used multiple filters with different window sizes in a single convolutional layer to learn the sentiment features at several fixed scales. Subsequently, CNNs developed more varieties in SA. The effectiveness of the convolutional filters is an important factor in ensuring the quality of the extracted features. To enhance the ability to extract important semantic features, Yao and Cai [20] used the naïve Bayes algorithm to initialize convolutional filters to identify the positions of important semantic information before training. The concept of multi-scale was also developed. A new feature extraction method was proposed by Soni et al. [21]. The method constructed a text as a three-dimensional paragraph matrix and explicitly applied two-dimensional convolution operation to the matrix to obtain intra-sentence and inter-sentence multi-scale features. Dependency trees model the syntactic relationship between words and are used to improve the performance of models for SA. Graph convolutional networks (GCNs), which are an adaptation of the CNNs for handling unstructured data, can facilitate the handling of dependency trees. Zhang et al. [22] built a universal-syntax GCN over the syntactic dependencies with labels to achieve the goal of navigating richer syntax information for the best aspect-based SA robustness. With the development of deep learning, several strategies and approaches have been proposed for improving the ability of CNNs to extract sentiment features [23]. Of these, residual learning is an important approach and has been applied to SA tasks to improve the ability of CNNs to extract sentiment features. Conneau et al. [24] proposed VD-CNN, which is a pure ResNet that uses up to 29 layers to extract more and larger-scale sentiment features with minimal computational cost. Without relying solely on stacking convolutional layers, a CNN with dense connections was proposed by Wang et al. [6] to reuse existing multi-scale sentiment features and flexibly generate larger-scale features. Yan et al. [12] used a feature extraction block based on a convolution operation and a feature extraction block with dense connections as its feature extraction module, and their parallelism saved training time and reduced training iterations.

However, the aforementioned models must predefine and optimize the window sizes of convolutional filters, lack the interaction between sentiment features, or rely on deeper networks to synthesize more and larger-scale sentiment features. In addition, most of these models gradually lose more local information owing to convolution or pooling operations.

2.2. Attention Mechanisms in SA Tasks

Attention mechanisms are to simulate human attention and make models focus on task-related information to reduce computational complexity and improve performance [25]. Many models have attached different attention mechanisms to solve a wide range of SA tasks. An important role of attention mechanisms is to discover keywords and phrases that strongly contribute to sentiment classification. Lee et al. [26] implemented a word attention mechanism based on weakly supervised learning to identify keywords. Attention mechanisms can also capture behaviors related to the syntactic and semantic structures of a text [27]. Vaswani et al. [28] completely abandoned RNN and CNN structures and used only a multi-head self-attention mechanism to learn global dependencies for generating a text representation that is more relevant to semantics. Ambartsoumian and Popowich [29] explored two methods for combining multi-head self-attention based on the analysis of the characteristics of self-attention mechanisms and achieved competitive accuracy in multiple SA tasks. Attention mechanisms have also been widely used to enhance the aspect–opinion binding, which essentially solves aspect-based SA tasks. In order to pay more attention to the opinion expressions of aspects, Tan et al. [30] constructed a multi-graph fusion network based on GCNs and multiple attention mechanisms to exploit the syntax dependency relation label information and the affective semantic information of words. In addition, gating mechanisms, which control the flow of information through gating units according to the needs of a specific task, are an implementation form of attention mechanisms. Xue and Li [9] applied Tanh-ReLU gating units to the multi-scale sentiment features extracted by the top layer of a CNN to accurately select aspect- or target-related sentiment information. Liu et al. [31] used a convolutional layer and a gating mechanism before a pooling layer for generating attention weights, which helped the pooling layer to find genuinely critical features. Ren et al. [2] developed a gating mechanism similar to long short-term memory (LSTM) networks to control the flow of information between convolutional layers and improve the ability to extract features. Choi et al. [32] used gate mechanisms for the automatic calculation of the importance degrees of sentences in documents.

3. Material and Methods

3.1. Task Modeling

The sentiment classification of texts can be formulated as follows: given an input text $S = \{\text{Wrd}_1, \text{Wrd}_2 \ldots \text{Wrd}_L\}$ comprising L words, where each element denotes a word of a sentence, our task is to construct a sentiment classifier that predicts the whole sentiment polarity $y \in O$ of S, where $O = \{O_1, O_2, \cdots O_C\}$ denotes the sentiment categories of the current task.

3.2. Overview

This section presents the novel and effective model, which is fundamentally designed to obtain text sentiment representations from multi-scale sentiment features at a wide range. The creditable multi-scale sentiment features achieved through the interactive fusion of existing features provide the actual meaning of every token in optimized contexts. Then, high-quality text sentiment representations generated through selectively fusing all scales of sentiment features better retain sentiment information for improved sentiment prediction.

As illustrated in Figure 2, the framework of the model is divided into four processing parts. First, an embedding layer and a convolution block are used to map the text into a text matrix. The text matrix is then fed into a position-wise gated Res2Net (PG-Res2Net) module to obtain different levels of sentiment representations, each of which comprises a certain range of multi-scale sentiment features. Subsequently, the text matrix and these sentiment representations are sent to a selective fusing module through dense-like connections. The selective fusing mechanism of the module is applied to selectively fuse all sentiment features in these representations into a text sentiment representation. Finally, the representation is sent into a classifier for prediction.

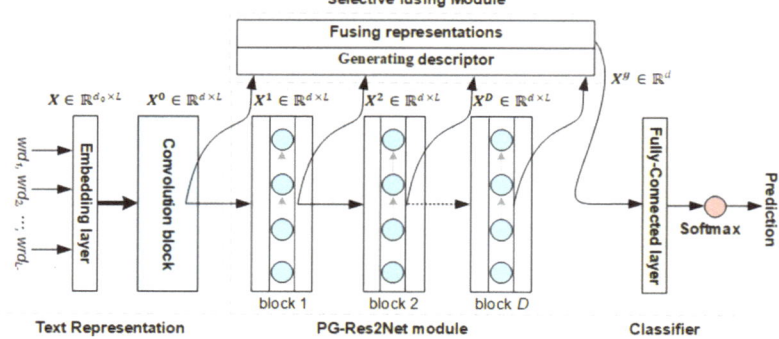

Figure 2. Overview framework of the proposed model.

3.3. Text Representation

Given a text $\{\text{Wrd}_1, \text{Wrd}_2 \ldots \text{Wrd}_L\}$ of length L, each word is first transformed into a word vector. Let $x_i \in \mathbb{R}^{d_0}$ denote the d_0-dimensional pre-trained word vector of Wrd_i, and the text is represented as an embedding matrix X by an embedding layer:

$$X = [x_1, \cdots, x_i, \cdots x_L]_{d_0 \times L}, \qquad (1)$$

Using pre-trained word vectors can improve the performance in the absence of a large supervised training set [33].

To facilitate the operation of the residual blocks in the subsequent PG-Res2Net module, a convolution block projects the feature dimension of X from d_0 to d and outputs a text matrix $X^0 \in \mathbb{R}^{d \times L}$, which is formulated as follows:

$$X^0 = ReLU\Big(BN\Big(conv\Big(X, W^0\Big)\Big)\Big) \qquad (2)$$

where $conv(\bullet)$ is a 1D convolution operation, $BN(\bullet)$ is batch normalization [34], and $ReLU$ is a rectified linear unit [35]. $\boldsymbol{W}^0 \in \mathbb{R}^{d \times d_0 \times 1}$ is the learnable weight.

3.4. PG-Res2Net Module

Conventional CNN-based models lack the interaction between multi-scale sentiment features, and the scale range of the sentiment features relies solely on the network depth of these models. Following Res2Net and its variants in computer vision and other fields [15,36], a PG-Res2Net module was proposed for SA tasks. It has a strong ability to effectively and efficiently learn more and larger-scale sentiment features. For comparison, the structures of the residual blocks in the Res2Net and PG-Res2Net modules are illustrated in Figure 3a,b, respectively. Notably, the number of convolution ways S is set to 4, 1×1 denotes a 2D convolution with window size 1×1, and "1" denotes a 1D convolution with window size 1. "FC" is the abbreviation for "Fully-Connected Layer". As shown in the two images, the most prominent difference between the two modules is that the residual-like connection between the two convolution ways in the Res2Net module is direct addition, whereas the residual-like connection in the PG-Res2Net module has a gate before addition. Different positions in the same text have different optimal scales to form new scale features. We expect that the gating mechanism gives priority to features at these optimal scales and suppresses less relevant features and then enhances the quality of new scale features.

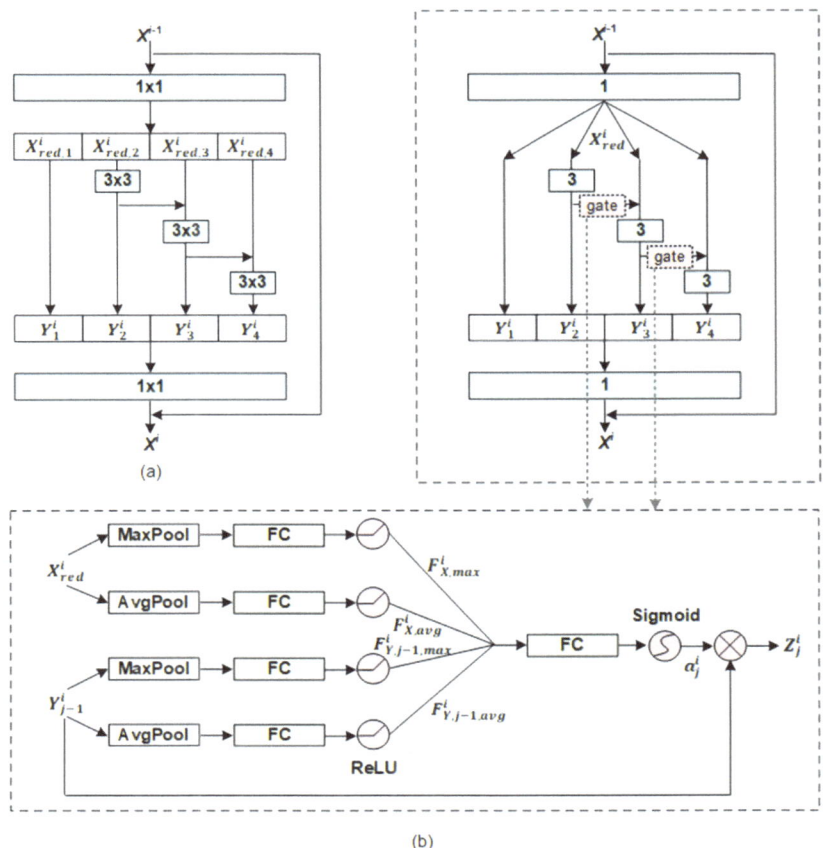

Figure 3. Structures of residual blocks in the two modules: (**a**) Res2Net and (**b**) PG-Res2Net.

As shown in the upper part of Figure 3b, for residual block i, its input X^{i-1} is first compressed by a convolution sub-block to reduce the computational cost and avoid overfitting. The calculation of the sub-block is as follows:

$$X_{red}^i = ReLU\left(BN\left(conv\left(X^{i-1}, W_{red}^i\right)\right)\right), \qquad (3)$$

where $X_{red}^i \in \mathbb{R}^{(d/r) \times L}$ denotes the output of the sub-block, r is the dimension reduction ratio, and W_{red}^i is the learnable weight. Notably, $i \in [1, D]$, where D is the number of residual blocks in the PG-Res2Net module.

Subsequently, X_{red}^i is fed into S convolution ways, respectively. As shown in Figure 3a,b, unlike the original Res2Net in computer vision tasks, X_{red}^i is not grouped because text semantics requires a complete feature space. The output $Y_j^i \in \mathbb{R}^{(d/r) \times L}$ of way j is derived as follows:

$$Y_j^i = \begin{cases} X_{red}^i, & j = 0 \\ ReLU\left(BN\left(conv(X_{red}^i, W_j^i)\right)\right), & j = 1 \\ ReLU\left(BN\left(conv(X_{red}^i + Z_{j-1}^i, W_j^i)\right)\right), & 1 < j \leq S \end{cases} \qquad (4)$$

$$Z_j^i = Y_j^i \otimes a_j^i, \qquad (5)$$

where $Z_j^i \in \mathbb{R}^{(d/r) \times L}$ is the amount of Y_j^i flowing into way $j+1$ through the position-wise gate a_j^i, and $\otimes$ denotes position-wise multiplication. $W_j^i \in \mathbb{R}^{(d/r) \times (d/r) \times 3}$ is the learnable weight. To improve the flexibility of the residual block in synthesizing a large-scale feature from various small-scale features, Z_j^i is implemented using a position-wise gate. Its operation is illustrated in the lower part of Figure 3b. The gate considers the statistics of both X_{red}^i and Y_{j-1}^i as references and prioritizes each position of Y_{j-1}^i. These priorities can highlight the sentiment information relevant to the feature extraction of way j and suppress less relevant information. Particularly, the information from X_{red}^i and Y_{j-1}^i is aggregated to generate four independent feature descriptors: $F_{Y,j-1,avg}^i$, $F_{Y,j-1,max}^i$, $F_{X,avg}^i$, and $F_{X,max}^i$. The calculation process is as follows:

$$F_{Y,j-1,avg}^i = ReLU\left(W_{Y,avg,j-1}^i AvgPool\left(Y_{j-1}^i\right) + b_{Y,avg,j-1}^i\right) \qquad (6)$$

$$F_{Y,j-1,max}^i = ReLU\left(W_{Y,max,j-1}^i MaxPool\left(Y_{j-1}^i\right) + b_{Y,max,j-1}^i\right) \qquad (7)$$

where $AvgPool$ and $MaxPool$ are the average-pooling and max-pooling operations in the feature dimension, respectively. $W_{Y,avg,j-1}^i \in \mathbb{R}^{(L/\gamma) \times L}$, $W_{Y,max,j-1}^i \in \mathbb{R}^{(L/\gamma) \times L}$, $b_{Y,avg,j-1}^i \in \mathbb{R}^{L/\gamma}$, and $b_{Y,max,j-1}^i \in \mathbb{R}^{L/\gamma}$ are the learnable weights. γ is the reduction ratio for compressing the dimensions of these descriptors and for avoiding overfitting. $F_{X,avg}^i$ and $F_{X,max}^i$ are derived in a manner similar to $F_{Y,j-1,avg}^i$ and $F_{Y,j-1,max}^i$. Notably, all of these are processed separately because their functionalities are not symmetric. All descriptors are then concatenated to produce $a_j^i \in \mathbb{R}^L$ as follows:

$$a_j^i = Sigmoid\left(W_{gate,j}^i \left[F_{Y,j-1,avg}^i, F_{Y,j-1,max}^i, F_{X,avg}^i, F_{X,max}^i\right] + b_{gate,j}^i\right) \qquad (8)$$

where $W_{gate,j}^i \in \mathbb{R}^{L \times (4*L/\gamma)}$ and $b_{gate,j}^i \in \mathbb{R}^L$ are the learnable weights. $Sigmoid$ is an activation function.

Finally, to better fuse the multi-scale sentiment features extracted by S convolution ways into the sentiment representation X^i of residual block i and to ensure that the input and output dimensions of the block are the same, these features are concatenated and fed into a convolution sub-block. X^i is calculated as follows:

$$X^i = ReLU\left(BN\left(conv\left(\left[Y_1^i, Y_2^i, \cdots Y_S^i\right], W_{fuse}^i\right)\right) + X^{i-1}\right) \qquad (9)$$

where $W_{fuse}^i \in \mathbb{R}^{d \times (d*S/r) \times 1}$ is the learnable weight.

There is a remarkable advantage of the PG-Res2Net module: Residual-like connections and position gates provide better interactions between existing multi-scale sentiment features to enhance the quality of new scale features. In fact, the first selection of multi-scale sentiment features is completed based on the guidance of local statistics. A new scale sentiment feature essentially stores the appropriate information contained in the different scales of the sentiment features.

3.5. Selective Fusing Module

A residual block in the PG-Res2Net module generates a level of sentiment representation containing multi-scale sentiment features within a limited range, and stacking multiple residual blocks enables the production of different levels of sentiment representations containing more multi-scale sentiment features over a large range. However, only the sequential connections between these blocks may not flexibly and accurately handle language composition. Drawing on the ideas of dense connections and selective kernel convolution [37,38], a selective fusing module was proposed. Its dense-like connections reuse all existing sentiment representations, and its selection operation adaptively adjusts the contribution of these sentiment representations to produce a text sentiment representation.

As shown in Figure 4a, the module first takes as input all levels of sentiment representations from the first convolution block and all residual blocks to generate a descriptor $z^f \in \mathbb{R}^d$. The descriptor provides global information as a guide for selection. Its calculation is formulated as follows:

$$z^f = ReLU\left(BN\left(W_1^f AvgPool\left(\sum_{l=0}^{D} X^l\right) + b_1^f\right)\right) \qquad (10)$$

where $W_1^f \in \mathbb{R}^{d \times d}$ and $b_1^f \in \mathbb{R}^d$ are the learnable weights. The module then uses soft selection, which is guided by z^f, to select different sentiment information into a text representation $X^g \in \mathbb{R}^d$. This process is shown in Figure 4b. Particularly, $A^f \in \mathbb{R}^{(D+1) \times d}$ is a selective matrix, and any vector $a_i^f \in \mathbb{R}^d$ in the matrix represents the selective weights of X^i in the feature dimension. The selective matrix is formulated as follows:

$$A^f = \left[a_0^f, a_1^f, \cdots, a_d^f\right]_{(D+1) \times d} \qquad (11)$$

$$a_i^f = Softmax\left(W_{2,i}^f z^f\right) = \frac{exp\left(W_{2,i}^f z^f + b_{2,i}^f\right)}{\sum_{j=0}^{D} exp\left(W_{2,j}^f z^f + b_{2,j}^f\right)} \qquad (12)$$

where Softmax is a normalized exponential function and $exp(\bullet)$ is an exponential function based on the natural constant e. $W_{2,i}^f \in \mathbb{R}^{d \times d}$ and $b_{1,i}^f \in \mathbb{R}^d$ are the learnable weights. Finally, X^g is defined as follows:

$$X^g = AvgPool\left(Sum\left(\left[X^0, X^1, \cdots X^D\right] \otimes A^f\right)\right) \qquad (13)$$

where $\otimes$ is a level-wise product, and Sum is a sum function on the level dimension.

Each sentiment representation contains a certain range of selected multi-scale sentiment features. Essentially, the selective fusing module performs the second selection for all multi-scale sentiment features based on global statistics.

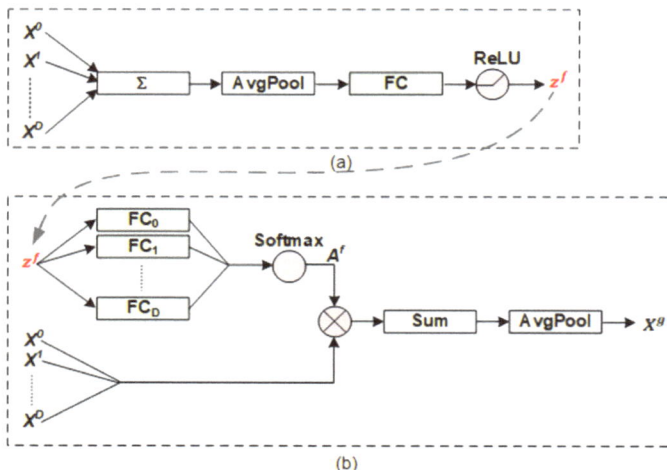

Figure 4. Structure of the selective fusing module. It includes two key operations: (**a**) generating a guidance descriptor and (**b**) fusing all sentiment representations based on the descriptor.

3.6. Objective Function

The classifier in our model was implemented using one fully-connected layer and used X^g as its input. It outputs the prediction $y \in \mathbb{R}^c$ as follows:

$$y = Softmax(W^c X^g + b^c) \qquad (14)$$

where $W^c \in \mathbb{R}^{C \times d}$ and $b^c \in \mathbb{R}^C$ are the learnable weights. C is the number of sentiment categories in a dataset. The cross-entropy function ε is used as the training objective and minimized as follows:

$$\varepsilon = -\sum_{i=1}^{C} \hat{y}_i * log(y_i) \qquad (15)$$

where $\hat{y} \in \mathbb{R}^C$ denotes the referenced distribution.

In this model, the supervision signals are more directly propagated back to the upstream blocks through dense-like connections. Such connections force upstream blocks to learn task-friendly sentiment features, also known as "deep supervision" [37]. Given a sample, the gradient $\frac{\partial \varepsilon}{\partial X^i}$ is decomposed into $D - i + 1$ additive terms as follows:

$$\frac{\partial \varepsilon}{\partial X^i} = \frac{\partial \varepsilon}{\partial y} \frac{\partial y}{\partial X^g} \frac{\partial X^g}{\partial X^i} + \frac{\partial \varepsilon}{\partial y} \frac{\partial y}{\partial X^g} \frac{\partial X^g}{\partial X^{i+1}} \frac{\partial X^{i+1}}{\partial X^i} + \cdots + \frac{\partial \varepsilon}{\partial y} \frac{\partial y}{\partial X^g} \frac{\partial X^g}{\partial X^D} \frac{\partial X^D}{\partial X^i} \qquad (16)$$

$$= \frac{\partial \varepsilon}{\partial y} \frac{\partial y}{\partial X^g} \left(\sum_{m=i}^{D} \frac{\partial X^g}{\partial X^m} \prod_{n=i}^{m-1} \frac{\partial X^{n+1}}{\partial X^n} \right) \qquad (17)$$

where $i \in [0, D]$. The first term of Equation (16) indicates that the supervision information is directly propagated back to any upstream block i through only a few blocks or layers. Therefore, the block is forced to learn directly under the supervision signals. These additive terms also intuitively show that the training behavior is similar to the simultaneous training of a series of neural networks, the structures of which range from shallow to deep. In this manner, the learning of sentiment features is carried out under multiple supervision signals from multiple neural networks. These features better consider both feature synthesis and direct task purpose, which are reflected in the two terms inside and outside the brackets in Equation (17).

4. Results and Discussion

This section first describes the five public datasets used in our experiments, as well as the experimental setup and models for comparison. Next, the experimental results of the proposed model and other models on these datasets are presented. Finally, the effectiveness of the model is demonstrated through ablation studies and visualization.

4.1. Datasets

To verify the performance of the model in short-text-level and document-level SA tasks, the experiments were conducted on five datasets. The binary-category short-text-level datasets included MR [39] and SST-2 [40], and the multi-category document-level datasets consisted of Yelp.F [7], Sports & Outdoors (S&O), and Toys & Games (T&G) from SNAP [41].

- MR: The dataset was built by searching for movie reviews from review websites. In this dataset, 10,662 samples are separated into two categories.
- SST-2: The dataset is a binary version of the Stanford Sentiment Treebank dataset, which is an extension of MR. It comprises 9163 samples, which are separated into two categories.
- Yelp.F: The Yelp review dataset was obtained from the 2015 Yelp Dataset Challenge. It has five-star polarity labels. Each star label contains 130,000 training samples and 10,000 testing samples.
- S&O and T&G: These two datasets contain product reviews and metadata from SNAP, including 142.8 million reviews from Amazon. In this study, only reviews of Sports & Outdoor and Toy & Game products were used.

The complete details and statistics of these datasets are listed in Table 1. Note that S&O and T&G have no standard training/test split, and their split refers to [42].

Table 1. Data statistics. Training, training set size; Testing, test set size; Classes, number of classes; Avg-Len, average text length; Max-Len, maximum text length.

Dataset	MR	SST-2	Yelp.F	S&O	T&G
Training	7.1 K	6.9 K	650 K	294.0 K	165.4 K
Testing	3.6 K	1.8 K	50 K	1 K	1 K
Classes	2	2	5	5	5
Avg-Len	21	19	155	99	114
Max-Len	62	56	1214	6467	6224

4.2. Models for Comparison

To evaluate the performance of the model, it was compared with baseline and state-of-the-art models. The baseline methods are as follows:

- *Bi-LSTM* [43] directly inputs the entire document as a single sequence into a bi-directional LSTM network for SA.
- *HAN* [44] uses hierarchical attention networks to classify documents.
- *Classical CNN* [11] uses multiple filters with different window sizes in a single convolutional layer to learn the sentiment features.
- *VDCNN* [24] uses only small convolution and pooling operations at the character level with a depth of 29 convolutional layers.
- *Word-DenseNet* [45] is an adaptation of DenseNet for text classification.

The state-of-the-art models are as follows:

- *HUSN* [46] utilizes user review habits to enhance an LSTM-based hierarchical neural network for SA.
- *CAHAN* [47] is a modification of HAN that can make context-aware attentional decisions.
- *AGCNN* [31] introduces an attention-gated layer before the pooling layer to help the CNN focus on critical abstract features.

- *TextConvoNet* [21] applies multidimensional convolution to extract inter-token and inter-sentence N-gram features.
- *DenseNet with multi-scale feature attention* [6] is an improved version of DenseNet and is equipped with multi-scale feature attention.
- *SAHSSC* [48] is a self-attentive hierarchical model for text summarization and sentiment classification.
- *Sentiment-Aware Transformer* [49] is a new type of transformer model designed to predict both word and sentence sentiment.

4.3. Experimental Setup

The experimental setup of the proposed model involved three parts:

(1) **Input.** Data preprocessing was performed because the datasets were obtained from web reviews and had complex and arbitrary characteristics. Anomalous symbols were eliminated, and upper-case letters were converted to lower-case letters. A word embedding corpus pre-trained by GloVe was used [50]. Words in a target dataset that were not in the corpus were initialized using a random vector with element values between -0.01 and 0.01. Because the input of the model requires a constant length L, all samples whose length was not L were padded with zero vectors or truncated. In the experiments, L was set to 50 for MR and SST-2 and 500 for the other datasets.

(2) **Architecture configuration.** The feature dimension d of the output of the first convolutional block was set to 128. For the PG-Res2Net module, the reduction ratio γ was set to 2, and the number S of convolution ways of a residual block was set to 4. The number D of residual blocks was set to 2 for MR and SST-2, 4 for S&O and T&G, and 7 for Yelp.F. S and D were determined by the experimental results.

(3) **Training setting.** The objective function was minimized by stochastic gradient descent (SGD) with a batch size of 256, a learning rate of 0.01, and a momentum of 0.99. For all datasets except SST-2, the learning rate dropped to 0.1 times every 5 epochs. For SST-2, the period was 10 epochs. L_2 regularization was also added to the objective function, and its coefficient was set to 0.0001. Random dropout [51] with a drop rate of 0.5 was applied to the input of the classifier. The training processes lasted for at most 20 epochs on all datasets, and all experiments were conducted using PyTorch v1.9 (Linux Foundation, San Francisco, CA, USA).

In the experiments, the above datasets were not processed by any pre-trained transformer model, such as BERT [52]. There are two reasons. First, the above datasets contain numerous long texts. The memory usage and computational complexity caused by the self-attention mechanism in pre-training models grow quadratically with the text length [53]. This can lead to excessive costs when processing long texts. Second, the proposed model aims to improve the ability to extract credible features, while pre-training models are usually used to initialize the feature vector for each word in the SA tasks. Therefore, whether or not pre-training models are used does not affect the demonstration for the innovation of the proposed model. In essence, the modules in the proposed model can be easily incorporated into several existing CNN-based models to improve their ability to extract multi-scale features.

4.4. Experimental Results

The results of the proposed model and the other models for the five datasets are listed in Table 2. The proposed model achieved superior or comparable results to all other models. For the Yelp.F, S&O, and T&G datasets, the proposed model achieved the best accuracy, which was at least 0.5%, 1.2%, and 0.7% higher than those of the other models, respectively. Most of the samples in the three datasets are at the document level and have more complex sentiment semantic dependencies than short texts. Compared with those RNNs, the proposed model exhibited the ability to explicitly capture more and larger-scale sentiment features. Compared with those shallow CNNs, the proposed model could flexibly synthesize sentiment features on various scales and alleviate the problem of sentiment information utilization. Compared with other ResNets, the proposed model improved the interactions between multi-scale features and exhibited the capability to fuse different scales of sentiment features. For those transformer-based models, their self-attention may miss local meaningful semantic relationships over long sequences, and the proposed model is better able to extract and preserve these relationships. For MR and SST-2, the accuracy of the proposed model was comparable to that of the other models. We propose two reasons for the weakening of the advantages of the proposed model. First, most of the samples in the two datasets are short texts, which are less dependent on the ability to extract multi-scale features than document-level texts. Second, the small sample sizes of the two datasets limit the training of the proposed model.

Table 2. Test accuracy (%) of the proposed model and other models on the five datasets. The results marked with * are obtained by our re-implementation.

	Model	MR	SST-2	Yelp.F	S&O	T&G
RNN	Bi-LSTM [43]	79.7	83.2	54.8	71.9	70.7
	HAN [44]	77.1	-	-	72.3	69.1
	CAHAN [47]	-	79.8	-	73.0	70.8
	HUSN [46]	81.5 *	82.2	-	-	-
CNN	Classical CNN [11]	81.5	87.2	65.5	72.0	70.5
	AGCNN [31]	81.9	87.4	62.4	-	-
	TextConvoNet [21]	-	-	63.1	71.3 *	73.2 *
ResNet	VDCNN (29 layers) [24]	72.8	78.2	64.7	72.3 *	74.8 *
	Word-DenseNet [45]	79.6 *	82.2 *	64.5	67.6 *	72.6 *
	DenseNet with Multi-scale Feature Attention [6]	81.5	84.3 *	66.0	71.6 *	74.2 *
Transformer	SAHSSC [48]	-	-	-	73.6	72.5
	Sentiment-Aware Transformer [49]	79.5	84.3	-	-	-
This work	CNN with PG-Res2Net and Selective fusing	82.3 (D = 2)	85.5 (D = 2)	66.5 (D = 7)	74.8 (D = 4)	75.5 (D = 4)

4.5. Study of PG-Res2Net

4.5.1. Tuning of Hyperparameters

The position-wise gating mechanism in the PG-Res2Net module is critical to determining the performance of the proposed model. To verify the effectiveness of the gating mechanism, we conducted a comparison of the proposed model with Res2Net and the proposed model with PG-Res2Net. The comparison results are given in Table 3. The highest accuracy on each dataset was achieved by the proposed model with PG-Res2Net. Except $S = 3$ on Yelp.F and $S = 3$ on T&G, the accuracy with PG-Res2Net was higher than that with Res2Net under the same S. It means that the gating mechanism can select the optimized scales of features that are more effective to improve the performance of the proposed model.

Table 3. Test accuracy (%) of the proposed model with Res2Net and PG-Res2Net on the five datasets.

	S	MR (D = 2)	SST-2 (D = 2)	Yelp.F (D = 7)	S&O (D = 4)	T&G (D = 4)
with ResNet	3	81.0	84.4	66.1	73.3	75.0
	4	82.0	84.6	65.9	73.6	74.7
	5	81.2	83.9	66.1	72.3	74.4
	6	81.2	84.1	66.2	72.6	74.6
with PG-Res2Net	3	81.5	84.6	65.6	73.8	74.2
	4	82.3	85.5	66.5	74.8	75.5
	5	81.7	84.0	66.3	72.8	75.2
	6	82.1	84.2	66.3	73.0	74.8

Table 3 also shows how the performance is influenced by the number S of convolution ways of a residual block. S is varied among {3, 4, 5, 6}. For different datasets, the value of S for which the model with Res2Net accomplished the best accuracy was not fixed for different datasets, and the value of S for which the model with PG-Res2Net achieved the best accuracy was fixed at 4. Without the help of the gating mechanism, the selection of feature scales is more dependent on the variation of S. A smaller value of S limits the range of feature scales. While a larger value of S allows learning with a wider range of features, it also introduces more noise. Thus, the gating mechanism reduces the dependence of the proposed model on S.

4.5.2. Visualization of Multi-Scale Sentiment Features

In this subsection, we demonstrate the effectiveness of the residual blocks of the PG-Res2Net module in the proposed model. Considering residual block 1 trained by MR as an example, Figure 5 shows the heatmaps of its multi-scale sentiment features and sentiment representations generated by the two texts. For each image, the first four rows correspond to the sentiment features extracted by the four convolution ways of the block, respectively. The upper part of each row shows the heatmap of a sentiment feature, and the lower part shows the phrases corresponding to the positions of the feature. The last row shows the heatmap of a sentiment representation. These sentiment features and representations were first transformed into intensity vectors and then visualized.

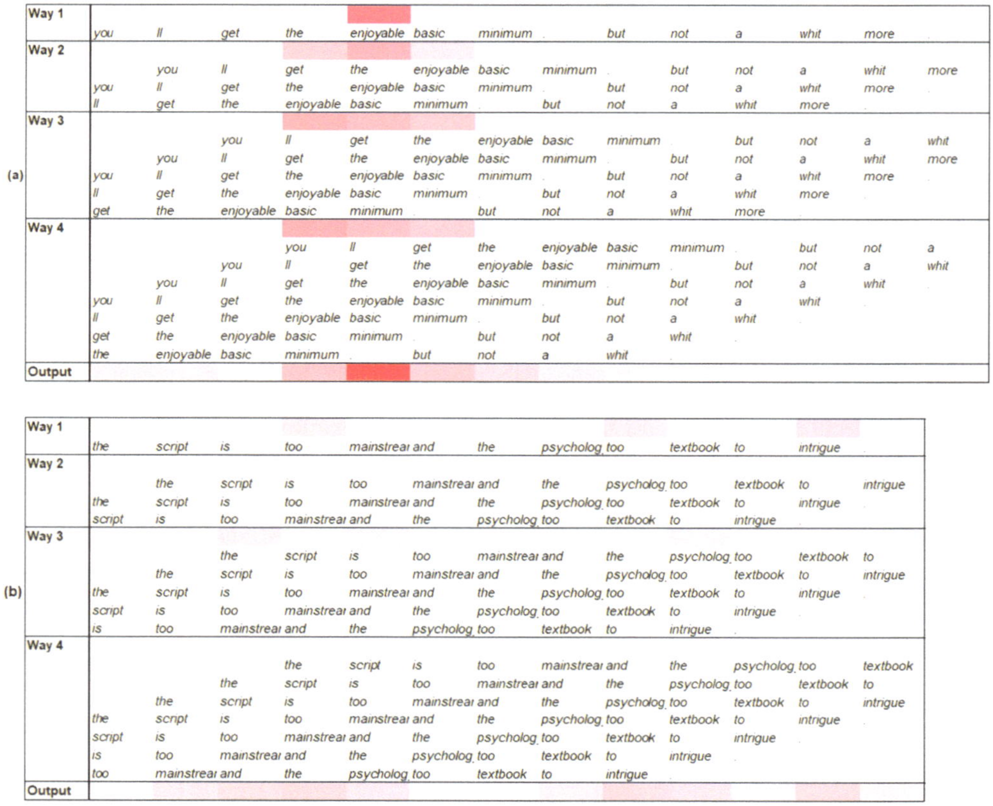

Figure 5. Heatmaps of multi-scale sentiment features and representations of residual block 1 in the PG-Res2Net. (**a**,**b**) show two texts with positive and negative sentiment polarities, respectively.

For the text shown in Figure 5a, Way 1 in the block captured *"enjoyable"* (1-scale), which has a strong positive sentiment intensity and is an important influence on the sentiment polarity of the text. Ways 2, 3, and 4 also captured the phrases of 3-scale, 5-scale, and 7-scale with strong sentiment intensity. All of these ways contain *"enjoyable"*. When the phrases including *"enjoyable"* contain the conjunction word *"but"* or the negative word *"not"*, their sentiment intensity is evidently weakened, such as *"enjoyable basic minimum. but"* (5-scale) and *"enjoyable basic minimum. but not a"* (7-scale). This indicates that a single residual block in the PG-Res2Net module can accurately extract sentiment features at different scales using multiple convolution ways, residual-like connections, and gates between ways.

For the text shown in Figure 5b, the sentiment intensity of each word (1-scale), which was captured by Way 1, was not very strong. Although Ways 2, 3, and 4 gradually captured more phrases with a certain sentiment intensity, such as *"the script is too mainstream"* (5-scale) and *"the psychology too textbook to intrigue"* (7-scale), their sentiment intensity is still weak. This phenomenon is not conducive to judging text sentiment polarity. However, the overall sentiment intensity of its sentiment representation is significantly enhanced and can determine the sentiment polarity of the text. This illustrates that a residual block in the PG-Res2Net module can effectively select multi-scale sentiment features to generate task-friendly sentiment representations. As mentioned in Section 3.4, the sentiment representation of a block selectively contains the multi-scale features extracted by the block.

4.6. Effectiveness of Selective Fusing Module

To investigate the effect of the selective fusing module in the proposed model, ablation experiments were conducted on MR and Yelp.F, which represent 2-category short-text-level and 5-category document-level datasets, respectively. The four structures were constructed as follows, and the results are listed in Table 4.

- 3-Blocks-W-SF: The structure has a PG-Res2Net module containing 3 residual blocks and a selective fusing module for MR.
- 3-Blocks-WO-SF: The structure is similar to 3-Blocks-W-SF except that an average method replaces the selective fusing module.
- 7-Blocks-W-SF: The structure has a PG-Res2Net module containing 7 residual blocks and a selective fusing module for Yelp.F.
- 7-Blocks-WO-SF: The structure is similar to 7-Blocks-W-SF except that an average method replaces the selective fusing module.

Table 4. Ablation study on the selective fusing module of the proposed model. Test accuracy (%) is used as an evaluation metric.

	3-Blocks-W-SF	3-Blocks-WO-SF	7-Blocks-W-SF	7-Blocks-WO-SF
MR	81.7	81.4	-	-
Yelp.F	-	-	66.5	64.3

As shown in Table 4, for both MR and Yelp.F, the removal of the selective fusing module led to a decline in accuracy, particularly for Yelp.F. We further used t-SNE to visualize the text sentiment representations of the four structures, which were the outputs of the selective fusing modules or the alternative average methods. The corresponding results are shown in Figure 6, where every point represents a sample, and different colors represent different classes. For MR, Figure 6a shows that the text sentiment representations of 3-Blocks-W-SF and 3-Blocks-WO-SF form different clusters. However, the boundary between the different clusters of 3-Blocks-W-SF is more evident than that of 3-Blocks-WO-SF. For Yelp.F, Figure 6b shows that the text sentiment representations of 7-Blocks-W-SF and 7-Blocks-WO-SF do not form different clusters well. We suggest that this phenomenon might be caused by the difficulty of multi-category document-level datasets and the similar sentiment representation projections of texts adjacent to the sentiment polarity. The clusters of Classes 2, 3, and 4 of 7-Blocks-WO-SF almost overlapped. However, the clusters of

7-Blocks-W-SF can be distinguished and distributed in space in the order of sentiment polarity. Overall, the selective fusing module can optimally select sentiment features from different levels of sentiment representations to generate a task-friendly text sentiment representation.

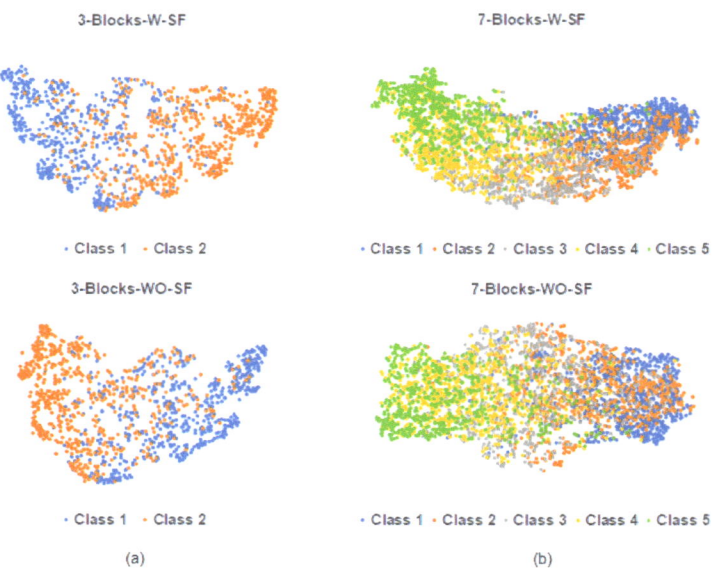

Figure 6. Two-dimensional t-SNE visualization of text sentiment representations. (**a**) Text sentiment representations produced by 3-Blocks-W-SF and 3-Blocks-WO-SF on MR. (**b**) Text sentiment representations produced by 7-Blocks-W-SF and 7-Blocks-WO-SF on Yelp.F.

4.7. Analysis of Model Scalability

The proposed model can better handle target datasets with different text length distributions and sample sizes by scaling the number D of its residual blocks. In this subsection, we assess how the scaling of the model influences its performance. The model had two forms in this experiment. When processing 2-category short-text-level datasets, $C = 2$ and $L = 50$, and when processing 5-category document-level datasets, $C = 5$ and $L = 500$. Figure 7a shows the accuracy of the model for the five datasets for different D values. For Yelp.F, S&O, and T&G, the accuracy continuously improved with an increase in D until $D = 7$, 4, and 4, respectively. This is because the three datasets are document-level and dependent on multi-scale sentiment features in a larger range, whose extraction requires more residual blocks. For the short-text-level datasets MR and SST-2, the accuracy reached the maximum when $D = 2$ and 3, respectively. We suggest that the sentiment classification of short texts depends more on small-scale sentiment features, which may be obtained using only a few residual blocks. Moreover, a single residual block in the PG-Res2Net module can learn a certain range of sentiment features.

Figure 7a also shows that, for all datasets except Yelp.F, the accuracy begins to decrease and fluctuate when D exceeds a certain value. This may be caused by overfitting, which is triggered by the relatively small sample size of a training set and the more learnable weights of a model. As shown in Figure 7b, although the number of the learnable weights of the model ($C = 5$ and $L = 50$) did not increase significantly with an increase in D, the training sample size of MR and SST-2 were small enough to easily cause overfitting. For S&O and T&G, the training sample size satisfied the increase in the number of the learnable weights ($C = 5$ and $L = 500$) when D was not too large. For Yelp.F, the accuracy always increased when D increased from 2 to 7 because the dataset had sufficient training samples to train more learnable weights. Overall, increasing D within a certain range may improve the accuracy of the model for document-level datasets.

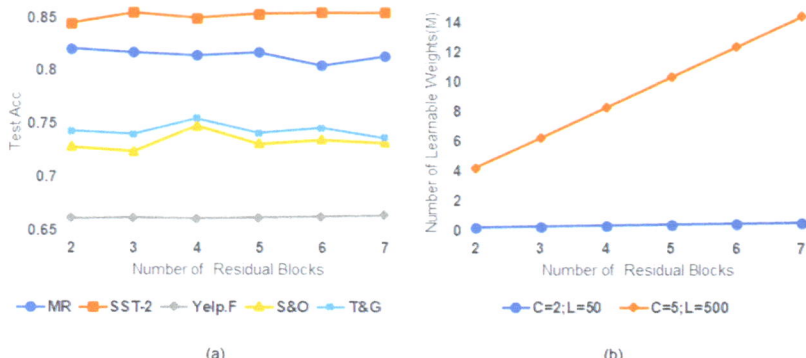

Figure 7. Impact with a different number of residual blocks. (**a**) Test accuracy with a different number of residual blocks. (**b**) Relationship between the number of residual blocks and the number of learnable weights.

4.8. Error Analysis

An error analysis of the proposed model was conducted, and it was found that most of the errors could be summarized as follows. The first factor is a lack of background knowledge. An example is *"ethan hawke has always fancied himself the bastard child of the beatnik generation and it's all over his chelsea walls."*, whose representation of residual block 1 is shown in Figure 8a. As observed in the representation, the most emphasized phrase is *"ethan hawke has always fancied himself the"*. However, it does not have a strong sentiment. *"beatnik"* and *"chelsea walls"*, which are decisive for the sentiment judgment of the text, require relevant background knowledge to be understood. The second factor is the mutual interference between different sentiment tendencies in a text with less prominent sentiment, such as *"an otherwise intense, twist-and-turn thriller that certainly shouldn't hurt talented young gaghan's resume."*. From Figure 8b, while the phrase *"an otherwise intense, twist-and-turn thriller"* with negative sentiment is emphasized, the phrase *"shouldn't hurt talented young gaghan's"* with positive sentiment is also emphasized. These two phrases with different sentiment tendencies make it difficult to judge the less prominent sentiment of the whole text.

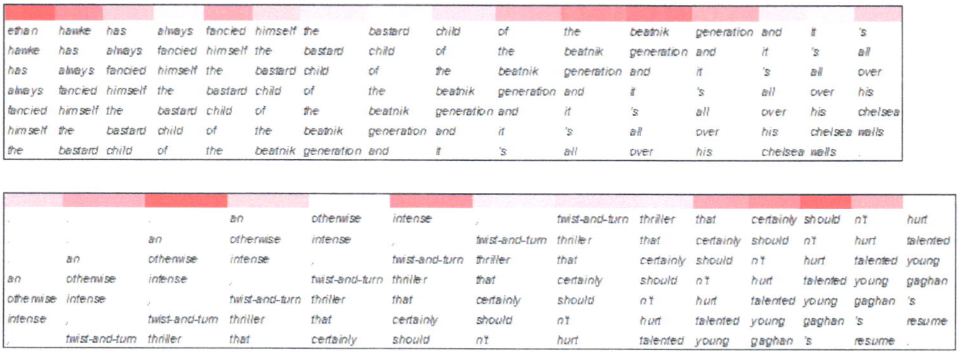

Figure 8. Heatmaps of representations of residual block 1 in the PG-Res2Net module. (**a**,**b**) are the representative texts of two factors that cause incorrect predictions.

5. Conclusions

In this study, a novel CNN model is proposed for sentiment analysis of short texts and documents, in which a PG-Res2Net module and a selective fusing module are defined. This model is intuitively designed to earn credible text sentiment representations through the interaction and fusion of various scale features for predicting the right sentiment of a text, where multi-scale sentiment features are achieved by developing the optimized interaction among various small-scale sentiment features. Furthermore, text sentiment representations are produced by selectively fusing multi-scale features over a large range. Compared with other CNN-based models, the proposed model can obtain more abundant multi-scale sentiment features and alleviate the loss of local detailed information caused by a convolution operation. The model achieved comparable or better performance on the five benchmark datasets compared with the other models. The comparison results, ablation studies, and visualizations also demonstrated the proposed model's ability to optimize the interaction among multi-scale features and selectively fuse multi-scale features.

Although this model achieves marginal improvement over other models, several research areas warrant further investigation. First, sentiment datasets often show category imbalances, and we attempt to handle the imbalances using the reuse of multi-scale sentiment features across samples. Second, there is interference between the features with different sentiment tendencies in a text with less prominent sentiment, and we try to use computational intelligence algorithms, such as monarch butterfly optimization and differential evolution, to further optimize and improve the feature selection operator. Third, there is other information associated with texts, such as user and product information [54,55], and we are exploring further how this information can be used.

Author Contributions: Conceptualization, X.Z. and J.Z.; methodology, J.Z.; software, J.Z.; validation, X.Z., Y.Z. and J.Z.; formal analysis, J.Z. and H.Z.; investigation, J.Z. and Y.Z.; resources, H.Z.; data curation, Y.Z.; writing—original draft preparation, J.Z. and X.Z.; writing—review and editing, J.Z.; visualization, Y.Z.; supervision, X.Z. All authors have read and agreed to the published version of the manuscript.

Funding: This research received no external funding.

Institutional Review Board Statement: Not applicable.

Data Availability Statement: Not applicable.

Conflicts of Interest: The authors declare no conflict of interest.

References

1. Park, J.H.; Choi, B.J.; Lee, S.K. Examining the impact of adaptive convolution on natural language understanding. *Expert Syst. Appl.* **2022**, *189*, 49–69. [CrossRef]
2. Ren, J.; Wu, W.; Liu, G.; Chen, Z.; Wang, R. Bidirectional gated temporal convolution with attention for text classification. *Neurocomputing* **2021**, *455*, 265–273. [CrossRef]
3. Tan, C.; Ren, Y.; Wang, C. An adaptive convolution with label embedding for text classification. *Appl. Intell.* **2022**, *33*, 804–812. [CrossRef]
4. Zou, H.; Xiang, K. Sentiment classification method based on blending of emoticons and short texts. *Entropy* **2022**, *24*, 398. [CrossRef]
5. Liu, Y.; Wang, L.; Shi, T.; Li, J. Detection of spam reviews through a hierarchical attention architecture with N-gram CNN and Bi-LSTM. *Inf. Syst.* **2022**, *103*, 101865. [CrossRef]
6. Wang, S.; Huang, M.; Deng, Z. Densely connected CNN with multi-scale feature attention for text classification. In Proceedings of the 28th International Joint Conference on Artificial Intelligence (IJCAI), Stockholm, Sweden, 13–19 July 2018; pp. 4468–4474.
7. Xiang, Z.; Zhao, J.; LeCun, Y. Character-level convolutional networks for text classification. In Proceedings of the 28th Advances in Neural Information Processing Systems (NIPS), Montreal, QC, Canada, 7–12 December 2015; pp. 649–657.
8. Dashtipour, K.; Gogate, M.; Adeel, A.; Larijani, H.; Hussain, A. Sentiment analysis of persian movie reviews using deep learning. *Entropy* **2021**, *23*, 596. [CrossRef]
9. Xue, W.; Li, T. Aspect based sentiment analysis with gated convolutional networks. In Proceedings of the 56th Annual Meeting of the Association for Computational Linguistics (ACL), Melbourne, VIC, Australia, 15–20 July 2018; pp. 2514–2523.

10. Liu, F.; Zheng, J.; Zheng, L.; Chen, C. Combining attention-based bidirectional gated recurrent neural network and two-dimensional convolutional neural network for document-level sentiment classification. *Neurocomputing* **2020**, *371*, 39–50. [CrossRef]
11. Kim, Y. Convolutional neural networks for sentence classification. In Proceedings of the Conference on Empirical Methods in Natural Language Processing (EMNLP), Doha, Qatar, 25–29 October 2014; pp. 1746–1751.
12. Yan, L.; Han, J.; Yue, Y.; Zhang, L.; Qian, Y. Sentiment analysis of short texts based on parallel densenet. *Comput. Mater. Contin.* **2021**, *69*, 51–65. [CrossRef]
13. Ma, Q.; Yan, J.; Lin, Z.; Yu, L.; Chen, Z. Deformable self-attention for text classification. *IEEE/ACM Trans. Audio Speech Lang. Process.* **2021**, *29*, 1570–1581. [CrossRef]
14. Xu, Y.; Yu, Z.; Cao, W.; Chen, C.L.P. Adaptive dense ensemble model for text classification. *IEEE Trans. Cybern.* **2022**, *52*, 7513–7526. [CrossRef]
15. Gao, S.H.; Cheng, M.M.; Zhao, K.; Zhang, X.Y.; Yang, M.H.; Torr, P. Res2net: A new multi-scale backbone architecture. *IEEE Trans. Pattern Anal. Mach. Intell.* **2021**, *43*, 652–662. [CrossRef]
16. Shi, W.; Li, F.; Li, J.; Fei, H.; Ji, D. Effective token graph modeling using a novel labeling strategy for structured sentiment analysis. In Proceedings of the 60th Annual Meeting of the Association for Computational Linguistics (ACL), Dublin, Ireland, 22–27 May 2022; pp. 4232–4241.
17. Chen, S.; Shi, X.; Li, J.; Wu, S.; Fei, H.; Li, F.; Ji, D. Joint alignment of multi-task feature and label spaces for emotion cause pair extraction. In Proceedings of the 27th International Conference on Computational Linguistics (COLING), Gyeongju, Republic of Korea, 12–17 October 2022; pp. 6955–6965.
18. Fei, H.; Li, F.; Li, C.; Wu, S.; Li, J.; Ji, D. Inheriting the wisdom of predecessors: A multiplex cascade framework for unified aspect-based sentiment analysis. In Proceedings of the 31st International Joint Conference on Artificial Intelligence (IJCAI), Vienna, Austria, 23–29 July 2022; pp. 4121–4128.
19. Yan, H.; Dai, J.; Ji, T.; Qiu, X.; Zhang, Z. A unified generative framework for aspect-based sentiment analysis. In Proceedings of the 59th Annual Meeting of the Association for Computational Linguistics and the 11th International Joint Conference on Natural Language Processing (ACL-IJCNLP), Bangkok, Thailand, 1–6 August 2021; pp. 2416–2429.
20. Yao, C.; Cai, M. A novel optimized convolutional neural network based on attention pooling for text classification. *J. Phys. Conf. Ser.* **2021**, *1971*, 012079. [CrossRef]
21. Soni, S.; Chouhan, S.S.; Rathore, S.S. TextConvoNet: A convolutional neural network based architecture for text classification. *Appl. Intell.* **2022**, *33*, 1–12. [CrossRef]
22. Fei, H.; Chua, T.-S.; Li, C.; Ji, D.; Zhang, M.; Ren, Y. On the robustness of aspect-based sentiment analysis: Rethinking model, data, and training. *ACM Trans. Inf. Syst.* **2023**, *41*, 1–32. [CrossRef]
23. Chen, Y.; Dai, X.; Liu, M.; Chen, D.; Yuan, L.; Liu, Z. Dynamic convolution: Attention over convolution kernels. In Proceedings of the 14th IEEE Computer Society Conference on Computer Vision and Pattern Recognition (CVPR), Seattle, WA, USA, 14–19 June 2020; pp. 11027–11036.
24. Conneau, A.; Schwenk, H.; Cun, Y.L.; Barrault, L. Very deep convolutional networks for text classification. In Proceedings of the 15th Conference of the European Chapter of the Association for Computational Linguistics (EACL), Valencia, Spain, 3–7 April 2017; pp. 1107–1116.
25. Brauwers, G.; Frasincar, F. A general survey on attention mechanisms in deep learning. *IEEE Trans. Knowl. Data Eng.* **2021**, *1*, 3279–3298. [CrossRef]
26. Lee, G.; Jeong, J.; Seo, S.; Kim, C.Y.; Kang, P. Sentiment classification with word localization based on weakly supervised learning with a convolutional neural network. *Knowledge-Based Syst.* **2018**, *152*, 70–82. [CrossRef]
27. Liu, P.; Chang, S.; Huang, X.; Tang, J.; Cheung, J.C.K. Contextualized non-local neural networks for sequence learning. In Proceedings of the 33rd Innovative Applications of Artificial Intelligence Conference (AAAI), Honolulu, HI, USA, 27 January–1 February 2019; pp. 6762–6769.
28. Vaswani, A.; Shazeer, N.; Parmar, N.; Uszkoreit, J.; Jones, L.; Gomez, A.N.; Kaiser, Ł.; Polosukhin, I. Attention is all you need. In Proceedings of the 31st Advances in Neural Information Processing Systems (NIPS), Long Beach, CA, USA, 4–9 December 2017; pp. 5999–6009.
29. Ambartsoumian, A.; Popowich, F. Self-attention: A better building block for sentiment analysis neural network classifiers. In Proceedings of the 9th Workshop on Computational Approaches to Subjectivity, Sentiment and Social Media Analysis (WASSA), Brussels, Belgium, 31 October 2018; pp. 130–139.
30. Tang, S.; Chai, H.; Yao, Z.; Ding, Y.; Gao, C.; Fang, B.; Liao, Q. Affective knowledge enhanced multiple-graph fusion networks for aspect-based sentiment analysis. In Proceedings of the 7th Conference on Empirical Methods in Natural Language Processing (EMNLP), Abu Dhabi, United Arab Emirates, 7–11 December 2022; pp. 5352–5362.
31. Liu, Y.; Ji, L.; Huang, R.; Ming, T.; Gao, C.; Zhang, J. An attention-gated convolutional neural network for sentence classification. *Intell. Data Anal.* **2019**, *23*, 1091–1107. [CrossRef]
32. Choi, G.; Oh, S.; Kim, H. Improving document-level sentiment classification using importance of sentences. *Entropy* **2020**, *22*, 1336. [CrossRef]
33. Xianlun, T.; Yingjie, C.; Jin, X.; Xinxian, Y. Deep global-attention based convolutional network with dense connections for text classification. *J. China Univ. Posts Telecommun.* **2020**, *27*, 46–55. [CrossRef]

34. Ioffe, S.; Szegedy, C. Batch normalization: Accelerating deep network training by reducing internal covariate shift. In Proceedings of the 32nd International Conference on Machine Learning (ICML), Lille, France, 7–9 July 2015; pp. 448–456.
35. Hinton, G.E. Rectified linear units improve restricted boltzmann machines. *J. Appl. Biomech.* **2017**, *33*, 384–387.
36. Li, X.; Wu, X.; Lu, H.; Liu, X.; Meng, H. Channel-wise gated res2net: Towards robust detection of synthetic speech attacks. In Proceedings of the Annual Conference of the International Speech Communication Association (INTERSPEECH), Brno, Czech Republic, 30 August–3 September 2021; pp. 4314–4318.
37. Huang, G.; Liu, Z.; Van Der Maaten, L.; Weinberger, K.Q. Densely connected convolutional networks. In Proceedings of the IEEE Computer Society Conference on Computer Vision and Pattern Recognition (CVPR), Honolulu, HI, USA, 21–26 July 2017; pp. 2261–2269.
38. Li, X.; Wang, W.; Hu, X.; Yang, J. Selective kernel networks. In Proceedings of the IEEE Computer Society Conference on Computer Vision and Pattern Recognition (CVPR), Long Beach, CA, USA, 15–20 June 2019; pp. 510–519.
39. Socher, R.; Perelygin, A.; Wu, J.Y.; Chuang, J.; Manning, C.D.; Ng, A.Y.; Potts, C. Recursive deep models for semantic compositionality over a sentiment treebank. In Proceedings of the Conference on Empirical Methods in Natural Language Processing (EMNLP), Seattle, WA, USA, 18–21 October 2013; pp. 1631–1642.
40. Pang, B.; Lee, L. Seeing stars: Exploiting class relationships for sentiment categorization with respect to rating scales. In Proceedings of the 43rd Annual Meeting of the Association for Computational Linguistics (ACL), Ann Arbor, MI, USA, 25–30 June 2005; pp. 115–124.
41. He, R.; McAuley, J. Ups and downs: Modeling the visual evolution of fashion trends with one-class collaborative filtering. In Proceedings of the 25th International World Wide Web Conference (WWW), Montreal, QC, Canada, 11–15 May 2016; pp. 507–517.
42. Wei, L.; Hu, D.; Zhou, W.; Tang, X.; Zhang, X.; Wang, X.; Han, J.; Hu, S. Hierarchical interaction networks with rethinking mechanism for document-level sentiment analysis. In Proceedings of the European Conference on Machine Learning and Principles and Practice of Knowledge Discovery in Databases (ECML PKDD), Ghent, Belgium, 14–18 September 2020; pp. 633–649.
43. Zhao, J.; Zhan, Z.; Yang, Q.; Zhang, Y.; Hu, C.; Li, Z.; Zhang, L.; He, Z. Adaptive learning of local semantic and global structure representations for text classification. In Proceedings of the 27th International Conference on Computational Linguistics (COLING), Santa Fe, NM, USA, 20–26 August 2018; pp. 2033–2043.
44. Yang, Z.; Yang, D.; Dyer, C.; He, X.; Hovy, E. Hierarchical attention networks for document classification. In Proceedings of the Conference of the North American Chapter of the Association for Computational Linguistics: Human Language Technologies (NAACL), San Diego, CA, USA, 12–17 June 2016; pp. 1480–1489.
45. Le, H.T.; Cerisara, C.; Denis, A. Do convolutional networks need to be deep for text classification? *arXiv* **2017**, arXiv:1707.04108.
46. Chen, J.; Yu, J.; Zhao, S.; Zhang, Y. User's review habits enhanced hierarchical neural network for document-level sentiment classification. *Neural Process. Lett.* **2021**, *53*, 2095–2111. [CrossRef]
47. Remy, J.-B.; Tixier, A.J.-P.; Vazirgiannis, M. Bidirectional context-aware hierarchical attention network for document understanding. *arXiv* **2019**, arXiv:1908.06006.
48. Wang, H.; Ren, J. A self-attentive hierarchical model for jointly improving text summarization and sentiment classification. In Proceedings of the 10th Asian Conference on Machine Learning (ACML), Beijing, China, 14–16 November 2018; pp. 630–645.
49. Huang, H.; Jin, Y.; Rao, R. Sentiment-aware transformer using joint training. In Proceedings of the 32nd International Conference on Tools with Artificial Intelligence (ICTAI), Baltimore, MD, USA, 9–11 November 2020; pp. 1154–1160.
50. Pennington, J.; Socher, R.; Manning, C.D. GloVe: Global vectors for word representation. In Proceedings of the Conference on Empirical Methods in Natural Language Processing (EMNLP), Doha, Qatar, 25–29 October 2014; pp. 1532–1543.
51. Hinton, G.; Krizhevsky, A.; Sutskever, I.; Salakhutdinov, R.; Srivastava, N. Dropout: A simple way to prevent neural networks from overfitting. *J. Mach. Learn. Res.* **2014**, *15*, 1929–1958.
52. Devlin, J.; Chang, M.W.; Lee, K.; Toutanova, K. BERT: Pre-training of deep bidirectional transformers for language understanding. In Proceedings of the Conference of the North American Chapter of the Association for Computational Linguistics (NAACL), Minneapolis, MN, USA, 2–7 June 2019; pp. 4171–4186.
53. Ding, S.; Shang, J.; Wang, S.; Sun, Y.; Tian, H.; Wu, H.; Wang, H. Ernie-Doc: A retrospective long-document modeling transformer. In Proceedings of the 59th Annual Meeting of the Association for Computational Linguistics and 11th International Joint Conference on Natural Language Processing (ACL-IJCNLP), Bangkok, Thailand, 1–6 August 2021; pp. 2914–2927.
54. Wu, Z.; Dai, X.Y.; Yin, C.; Huang, S.; Chen, J. Improving review representations with user attention and product attention for sentiment classification. In Proceedings of the 32nd Innovative Applications of Artificial Intelligence Conference on Artificial Intelligence (AAAI), New Orleans, LA, USA, 2–7 February 2018; pp. 5989–5996.
55. Fei, H.; Ren, Y.; Wu, S.; Li, B.; Ji, D. Latent target-opinion as prior for document-level sentiment classification: A variational approach from fine-grained perspective. In Proceedings of the 30th World Wide Web Conference (WWW), Ljubljana, Slovenia, 12–23 April 2021; pp. 553–564.

Disclaimer/Publisher's Note: The statements, opinions and data contained in all publications are solely those of the individual author(s) and contributor(s) and not of MDPI and/or the editor(s). MDPI and/or the editor(s) disclaim responsibility for any injury to people or property resulting from any ideas, methods, instructions or products referred to in the content.

Article

PyDTS: A Python Toolkit for Deep Learning Time Series Modelling

Pascal A. Schirmer *,† and Iosif Mporas †

School of Physics, Engineering, and Computer Science, University of Hertfordshire, Hatfield AL10 9AB, UK; i.mporas@herts.ac.uk
* Correspondence: p.schirmer@herts.ac.uk
† These authors contributed equally to this work.

Abstract: In this article, the topic of time series modelling is discussed. It highlights the criticality of analysing and forecasting time series data across various sectors, identifying five primary application areas: denoising, forecasting, nonlinear transient modelling, anomaly detection, and degradation modelling. It further outlines the mathematical frameworks employed in a time series modelling task, categorizing them into statistical, linear algebra, and machine- or deep-learning-based approaches, with each category serving distinct dimensions and complexities of time series problems. Additionally, the article reviews the extensive literature on time series modelling, covering statistical processes, state space representations, and machine and deep learning applications in various fields. The unique contribution of this work lies in its presentation of a Python-based toolkit for time series modelling (PyDTS) that integrates popular methodologies and offers practical examples and benchmarking across diverse datasets.

Keywords: time series modelling; forecasting; nonlinear modelling; denoising; anomaly detection; degradation modelling; deep learning; machine learning

Citation: Schirmer, P.A.; Mporas, I. PyDTS: A Python Toolkit for Deep Learning Time Series Modelling. *Entropy* **2024**, *26*, 311. https://doi.org/10.3390/e26040311

Academic Editors: Shuangming Yang, Shujian Yu, Luis Gonzalo Sánchez Giraldo, Badong Chen and Boris Ryabko

Received: 27 February 2024
Revised: 20 March 2024
Accepted: 29 March 2024
Published: 31 March 2024

Copyright: © 2024 by the authors. Licensee MDPI, Basel, Switzerland. This article is an open access article distributed under the terms and conditions of the Creative Commons Attribution (CC BY) license (https://creativecommons.org/licenses/by/4.0/).

1. Introduction

Time series modelling has gained significant interest in the last decades due to the rise of machine learning and big data. It stands out as a crucial domain with diverse applications, ranging from financial forecasting to climate modelling [1,2]. The ability to analyse and forecast time series data has become increasingly important for timely informed decision making in various fields. Five different areas of applications can mainly be identified: first, denoising (or source separation), where the signal ground truth is isolated from a noisy observation, e.g., speech denoising [3] or separation of energy signals [4]; second, forecasting, where future signal values are predicted based on the signal's history, e.g., grid load or weather forecasting [5]; third, nonlinear transient modelling, where nonlinear and possibly underdetermined problems are solved for time series inputs, e.g., transient thermal, structural, or fluid modelling [6]; fourth, anomaly detection, where outliers are identified in a large population of time series data, e.g., faulty samples in production sequences or failures under thermal/mechanical stress [7]; and fifth, degradation modelling, where a variable changes slowly over time, e.g., ageing of electric components and structures or expiration of food [8,9].

To model the above phenomena in time series signals, several mathematical approaches have been proposed in the literature. These approaches can be fundamentally split into three categories, namely, statistical, linear algebra, and machine- or deep-learning (ML, DL)-based ones. The dimensionality of the problem, i.e., the input and output dimension, as well as the problem evaluation over time, i.e., if the data have a constant mean value, highly determines which of the above techniques can be used to model the time series problem. For example, statistical models like autoregression or moving average processes are restricted to one-dimensional time series and have been applied to linear statistical problems and short-term ahead prediction [10]. Conversely, in the case of two or more variables, linear algebra models like state-space (SS) systems can be used to capture the input and output relation of multidimensional time series [11]. Most recently, machine and deep learning models have been used to capture complex multidimensional and possibly nonlinear relations between input and output samples of time series data [12], like long short-term memory (LSTM) [13], one-dimensional convolutional neural networks (CNNs) [14], or transformer models [15].

The topic of time series modelling has also been studied extensively in the literature. Modelling of statistical processes has been discussed in [16], with specific applications like wind speed modelling [17] or electricity or emission forecasting [18,19]. Similarly, state-space representations have been reviewed in [20]. In detail, state-space models have been proposed for thermal modelling in buildings [21] or battery electric vehicles [22], as well as in methodologies for solar irradiance forecasting in combination with exponential smoothing [23]. Moreover, numerous articles on machine and deep learning have been published covering the topics of feature extraction [24] and modelling approaches [25,26]. In specific, machine and deep learning approaches have been used for forecasting in applications like renewable energies [27], grid loads [28], and weather events [29]. Furthermore, deep learning models have been used for denoising in medical applications [30] and in renewable energy generation [31]. Similarly, nonlinear applications have been studied including structural dynamic problems [32], time delay approximations in optical systems [33], or transient thermal modelling [34]. Deep learning approaches have also been used in anomaly detection [35] and degradation modelling [36]. Most recently, also combinations of these approaches, e.g., deep state space models [37], or informed neural networks have been proposed [38]. Moreover, federated learning applications sharing one common model and approaches implemented on microprocessor hardware have been investigated [39].

Several different toolkits for time series modelling have been proposed previously, including Nixtla [40], AutoTS, Darts [41], and Sktime [42]. Each of these toolkits has a different purpose and different functionalities. While Nixtla and AutoTS only implement time series forecasting, Darts additionally implements anomaly detection, while Sktime implements forecasting, classification, regression, and data transformations. Likewise, PyDTS offers forecasting, classification, and regression functionalities, but additionally focuses on specific applications like denoising, nonlinear modelling, or degradation. The aim is to reduce the threshold of using deep-learning-based modelling as far as possible by offering a one-click functionality without needing to copy code, download, and preprocess data or plot results. The contributions of this article are as follows: First, the topic of time series modelling is reviewed. Second, a Python-based toolkit for time series modelling (PyDTS) with deep learning is presented, which incorporates the most used approaches and provides time series modelling examples for a wide range of datasets and benchmarking results. The results of these examples can be reproduced by calling one single function. Third, the article explains the effect of the free parameters, and the user can try these changes by simply changing one parameter without the need for changing the code while observing the changes based on a standard set of accuracy metrics and plots. Fourth, all results are evaluated on real-world datasets without the use of any synthetic or exemplary datasets. The toolkit is available on GitHub (https://github.com/pascme05/PyDTS, accessed on 27 February 2024).

The remainder of the article is structured as follows: In Section 2, a generalized architecture for time series modelling is described, also introducing the different applications of time series modelling. In Section 3, different modelling approaches are presented. An experimental setup and results for different datasets and applications are presented in Section 4. Finally, discussion and conclusions are provided in Sections 5 and 6, respectively.

2. Time Series Modelling Architecture

As outlined in Section 2, time series modelling has several applications. In this section, a generalized modelling architecture is introduced, while specific approaches including their mathematical formulation are presented in Sections 2.1–2.5. Let us consider an input time series signal $x \in \mathbb{R}^{T \times M}$ with T time samples of M input values each and a multivariate output signal $y \in \mathbb{R}^{T \times N}$ with the same number of time samples and N output values; we can formulate the input–output relation as follows (1):

$$y(t) = f_\Theta(x(t)), \quad (1)$$

where $f_\Theta(\cdot)$ is an arbitrary nonlinear function parametrized by a set of free parameters Θ. The goal of a time series modelling architecture is to model the input and output relation as in (2):

$$\hat{y}(t) = g(x(t)) \\ s.t. \ min\|y - \hat{y}\|_2 \quad (2)$$

where $g(\cdot)$ is an arbitrary regression or classification function aiming to approximate $f_\Theta(\cdot)$ and its free parameters, and $\hat{y} \in \mathbb{R}^{T \times N}$ is the predicted output. The generalized architecture is illustrated in Figure 1:

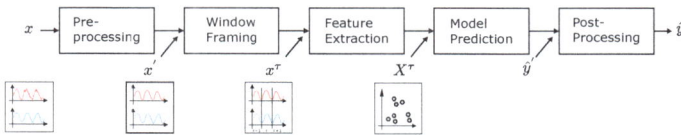

Figure 1. Generalized time series architecture.

As illustrated in Figure 1, the general architecture consists of five steps: first, preprocessing, e.g., resampling or filtering, of the raw feature input vector, x resulting into x'; second, window framing x' into time frames $x^\tau \in \mathbb{R}^{W \times M}$ with a window length W; third, feature extraction based on the time frame signals converting x^τ to a feature input vector $X^\tau \in \mathbb{R}^{W \times F}$ with F input features; and finally, predicting and optionally postprocessing the model output $\hat{y}$. In specific, when predicting time series signals, the input and output relation can be modelled using three different approaches, which can be distinguished by their input and output dimensionality in the temporal domain. The three approaches are sequence-to-point modelling, sequence-to-subsequence modelling, and sequence-to-sequence modelling [43] and are conceptually illustrated in Figure 2.

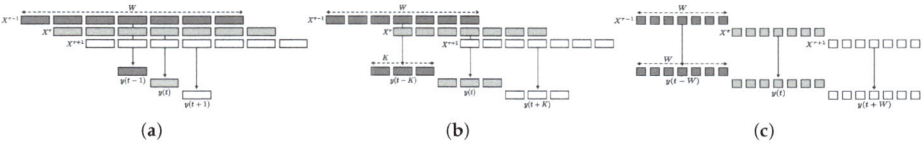

Figure 2. Relation between input and output dimensionality for frame-based time series modelling: (**a**) sequence-to-point, (**b**) sequence-to-subsequence, and (**c**) sequence-to-sequence.

The PyDTS toolkit replicates the above structure, providing modules for preprocessing, framing, feature extraction, modelling approach, and postprocessing. The different modules offered by PyDTS and the flow diagram for the different operations are illustrated in Figures 3 and 4.

In the following, the mathematical formulation of time series modelling with application in denoising, forecasting, nonlinear modelling, anomaly detection, and degradation modelling are provided.

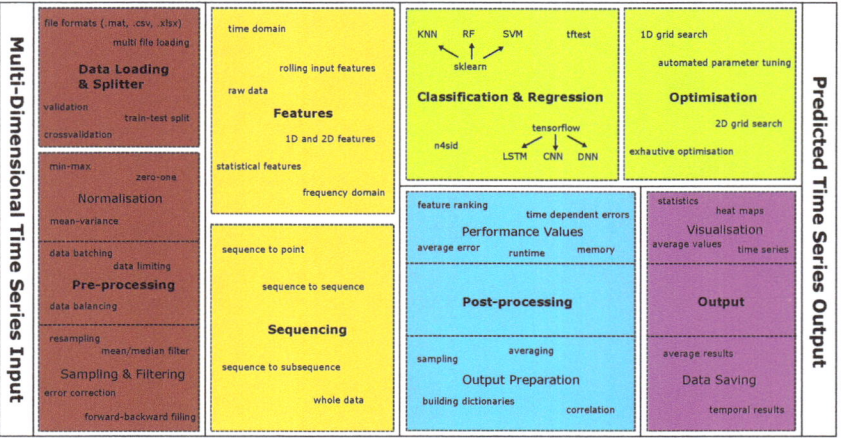

Figure 3. Overview of implemented modules and functionalities in the PyDTS toolkit. Inputs and preprocessing are indicated in red, features and data sequencing in yellow, modelling in green, postprocessing in blue, and visual elements and outputs in purple.

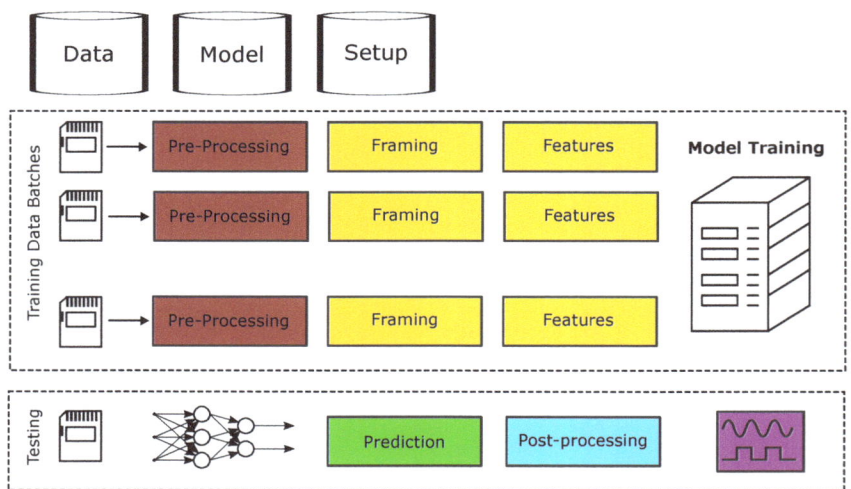

Figure 4. Internal data pipeline of PyDTS including training and testing modules and external data, model, and setup databases.

2.1. Denoising

One of the most common time series prediction tasks is denoising, where the ground-truth data are retrieved based on a distorted observation. Without loss of generality, the problem can be formulated as in (3):

$$y(t) = x(t) + \epsilon(t), \tag{3}$$

where $y(t)$ is the output signal, $x(t)$ is the input signal, and $\epsilon(t)$ is the noise. Here, we use as an example of denoising the energy disaggregation task, where appliance energy signatures (clean signal) are extracted from the aggregated data (noisy signal) [44]. Since multiple signals are extracted from a single observation, it is a single-channel blind source separation problem, i.e., a problem with very high signal-to-noise ratio. The problem can be mathematically formulated as in (4):

$$y(t) = f(x_m(t), \epsilon(t)) = \sum_{m=1}^{M} x_m(t) + \epsilon(t), \qquad (4)$$

where $y(t)$ is the aggregated signal, $x_m(t)$ is the m-th appliance signal, and $\epsilon(t)$ is additive noise from unknown devices, from electromagnetic interference on the transmission lines and from line coupling. The goal is to denoise the signal $y(t)$ by isolating the signature $\hat{x}_m(t)$ of each appliance.

2.2. Forecasting

Load forecasting is a task where future values, e.g., weather, energy consumption, or power draw, are predicted based on previous values of the same time series signal [45]. The aim is to model temporal information based on previous samples and accurately predict future values. Assuming linearity, the problem can be mathematically formulated as in (5):

$$y(t) = \alpha y(t-1) + \beta x(t) + \epsilon(t), \qquad (5)$$

where $y(t)$ is the signal of interest, $x(t)$ are signals with additional information and α, β are constant in the linear case, and $\epsilon(t)$ is stochastic noise. In this article, energy consumption prediction has been used as an example; i.e., future energy consumption values are predicted based on the consumption of previous days and additional information, e.g., weather or socioeconomic information [46].

2.3. Nonlinear Modelling

Nonlinear modelling is a task where the relation between input and output values is nonlinear. As an example application of nonlinear modelling, thermal modelling of power electronics and electric machinery is considered [47]. In this application, the fundamental heat conduction equation itself is linear, but nonlinearities are introduced through thermal coupling or losses, which are themselves a nonlinear function of temperature. Fundamentally, the temperature on a component can be modelled as in (6) and (7):

$$\dot{q}(t) = R(\vartheta) \cdot I_{rms}^2, \qquad (6)$$

where $\dot{q}(t)$ is a time-dependent heat source that is generated by a current I_{rms} flowing through a nonlinear temperature-dependent resistance $R(\vartheta)$. The temperature is then calculated using (7):

$$\rho c_p \frac{\partial T}{\partial t} - \nabla \cdot (k \nabla T) = \dot{q}(t) \varphi(\vec{r}), \qquad (7)$$

where ρ is the mass density, c_p the specific heat capacity, and k the thermal conductivity. Furthermore, $\varphi(\vec{r})$ is a spatial function projecting the heat source $\dot{q}(t)$ on the respective volume.

2.4. Anomaly Detection

Anomaly detection describes the task of finding outliers within the data. Often, these data are highly unbalanced; i.e., there are much more positive than negative values or vice versa. The aim is to efficiently detect a small number of outliers within large amounts of time series data. The problem can be mathematically formulated as follows (8):

$$\hat{y}(t) = \varphi(f_\Theta(x(t))), \qquad (8)$$

where $\hat{y}(t) \in {0, 1}$ is the anomaly detection status of the signal; i.e., if a sample at time t is normal or anomalous, $x(t)$ are the input signals that provide indication for the status signal, $f(\cdot)$ is a function calculating the probability for a sample to be anomalous, and $\varphi(\cdot)$

is a threshold to convert the prediction into a binary variable. In this article, we used as an example model motor faults based on vibration data.

2.5. Degradation Modelling

Degradation modelling is a task where a relation between input parameters, time, and slow-varying output parameters exists. The aim is to describe the slow-varying degradation based on the initial state and the loads applied over time. The problem can be mathematically formulated as in (9):

$$y(t) = y_0 + \beta x(t) + \epsilon(t), \tag{9}$$

where $y(t)$ is the degradation signal; $x(t)$ are load signals stressing the component, e.g., temperature or mechanical stress; and $\epsilon(t)$ is stochastic noise. It must be noted that this problem depends on the initial state of y_0. In this article, the example case is to predict degradation data of lithium-ion batteries, i.e., the change of cell capacitance over time, using temperature, current, and voltage as input features.

3. Modelling Approaches

To implement the classification or regression function $f(\cdot)$ from (1), three approaches exist, namely, statistical, linear algebra, and machine or deep learning (ML, DL). In the following subsections, each of these three approaches is briefly explained.

3.1. Statistical Modelling

Assuming that the output function $y(t)$ is a one-dimensional time series and only depends on previous values $y(t-1)$ and stochastic white noise $\epsilon(t)$, then the relation between input and output can be expressed using statistical models based on autoregression and averaging (ARMA) [48], as described in (10):

$$y(t) = c + \sum_{i=1}^{p} \phi_i y(t-1) + \sum_{j=1}^{q} \theta_j \epsilon(t-j) + \epsilon(t), \tag{10}$$

where c is a constant, ϕ_i is a weighting factor for the autoregression term, and θ_j is a weighting factor for the moving average.

3.2. Linear Algebra Modelling

If there are two processes, with one process being latent, thus describing a hidden time-varying structure, state-space representations have been used for the system identification of first-order systems with M inputs and N outputs [49]. The mathematical formulation for continuous parameter time-invariant coefficients is shown in (11):

$$\dot{s}(t) = As(t) + Bx(t) \tag{11a}$$

$$y(t) = Cs(t) + Dx(t) \tag{11b}$$

where $s(t) \in \mathbb{R}^L$ and $\dot{s}(t) \in \mathbb{R}^L$ are the internal system states and the derivatives with L being the number of states, $A \in \mathbb{R}^{L \times L}$ is the system matrix, $B \in \mathbb{R}^{L \times M}$ is the input matrix, $C \in \mathbb{R}^{N \times L}$ is the output matrix, and $D \in \mathbb{R}^{N \times M}$ is the feed-forward matrix. This model belongs to the category of white box modelling [50], where the states and the evolution of the states can be physically interpreted and, most importantly, also observed (12) and controlled (13) if the following restrictions are satisfied [49]:

$$rank\left[B,\ AB,\ A^2B, \ldots, A^{n-1}B\right] = L, \tag{12}$$

$$rank \begin{bmatrix} C \\ CA \\ \vdots \\ CA^{n-1} \end{bmatrix} = L, \qquad (13)$$

3.3. Machine and Deep Learning

While the above techniques have limitations regarding the dimensionality of the input and output channels or the nonlinearity of the relation between input and output features, machine and deep learning models offer the highest flexibility in modelling an arbitrary function. In detail, the output of an artificial neural network with one hidden layer is shown in (14):

$$\hat{y}_n(t) = \varphi_2 \left(\sum_{j=1}^{J} w_{nj}^{(2)} \varphi_1 \left(\sum_{m=1}^{M} w_{jm}^{(1)} x_m(t) \right) \right), \qquad (14)$$

where $\varphi_{1,2}(\cdot)$ and $w_{1,2}$ are the activation functions and the weights of the respective layer, and J is the number of nodes in the hidden layer. The weights can then be determined iteratively using backpropagation and a loss function, as shown in (15):

$$E = \frac{1}{2n} \sum_x \|y - \hat{y}\|_2^2, \qquad (15)$$

3.4. Comparison

Each of the above modelling approaches has its advantages and disadvantages. A comparison list of relevant properties is shown in Table 1. Whenever, the respective property can be deducted directly from the model equation in Sections 3.1–3.3, e.g., the dimensionality of the input/output or the interpretability of the internal state. Table 1 lists the respective equation; otherwise, relevant literature is provided.

Table 1. Comparison of relevant properties between different modelling approaches: (+): comparatively better, (o): neutral, and (-): comparatively worse.

Properties	Ref. and Eq.	Linear Algebra	Statistical Modelling	Machine Learning
Runtime	[51]	o	+	-
Memory	[51]	o	+	-
Interpretability	(12)–(14)	+	o	-
Dimensionality	(10), (11), (14)	o	-	+
Transferability	[52]	o	-	+
Nonlinear	(10), (11), (14)	o	-	+
Hyperparameters	(10), (11), (14)	o	+	-
Training data	[53]	+	o	-

As can be seen in Table 1, machine and deep learning approaches suffer especially from larger computational complexity, memory requirements, and a lack of physical interpretation of the model parameters [50,51]. Statistical models present advantages, but at the same time, they are limited in 1D-only input and output dimensionality [48], as can be also seen from (10). This restriction makes statistical modelling approaches not feasible for most of the presented tasks in Section 2. In terms of transferability, deep learning approaches have very good transferability properties working as automated feature extraction engines [52]; however, they require extensive amounts of training data and have many hyperparameters to optimize [50,53]. Finally, as explained in Section 3.3, machine and deep learning models enable nonlinear modelling due to the nonlinear activation functions in (14). Because of the limitation of statistical and linear algebra models with respect to the input and output dimension in the following sections, the focus will be on machine and deep learning approaches.

4. Experimental Setup

The time series modelling architecture described in Section 2 was evaluated using the datasets, models, and experimental protocols presented below.

4.1. Datasets

The proposed time series prediction methods have been evaluated using publicly available datasets consisting of real-world data; i.e., no synthetic data have been used. In the following, each of the datasets is briefly explained. For disaggregation energy data (denoising), the AMPds2 dataset has been used, which includes 20 electrical appliances and the aggregated energy consumption of a Canadian household measured between 2012 and 2014 [54]. For energy consumption forecasting, the energy consumption of Tetouan, a city in the north of Morocco, has been used [55]. For nonlinear modelling, the motor temperature dataset in [47] has been used, which includes 185 h of measured temperatures of a state-of-the-art permanent magnet synchronous machine from a Tesla Model 3. To predict anomalies, motor vibration data have been used, which were previously classified into faulty and faultless motors [56]. To model degradation, the dataset from [57] was used, which includes lithium-ion battery cells measured over several cycles of charging and discharging under different conditions. The datasets, including their most important properties, are summarized in Table 2.

Table 2. Short description of the datasets. The feature column includes the following abbreviations: active power (P), reactive power (Q), apparent power (S), current (I), voltage (V), temperature (T), relative humidity (RH), solar irradiance (IRR), wind speed (Ws), rotational speed (n), torque (M), and acceleration (A). Similarly, the outputs include the appliance current (I_{app}), the per-phase power (P_{L_x}), the stator winding and rotor magnet temperatures (ϑ), the motor state, and the remaining battery charge (Q_{bat}).

Name	Ref.	Scenario	Length	Sampling	Features	Output	Max	Mean	Std
AMPds2	[54]	Denoise	2 y	60 s	P, Q, S, I	I_{app}	105	0.8	10.9
Energy	[55]	Forecast	1 y	10 min	$P, T, RH, Ws\ Irr$	P_{L_1, L_2, L_3}	52.2	23.7	12.2
Motor Temp.	[47]	Nonlinear	185 h	0.5 s	V, I, T, M, n	ϑ	141.4	57.5	22.7
Ford Motor	[56]	Anomaly	1.4 h	2 ms	$A_{x,y,z}$	s	1.0	0.49	0.50
Battery Health	[57]	Degradation	57 days	2.5 s	V, I, T	Q_{bat}	1.92	1.54	0.17

As can be seen in Table 2, the datasets cover a wide range of sampling frequencies, total number of samples, and input features, allowing for testing the PyDTS toolkit on different data inputs. Additionally, for the input features, the output that will be predicted is shown, as well as the max, mean, and standard deviation of the output. These values are included to provide a standard to the performance of the regression or classification models. For example, if the standard deviation of a dataset is close to zero, there are very few changes in the output signal; thus, a naive predictor would be sufficient to predict the outputs. Similarly, if the maximum predicted error of a model is equal to the maximum value of the output signal, while the average is close to zero, that indicates that the model is predicting well on average, but there are instances in which it fails to make an accurate prediction.

4.2. Preprocessing

During preprocessing, the input data have been normalized using mean–std normalization for input features (16):

$$x' = \frac{x - \mu_{train}}{\sigma_{train}}, \tag{16}$$

where x' is the input feature scaled by the mean (μ_{train}) and standard deviation (σ_{train}) of the training data. Similarly, min–max normalization has been used for the output features (17):

$$y' = \frac{y - min(y_{train})}{max(y_{train}) - min(y_{train})}, \qquad (17)$$

where y' is the output feature scaled by the minimum and maximum values of the training data. Furthermore, the optimal number of samples for the input window has been determined by grid search for each of the datasets tabulated in Table 1 with the exception of the anomaly detection as it is predefined in that dataset. The results are shown in Figure 5.

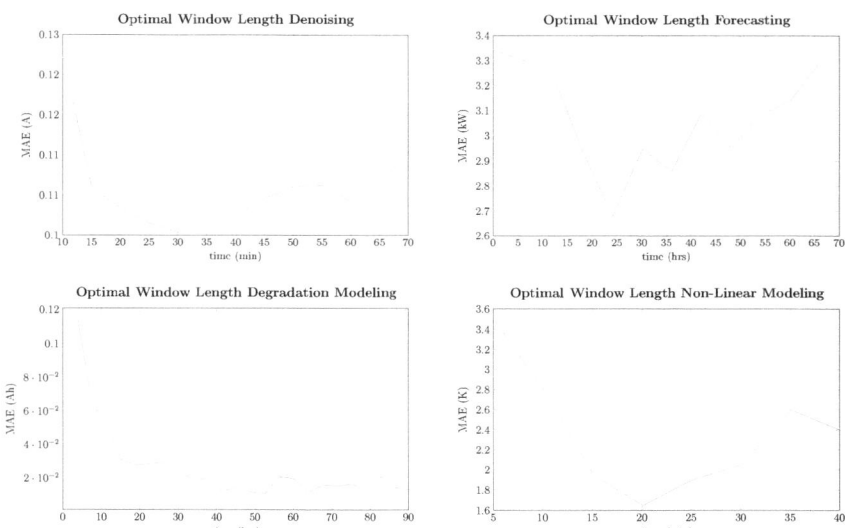

Figure 5. Grid search for the optimal number of input samples depending on the time series problem.

As can be seen in Figure 5, the optimal number of input samples strongly varies with the problem under investigation. In detail, when denoising electrical appliances signatures, the optimal input length is around 30 min, which is a typical operational duration for electrical appliances [58]. For the forecasting of electrical power consumption, the optimal input length was found to be around 24 h, which is typical due to working and living habits. It can also be observed that at around 12 h, 36 h, and 48 h, there are significant improvements. For modelling degradation data, no upper limit could be found since the degradation is a slow-varying property and it would be best to feed the complete degradation cycle at once, which is not possible due to the number of samples. The optimal input length for modelling the thermal behaviour of the electrical machine was found to be 20 min, which is in the order of the thermal time constant of the machine, and it is in line with [59]. Unless otherwise stated, the modelling approaches are based on sequence-to-point modelling using the optimized length of input samples from Figure 5, with one sample overlap between consecutive frames.

4.3. Model Structure and Parametrization

To implement the regression function $f(\cdot)$ for the approaches discussed in Section 2, different ML and DL approaches have been used. For ML approaches especially, random forest (RF) and K-nearest neighbours (KNN) have been evaluated, while for anomaly detection, also support vector machine (SVM) has been tested. The free parameters have been found using exhaustive automated parameter optimization on a bootstrap training dataset. The results are presented in Table 3.

Table 3. Optimized model parameters for ML approaches including KNN, RF, and SVM.

Model	Parameter	Optimal	Range	Step
KNN	Neighbors	140	10–200	5
RF	Max. Depth	10	5-25	5
	Split	4	2–10	2
	#-Trees	128	2–256	2^n
SVM	Kernel	rbf	linear, rbf, poly	-
	C	100	1–200	20
	Gamma	0.1	0.001–1	10^n

Similarly, for DL models, DNN, LSTM, and CNN architectures have been evaluated. The architectures are illustrated in Figure 6.

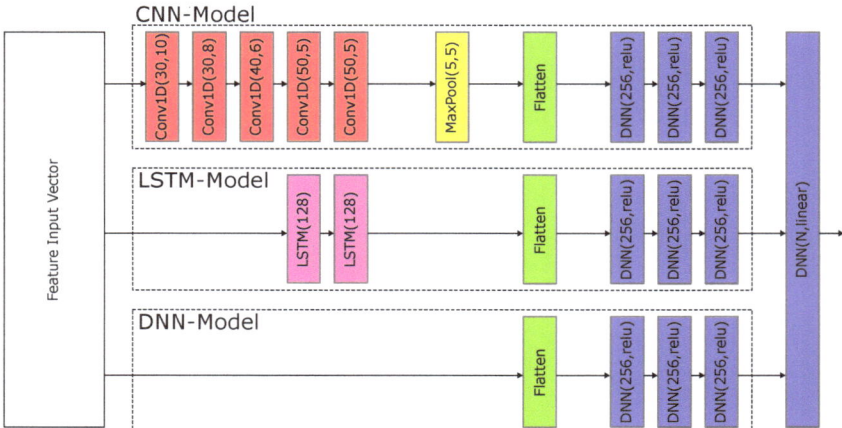

Figure 6. DL layer architectures for DNNs, LSTM, and CNN models. For CNNs, the notation of the convolutional layer is Conv1D(x,y) with x being the number of filters and y being the kernel size. For pooling layers MaxPool(x,y), x is the size and y the stride, while for LSTM and DNN layers, x denotes the number of neurons.

Unless otherwise stated, the above architectures have been used when being referred to CNN, LSTM, and DNN. For specific applications, the free parameters, i.e., the number of hidden layers, neurons, the kernel sizes, and the filters, have been optimized using the hyperband tuner from Keras. Additionally, the hyperparameters and solver parameters tabulated in Table 4 have been used.

Table 4. Hyper- and solver parameters for deep learning models including DNN, CNN, and LSTM.

Hyperparameters		Solver Parameters	
Batch	1000	optimizer	adam
Epochs	50–200	loss	mae
Patience	15	Learning rate	1×10^{-3}
Validation steps	50	Beta1	0.9
Shuffle	False	Beta2	0.999

5. Experimental Results

In this section, the experimental results are presented when using the data, the parametrizations, and models from Section 4. The results are evaluated in terms mean absolute error (MAE), root mean square error (RMSE), mean square error (MSE), and the normalized mean square error (NMSE):

$$\text{MAE} = \frac{1}{T} \sum_{t=1}^{T} |y(t) - \hat{y}(t)|, \tag{18}$$

$$\text{RMSE} = \sqrt{\text{MSE}} = \sqrt{\frac{1}{T} \sum_{t=1}^{T} (y(t) - \hat{y}(t))^2}, \tag{19}$$

$$\text{NMSE} = 1 - \frac{\sum_{t=1}^{T} |y(t) - \hat{y}(t)|}{2 \cdot \sum_{t=1}^{T} |y(t)|}, \tag{20}$$

where $y(t)$ is the true signal, $\hat{y}(t)$ is the predicted value, and T is the total number of samples. Since not all modelling approaches are applicable for each of the scenarios, due to their limitations with respect to the input and output dimensionality, the following results are presented for machine and deep learning approaches. Each of these approaches can be reproduced with the PyDTS toolkit using the predefined configuration stored under the setup directory (https://github.com/pascme05/PyDTS/tree/main/setup/journal, accessed on 26 February 2024). Unless otherwise stated, the results were calculated using fivefold cross-validation using 10% of the training data for validation.

5.1. Denoising

For the denoising task, the energy of a Canadian household [54] has been disaggregated; i.e., the appliance-specific energy consumption has been extracted based on the observation of the total energy consumption of the household. Specifically, we focused on five different appliances: the dishwasher (DWE), the fridge (FRE), the heat pump (HPE), the wall oven (WOE), and the cloth dryer (CDE). For input features, active power (P), reactive power (Q), apparent power (S), and current (I) were used, while the output feature was the current for each device. The average results for all the five appliances and different machine and deep learning models are tabulated in Table 5.

Table 5. Average results (A) for the energy disaggregation task for fivefold cross-validation using different models and accuracy metrics. The best performances are indicated with bold notation.

Model	NMSE	RMSE	MSE	MAE	MAX
CNN	92.48	0.64	0.41	0.08	29.01
LSTM	**94.51**	**0.60**	**0.36**	**0.08**	30.54
DNN	94.39	0.66	0.44	0.08	31.85
RF	81.39	0.63	0.40	0.10	**28.60**
KNN	74.11	1.15	1.32	0.21	31.09

As can be seen in Table 5, LSTM outperforms all other regression models for all accuracy metrics except for the maximum error. In this scenario, only 1D time series inputs were used to disaggregate the signals, and LSTM has shown outperforming results in application with 1D time series, including temporal information, i.e., where future samples depend on previous samples. Furthermore, the results for the best-performing model (LSTM) have been evaluated at the device level and are presented in Table 6.

As can be seen in Table 6, all appliances show low disaggregation errors, except the dishwasher, which shows poor performance that could be attributed to its lower activity, which is in line with other approaches reported on the same dataset [58]. Moreover, the results have been compared with the state-of-the-art approaches in the literature. The results are presented in Table 7.

Table 6. Per-device results (A) for the energy disaggregation task for fivefold cross-validation using LSTM as regression model and different accuracy metrics.

Device	NMSE	RMSE	MSE	MAE	MAX
DWE	49.79	0.87	0.76	0.12	6.76
FRE	95.15	0.24	0.06	0.13	3.41
HPE	97.55	0.63	0.40	0.07	7.21
WOE	91.50	0.63	0.40	0.03	30.61
CDE	97.66	0.62	0.38	0.02	40.73
Avg	94.51	0.60	0.36	0.08	30.54

Table 7. Comparison with the literature for the energy disaggregation task.

Ref.	Year	Model	NMSE	RMSE	MAE
[60]	2016	HMM	94.1%	-	-
[61]	2019	CNN	93.9%	-	-
[62]	2020	CNN	94.7%	-	-
[58]	2021	CNN	95.8%	-	-
[43]	2022	CNN	94.7%	0.48	0.06
This Work	2023	LSTM	94.5%	0.60	0.08

As can be seen in Table 7, the PyDTS toolkit reports results similar to the ones from previously reported approaches on the same dataset and is only outperformed by specifically optimized approaches for the energy disaggregation task. Moreover, a set of numerical predictions and ground-truth data is illustrated in Figure 7 for the best-performing LSTM model from PyDTS. In detail, a 12 h period with high appliance activity on 9 January 2013 at 12:00 p.m. was selected, where FRE, HPE, and CDE are active at the same time.

As can be seen in Figure 7, the LSTM model is able to extract all three appliance signatures from the aggregated data with high accuracy. There are only minor errors during the active periods where the current ripple is not precisely predicted.

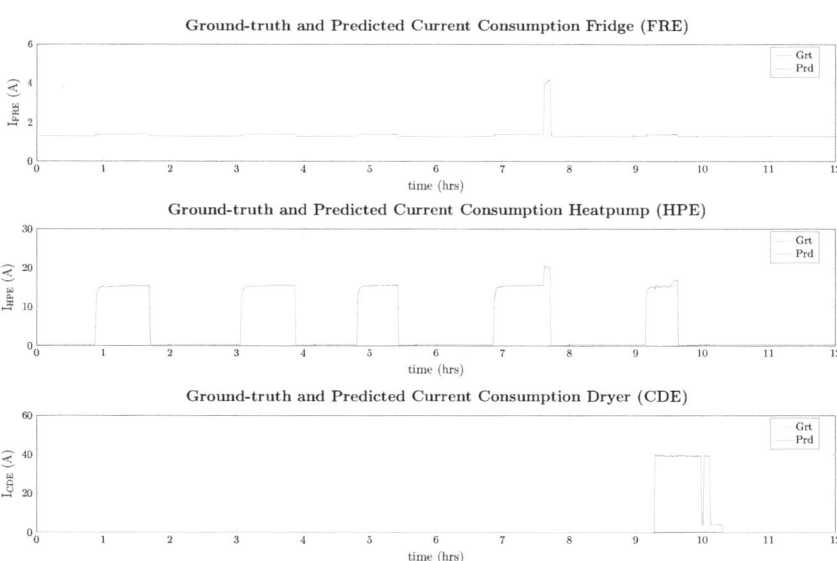

Figure 7. Predicted appliance current draw for 12 h for three different (FRE, HPE, and CDE) appliances from the AMPds2 dataset on 9 January 2013 at 12:00 p.m.

5.2. Forecasting

For the forecasting task, the energy consumption of a city in Morocco [55] has been used. As input features, the previous power consumption values of the three-phase grid have been chosen. Additionally, these values have been extended by environmental features, namely, the ambient temperature, the wind speed, the relative humidity, and the solar irradiance. The output feature, which is predicted, is the power consumption on phase-leg L1. The results for an ahead forecast of 24 h are presented for different regression models in Table 8 using Seq2Point and in Table 9 using Seq2Seq approaches.

Table 8. Forecasting errors (kW) using Seq2Point for a 24 h ahead prediction window with different models and accuracy metrics using fivefold cross-validation. The best performances are indicated with bold notation.

Model	NMSE	RMSE	MSE	MAE	MAX
CNN	95.72	3.62	13.10	2.77	18.49
LSTM	95.55	3.85	14.82	2.88	18.19
DNN	95.61	3.74	13.99	2.85	17.90
RF	**97.50**	**2.42**	**5.87**	**1.60**	**17.88**
KNN	93.98	4.96	24.60	3.88	18.63

Table 9. Forecasting errors (kW) using Seq2Seq for a 24 h ahead prediction window with different models and accuracy metrics using fivefold cross-validation. The best performances are indicated with bold notation.

Model	NMSE	RMSE	MSE	MAE	MAX
CNN	95.88	3.54	12.53	2.67	18.61
LSTM	**95.99**	**3.01**	**9.06**	**2.36**	**12.12**
DNN	95.66	3.71	13.76	2.81	17.26

As can be seen in Tables 8 and 9, Seq2Seq approaches outperform Seq2Point approaches for all deep learning approaches with LSTM being able to capture the temporal relation reporting an average error equal to 2.36 kW. However, when considering Seq2Point approaches, RF shows improved performance reporting an average error of 1.60 kW but showing a significantly higher maximum error of 17.88 kW compared with the best-performing LSTM approach, which has a maximum error of 12.12 kW. The best performance is illustrated for 1 week in Figure 8.

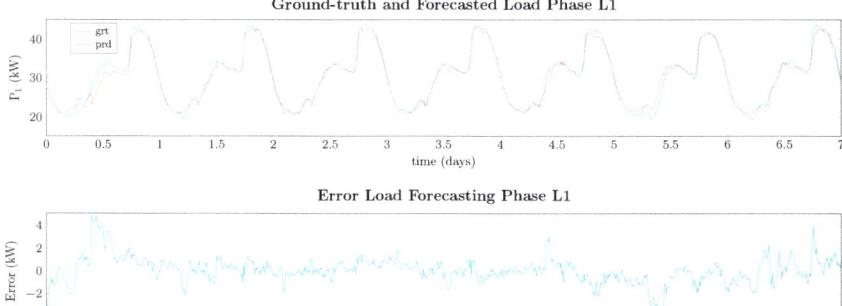

Figure 8. Forecasted power consumption and error for phase L1 for 1 week using RF as regression model.

As can be seen in Figure 8, the predicted power consumption is close to the actual value with errors between 1 and 5 kW. Interestingly, the errors at the beginning and ending of the week are higher than at the middle of the week, which is probably due to a higher fluctuation of power demand at these times.

5.3. Nonlinear Modelling

For the nonlinear modelling task, the temperature prediction of a permanent magnet synchronous machine [47] has been considered. In detail, four different temperature hot spots have been evaluated, namely, the stator winding, the stator tooth, the stator yoke, and the magnet temperature inside the rotor. As input features, the ambient and the coolant temperature, the stator current and voltages, and the mechanical torque as well as the rotational speed have been used. The output is the maximum stator winding (ϑ_{sw}) and the rotor magnet (ϑ_{pm}) temperature. The results in terms of MAE, RMSE, and MAX error are tabulated in Table 10 for stator and rotor temperatures, respectively.

Table 10. Temperature prediction results for 5-fold cross validation using different regression models and performance metrics. Due to memory restrictions the LSTM input was reduced to 500 samples. The best performances are indicated with bold notation.

Model	NMSE		RMSE		MSE		MAE		MAX	
	ϑ_{sw}	ϑ_{pm}	ϑ_{sw}	ϑ_{pm}	ϑ_{sw}	ϑ_{pm}	ϑ_{sw}	ϑ_{pm}	ϑ_{sw}	ϑ_{pm}
CNN	97.67	95.19	**4.54**	**7.59**	**20.61**	**57.61**	**3.06**	5.53	76.43	54.18
LSTM	96.71	93.23	6.39	10.6	40.83	112.4	4.28	7.85	77.15	60.05
DNN	**97.37**	**95.21**	5.32	7.81	28.30	61.00	3.43	5.59	76.52	59.20
RF	96.04	94.66	7.63	8.30	58.22	68.89	5.26	**4.43**	**73.73**	**47.87**
KNN	86.40	89.85	22.79	14.98	519.4	224.4	17.39	11.45	82.24	57.96

As can be seen in Table 10, the rotor temperature shows worse performances across all models in terms of accuracy as its losses and thus temperatures are much more difficult to model based on the available inputs. Furthermore, deep learning models outperform machine learning models due to their ability to better capture the nonlinear relationship between the input feature vector and the temperature rise of the electric machine. To further compare the results, the experiments from [59] have been repeated using the same split for training, testing, and validation data. The results for the best-performing CNN model are tabulated in Table 11.

Table 11. Results for MSE (K²) and MAX (K) errors for different testing IDs, their respective time (hr), and temperature hot spots using a CNN regression model per hot spot.

ID	Time	Stator Winding		Stator Tooth		Stator Yoke		Magnet	
		MSE	MAX	MSE	MAX	MSE	MAX	MSE	MAX
60	1.7	2.41	5.03	1.68	4.28	1.16	3.14	22.62	9.90
62	3.3	2.75	6.23	1.25	3.78	1.22	3.96	17.49	9.74
74	3.0	3.33	6.18	2.42	5.43	1.80	5.00	14.47	10.81
Avg	8.0	2.90	6.23	1.78	5.43	1.42	5.00	17.45	10.81

As can be seen in Table 11, the difficulty in estimating the temperatures in the different test IDs varies significantly, with the lowest errors being found in test ID 62 and the highest in test ID 72. On average, the results are better for the stator temperatures, which is in line with the input features being mostly stator quantities. In Figure 9, the temperature predictions for stator winding and magnet temperature are illustrated for all three testing IDs.

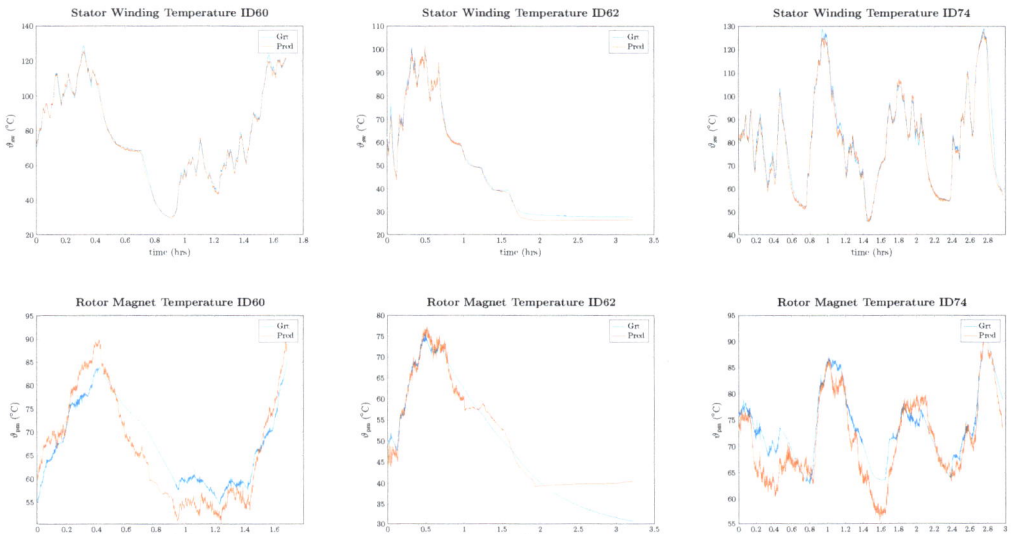

Figure 9. Predicted temperature for stator winding and rotor magnet for IDs 60, 62, and 72.

As can be seen in Figure 9, stator temperatures are much better predicted than rotor temperatures. Especially during heat-up and cool-down phases, the rotor temperature is not correctly predicted. This is probably due to the change in the heat transfer coefficient and the fact that the rotor is thermally isolated through the air gap; thus, the heat path is not based on heat conduction as in the stator, but a combination of heat convection and conduction. To compare the results with the previously published literature, a comparison of average errors was made in Table 12.

As can be seen in Table 12, the results obtained from the baseline CNN model implemented in PyDTS are comparable to the results obtained from other machine or deep learning architectures. Only physical informed approaches like thermal neural networks [59] perform significantly better.

Table 12. Comparison for temperature prediction using different models and number of input features.

Ref.	Year	Model	MSE	MAX	Features
[63]	2021	MLP	5.58	14.29	81
[63]	2021	OLS	4.47	9.85	81
[47]	2020	CNN	4.43	15.54	81
[59]	2023	TNN	2.87	6.02	5
This Work	2023	CNN	5.89	10.81	13

5.4. Anomaly Detection

For the anomaly detection task, the vibration data of combustion engines, in normal and faulty states, have been used. As an input feature, the acceleration signal has been used, while the output is a binary variable indicating the healthy or faulty state of the motor [56]. Since, in this dataset, the training and test scenarios are presplit, the results will not be presented for fivefold cross-validation as in the previous experiments but using the predefined splitting of the data. In detail, the results were calculated three times, using raw input samples of the acceleration data, using statistical features of the acceleration data (mean, min, max, std, range, etc.) [44], and using frequency domain features (e.g., magnitudes of the Fourier transform signal or wavelets) [64,65]. The results in terms of accuracy (ACC) and F1-score (F1) are tabulated in Table 13 for different classification models.

Table 13. Classification results in terms of ACC and F1 for anomaly detection using different classification models. The best performances are indicated with bold notation.

Model	Raw		Statistical		Frequency	
	ACC	F1	ACC	F1	ACC	F1
CNN	**92.35**	**92.34**	56.52	55.87	**94.85**	**94.85**
LSTM	51.06	50.52	55.30	54.90	51.59	35.12
DNN	80.15	80.15	56.52	56.13	94.77	94.77
RF	72.80	72.77	**59.09**	**59.10**	92.42	92.42
KNN	72.80	72.76	58.11	58.12	88.94	88.90
SVM	51.59	35.12	58.41	58.01	94.47	94.47

As can be seen in Table 13, DL approaches clearly outperform ML-based approaches when using raw data operating as automated feature extraction engines. ML techniques show good results on frequency domain features as the relevant information is extracted when computing the Fourier coefficients. When using statistical features, none of the classification models can perform well, as the averaging effect in the time domain eliminates the vibration signatures discriminating healthy and faulty samples. To give more insights into the prediction accuracy, the confusion matrix of the best-performing CNN model is illustrated in Figure 10 for all three different feature setups.

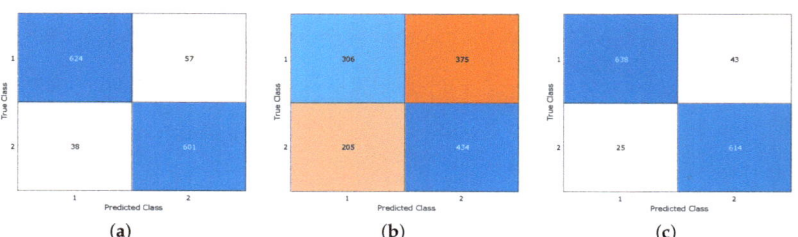

Figure 10. Confusion matrices for (**a**) raw, (**b**) statistical, and (**c**) frequency domain features for the CNN model.

5.5. Degradation Modelling

For the degradation modelling task, the ageing data of lithium-ion battery cells [57] have been used during charging and discharging. As input features, the cell current and voltage as well as the cell temperature have been used. The output is the degradation curve of the maximum remaining cell capacity for each charging and discharging cycle. The results for different regression models and accuracy metrics are tabulated in Table 14 for Seq2Point learning and in Table 15 for Seq2Seq learning. It must be noted that machine learning approaches are not able to perform Seq2Seq learning due to their restriction of the input dimensionality.

Table 14. Degradation errors for different regression models and performance metrics using Seq2Point learning. The best performances are indicated with bold notation.

Model	NMSE	RMSE	MSE	MAE	MAX
CNN	98.00	0.08	0.01	0.06	0.36
LSTM	97.85	0.08	0.01	0.07	0.39
DNN	**98.64**	**0.06**	**0.01**	**0.04**	0.49
RF	95.15	0.16	0.03	0.15	0.38
KNN	97.43	0.10	0.01	0.08	**0.35**

Table 15. Degradation errors for different regression models and performance metrics using Seq2Seq learning. The best performances are indicated with bold notation.

Model	NMSE	RMSE	MSE	MAE	MAX
CNN	**98.26**	**0.07**	**0.01**	**0.05**	**0.34**
LSTM	97.74	0.09	0.01	0.07	0.41
DNN	97.85	0.09	0.01	0.07	0.41

As can be seen in Tables 14 and 15, deep learning approaches are significantly outperforming machine learning approaches due to their ability to model longer temporal characteristics. In detail, DNNs outperform all other models for all performance metrics except for the maximum error. The predicted degradation curve is illustrated in Figure 11.

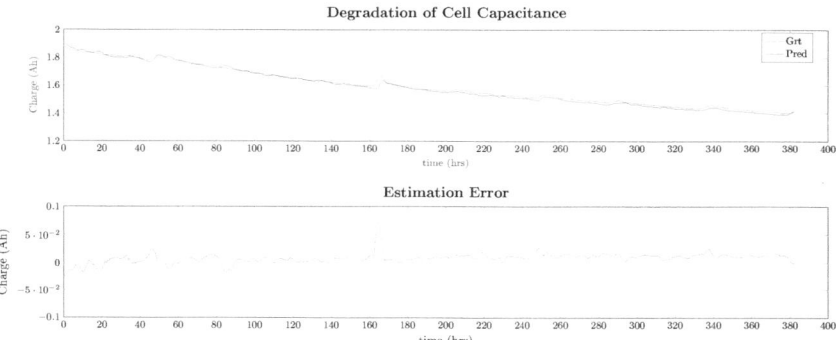

Figure 11. Ground-truth and predicted remaining cell charge and prediction error using the best-performing DNN model (for visibility, the predicted output has been filtered with a median filter of a length of 100 samples).

As shown in Figure 11, the predicted output closely follows the measured degradation curve and is also capturing the frequent relaxation of the cell material, e.g., after 50 h. The maximum error is approximately 0.075 Ah being 12.3% of the remaining cell capacitance. On average, the model is underestimating the remaining capacity with around 0.01 Ah being 1.7% of the average cell capacitance.

6. Discussion

In this section, discussion on transferability is provided in Section 6.1, execution time and model size in Section 6.2, and model optimization and model order reduction in Section 6.3.

6.1. Transfer Learning

In transfer learning, the aim is to predict the output of new data based on a model that was pretrained on other data for a usually similar application. Two different approaches are investigated, namely, the intratransferability and the intertransferability. During intratransferability, the new data come from the same data domain, e.g., a different phase of the same electrical grid, while in intertransferability, the data only come from the same application domain, e.g., the same type of electrical appliance in a different consumer household. Both types of transferability will be considered in this subsection. The intratransferability setup is based on the electrical load forecasting of Section 5.2, predicting the load of phase 2 using a model trained on phase 1. The intertransferability setup is based on the disaggregation setup of Section 5.1 and [52], extracting the load signatures of a fridge, microwave, and dishwasher in a different household using the REDD dataset [66] (houses 1 and 2). The results for the intratransferability setup are tabulated in Table 16.

Table 16. Intratransferability scenario based on load forecasting between phases 1 (L1) and 2 (L2). The best performances are indicated with bold notation.

Model	L2 (Train L2)			L2 (Train L1)			Loss (%)		
	NMSE	RMSE	MAE	NMSE	RMSE	MAE	NMSE	RMSE	MAE
CNN	92.02	4.22	3.36	87.61	6.34	5.19	4.79	50.24	54.46
LSTM	93.21	3.58	2.81	92.88	3.70	2.94	**0.35**	**3.35**	**4.63**
DNN	92.81	3.86	3.03	87.44	6.40	5.25	5.79	65.80	73.27
RF	**96.02**	**2.35**	**1.71**	**93.28**	**3.44**	**2.78**	2.85	46.38	62.57
KNN	91.66	4.37	3.49	89.07	5.58	4.56	2.83	27.69	30.66

As can be seen in Table 16, the performance when predicting phase 2 based on a model of phase 1 leads to a decrease in all evaluated accuracy metrics and all regression models with a loss between 0.35% and 73.27%. However, due to the data coming from the same domain, the average accuracy is still relatively high between 87.44% and 93.28%. In detail, LSTM shows better performance capturing the temporal information of phase 1 and transferring it to phase 2, showing significantly lowest loss in accuracy by only 0.35–4.63%. The results for the intertransferability setup are tabulated in Table 17.

Table 17. Intertransferability scenario based on energy disaggregation between different consumer households (REDD-1,2). The best performances are indicated with bold notation.

Model	REDD2 (Train REDD2)			REDD2 (Train REDD1)			Loss (%)		
	NMSE	RMSE	MAE	NMSE	RMSE	MAE	NMSE	RMSE	MAE
CNN	**92.60**	39.44	**5.45**	**76.12**	70.83	**16.57**	16.48	79.59	204.0
LSTM	86.65	84.36	9.83	71.26	94.88	19.95	15.39	**12.47**	**102.9**
DNN	85.02	76.83	11.03	55.19	106.4	31.10	29.83	38.49	181.9
RF	89.19	41.38	7.96	75.88	**67.77**	16.74	**13.31**	63.77	110.3
KNN	92.48	**31.32**	5.54	70.09	79.57	20.76	22.39	154.1	274.7

As can be seen in Table 17, the loss in performance is substantially increased compared with the intratransferability setup by 13.31–204.00%. This is due to the much more complex task of modelling similar devices in a completely different environment. Overall, CNN is achieving the best absolute performance for both the baseline and the transferability scenario.

6.2. Execution Time and Model Size

Model size and execution time determine the real-time capability and the utilization on hardware applications. Different models and application scenarios have been benchmarked on a personal computer using an AMD Ryzen 3700, an Nvidia RTX3070, and 32 GB of 3600 MHz DDR4 RAM. The model sizes after training are tabulated in Table 18.

Table 18. Model size of the trained model including all parameters for different scenarios.

Model	Denoise	Forecast	Nonlinear	Anomaly	Degradation
	30 × 4	144 × 8	1000 × 13	500 × 1	140 × 3
CNN	2.91 MB	6.37 MB	32.0 MB	9.49 MB	6.20 MB
LSTM	4.29 MB	4.30 MB	4.34 MB	4.26 MB	4.27 MB
DNN	1.92 MB	5.00 MB	40.6 MB	2.30 MB	2.81 MB
RF	37.7 MB	12.1 MB	58.4 MB	2.80 MB	9.16 MB
KNN	3.94 GB	0.33 GB	26.9 GB	7.05 MB	162.4 MB

From Table 18, it is observed that while the model size of CNN, LSTM, and DNN only depends on the size of the feature input vector, KNN stores all training samples to compute neighbouring distances and RF creates more trees, thus having significantly higher memory requirements for large datasets. Additionally, while the DNN and CNN models are sensitive to the window length of the input feature vector, the LSTM model has barely increased in model size due to its long short-term memory cells. The training and inference times are reported in Table 19.

Table 19. Training (T) and inference time (I) per sample (μs) for different models and scenarios.

Model	Denoise		Forecast		Non-Linear		Anomaly		Degradation	
	T	I	T	I	T	I	T	I	T	I
CNN	530	59	2570	120	2610	190	8650	478	1540	109
LSTM	540	87	6790	255	10,300	556	6540	893	2410	232
DNN	310	22	1500	33	3070	95	3760	76	1510	31
RF	9×10^3	15	5710	5.5	20×10^3	24	90	20	2170	3.1
KNN	0	6×10^3	0	967	0	42×10^3	0	97	0	854

As can be seen in Table 19, the training time per sample of deep learning approaches depends mainly on the convergence of the model. Conversely, the training time per sample for RF depends on the complexity and the number of different states that are extracted, while it is close to zero for KNN, which does not have any trainable parameters. Considering inference time, deep learning approaches are mostly dependent on the model size and the size of the input feature vector. Conversely, RF has very low inference time as it only performs comparison at the branches of the different decision trees, while KNN has large inference times because it compares every sample in the testing data with the training data.

6.3. Optimal Models and Model Order Reduction

To further improve the performance of a deep learning model in terms of model size and/or performance, the input feature vector and the model parameters can be optimized. To optimize the input feature vector, the importance of the input with respect to the output can be evaluated. Possible ranking algorithms include principal component analysis (PCA), correlation coefficients, or the ReliefF algorithm [67]. The feature ranking for the nonlinear modelling task is illustrated in Figure 12.

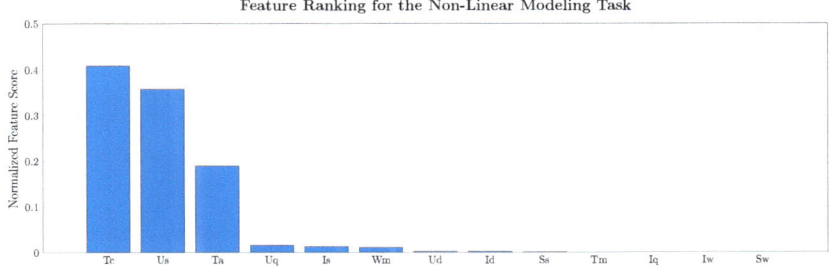

Figure 12. Feature ranking for the nonlinear modelling task for 13 features: coolant/ambient temperature (T_c, T_a), stator voltages (U_s, U_d, U_q), stator currents (I_s, I_d, I_q), torque (T_m), rotational speed (ω_m), apparent power (S_s), and products or current/power and rotational speed (I_ω, S_ω).

As can be seen in Figure 12, the stator and rotor temperature are dominated by the cooling temperature (heat conduction to the coolant), the ambient temperature (heat convection to the ambient), the stator voltage and stator current (ohmic and iron losses), and the rotational speed (coupling or stator and rotor temperature through airflow inside the machine). Furthermore, a Keras hyperparameter tuner can be used to optimize the parameters of the CNN model to account for the changed input feature dimensionality. The results of the reduced-order model using 6 input features instead of 13 are tabulated in Table 20.

Table 20. Temperature prediction results for stator winding and magnet temperature in terms of MSE (K^2) for different testing IDs and models. Baseline scenarios are denoted with 'Base', while reduced-order configurations are denoted with 'MOR'.

ID	Time (h)	Stator Winding		Rotor Magnet	
		Base	MOR	Base	MOR
60	1.7	2.41	1.34	22.62	16.68
62	3.3	2.75	1.79	17.49	31.11
74	3.0	3.33	2.37	14.47	15.39
Avg	8.0	2.90	1.91	17.45	22.15

As can be seen in Table 20, a reduced-order model reports even better performances for stator quantities, showing improvement by 34.1%. Conversely, the rotor performance decreased by 26.9%, which is probably due to the missing torque values and the complex power as these quantities are directly related to the rotor shaft.

7. Conclusions

A machine and deep learning Python toolkit for modelling time series data has been introduced. Five different scenarios, namely, denoising, forecasting, nonlinear modelling, anomaly detection, and degradation modelling, have been evaluated using real-word datasets and different machine and deep learning models. It was shown that the PyDTS toolkit and the models implemented in the toolkit can achieve performance close to the state of the art of the respective approach. Additionally, to benchmark the different approaches, the topics of transfer learning, hardware requirements, and model optimization have been discussed. The authors hope that the paper, accompanied by the PyDTS toolkit, will help new researchers entering the area of time series modelling and hopefully will create new ideas.

Author Contributions: Conceptualization, P.A.S.; methodology, P.A.S.; software, P.A.S.; writing—original draft preparation, P.A.S. and I.M.; writing—review and editing, I.M. All authors have read and agreed to the published version of the manuscript.

Funding: This research received no external funding.

Institutional Review Board Statement: Not applicable.

Data Availability Statement: The data on code are publicly available on GitHub at https://github.com/pascme05/PyDTS (accessed on 26 February 2024).

Conflicts of Interest: The authors declare no conflicts of interest.

References

1. Barra, S.; Carta, S.M.; Corriga, A.; Podda, A.S.; Recupero, D.R. Deep learning and time series-to-image encoding for financial forecasting. *IEEE/CAA J. Autom. Sin.* **2020**, *7*, 683–692. [CrossRef]
2. Mudelsee, M. *Climate Time Series Analysis*; Atmospheric and Oceanographic Sciences Library; Springer: Cham, Switzerland, 2010; Volume 397.
3. Mporas, I.; Ganchev, T.; Kocsis, O.; Fakotakis, N. Context-adaptive pre-processing scheme for robust speech recognition in fast-varying noise environment. *Signal Process.* **2011**, *91*, 2101–2111. [CrossRef]
4. Rasul, K.; Seward, C.; Schuster, I.; Vollgraf, R. Autoregressive denoising diffusion models for multivariate probabilistic time series forecasting. In Proceedings of the International Conference on Machine Learning, PMLR, Virtual, 18–24 July 2021; pp. 8857–8868.
5. Almalaq, A.; Edwards, G. A review of deep learning methods applied on load forecasting. In Proceedings of the 2017 16th IEEE International Conference on Machine Learning and Applications (ICMLA), Cancun, Mexico, 18–21 December 2017; pp. 511–516.
6. Osorio, J.D.; Wang, Z.; Karniadakis, G.; Cai, S.; Chryssostomidis, C.; Panwar, M.; Hovsapian, R. Forecasting solar-thermal systems performance under transient operation using a data-driven machine learning approach based on the deep operator network architecture. *Energy Convers. Manag.* **2022**, *252*, 115063. [CrossRef]
7. Hsieh, R.J.; Chou, J.; Ho, C.H. Unsupervised online anomaly detection on multivariate sensing time series data for smart manufacturing. In Proceedings of the 2019 IEEE 12th Conference on Service-Oriented Computing and Applications (SOCA), Kaohsiung, Taiwan, 18–21 November 2019; pp. 90–97.

8. Vichard, L.; Harel, F.; Ravey, A.; Venet, P.; Hissel, D. Degradation prediction of PEM fuel cell based on artificial intelligence. *Int. J. Hydrogen Energy* **2020**, *45*, 14953–14963. [CrossRef]
9. Fengou, L.C.; Mporas, I.; Spyrelli, E.; Lianou, A.; Nychas, G.J. Estimation of the microbiological quality of meat using rapid and non-invasive spectroscopic sensors. *IEEE Access* **2020**, *8*, 106614–106628. [CrossRef]
10. Contreras, J. ARIMA models to predict next-day electricity process. *IEEE Trans. Power Syst.* **2004**, *19*, 366–374.
11. Chen, K.; Yu, J. Short-term wind speed prediction using an unscented Kalman filter based state-space support vector regression approach. *Appl. Energy* **2014**, *113*, 690–705. [CrossRef]
12. Lim, B.; Zohren, S. Time-series forecasting with deep learning: A survey. *Philos. Trans. R. Soc. A* **2021**, *379*, 20200209. [CrossRef]
13. Siami-Namini, S.; Tavakoli, N.; Namin, A.S. The performance of LSTM and BiLSTM in forecasting time series. In Proceedings of the 2019 IEEE International Conference on Big Data (Big Data), Los Angeles, CA, USA, 9–12 December 2019; pp. 3285–3292.
14. Koprinska, I.; Wu, D.; Wang, Z. Convolutional neural networks for energy time series forecasting. In Proceedings of the 2018 International Joint Conference on Neural Networks (IJCNN), Rio de Janeiro, Brazil, 8–13 July 2018; pp. 1–8.
15. Chen, Y.; Ren, K.; Wang, Y.; Fang, Y.; Sun, W.; Li, D. ContiFormer: Continuous-time transformer for irregular time series modeling. *Adv. Neural Inf. Process. Syst.* **2024**, *36*.
16. Alwan, L.C.; Roberts, H.V. Time-series modeling for statistical process control. *J. Bus. Econ. Stat.* **1988**, *6*, 87–95. [CrossRef]
17. Lojowska, A.; Kurowicka, D.; Papaefthymiou, G.; van der Sluis, L. Advantages of ARMA-GARCH wind speed time series modeling. In Proceedings of the 2010 IEEE 11th International Conference on Probabilistic Methods Applied to Power Systems, Singapore, 14–17 June 2010; pp. 83–88.
18. Chujai, P.; Kerdprasop, N.; Kerdprasop, K. Time series analysis of household electric consumption with ARIMA and ARMA models. In Proceedings of the International Multiconference of Engineers and Computer Scientists, IAENG, Hong Kong, China, 13–15 March 2013; Volume 1, pp. 295–300.
19. Mahla, S.K.; Parmar, K.S.; Singh, J.; Dhir, A.; Sandhu, S.S.; Chauhan, B.S. Trend and time series analysis by ARIMA model to predict the emissions and performance characteristics of biogas fueled compression ignition engine. *Energy Sources Part A Recover. Util. Environ. Eff.* **2023**, *45*, 4293–4304. [CrossRef]
20. Durbin, J.; Koopman, S.J. *Time Series Analysis by State Space Methods*; OUP: Oxford, UK, 2012; Volume 38.
21. Yang, S.; Wan, M.P.; Ng, B.F.; Zhang, T.; Babu, S.; Zhang, Z.; Chen, W.; Dubey, S. A state-space thermal model incorporating humidity and thermal comfort for model predictive control in buildings. *Energy Build.* **2018**, *170*, 25–39. [CrossRef]
22. Hu, X.; Lin, S.; Stanton, S.; Lian, W. *A State Space Thermal Model for HEV/EV Battery Modeling*; Technical Report, SAE Technical Paper; SAE: Warrendale, PA, USA, 2011.
23. Dong, Z.; Yang, D.; Reindl, T.; Walsh, W.M. Short-term solar irradiance forecasting using exponential smoothing state space model. *Energy* **2013**, *55*, 1104–1113. [CrossRef]
24. Längkvist, M.; Karlsson, L.; Loutfi, A. A review of unsupervised feature learning and deep learning for time-series modeling. *Pattern Recognit. Lett.* **2014**, *42*, 11–24. [CrossRef]
25. Gamboa, J.C.B. Deep learning for time-series analysis. *arXiv* **2017**, arXiv:1701.01887.
26. Han, Z.; Zhao, J.; Leung, H.; Ma, K.F.; Wang, W. A review of deep learning models for time series prediction. *IEEE Sens. J.* **2019**, *21*, 7833–7848. [CrossRef]
27. Wang, H.; Lei, Z.; Zhang, X.; Zhou, B.; Peng, J. A review of deep learning for renewable energy forecasting. *Energy Convers. Manag.* **2019**, *198*, 111799. [CrossRef]
28. Hafeez, G.; Alimgeer, K.S.; Khan, I. Electric load forecasting based on deep learning and optimized by heuristic algorithm in smart grid. *Appl. Energy* **2020**, *269*, 114915. [CrossRef]
29. Hewage, P.; Trovati, M.; Pereira, E.; Behera, A. Deep learning-based effective fine-grained weather forecasting model. *Pattern Anal. Appl.* **2021**, *24*, 343–366. [CrossRef]
30. Antczak, K. Deep recurrent neural networks for ECG signal denoising. *arXiv* **2018**, arXiv:1807.11551.
31. Peng, Z.; Peng, S.; Fu, L.; Lu, B.; Tang, J.; Wang, K.; Li, W. A novel deep learning ensemble model with data denoising for short-term wind speed forecasting. *Energy Convers. Manag.* **2020**, *207*, 112524. [CrossRef]
32. Peng, H.; Yan, J.; Yu, Y.; Luo, Y. Time series estimation based on deep learning for structural dynamic nonlinear prediction. *Structures* **2021**, *29*, 1016–1031. [CrossRef]
33. Gao, X.; Zhu, W.; Yang, Q.; Zeng, D.; Deng, L.; Chen, Q.; Cheng, M. Time delay estimation from the time series for optical chaos systems using deep learning. *Opt. Express* **2021**, *29*, 7904–7915. [CrossRef]
34. Padrós, M.S.; Schirmer, P.A.; Mporas, I. Estimation of Cooling Circuits' Temperature in Battery Electric Vehicles Using Karhunen Loeve Expansion and LSTM. In Proceedings of the 2022 30th European Signal Processing Conference (EUSIPCO), Belgrade, Serbia, 29 August–2 September 2022; pp. 1546–1550.
35. Munir, M.; Siddiqui, S.A.; Dengel, A.; Ahmed, S. DeepAnT: A deep learning approach for unsupervised anomaly detection in time series. *IEEE Access* **2018**, *7*, 1991–2005. [CrossRef]
36. Zhang, W.; Li, X.; Li, X. Deep learning-based prognostic approach for lithium-ion batteries with adaptive time-series prediction and on-line validation. *Measurement* **2020**, *164*, 108052. [CrossRef]
37. Gedon, D.; Wahlström, N.; Schön, T.B.; Ljung, L. Deep state space models for nonlinear system identification. *IFAC-PapersOnLine* **2021**, *54*, 481–486. [CrossRef]

38. Bicer, E.A.; Schirmer, P.A.; Schreivogel, P.; Schrag, G. Electric Vehicle Thermal Management System Modeling with Informed Neural Networks. In Proceedings of the 2023 25th European Conference on Power Electronics and Applications (EPE'23 ECCE Europe), Aalborg, Denmark, 4–8 September 2023; pp. 1–8.
39. Schwermer, R.; Bicer, E.A.; Schirmer, P.; Mayer, R.; Jacobsen, H.A. Federated Computing in Electric Vehicles to Predict Coolant Temperature. In Proceedings of the 24th International Middleware Conference: Industrial Track, Bologna, Italy, 11–15 December 2023; pp. 8–14.
40. Garza, F.; Canseco, M.M.; Challú, C.; Olivares, K.G. *StatsForecast: Lightning Fast Forecasting with Statistical and Econometric Models*; PyCon: Salt Lake City, UT, USA, 2022.
41. Herzen, J.; LÃ¤ssig, F.; Piazzetta, S.G.; Neuer, T.; Tafti, L.; Raille, G.; Pottelbergh, T.V.; Pasieka, M.; Skrodzki, A.; Huguenin, N.; et al. Darts: User-Friendly Modern Machine Learning for Time Series. *J. Mach. Learn. Res.* **2022**, *23*, 1–6.
42. Löning, M.; Bagnall, A.; Ganesh, S.; Kazakov, V.; Lines, J.; Király, F.J. sktime: A unified interface for machine learning with time series. *arXiv* **2019**, arXiv:1909.07872.
43. Schirmer, P.A.; Mporas, I. Non-Intrusive Load Monitoring: A Review. *IEEE Trans. Smart Grid* **2023**, *14*, 769–784. [CrossRef]
44. Schirmer, P.A.; Mporas, I. Statistical and Electrical Features Evaluation for Electrical Appliances Energy Disaggregation. *Sustainability* **2019**, *11*, 3222. [CrossRef]
45. Schirmer, P.A.; Mporas, I.; Paraskevas, M. Evaluation of Regression Algorithms and Features on the Energy Disaggregation Task. In Proceedings of the 2019 10th International Conference on Information, Intelligence, Systems and Applications (IISA), Patras, Greece, 15–17 July 2019; pp. 1–4. [CrossRef]
46. Schirmer, P.A.; Geiger, C.; Mporas, I. Residential Energy Consumption Prediction Using Inter-Household Energy Data and Socioeconomic Information. In Proceedings of the 2020 28th European Signal Processing Conference (EUSIPCO), Patras, Greece, 18–21 January 2020.
47. Kirchgässner, W.; Wallscheid, O.; Böcker, J. Estimating electric motor temperatures with deep residual machine learning. *IEEE Trans. Power Electron.* **2020**, *36*, 7480–7488. [CrossRef]
48. Shumway, R.H.; Stoffer, D.S. *Time Series Analysis and Its Applications*; Springer: Cham, Switzerland, 2000.
49. Chen, C.T. *Linear System Theory and Design*, 3rd ed.; Oxford University Press, Inc.: Cary, NC, USA, 1998.
50. Loyola-González, O. Black-Box vs. White-Box: Understanding Their Advantages and Weaknesses From a Practical Point of View. *IEEE Access* **2019**, *7*, 154096–154113. [CrossRef]
51. Zheng, H.S.; Liu, Y.Y.; Hsu, C.F.; Yeh, T.T. StreamNet: Memory-Efficient Streaming Tiny Deep Learning Inference on the Microcontroller. In Proceedings of the Thirty-Seventh Conference on Neural Information Processing Systems, 2023. Available online: https://nips.cc/media/neurips-2023/Slides/72782_KsNdwFo.pdf (accessed on 26 February 2024).
52. Schirmer, P.A.; Mporas, I. Device and Time Invariant Features for Transferable Non-Intrusive Load Monitoring. *IEEE Open Access J. Power Energy* **2022**, *9*, 121–130. [CrossRef]
53. Chen, X.W.; Lin, X. Big Data Deep Learning: Challenges and Perspectives. *IEEE Access* **2014**, *2*, 514–525. [CrossRef]
54. Makonin, S.; Ellert, B.; Bajić, I.V.; Popowich, F. Electricity, water, and natural gas consumption of a residential house in Canada from 2012 to 2014. *Sci. Data* **2016**, *3*, 1–12. [CrossRef] [PubMed]
55. Soriano, F. Electric Power Consumption Dataset. 2023. Available online: https://www.kaggle.com/datasets/fedesoriano/electric-power-consumption (accessed on 26 February 2024).
56. Wichard, J.D. Classification of Ford Motor Data. *Comput. Sci.* **2008**. Available online: http://www.j-wichard.de/publications/FordPaper.pdf (accessed on 26 February 2024).
57. Bills, A.; Sripad, S.; Fredericks, L.; Guttenberg, M.; Charles, D.; Frank, E.; Viswanathan, V. A battery dataset for electric vertical takeoff and landing aircraft. *Sci. Data* **2023**, *10*, 344. [CrossRef] [PubMed]
58. Schirmer, P.A.; Mporas, I. Low-Frequency Energy Disaggregation based on Active and Reactive Power Signatures. In Proceedings of the 2021 29th European Signal Processing Conference (EUSIPCO), Dublin, Ireland, 23–27 August 2021; pp. 1426–1430. [CrossRef]
59. Kirchgässner, W.; Wallscheid, O.; Böcker, J. Thermal neural networks: Lumped-parameter thermal modeling with state-space machine learning. *Eng. Appl. Artif. Intell.* **2023**, *117*, 105537. [CrossRef]
60. Makonin, S.; Popowich, F.; Bajic, I.V.; Gill, B.; Bartram, L. Exploiting HMM Sparsity to Perform Online Real-Time Nonintrusive Load Monitoring. *IEEE Trans. Smart Grid* **2016**, *7*, 2575–2585. [CrossRef]
61. Harell, A.; Makonin, S.; Bajic, I.V. Wavenilm: A Causal Neural Network for Power Disaggregation from the Complex Power Signal. In Proceedings of the ICASSP 2019—2019 IEEE International Conference on Acoustics, Speech and Signal Processing (ICASSP), Brighton, UK, 12–17 May 2019; pp. 8335–8339. [CrossRef]
62. Schirmer, P.A.; Mporas, I. Energy Disaggregation Using Fractional Calculus. In Proceedings of the ICASSP 2020—2020 IEEE International Conference on Acoustics, Speech and Signal Processing (ICASSP), Barcelona, Spain, 4–8 May 2020; pp. 3257–3261. [CrossRef]
63. Kirchgässner, W.; Wallscheid, O.; Böcker, J. Data-driven permanent magnet temperature estimation in synchronous motors with supervised machine learning: A benchmark. *IEEE Trans. Energy Convers.* **2021**, *36*, 2059–2067. [CrossRef]
64. Schirmer, P.A.; Mporas, I. Energy Disaggregation from Low Sampling Frequency Measurements Using Multi-Layer Zero Crossing Rate. In Proceedings of the ICASSP 2020—2020 IEEE International Conference on Acoustics, Speech and Signal Processing (ICASSP), Barcelona, Spain, 4–8 May 2020; pp. 3777–3781. [CrossRef]

65. Schirmer, P.A.; Mporas, I. A Wavelet Scattering Approach for Load Identification with Limited Amount of Training Data. In Proceedings of the ICASSP 2023—2023 IEEE International Conference on Acoustics, Speech and Signal Processing (ICASSP), Rhodes Island, Greece, 4–10 June 2023; pp. 1–5. [CrossRef]
66. Kolter, J.Z.; Johnson, M.J. REDD: A public data set for energy disaggregation research. In *Workshop on Data Mining Applications in Sustainability (SIGKDD)*; Citeseer: San Diego, CA, USA, 2011; Volume 25, pp. 59–62.
67. Robnik-Šikonja, M.; Kononenko, I. Theoretical and empirical analysis of ReliefF and RReliefF. *Mach. Learn.* 2003, 53, 23–69. [CrossRef]

Disclaimer/Publisher's Note: The statements, opinions and data contained in all publications are solely those of the individual author(s) and contributor(s) and not of MDPI and/or the editor(s). MDPI and/or the editor(s) disclaim responsibility for any injury to people or property resulting from any ideas, methods, instructions or products referred to in the content.

MDPI AG
Grosspeteranlage 5
4052 Basel
Switzerland
Tel.: +41 61 683 77 34

Entropy Editorial Office
E-mail: entropy@mdpi.com
www.mdpi.com/journal/entropy

Disclaimer/Publisher's Note: The title and front matter of this reprint are at the discretion of the Guest Editors. The publisher is not responsible for their content or any associated concerns. The statements, opinions and data contained in all individual articles are solely those of the individual Editors and contributors and not of MDPI. MDPI disclaims responsibility for any injury to people or property resulting from any ideas, methods, instructions or products referred to in the content.